D0498518

ROOTED COSMOPOLITANS

JAMES LOEFFLER

Rooted Cosmopolitans

JEWS AND HUMAN RIGHTS IN
THE TWENTIETH CENTURY

Yale

UNIVERSITY PRESS

NEW HAVEN & LONDON

Published with assistance from the foundation established in memory
of Calvin Chapin of the Class of 1788, Yale College.

Yale University Press books may be purchased in quantity
for educational, business, or promotional use. For information,
please e-mail sales.press@yale.edu (U.S. office) or
sales@yaleup.co.uk (U.K. office).

Set in Scala type by Westchester Publishing Services. Printed in the
United States of America.

Library of Congress Control Number: 2017964065
ISBN 978-0-300-21724-7 (hardcover : alk. paper)

A catalogue record for this book is available from the British Library.

This paper meets the requirements of ANSI / NISO Z39.48-1992
(Permanence of Paper).

10 9 8 7 6 5 4 3 2 1

For David, Eli, and Talia

CONTENTS

THE PHOTOGRAPHER HEARD THE SOUNDS first. Gut-wrenching moans, muted sobbing, anguished gasps of Hebrew prayers, and bespittled Yiddish curses, all accompanied by the quiet crackling of dying flames. Next the darkened cityscape came into view: plumes of smoke rising from the buildings pockmarked with bullet holes. Then came the first ghostly apparitions, as survivors emerged from behind makeshift street barricades: "Their faces blue and full of expressions of human pain, they staggered about in stunned silence, like walking corpses. Every so often an anguished, heart-rending cry would ring out as a mother found the burnt remains of her daughter or a daughter collected the ashes of her mother's charred cadaver."

It was November 1918. The war to end all wars had just ended, to be replaced by a series of smaller yet equally brutal civil wars on the borderland ruins of the Austrian, German, and Russian Empires. As Polish and Ukrainian armies clashed for control of the city known as Lemberg to the Germans, Lwów to the Poles, and Lviv to the Ukrainians, the Jews found themselves singled out for a three-day orgy of violence at the hands of Polish soldiers and civilians. The assailants slashed, raped, murdered, and burned their way through the city's Jewish quarter. Initial Jewish reports spoke of 3,000 dead. The final number—between 73 and 150 Jews murdered, more than 450 casualties, and 100 million Austrian crowns' worth of property damage— still earned the Lemberg pogrom the grim distinction of the worst episode of civilian carnage in Eastern Europe since 1906. The photographer, dispatched by a Prague newspaper, returned home empty-handed. To photograph such an atrocity would be another crime in itself.[1]

Not everyone could afford to look away. The most immediate response came from the Zionist youth of the city, led by a young, bespectacled law student named Hersch Zvi Lauterpacht. Outraged by the violence, against which improvised Jewish self-defense brigades had proved largely helpless, Lauterpacht responded in a manner that today might seem curious. He made no tearful plea for tolerance. The man who would become known as the founding father of international human rights law did not even use the phrase "human rights" in his declarations. Instead, together with his fellow Zionists, he organized a boycott of local Polish schools. The only justifiable recompense from the murderous new regime would be the right for Jews to establish their own Jewish schools. Against Polish bullets, they demanded Hebrew books. Products of a polyglot university, they chose national autonomy. In a word, they opted for minority rights. What mattered most, what counted for justice in a violent and unstable world, was recognition in law by the Poles and the world at large that Jews were a nation entitled to run their own affairs. That modest, counterintuitive petition signaled the beginning of a now forgotten story: the strange, entangled pathways of Jewish politics and human rights across the twentieth century.[2]

The idea of recognizing a specific minority group's national rights as a response to violence flies in the face of how we think about atrocity and discrimination today. For us, human rights exist precisely in order to protect vulnerable individuals and communities outside the murkier precincts of nationalism. Human rights precede human politics. They are an appeal to the universal and a rejection of the particular. In this respect, we are heirs to the Enlightenment philosophers who imagined a world in which the strong help those who lack the means to help themselves. "If Dutchmen are injured and attacked, the Dutch have a nation, a Government and armies to redress or revenge their cause," Edmund Burke wrote at the end of the Napoleonic Wars, "Britons have armies and laws, the laws of nations . . . to fly to for protection and justice. But the Jews have no such power and no such friend to depend on. Humanity then must become their protector and ally." Burke's Jews were orphaned by history. Stripped of sovereignty, they could no longer practice the politics necessary for self-defense. Instead, the world needed to defend them.[3]

Between Burke's Law of Nations and our own world of contemporary human rights stand the Jews of post–World War I Eastern Europe. These wards of humanity had no wish to be protected as political invalids or naked individuals. They asked to be treated as an independent nation with legal rights and an equal share in the Law of Nations, even if they did not (yet) possess an army or a country. Their demand for rights was not an appeal beyond politics but an expression *of* politics. As Hannah Arendt once remarked about the Nazi rise to power: "If one is attacked as a Jew, one must defend oneself as a Jew. Not as a German, not as a world-citizen, not as an upholder of the Rights of Man." In the face of actual tyranny, any theoretical notion of general humanity quickly vanishes. Human rights prove a mere abstraction. Arendt understood that self-defense requires concrete politics, and politics begin with the assertion of specific identity. To be cosmopolitan, one must first be rooted.[4]

We live in an age in which human rights have become a source of great controversy in international affairs, and time and again the arguments converge on Zionism. The United States consistently threatens to resign from the United Nations Human Rights Council over its treatment of Israel. An internal civil war recently broke out at the organization Human Rights Watch over its handling of the Israeli-Palestinian conflict. The Government of Israel has drafted legislation to bar foreign activists from its shores and criminalize Israeli human rights organizations. The French president condemns anti-Zionism as antisemitism, while the European Union foreign policy chief defends the growing boycott-divestment-sanctions (BDS) movement. The International Criminal Court moots charges of war crimes for current and former Israeli political and military leaders. Despite all of these headlines, when it comes to Zionism and human rights, pundits and scholars alike remained locked in facile clichés: Israel as model democracy, Israel as rogue regime, Jews as social justice warriors, Jews as partisan defenders of Israel's interests.

The strangest thing about these clichés, besides how frequently they reappear, is the way they cancel each other out. Like all stereotypes, they reveal more about the needs and anxieties of our own moment than the ideas and events that brought us here. As a result, it proves nearly impossible to have a sustained conversation today about Israel and human rights without devolving into emotionally charged debates about the Israeli Occupation and Palestinian terrorism or the Holocaust and the Nakba. What is missing from these heated discussions is any awareness of the actual history linking the emergence of modern human rights to Jewish political activism.

"We are all historians of human rights," the president of the American Historical Association announced in 2006. Her self-conscious comment reflects the newfound scholarly interest in the historical origins of contemporary human rights. Where did our world of international legal treaties and NGOs (nongovernmental organizations) come from? How did we reach a point where even dictators who reject liberal democracy pledge their commitment to human rights? Most historians answer these questions by reference to a simple narrative. Modern international human rights emerged after World War II as a global response to the horrors of the Holocaust. We read frequently of how the world's statesmen came together in the shadows of Auschwitz and Birkenau to build a new vision of protecting humanity through international law. The result was the Universal Declaration of Human Rights approved by the United Nations (UN) on December 10, 1948, one day after the UN Genocide Convention was adopted by the same body. So linked are the Holocaust and human rights in our imaginations that we routinely assume that the Nazi mass murder of the Jews was the main impetus for the global advance in law and ethics. The ultimate wartime atrocity yielded a postwar bounty of human freedom.[5]

Yet human rights did not spring fully formed from the foreheads of diplomats. Nor were they merely the product of moral idealism or even the shock of a crime without precedent. Left out of the history of human rights, ironically, are the voices of the rightless. And when we pause to peer behind the United Nation's diplomatic tableaux, we find a very different story of the birth of human rights—and the place of Jews within it. This history begins well before World War II. Its origins are to be found not in the Nazi death camps of Poland but in the living shtetls of Eastern Europe.

Much of what we think of today as post–World War II international human rights began life as a specifically Jewish pursuit of minority rights in the ravaged borderlands of post–World War I Eastern Europe. This vision came couched in the political language of early twentieth-century Zionism. It was less the nightmare of the Holocaust than the dreams and dilemmas of Jewish nationhood that inspired a generation of Jewish lawyers, rabbis, and politicians to leave their mark on the emerging idea of human rights.

In this book, I recover this unknown history through the intersecting biographies of five remarkable men: Hersch Zvi Lauterpacht, the Polish-born international lawyer who drafted early versions of both the International Bill of Human Rights and the Israeli Declaration of Independence; Jacob Blaustein, the Baltimore oilman who brought human rights into U.S. foreign policy and first tried to solve the Arab-Israeli conflict; Rabbi Maurice Perlzweig, the British Zionist leader who created the modern international NGO at the League of Nations and the UN; Jacob Robinson, the Lithuanian Zionist leader who helped design the UN Commission on Human Rights and the Nuremberg and Eichmann trials; and Peter Benenson, the British Zionist youth activist who converted to Catholicism and founded Amnesty International. Their lives spanned continents. Their ideas reshaped the legal fabric of international society. Their language has become our language. They coined the very words we use today—crimes against humanity, prisoners of conscience—to speak about international law and global justice. But their Jewish political backstories are missing from the history of human rights.[6]

There is a simple reason for this lacuna. The lofty rhetoric of universality that hovers over our common conceptions of human rights tends to conceal more than it reveals. Behind this pristine concept lies a much richer, if counter-intuitive story of how Jews navigated the tumultuous currents of twentieth-century history. Charting these intersecting Jewish paths discloses an alternative map of the modern moral imagination. Where we might expect to find utopian idealists and socialist revolutionaries on the margins of Western society, instead we meet a global network of Jewish activists deeply enmeshed in the central dramas of European and American Jewish communal life. Where we might anticipate that Jewish religious traditions shaped the Jewish ethical horizon, we encounter a cadre of thinkers little concerned with rabbinic precepts or prophetic teachings. Instead, these forgotten Jewish journeys show how—despite the universalist cast of their language and ideas—the international human rights regime was born of their particular engagements with the rigors and rhapsodies of modern Jewish politics.

If pre–World War II Zionism paved the Jewish path into human rights, it also guaranteed that the rise of Israel would transform the meaning of that Jewish activism in the second half of the twentieth century. After tracking the intertwined fates of international minority rights and Zionism throughout the 1920s and 1930s, I turn in the middle section of this book to the crucial decade of the 1940s, in which the postwar international order as we know it was created. The twin births of the State of Israel and the Universal Declaration of Human Rights in 1948 do not typically appear in the same historical frame. Yet the pairing of their stories together restores a crucial context to each, revealing the deep interdependence of human rights and nationalism that is so often overlooked in accounts of the period. That key connection between rights and nationhood in 1948 helps explain the persistence of so many problems that have plagued the international human rights movement and the Israeli-Palestinian conflict alike down to the present.[7]

In the final third of this book, I turn to the fate of postwar human rights in the Cold War Middle East. This section begins in the early 1950s as Israeli government lawyers and diaspora Jewish activists pursued a new kind of human rights diplomacy across the geopolitical chessboard of the early Cold War. It moves on to the post-Suez War origins of Amnesty International, showing how a human rights organization born of a Jewish desire to transcend Zionism nevertheless retained an umbilical connection to its Jewish roots. The story then turns to the two seismic events of 1960, one famous, the other forgotten, that have defined much of the relationship between Zionism and international law: the Eichmann trial in Jerusalem and the global Swastika Epidemic. In different ways, each of these events set the stage for a wholesale crisis in the Jewish human rights world that only worsened in the aftermath of the 1967 Six-Day War. The final chapter looks at the little-known attempt by Amnesty International and the Government of Israel to conduct a joint investigation of alleged Israeli human rights violations against Palestinians in the late 1960s. The failure of that venture established a pattern of mutual recrimination between Israel and the human rights community that has repeated itself at regular intervals ever since. It also coincided with the formal departure of Israel and Jewish organizations from the international human rights arena in the 1970s and with the 1975 UN General Assembly Resolution that labeled "Zionism as Racism." The legacies of that controversial moment remain with us today.

Stalin's propagandists famously coined the term "rootless cosmopolitans" after World War II as an antisemitic euphemism for Jews. In the strange dialectics of Soviet ideology, all Jews were simultaneously bourgeois Zionists, wedded to their particular nation, and deracinated cosmopolitans who stood perennially apart, incapable of truly belonging to any one country or culture. "Rootless cosmopolitans," in other words, were charged with contradictory sins: both retrograde particularism and dangerous universalism. Jews could claim no legitimate country of their own yet they persisted in clannish ways wherever they went. As we shall see, this slur followed Jews into the world of human rights. It persists today in various forms, including among those Jewish intellectuals who have refashioned the antisemitic libel into a proud trademark of diasporic universalism. At the other end of the political spectrum, the same smear has surfaced among Jewish conservative voices in American politics who gleefully brandish it against liberal opponents—in a dangerously cynical flirtation with contemporary right-wing antisemitism. Both of these would-be Jewish cosmopolitans and Jewish populists have misread history. A better characterization of the Jewish pathways through twentieth-century international human rights would be as *rooted* cosmopolitans, braiding together the ethnos and ethical in a distinctively Jewish model of universalism.[8]

It is always the case that we go hunting in the past for evidence to confirm our intuitions and ease our worries about the present. But if we want an honest reckoning with the dilemmas of human rights now confronting the world at large and the State of Israel more specifically, we must begin with a critical engagement with this complicated history. Ultimately, the Jews who played leading roles in the story of modern human rights never rested at one extreme of either the particular or the universal. Like so many other dreamers and dissidents in the modern world, they sought to balance rootedness and cosmopolitanism in quest of a pragmatic idealism. Sometimes they succeeded, sometimes they did not. Regardless, they persevered. Their inspiration and their struggle remain before us today.

PART ONE

EMERGENCE

Don't think that the sky is a curtain,
made so God won't see,
the clouds made to hide your hands,
the wind to muffle the wild cries,
the earth to soak up the blood of the victims . . .
All will be measured, all will be weighed!
No tear, no drop of blood ever vanishes.
No spark is extinguished, no eye blotted out!
From tears come rivers, from rivers come oceans,
From oceans—a flood; from sparks—thunder—
Oh, don't think, that there is no Judge and no Judgement!
                    —Y. L. Peretz, "Don't Think," 1905

Every treaty contains within it a basic paradox: each contract
obligates the signatories and ensures the fulfillment of the
obligations notwithstanding the will of one side. But when each
side can decide whether the obligation has been fulfilled, how can
one speak of a binding obligation?
        —Hersch Zvi Lauterpacht, "Agreement to Disagree," 1925

Just as in the Declaration of the Rights of Man of more than a
hundred years ago the human rights of individuals were
proclaimed, now after another enormous world-rupture that the
World War has brought us, so too a new concept of the Rights of
Groups of national minorities have been proclaimed.

—Emil Margulies, Speech at the European Congress of
National Minorities, 1929

You've become
inanimate, brother
Jesus. You've
had 2,000 years
of tranquility on
the cross.
All around you, meanwhile, the world expires. But damn it, you've
forgotten everything. Your frozen brain cannot think: a Star of David
above your head, over the star—hands held in priestly blessing.
Below lie olive trees
and etrog gardens.
Your frozen eyes
cannot see. At your
feet: a pile of Jewish
heads. . . . It is
Golgotha, my brother,
which you do not
see. Golgotha is
here—all around.
Pilate lives, and in
Rome they chant
Psalms in churches.

—Uri Zvi Greenberg, "Uri Zvi in Front of the Cross," 1922

1

A Jewish Magna Carta

ONE MONDAY MORNING IN PARIS IN June 1919, a curious argument broke out in the elegant, wood-paneled hotel chambers of President Woodrow Wilson. While anti-Jewish violence raged half a continent away, the American leader listened as British prime minister David Lloyd George complained about the obstinacy of Polish Jews. He was all for the protection of minorities, Lloyd George explained, but there must be a limit: "Our desire to protect the Jews doesn't have to go so far as to make them into a state within a state." What irked the British statesman was the Jewish demand that the Poles guarantee them their own Yiddish-language schools. Why all this bother, to the point of alienating the Poles, over a folk jargon that was not even a real language but "only corrupt German"? That denigrating comment was too much, Wilson protested. The American president, who likely had never heard a word of Yiddish in his life, rose to its defense. Yiddish was the thousand-year-old mother tongue of the East European Jewish masses. They even spoke it in New York, so much so that public schools employed Yiddish-speaking teachers to teach immigrant Jewish children. Lloyd George sniffed at that answer. That Jewish boys and girls learned their ABCs in Yiddish did not make of it a language of learning.[1]

Had he been less diplomatic, Wilson might have asked Lloyd George, a native Welsh speaker, how he had lost his own "foreign" accent in his journey through British politics. Or he might have cited the famous Yiddish dictum "A language is but a dialect with an army and a navy." It would have made little difference. Lloyd George admonished him that their mission was not to placate small nations, but to drag them into the civilized world. "As the real representatives of the League of Nations today," he said, "we are considering the situation of backward countries, and we think we must do for them what Rome did for us: without the Romans, we would have remained half savages for centuries longer."[2]

Were the founders of the League of Nations really latter-day Romans? The quarrel over Yiddish highlighted the root tension in the League between power and idealism. Wilson believed that bestowing national dignity on European minorities was an important part of democracy. Solving the problem of nationalism via law would pave the way for international liberalism. Lloyd George, by contrast, saw the League as the vehicle of an updated liberal imperialism whose first function was to provide stability in European continental affairs. By putting Pax Anglo-Britannica before all else, Western civilization would remake the world in its own Victorian image for the benefit of humankind. These contradictory visions of international order were built into the League's very structure. They also formed the starting point for Jewish thinking about what kind of justice was possible for themselves and others in the postwar world.[3]

The League of Nations may today seem like a quaint idea, a distant and ill-starred antique. But to understand the story of human rights in the twentieth century, we have to realize how forcefully it captured the imagination of a rising generation of Zionist youth in the ongoing war zone of post–World War I Eastern Europe—first and foremost Hersch Zvi Lauterpacht himself. "The history of the colonial conquests of the European powers," he wrote in 1921, "has in fact been a history of the most ruthless economic exploitation of native peoples, maintained by the despotic rule of military administrations." Now, however, the Paris Peace Conference marked a turning point in world affairs. For the first time ever, the Great Powers had devised a system premised on modern international law that would be equally binding on countries large and small. The fact that England, France, and the United States were willing to accede to the League's Covenant alongside Poland, Lithuania, and other fledging states was a breakthrough for the global rule of law, he claimed. When sovereign power accepted limits, international law acquired a new authority. Where once law had merely ratified the results of force, it now heralded the victory of enlightened "public opinion in a democratic age."[4]

For the Jews in particular, the League of Nations promised a world in which neither size nor power would determine a people's right to national existence. The proof of this promise was its two most controversial legal innovations, each of which might radically reshape the lives of millions of Jews across Europe and the Middle East. The Minorities Treaties extended linguistic, cultural, and other group rights to national minorities living in the belt of post-imperial states from Austria, Poland, and Lithuania southeast to Romania, Greece, and Turkey. The mandate system carved up large swaths of the non-Western world into territorial mandates, which the "advanced nations" of Europe would magnanimously govern on behalf of local peoples "not yet able to stand by themselves under the strenuous conditions of the modern world," until such time as these "independent nations" could be fully released from their political and administrative "tutelage." Among these mandates was British Palestine, where, according to Britain's own wartime Balfour Declaration, the world's Jews now had their own "national home."

Both the Minorities Treaties and the mandate system rested on an uneasy foundation of imperial largesse combined with democratic internationalism. Independence for new postwar nation-states in Central and Southeastern Europe was conditioned on their proper treatment of their national minorities; national freedom for the peoples of the Middle East and, more distantly, for Africans and Pacific Islanders, would come only after they had proved themselves to be sufficiently civilized in the eyes of the West. In effect, the Great Powers sought to accommodate nationalism in Europe and pacify local political demands abroad through a mix of colonial rule and newer ideas of self-determination and minority rights. In between Europe and the world, straddling the categories of mandate and minority, stood the Jews.[5]

To Jews like Lauterpacht, these compromises did not detract from the enormous revolution at hand. Poland and Palestine together offered proof of the fundamental change in human history. In the enduring East European heartland, three million Jews now embarked on an experiment as a model minority with international legal protection. Meanwhile, in their emerging Middle Eastern homeland, the Jewish people laid claim to national self-determination as a model majority. These dual inventions shaped Lauterpacht's mission throughout the 1920s: to fight for Jewish rights via international law and, at the same time, to defend international law itself from its doubters. The former task he pursued as a youth leader in the Polish Zionist movement and founder of the World Union of Jewish Students, an international movement to combat antisemitism in European universities. The latter he undertook as a rising legal scholar and chief theoretician of the new League of Nations mandate system. In the opening years of the decade, Lauterpacht became the man who argued that the British promise of Palestine to the Jews was not a tactical concession or wartime propaganda tactic but the very beginning of modern international justice.

During the 1920s, this remarkable admixture of idealism and pragmatism would be repeatedly tested by violence in both Poland and Palestine, antisemitic exclusion at the League of Nations, and deep ambivalence from Great Britain itself. Ultimately, Lauterpacht discovered, betting on the empire to promulgate international law and safeguard Jewish rights was a risky proposition. The events of the 1920s made him one of the first thinkers to grapple with a question that has plagued lawyers and activists ever since: Can international law be separated from the politics necessary to forge it?[6]

A Son of the Nation

Before it was twenty-first-century Ukrainian Lviv, before it was twentieth-century Polish Lwów, Lemberg was a quiet Austrian border city perched on the banks of the Poltva River, a hundred miles east of the Carpathian Mountains. The city hosted a university founded in 1661 by the Polish king John II Casimir. Depending on the political climate, courses were taught in Polish, Ukrainian, or German—sometimes in all three. In the streets one could also hear Yiddish, Hebrew, and Russian. This linguistic diversity testified to the confluence of nationalities in the late Hapsburg Empire's Galician region. It also ensured that, during World War I, a large number of nations wished to claim the land.

The Austrian forces mobilized in 1914. The Russians quickly invaded, only to be driven back out by the Austrians, and for the rest of the war, the city remained caught between the two sides. Mass expulsions and brutal massacres tore apart Jewish Galicia. The violence and chaos also shattered the Jews' delicate political position in the region's ethnoreligious landscape. One result was a generation of Zionist leaders who came of age acutely sensitive to the politics of national identity.

Hersch Zvi Lauterpacht was born in 1897 in the nearby townlet of Zolkiew. The middle child of three, he grew up the son of a father who ran a local timber factory, in a home where the Torah coexisted easily with modern European education. The family spoke Polish outside the house, Yiddish within it. Hebrew was reserved for prayer and religious study. When he was thirteen years old, his parents relocated to Lemberg to enroll him in a German-style Gymnasium.

The move also marked the bar mitzvah boy's political coming of age. In high school, Lauterpacht joined a local Zionist youth group, *Ha-sha<u>h</u>ar* (The Dawn). Members met early mornings and weekends to study Jewish history and to drill themselves in modern conversational Hebrew. Their goal was to strengthen their Jewish self-knowledge and language skills and to master Jewish self-defense in order to advance the cause of national rebirth. With his "penetrating eyes, unshakeable logic, sober rationalism and ironic style," the confident teenager proved a captivating public speaker and natural leader. He preached a combination of moderate socialism, equal rights, and national autonomy for Jews in a future Polish state and, most of all, preparation for migration to a future Jewish Palestine. His generation was "the last of the enslaved," in the words of his favorite Hebrew poem, and was destined to become the first to redeem the "new land" of Israel.[7]

In 1915, Lauterpacht was drafted into the Austrian army. Yet he managed to secure a military support position at his father's factory, where he spent many happy days in the sawmill's engine room reading English economics, German philosophy, and Jewish political thought. In November 1917, the British issued the famous Balfour Declaration. In carefully worded language, Foreign Secretary Lord Arthur James Balfour promised his country's support for the establishment after the war of a Jewish national home in Palestine (though not a full-fledged sovereign state). Defying martial law and risking a charge of treason, Lauterpacht joined his Zionist friends in the city's streets to celebrate. As he saw it, the Balfour Declaration was more than a promissory note for a Jewish return to Zion. It was also an acknowledgment by the most powerful country in the world that Jews were a modern nation entitled to full recognition under international law. The same year saw another shock: the Russian Revolution, which brought down the world's greatest antisemitic autocrat. Then the Americans plunged into the war. By the time the Central Powers surrendered in November 1918, a new world seemed at hand. It was one of history's "plastic hours," in the phrase of another young Zionist intellectual, Gershom Scholem: one of those "crucial moments . . . [when] it is possible to act" to shape history. "If you move then," Scholem declared, "something happens."[8]

In postwar Lemberg, Lauterpacht was determined to move. He had become the local head of two Zionist youth groups, *He-haluts* (The Pioneer) and *Tseir'ei Tsion* (The Youth of Zion). By day, he and his friends memorized Hebrew poems by the great Zionist bard, Chaim Nachman Bialik. At night they ran street patrols to protect Jews from the mounting violence. Lauterpacht launched yet a third Zionist group for Jewish college students at the University of Lemberg, the Herzliah Society, designed to protect their "academic" rights and combat the dangers of "assimilation." In the fall of 1918, he began organizing rallies to demand recognition of their nationality by the administration. "Jewish university students are convinced," he wrote in a manifesto that October, "that in the moment when the whole civilized world has recognized the rule of self-determination of nations, it is unthinkable that our *almae matris* would be the only refuge of reaction and obscurantism. Therefore, we firmly demand that the Jewish nationality be immediately recognized at universities, and that departments of Jewish Studies, Jewish History, and Hebrew be created." This call for minority rights, he hastened to add, was not meant to diminish the national ambitions of Poles or Ukrainians. "We, the sons of the nation that has passed through the two-millennia hell of oppression, torment, and autos-da-fé, welcome the nations now emancipating themselves from the yoke of bondage and send a brotherly salute to the resurrected Polish nation, rousing itself from a hundred-years-plus slumber, and to the Ukrainian nation, stirring itself to new life."[9]

Lauterpacht's impassioned plea for pluralism was genuine enough, but it also possessed a tactical dimension. In the face of the rising conflict between Ukrainian and Polish nationalist movements, each of which now sought to claim Lemberg as part of its planned state, the city's Zionists tried to preserve Jewish neutrality. Unfortunately, the Poles took Jewish neutrality as a mark of disloyalty in their war with the Ukrainians, and after capturing the city they answered with the infamous November 1918 pogrom. Even for a people well used to the tidal rhythms of invasion and periodic spasms of anti-Jewish violence, the three-day murderous rampage through the Jewish quarter elicited biblical metaphors of catastrophe and ruin. The poet Uri Zvi Greenberg recalled Polish soldiers lining him and his family up against a wall to be shot. When he dared to ask them why, the answer was simple: "Because you are Jews who carry dogs' blood in your veins." Miraculously, Greenberg survived, and he turned his grief and rage into a searing Yiddish poem written in the shape of a crucifix, in which he denounced Jesus for ignoring the suffering of his own people at the hands of Christian terror.[10]

The Lemberg pogrom acquired instant notoriety around the world. To the Great Powers then contemplating the future map of Central Europe, it was taken as a sign of the Poles' political immaturity and barbarism. To the Poles, who denied responsibility for the atrocities, it was evidence of a sinister conspiracy directed against them by international Jewish propagandists. To Jewish communities around the world, the pogrom provided a stark reminder that the war's end had not stopped the dire threat to the Jews of Eastern Europe. It prompted them to ask who and what would protect them in the postwar world. These questions passed directly onto the agenda of the Paris Peace Conference, which opened just two months later.[11]

In Lemberg itself, the city's Jews remained in a state of mortal terror. The burnt-down Jewish quarter with its ruined Great Synagogue reminded them of what might yet come again. The city still lacked electricity and a regular water supply. Food and coal sold at famine prices. The Ukrainians continued their daily bombardment, leaving many people dead in the street. In these terrible circumstances, local Polish leaders announced a boycott of Jewish-owned businesses. Poles caught patronizing Jewish shops were accosted in the street and forced to wear tags on their clothes that read, "This pig has dealt with a Jew." Mock funeral notices around town listed them as "dead to the Polish race."[12]

Lauterpacht was outraged by the murderous violence and barbaric discrimination. He and three other young Zionist leaders, Szymon Wolf, Issachar Reiss, and David Horovitz, briefly contemplated an assassination operation against the Polish commanding officer. Instead, they opted for the nonviolent boycott of Polish schools and further demands for minority rights. Yet these calls too were perilous acts of defiance. The Polish authorities looked on Lauterpacht and his comrades as militant rebels illegally conspiring against the local government. They would hardly alter course because of a symbolic action by Jewish students. But the Poles were not Lauterpacht's target. He had already realized that Jewish hopes for justice required international recognition that could only come from the Great Powers gathering at the Paris Peace Conference, then just weeks away.[13]

Neither Sovereignty nor Special Privileges

They came from every corner of the globe, peoples small and large, some already living in independent states, others chafing under colonial rule. Beginning in January 1919 and continuing for six months, Arab princes, Chinese intellectuals, African politicians, and scores of other leaders gathered in Paris to plead their cases before the trio of U.S. president Woodrow Wilson, British prime minister David Lloyd George, and French prime minister Georges Clemenceau. Many of the loudest voices emerged from the heart of Europe, where Poles, Lithuanians, Ukrainians, and others petitioned for the prize of national sovereignty and the land to go with it. They laid claim to overlapping swaths of territory in the corridor between a shrunken, defeated Germany and a disintegrating Russia convulsed by civil war and revolution. Like heirs to "a large estate," observed American Jewish diplomat Henry Morgenthau, they crowded into court to squabble over the "division of the spoils."[14]

Lauterpacht, one semester short of graduation, could not leave Lemberg. But there was no shortage of Jewish voices at Paris, including some of his close comrades from Eastern Galicia. They poured in as well from New York, Jerusalem, Zurich, Vilnius, Prague, and London. The end of World War I had brought a unique moment in which Jewish communities around the world convened their own political congresses to formulate their demands for the postwar international order. All told, some thirty such gatherings took place, each amounting to a miniature constitutional moment of political self-definition. "With the creation of the League of Nations," declared Polish Zionist leader Leon Reich, "the world has changed vis-à-vis nations, and Jews must demand our national rights." From Copenhagen, the Zionist movement leadership echoed this sentiment with an official manifesto whose demands would come to be known as the "Famous Trinity of 1917":

(a) the recognition of Palestine as the national home of the Jewish people;
(b) complete equal rights for Jews in all countries;
(c) national autonomy in cultural, social, and political spheres in the countries where Jews live in compact masses and in lands where the Jewish communities seek these rights.[15]

The Copenhagen manifesto is barely noted in the annals of Zionism today. Yet in its time it conveyed a crucial, now-forgotten truth about the breadth of the interwar Zionist movement's goals in the international sphere. Conventional wisdom holds now that Zionist leaders wished only to dissolve the diaspora and gather as many Jews as possible in Palestine. This idea is embodied in the Hebrew slogan "Shelilat ha-galut," or "Negation of the Exile." In reality, however, for many interwar Zionist leaders, Jewish nation-building in the homeland went hand in hand with a fight for minority rights abroad. Building a Jewish country would not invalidate Jewish minority status abroad, but rather safeguard it.[16]

This position found support at each of the thirty-some postwar gatherings held in anticipation of the Paris Peace Conference. In Philadelphia, for instance, American Zionist leaders Rabbi Stephen S. Wise and Supreme Court Justice Louis Brandeis joined with noted civil rights lawyer Louis Marshall to incorporate these demands into a "Jewish Bill of Rights." They mobilized their country's Jews in an act of bold political self-assertion. In mid-December 1918, four hundred delegates chosen by some 325,000 American Jews in countrywide elections gathered for a massive convention to approve the platform and authorize a delegation to seek inclusion of Jewish rights in the peace treaties to be negotiated in Paris. As Brandeis declared, "The new nationalism proclaims that each race or people, like each individual, has a right and duty to develop, and that only through such differentiated development will high civilization be attained. Not until these principles of nationalism, like those of democracy, are generally accepted will liberty be fully attained, and minorities be secure in their rights."[17]

At Vilnius the same month, Zionists approved the same principles, with a twist: Jews should be admitted to the League as an independent nation regardless of where they lived. After centuries of "politics for the Jews" conducted on their behalf by Gentiles, the moment of true "Jewish politics" had arrived. The Lithuanian Jewish position hit on precisely what was novel about these Jewish rights claims. In the nineteenth century, the "Jewish Question" had been raised and debated at the international diplomatic conferences held in Vienna in 1815, Paris in 1856, and Berlin in 1878. In the latter two instances West European Jewish notables had quietly interceded on behalf of vulnerable Jews around the globe. European diplomats responded to these pleas for humanitarian intervention with selective campaigns for Jewish relief from discrimination and violence and limited treaties with Turkey, Romania, and Bulgaria to guarantee Jewish civil rights. Yet both the self-appointed imperial watchmen and the resentful small states freely violated the agreements. The Jewish masses themselves were left voiceless and defenseless. No one cared to hear what the victims themselves had to say.[18]

All that promised to change with President Wilson's famous "Fourteen Points" speech of January 1918, in which he reframed his domestic progressive policies into a blueprint for a new liberal world order. Free trade, transparent diplomacy, territorial integrity, global democracy, and, most crucially, self-determination for nations big and small: these building blocks, once assembled, would produce a new kind of international society. "Peoples and provinces are not to be bartered about from sovereignty to sovereignty," he said in a follow-up speech, "as if they were mere chattels and pawns in a game." Though crucial practical details remained obscure, Jews around the world saw in Wilson's vision a blueprint for their claims to minority rights. With Central Europe in tatters, Russia engulfed in civil war, and Britain and France locked in a bitter imperial rivalry for the Middle East, Jewish eyes turned hopefully to the rising power of the United States. "America in one word has become not simply a world-power," declared one American Jewish leader in 1918, "but a power for world good and world liberty."[19]

By March 1919, Jewish delegations from across the world had arrived in Paris. At the initiative of Russian Zionist leader Leo Motzkin, they voted to band together as a single diplomatic organization. The Comité des Délégations Juives auprès de la Conférence de la Paix, as it came to be known, included several European and Middle Eastern Zionist delegations along with the Americans. Yet not all would-be Jewish diplomats agreed with its agenda. A few more genteel American Jewish leaders associated with the non-Zionist American Jewish Committee (AJC) hoped to secure individual civil rights for Jews, but staunchly opposed any suggestion of Jewish nationalism. New York Jewish philanthropists had organized the AJC back in 1906 to respond to Russian pogroms without the unseemly spectacle of Jewish national politics. They were joined in Paris by similarly minded British and French Jewish leaders like English journalist Lucien Wolf and French Orientalist Sylvain Lévi, who also preferred a liberal Jewish international advocacy that did not identify Jews as a separate ethnic nationality. Doing so would lend credence to the charges of antisemites and jeopardize the hard-won civil emancipation achieved over the course of the nineteenth century. This position infuriated the Polish Zionists. "Civil rights without national rights," shouted Lauterpacht's friend Joseph Tenenbaum at one meeting, "would turn the Jews into Polish slaves."[20]

Channeling this sentiment, Wise and Marshall formally requested in an early March memo a guarantee of "fundamental human rights" for Jews in countries like Poland and Romania after the war. Such a guarantee, they explained to Wilson and his compatriots, must include "autonomous management of their own communal institutions," language rights, religious freedom, and "minority representation" based on proportional voting. These "national rights" were not, they stressed, intended as a pretext for political irredentism. "Nothing is further removed from our purpose than to countenance the establishment of an *imperium in imperio*," they explained, batting away the hoary charge that Jews sought a "state-within-a-state." They

sought neither "sovereignty [n]or special privileges, but merely justice."
Just treatment would help tame the wild spirit of nationalism.

> [We must acknowledge] the intense desire of all the various ethnic minori-
> ties in Eastern Europe to preserve their cultural identity. . . . Practically all
> of the new and enlarged States which are to be organized will be composed
> of Jews, Ruthenians [Ukrainians], Lithuanians, Letts [Latvians], and Rus-
> sians. The same is true of Ukrainia, Lithuania, and Roumania. Most of the
> Jews of these lands share with their fellow-countrymen the desire for cul-
> tural autonomy, and the most advanced statesmen in these lands sympa-
> thize with this feeling and favor the granting of these rights.[21]

As Europe's quintessential minority group, the Comité delegates argued,
Jews were ideally positioned to articulate what was needed to secure the
rights of *all* minorities: "Without these minority rights, Jews, Ukrainians,
Lithuanians and others within the new Polish, Rumanian and other States
would incur the danger of the annihilation of their ancient civilization, the
destruction of their schools, and the suppression of their languages." In the
Jewish political imagination of 1919, practical and moral reasoning went
hand in hand.[22]

Wilson personally favored the idea of minority rights. It was an elegant
solution to the problem of nationalism, a way to deliver on his promise of
national self-determination without full-fledged sovereignty. Realizing minority rights would not weaken the international system, but strengthen it.
After all, the Versailles Treaties promised some sixty million people states
of their own, but in the process turned another twenty-five million into
minority populations. Massive numbers of ethnic Poles, Germans, and
others were left stranded outside the redrawn borders of their new nation-
states. However, Wilson's arguments fell on deaf ears. The British and
French stood to gain little by granting legal privileges to Jews or other minorities. Clemenceau, despite his opposition to colonialism, wondered why
Jews in Poland and Russia could not integrate as individual citizens as they
had in France. Lloyd George grudgingly accepted some protections for minorities, but pointedly dismissed the possibility of allowing them to petition the League's judicial system directly, which he thought would create
an endless stream of diplomatic headaches. "If they are persecuted, the

Jews of Poland will find a member state of the League of Nations to take up their cause. . . . We cannot allow propagandistic associations and societies from all over the world to flood the League with their complaints. . . . The Jews, in particular, are very litigious."[23]

Wilson pushed back. Ready proof that something had to be done came in the form of the rash of postwar pogroms. By March the delegates had received reports of 150 separate attacks, with thousands upon thousands of Jews killed. Yet the Polish delegation continued to suggest that Jews exaggerated their suffering—or brought it on themselves by exploiting defenseless Polish peasants and aligning with the Bolsheviks. At one meeting with Polish Jewish representatives in Paris, President Ignacy Jan Paderewski bluntly proclaimed that no Polish government would ever grant the Jews the rights they sought. Any idea of internationally protected Jewish rights was a direct attack on hard-won Polish sovereignty. Finally, in a secret, closed-door plenary meeting on May 31, Wilson proposed conditioning Polish independence on their acquiescence to some tangible measure of minority rights. It was not only a Jewish issue, he reminded Clemenceau and Lloyd George. Huge numbers of ethnic Germans would remain in the postwar Polish state. They too had to be given legal protections from the lethal force of nationalism.[24]

As with many matters involving the League, Wilson won the battle but lost the war. The Poles calculated correctly that minority rights were not as crucial to the Great Powers' League plan as peace with Germany and a solid Polish state to serve as buffer against the Bolshevik expansion. Then too, the American president's own racial chauvinism undermined his bargaining position. When the Japanese brought a related international measure that would have banned racial and religious discrimination, Wilson balked for fear of exposing American segregation to sanction. A modest deal was struck that whittled down the scope of the minority rights in question. The Great Powers agreed to give the Poles Lemberg and the surrounding region in exchange for some limited provisions regarding national minorities in the Polish constitution.[25]

On June 28, 1919, Paderewski signed the first of the Minorities Treaties, known as the Little Versailles Treaty. It would become the template for similar agreements signed by the new states of Albania, Austria, Bulgaria,

Czechoslovakia, Estonia, Finland, Greece, Hungary, Iraq, Latvia, Lithuania, Romania, Turkey, and Yugoslavia. All accepted clauses in their new constitutions providing for individual religious freedom, the right to use minority languages, and various measures of minority self-control over schools, charities, and religion. Specific provisions for local Jewish communities to direct their own schooling and religious affairs and a restriction on holding elections on the Jewish Sabbath were also included.

The first Jewish reactions to news of the deal were decidedly favorable. Back in New York that summer, Marshall told an audience of three thousand at a Carnegie Hall rally that the treaties were a "Jewish Magna Carta." They ensured the "complete emancipation" of *all* minorities in Poland and beyond. Equally important, he added, was that "the observance of these treaties was made a matter of international concern . . . guaranteed by the League of Nations." Still, the rights in question remained tethered to land. Any international claim had to be made from within the specific political context of Poland, Lithuania, or any other state where Jews and other national minorities resided. Hence the innovation of minority rights arrived tempered by diplomatic compromise and constrained by demography and geography. Its fate remained tightly linked to unresolved questions about the map of Europe and the composition of the League. Lauterpacht quickly learned this lesson firsthand back home in newly independent Poland.[26]

A Higher Power

As Austrian Lemberg officially became Polish Lwów, Lauterpacht watched the Jewish "Magna Carta" fail its first test. Amidst the Polish-Ukrainian fighting, pogroms raged in nearby towns all around the city outskirts. The new Polish constitution guaranteed equal rights to all "Polish citizens," yet pointedly left "citizen" undefined. Many feared that much of the Jewish population would be deemed resident aliens on technical grounds. Nor were the Jews the only vulnerable group. One-third of the new state's population consisted of national minorities, including three million Jews, four million Ukrainians, and roughly one million Germans. The Polish Endeks (National Democratic) right-wing party, led by militant xenophobe Roman Dmowski, was determined to keep Poland Polish—which meant squeezing out the Jews and other minorities. Jews placed their trust in his left-wing rival, Józef Piłsudski, head of the Polish armed forces, whose expansive talk of rebuilding a Polish-Lithuanian Commonwealth inspired hopes for a multicultural society.

The early signs were not promising. At the university, an antisemitic Polonization campaign took place. Nearly the entire Jewish student body was expelled for failure to perform Polish army service. Thousands of students were locked out of classes, many, like Lauterpacht, just shy of graduation. As chairman of the regional Jewish university student association, he lodged numerous protests with Polish authorities, who responded by targeting him for arrest and imprisonment during a crackdown on the Galician Zionist leadership. Adding to the desperation, a famine broke out in Eastern Galicia, and the ongoing fighting prevented the U.S. government and Jewish groups from delivering emergency food supplies.[27]

During August and September 1919, the situation worsened. Having dispensed with the Ukrainians, Polish forces now fought the Bolshevik Red Army along the country's eastern border. In the process, they massacred about a thousand Jewish civilians. Similar atrocities occurred next door in war-torn Ukraine. It was a dismal start to two years of massive violence in the Polish-Russian war. The eventual Jewish death toll has been variously estimated at between 50,000 and 200,000.[28]

In November 1919, a U.S. government delegation led by Henry Morgenthau toured Lwów and surrounding areas to investigate the violence. Piłsudksi, on whom so many Jews pinned their hopes for a tolerant Poland, chided Morgenthau at length for his intrusive inquiry. What the Jews erroneously called "pogroms," he insisted, were merely "little mishaps." The real problem was international meddling in Poland's internal affairs. At Paris, America had humiliated Poland by insisting on a treaty that "creates an authority—a power to which to appeal—outside the laws of this country!" Article 93 of the Little Versailles Treaty, which obligated Poland to protect its minorities, constituted "a public insult to my country just as she was assuming her rightful place among the sovereign states of the world!"[29]

That was precisely the point, thought Lauterpacht. If the Polish government would not honor its legal commitments, Jews should appeal beyond it to the League of Nations for redress. In February 1920, he gave a public lecture

in the nearby town of Przemyśl (Pshemishl in Yiddish) in which he outlined a new plan to combat antisemitism in Poland and throughout all
European universities. It was time, he said, for Jews to internationalize
themselves and stand up for their rights as a nation. Others reached a similar conclusion. That same month, his Polish and Russian colleagues, still
in Paris for the tail end of the Peace Conference, announced the creation of
a permanent international body, the Council of Jewish Lands. Based in
Geneva and led by Leo Motzkin, it would "protect the civil, political, and
national rights of the Jews" everywhere, monitor their legal status in the
new independent states of Europe, and "defend Jewish interests before the
League of Nations." And it would do one other thing: the Council would
insist that the League formally recognize Palestine as the "Jewish national
home" and, eventually, as the Jewish "autonomous state."[30]

In December 1920, Lauterpacht presented his plan to combat antisemitism
to a larger group of Zionist leaders, many just back from Paris, at a meeting
in Vienna. The former Habsburg metropolis, now the capital of the Austrian
Republic, had become the seat of the regional Zionist movement. If the
Polish authorities refused to respond to Jewish legal demands, Lauterpacht
explained in an "extraordinary and important paper" delivered in Hebrew,
then Jews should turn to a larger European-wide "public opinion" campaign.
The first step was to organize the tens of thousands of Jewish university
students across the continent.[31]

Impressed by his drive and charisma, the regional Zionist leadership
encouraged him to remain in Vienna. Hundreds of thousands of Galician
Jews had streamed into the city, fleeing the fighting. Among them were
thousands of Jewish students shut out of Polish universities. They too
needed a voice and a leader, especially since antisemitic quotas had begun
to appear at the University of Vienna. At the urging of the city's Zionist
Chief Rabbi, Zvi Chajes, Lauterpacht ran in citywide communal elections
for Vienna's Jewish Student Association, "Judea," and won the presidency.
Now the official leader of 10,000-plus Jewish students, he set about launching
citywide political meetings to organize them and opening a communal
soup kitchen to feed them. (Ironically, the cook he employed for this job
was Adolf Hitler's sister.)

MANDATES

Under the Mandates system, created after the World War, certain territories in the Near East, Africa and Oceania, with a total population of about 19,500,000, are controlled or administered by various mandatory Powers in the name of the League of Nations and as a " sacred trust of civilisation " (Article 22 of the Covenant).

The mandatory Powers furnish to the Council an annual report on each of the mandated territories. These reports are examined and commented upon by the Permanent Mandates Commission.

Mandated territories are divided into three categories : A, B, and C, according to their stage of development.

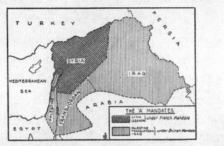

The Near East.

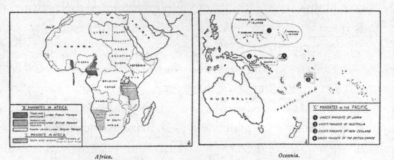

Africa. *Oceania.*

"A" MANDATES

These territories have reached a stage of development where their existence as independent nations can be provisionally recognised, subject to the rendering of administrative advice and assistance by the mandatory, until such time as they are able to stand alone.

"B" MANDATES

These territories are at such a stage of development that the mandatory Power must be responsible for the administration of the territory under certain specific guarantees for the welfare of the natives, and for the interests of other countries.

"C" MANDATES

These territories are to be administered under the laws of the mandatory as integral portions of its territory, under similar guarantees for the welfare of the natives.

The League of Nations mandate system

Pictorial Survey of the League of Nations (1931),
courtesy of the United Nations Office at Geneva

Meanwhile, the young lawyer enrolled himself as a student of the renowned jurist Professor Hans Kelsen, a Jewish convert twice over (first to Catholicism, then Lutheranism) and the greatest legal philosopher of the century. Kelsen had just written the Austrian Republic's postwar constitution. Under his tutelage, Lauterpacht deepened his academic researches into the nature of international law.[32]

Politics and law were not his only concerns. In Vienna he met a beautiful young pianist, Rachel Steinberg, a member of an illustrious Russian clan of early Zionist pioneers who had come from Jerusalem to study at the city's conservatory. Her nieces Suzi and Aura would go on to marry two major figures in the Israeli political establishment: diplomat Abba Eban and Ashkenazi Chief Rabbi Yitzhak HaLevi Herzog. Lauterpacht was entranced by Rachel's mixture of feminine grace and *sabra* grit; he won her over with his fluent Sephardi-accented Hebrew and calm confidence. In virtually the same breath, the young couple announced their engagement and their intention to settle in Palestine, "whose future," Lauterpacht wrote to his in-laws, "is the future of all of us."[33]

The moment seemed ripe for such a move. On July 24, 1922, the League of Nations formally authorized Great Britain to place Palestine under British Mandatory rule. A week earlier, Lauterpacht formally defended his dissertation in Vienna on the mandate system in international law. He began exploring legal career options in Jerusalem. However, even while planning his future in the Jewish homeland, Lauterpacht remained committed to protecting the rights of Jews in the European diaspora. The same year, while still in Vienna, he concluded that the time had come to launch an international Jewish student movement.[34]

Embracing the World

On April 30, 1924, 2,500 young men and women from across the world convened in Antwerp for the opening conference of the World Union of Jewish Students. In his inaugural presidential address, Lauterpacht addressed the crowd with evident satisfaction: "We see gathered here Jewish students from all over the world. We must harness our strength to fight against the dark forces that are at work everywhere to rob Jewish students of the opportunity to study." Speaking a combination of Yiddish, Hebrew, and French, he told the raucous crowd that the exclusion of Jewish youth from European universities not only contradicted "the ideas of justice and culture, but also constituted a breach" of the Minorities Treaties. This uncivilized "disgrace" must be rectified immediately via "political and legal action based on public law and international treaties, and by appealing to public opinion."[35]

In addition to expressing these goals, Lauterpacht made one other statement at Antwerp that proved controversial: "You, Zionists, must ensure that the World Union is created and remains apolitical, because this is a Zionist task: to organize the Jewish people and to unite them in the struggle for a better future." His exhortation signaled to many young European Zionists his expansive notion of what Jewish internationalism meant. All Jews, led by the vanguard of enlightened national leadership, would look beyond antisemitism and party politics to a cosmopolitan idea of Jewish nationhood. The battle for Jewish rights meant much more than extending "philanthropic or humanitarian aid" to fellow Jews in need or protesting "University antisemitism." Nor was it restricted to building Jewish Palestine. "Jewish international unity," he declared, required grounding in "the living foundation of world-embracing Jewish-community," which could only come via "cultural and national cooperation between all the Jewish students throughout the world." Only from that position, linking virtual arms "from Argentina to Latvia, from London to Melbourne," could Jews secure "the protection of the rights of men."[36]

Not all were convinced by Lauterpacht's lofty speech. His bid for national unity struck the Jewish socialist delegations as a thinly veiled Zionist plot to nationalize Jewish youth. His decision to have the congress sing "Hatikvah," the Jewish national anthem, only further angered them. A heated debate ensued in which the leftists denounced the "Bourgeois, nationalist-chauvinist Congress." Lauterpacht remained unapologetic. The World Union would work with any and all Jews, he declared, be they Zionists, non-Zionist, Orthodox, or secular. Only two kinds of Jews were off-limits: the "assimilationists" and the "Bundists," both of whom denied the existence of a global Jewish nation.[37]

Lauterpacht's liberal Zionism reflected not only his fierce Jewish national pride but also his internationalist sensibilities. The Jews were a global people. That was not a political defect but a moral asset. "When he is honest with himself," he said in another speech that year, the young Jew recognizes that "he is a member of two communities."

> He is bound to one with the memories of his life, with language, custom, education, with the ties of state and citizenship, he is bound with the other with memory of his past, with the elements of his blood, with the indestructible ties of his most inward—and some say—physical structure. He cannot, if he is true with himself, disregard this second, Jewish, community.

The Jewish quest for a homeland was not merely a chauvinist entitlement or a one-way exit strategy from an antisemitic Europe; it was a step toward the harmonious ordering of the world. The Jewish destiny relied on and affirmed the new spirit of international law. That congruence shaped the intellectual mission he undertook in his scholarly work. When no job was immediately forthcoming in Jerusalem, he changed course and made for London. There he enrolled in the law faculty of the University College of London (UCL) to take yet another doctoral degree. It was then that he began a quest to rewrite the script of British imperial power and international law.[38]

From Zion Will Come Forth the Law

Lauterpacht's choice of London as his next destination after Vienna reflected not only his struggles to find a fitting position in Palestine but also his keen political instincts about international relations. Back in 1920, an isolationist U.S. Congress had torpedoed Wilson's dream by voting against American membership in the League. The surprising turn of events deprived Jews not only of their best champion of minority rights but also of the clout of American Jews, who had proven influential at Paris. With Germany and Bolshevik Russia still outside the League's ranks, France and Great Britain were left as the two dominant powers. Of the two, it was the British, by virtue of their hold on Palestine and their dominance in Europe, who most directly held the fate of both Jewish rights and international law in their hands.

Despite knowing seven languages, Lauterpacht faced the challenge in London of simply being able to communicate. He had learned English strictly from books, and when he tried to speak it he was nearly unintelligible. His new advisor at UCL, the great Scottish lawyer Lord Arnold McNair, recalled his bafflement at the strange sounds emanating from his would-be pupil's mouth. Yet within weeks, Lauterpacht reappeared in the professor's office speaking a precise, astonishingly fluent English. He had trained himself by sitting day after day for eight-hour stretches in lecture halls listening to public talks on every conceivable subject. His dedication to this task left him with a decent British accent, though not without a trace of Mittleuropa that forever marked him as something of an outsider to the British establishment.

The next task was to select a topic for his research. Here Lauterpacht was well served by McNair's mentorship. The distinguished lawyer recognized a kindred spirit in the ambitious young immigrant. Soon he invited him to co-edit *Oppenheim's Digest of International Law,* a preeminent reference resource consulted by international lawyers around the world. Lauterpacht eventually succeeded McNair as the Whewell Chair in International Law at Cambridge University, and then once again as the British judge on the International Court of Justice. Working closely with McNair, he mastered the nuances of English academia even as he blazed his own revolutionary path in the realm of law, beginning with his second doctoral dissertation.

In Vienna, Lauterpacht had written a dissertation on the fundamental problem at the root of international law: whether or not it even existed. The consensus at the time was that absolute sovereignty was an irrefutable characteristic of states. The power of each sovereign over his or her territory and subjects was supreme. Hence no legal authority could be superimposed on states from outside to limit this autonomy. Inside a given country, the judiciary and the legislature might check state power, but no such institutions existed in the broader world. Who would be in a position to enforce a penalty against a king, an emperor, or even a prime minister who broke his word? "International law" was no more than a system of voluntary agreements or treaties that could be abrogated with impunity. This meant that individuals and groups had no recourse outside their own state, and no government could legitimately interfere in the internal affairs of another

country. Sovereignty raised a bar to all kinds of legal claims and protections. Diaspora groups, national minorities, and colonial peoples had no
legal standing.

Against this traditional view, Lauterpacht had argued in his 1922 Viennese
dissertation that the League of Nations Covenant had demonstrated once
and for all the reality of international law. The proof, he wrote, was the mandate system. In his formulation, the land of Palestine belonged to the Jews
by right. Though many dismissed the idea of a "mandate" as little more than
"a euphemism for the victors' imperialist annexation," he insisted they were
wrong. British sovereignty in Palestine (and in its other League mandates)
was but a legal fiction. The international community, in the form of the
League of Nations, actually possessed the land in trust for the Jewish nation via the British Empire, without making it part of the British state.[39]

Under McNair's guidance, Lauterpacht wrote another dissertation in 1924
on the theme of sovereignty, again with direct implications for Palestine.
He expanded his argument to claim that all state sovereignty was but a
fiction. Rather than being autonomous powers subject to no external,
higher authority, states functioned like individuals in society: they were
bound by laws—both customary and positive—that restricted their freedom. Likewise, the territory of a state was not intrinsic to its sovereignty. A
homeland was better understood as a piece of property owned by the state,
just as a private individual might own an object. Such ownership did not
exist outside the matrix of laws that governed the terms of private property. Building on this idea, Lauterpacht argued further that, where written
laws did not exist to govern international relations between states, they
could be determined through analogy to private laws.

When eventually published in book form in the 1930s, Lauterpacht's ideas
would prove controversial. In what has been called the first great debate of
twentieth-century international relations, the historian E. H. Carr attacked
him as the prime example of an obtuse "legalistic Utopianism" for his insistence that international law could contain politics and restrain states
from using force at will. Yet Lauterpacht insisted that a new order of human
affairs was at hand. Back in the mid-1920s, his chief exhibit in this argument was Zionism. Even as he settled into English academic life, he
continued to run the World Union of Jewish Students, and at University

Hersch Zvi Lauterpacht (third from left) with the founders
of the World Union of Jewish Students, 1924

Reproduced with permission of the Estate of Sir Elihu Lauterpacht

College London he served as president of the Zionist Section of the Jewish
Student Union and in the leadership of the Inter-University Zionist Federation. He also became the London correspondent for the Polish-language
Zionist newspaper *Nowy Dziennik,* published in Krakow. In near-weekly
columns over the next decade, he narrated international affairs for his fellow Jews back in Eastern Europe. In these columns and his public lectures,
he rhapsodized about the force of historical progress and the sensibility of
the British approach to law.[40]

In the spring of 1925, Lauterpacht and his wife led a delegation of two
hundred students from across Europe to attend the opening of the Hebrew
University of Jerusalem. There they mingled comfortably with British officials and led walking tours of the city. Lauterpacht watched approvingly
as Palestine's Governor-General Herbert Samuel and Attorney-General
Norman Bentwich, both Jews, joined Lord Balfour and other dignitaries in
the groundbreaking ceremony on Mount Scopus. Equally significantly,
Lauterpacht, Albert Einstein, Chaim Nachman Bialik, and several other
prominent Jewish intellectuals signed a Memorandum of Agreement for a

House of Jewish Students to be built in Jerusalem as lodging for Jewish students from all over the world.[41]

Lauterpacht returned to England with his spirits soaring. The university was not only a tangible sign of the "Jewish national renaissance"; it was further evidence of the moral and political partnership between Britain and the Jews. Zionism and international law had entered a symbiotic relationship. For the first time in history, the Jews were well on the way to regaining their national home thanks to the power of law, not naked force or imperial largesse.[42]

In the fall of 1925, Lauterpacht registered his approval as the Great Powers signed the Locarno Treaties. These agreements, negotiated between Britain, France, Germany, Italy, Belgium, Poland, Czechoslovakia, and the United States, normalized post–World War I political relations, setting the stage for the Weimar Republic to enter the League of Nations. The parties pledged not to attack one another, and Germany accepted its western border, the Rhineland, conceding France's rule over Alsace-Lorraine. Many thought the achievement heralded a new era of world peace: the foreign ministers of France, Germany, and England—Aristide Briand, Gustav Stresemann, and Austen Chamberlain, respectively—jointly received the 1926 Nobel Peace Prize for their efforts. Others took a darker view of Germany's quick rehabilitation. Polish prime minister Josef Beck quipped prophetically that "Germany was officially asked to attack the east, in return for peace in the west." Lauterpacht disagreed. Locarno, he told his readers, signaled "the beginning of a new, spiritual armistice, for which Europe has waited six years." He put his faith in Britain to lead the world "down the path of lasting peace."

> Peace is the main goal of the Empire's politics and a cardinal condition of its well-being. British Justice is a characteristic position not only for British judges. The history of the international courts of the last century indicates that Great Britain, with her sister United States, was the main pioneer of mediating international conflicts. In the last thirty years, Great Britain not once threw the fate of territories on the scale of mediating tribunals. The slogan "Parliament of Man, Federation of the World" . . . is a fitting example of the English character.[43]

Lauterpacht's confidence in the benevolence of British imperial power ran deep. It also pointed to the paradox at the root of his Zionism. The only way to fulfill a rightful Jewish claim to the land of Palestine was through an empire strong enough to seize the territory and hold it by force. International law and Jewish nationhood alike needed the backing of empire. What would happen, though, when British force met resistance? Or if Jewish claims clashed with those of the local Arab population? He did not have long to wait for an answer.

The British government never specified what the Jewish National Home would look like in its final form—or its relationship to Arab nationalist aspirations. The Balfour Declaration had spoken merely of "a national home for the Jewish people" in which "nothing shall be done which may prejudice the civil and religious rights of existing non-Jewish communities in Palestine." The 1922 League of Nations Covenant for Mandatory Palestine guaranteed that the British would safeguard "the civil and religious rights of all the inhabitants of Palestine, irrespective of race and religion." While most British colonial officials favored the Arab perspective, their policies overall proved more helpful to the Jewish cause. Nonetheless, both sides continued to offer dueling visions for the final disposition of the Palestinian Mandate throughout the 1920s, while the British gave few concrete policy signals about their intentions.

In Lauterpacht's view, Jews and Arabs could each be accommodated by the League's mandate system, which would "erect the independent Arab State of Mesopotamia and . . . a Jewish national home in Palestine." Events on the ground frustrated this tidy vision of political order. Throughout the early 1920s, the French repressed Arab democratic aspirations in Lebanon and Syria. The Palestinian Arabs, who feared becoming a minority—in both numerical and political senses—in a Jewish-dominated country, asserted their own claims to sovereignty. Meanwhile, deepening cracks appeared within the Zionist movement as leaders debated how far to accommodate Arab intransigence and their own people's nationalist passions. But the first real test of Lauterpacht's faith in the British commitment to Jewish rights did not come until 1929, when an unprecedented explosion of violence forced a major reckoning with the mandate system's political limits.[44]

"Basic Human Justice"

In September 1928, a conflict erupted at Jerusalem's Kotel, or Western Wall, when a British policeman interfered with Jewish prayer services on Yom Kippur, the holiest Jewish day of the year. The police were acting at the behest of Palestinian Arab leaders, who claimed that a newly installed screen separating Orthodox Jewish men and women constituted a provocative violation of the status quo agreement on prayer arrangements dating back to the Ottoman period. As Jewish authorities negotiated with the British to resolve the dispute, Haj Amin al-Husseini, the British-appointed Grand Mufti of Jerusalem, seized on the moment to spread false rumors of a Jewish plot to take over the Muslim-controlled Temple Mount. Seeking to consolidate his power in local Palestinian politics, Husseini inflamed the Arab masses with Islamist rhetoric. His strategy worked. Over the next year, tit-for-tat violence spread between Jewish and Arab communities.[45]

By August 1929, with Jewish and Arab mobs confronting each other openly in the streets of Jerusalem, Husseini instigated a larger Palestine-wide campaign of Arab violence. Jewish self-defense forces responded, but found themselves vastly outnumbered. Right-wing Zionist leaders called on their followers to carry out reprisal attacks. Both sides accused the British forces of standing idly by when not engaging in their own reckless violence. The tragic sequence of events culminated in six bloody days in late August, during which 472 Jews and 268 Arabs were either killed or wounded.[46]

In the aftermath, the British launched the Shaw Commission inquiry into the causes of the violence. British authorities attempted an evenhanded approach to assigning blame and de-escalating tensions. More than 800 people were charged with violent crimes, the vast majority of them Arabs, 55 of whom were convicted of murder. Heavy fines were imposed on various Arab communities for their role in widespread looting and destruction. In the eyes of the Shaw Commission members, however, the Arab attacks represented a natural reaction to the large-scale influx of Jews into Palestine. They therefore responded with a governing strategy for the next two decades that had dire consequences for Jewish claims to Palestine. To pacify Arab national passions, the British tightened controls on Jewish immigration and retreated on promises regarding Jewish political aims. The decision only emboldened radical elements in the Palestinian nationalist leadership, who realized their effectiveness in keeping the British from offering more concessions to the Jews lay in numbers and in the selective use of popular violence. Meanwhile, Zionists were left nursing the sting of a double betrayal by the Arabs and the British.[47]

Back in London, Lauterpacht was one of the first to condemn the 1929 attacks. By that time a newly appointed law professor at University College of London, he continued to believe that Zionism would help secure Jewish rights and advance international law. Both aims depended on the benevolent spirit of the British Empire. Absent a "racially allied existing State," the Jewish minority required the protection of international law, guaranteed by British power. Yet he now voiced fury at the British abandonment of the Jews. In his regular column for *Nowy Dziennik,* he spoke bluntly of the "feeling of terror" that left "one's blood running cold" at the carnage in Palestine. The Mufti and his Arab followers were criminals who bore full responsibility for the massacres. What had occurred, he asserted, was "a traitorous, massive, and terrible attack of uncivilized elements on the populace, who sought only peace and prosperity."[48]

Assigning primary responsibility for the violence was the easy part. Lauterpacht's greater challenge was to justify why the British government had acquiesced to this breakdown of the rule of law and, worse, why it had failed to ascribe full blame to the Arab side, the true culprit in his eyes. He felt compelled to defend British justice as a necessarily complex balancing act: "This obvious unwillingness to state who is guilty would be morally appalling, if it wasn't for the justification of the feeling of great responsibility which rests on the Empire, in which live the greatest number of Muslims in the world, even into the hundreds of millions." England, he explained to his Polish Jewish readers, was caught between its deep instinct "to defend minorities before deliberate physical attack" and its "reasonable fear" of criticizing a group "behind which stand tens and hundreds of millions fanatical co-believers, living in the countries of the Empire." Truth be told, he wrote, "A religious war by all of Islam is a thing before which even the British Empire must cower."[49]

Unable to bring himself to blame Her Majesty's Government or the Zionist right, as some of his colleagues did, Lauterpacht directed his ire at the

English press for minimizing Jewish casualties and refusing to take sides. The papers, he wrote, declined to state what everyone else knew: that "the Jewish people in Palestine are becoming an object of mass, bloody attack for which political expediency must make room for basic human justice."

> The situation has been presented in such a fashion as if there was a battle in Palestine, in which both sides are actively taking a role and in which both sides are willing participants, who must divide among themselves responsibility for what has occurred. . . . It is a naive act of closing one's eyes before the necessity of expressing a formal and moral judgment. Still today the press writes as if at present there was a religious conflict in Palestine, and only that, over the Wall of Tears. Even now it is being spoken of as an Arab-Jewish "conflict" in which both sides are involved. What comes to mind is the story about the unlucky man, who had all his fortunes stolen, but then was accused by his neighbors as having been involved in the theft.[50]

While Lauterpacht agonized in these dispatches, he reasserted his faith that the British sense of fairness would ultimately deliver justice to Jews and Arabs. Though shaken, he held to the belief that securing Jewish rights was not only the moral course of action but also redounded to Britain's benefit. "Intelligently conceived national interest," he wrote, "is identical with the general international good." British internationalism, certified by law, would ensure that the Jews eventually received their national home in Palestine.[51]

Lauterpacht ended the year bruised but not broken. For one thing, British politics was dynamic. The recent general elections had brought the Labour Party to power, and Lauterpacht felt hopeful that the new prime minister, Ramsay MacDonald, began his term with a consultation with his American counterpart, President Hoover. "Perhaps this conversation will be the first step on the road to actual cooperation with the United States in organizing the peace of the world, although in a different tempo and with different methods than those used by Wilson," he wrote in one of his Polish dispatches from London. "It is certainly true, that the civilized world makes up one great republic . . . [comprised of] the many members of the family of nations."[52]

While Lauterpacht clung to hopes for a renewed Anglo-American alliance, others openly dismissed Jewish reliance on British power to secure Jewish rights. In the days after the news of the 1929 massacres reached Lithuania, five thousand Jews gathered in Kovno, the capital city, to demand emergency intervention by the League of Nations. They were led by a young Lithuanian Zionist named Jacob Robinson, who had traveled the same path as Lauterpacht into international law in the aftermath of World War I. But unlike his London compatriot, Robinson minced no words in condemning what he saw as British malfeasance. "The hypocritical and criminal actions of the Palestine Administration," he declared in an urgent telegram to Geneva, had created "a situation where our elementary rights and interests in Palestine are scorned in the most brutal way." Robinson not only lambasted the British. He actively sought out help from their greatest rival. It turned out that the country most dedicated to advancing minority rights, and with them the Jewish cause, at the League of Nations in the late 1920s was none other than Weimar Germany.[53]

2

The Cry of the Peoples

THE VERY SAME WEEK IN LATE August 1929 that violence flared in the streets of Jerusalem, several Zionist leaders gathered in placid Geneva for the annual Congress of European National Minorities. For the past five years, the city's venerable Salle Centrale had played host to an oddball assortment of spokesmen for Europe's littlest diasporas—Hungarians from Czechoslovakia, Croats from Italy, Germans from Poland, and so forth. Thirty million people caught on the wrong side of the postwar borders had banded together to force the League of Nations to take action on the elusive promise of minority rights. Now, as word spread of the terrible events in Palestine, these minority leaders presented a remarkable display of pro-Jewish solidarity. One by one, the representatives of the different nationalities rose to pledge their support for "Jewish rights to self-defense in their motherland." The body's president, Dr. Josip Wilfan, a silver-tongued Slovenian lawyer from Italy, toasted the Jewish "freedom-struggle in Palestine." The fiery Catalan Joan Estelrich i Artigues from Spanish Mallorca proudly swore that his people would deploy their great "influence" to aid the cause of Jewish "national freedom."[1]

It was a moving sight. Yet the grand promise of help from tiny Catalonia underscored the quixotic character of the entire venture. The voices of Europe's minority groups might form an impressive multinational chorus, but neither numbers nor cultural diversity equaled diplomatic muscle on the international stage. The whole reason for the existence of the "Little

League of Nations," as it was nicknamed, was that ten years after the Paris Peace Conference, the actual League had failed to turn minority rights from ideal to reality.[2]

The man who best understood this failure was also the architect of the Jewish entrance into the interwar minority rights movement. From the moment the Paris Peace Conference ended, Jacob Robinson had fashioned himself into one of Europe's foremost champions of minority rights. He juggled multiple careers at home in Lithuania—as leader of the Jewish faction in the Lithuanian parliament, head of the country's Zionist movement, and publisher of a Jewish newspaper—with international work as a practicing lawyer, a leader of the Comité des Délégations Juives, and a co-founder of the Congress of European National Minorities. The ultimate internationalist, Robinson was no less a clear-eyed realist. "Never, ever believe a word you read that any public official says," he would remark, for "the essence of political discourse is deception." He knew this lesson from personal experience. The secret behind the Congress of European National Minorities was a hidden alliance between Europe's weakest minority, the Jews, and a resurgent state power: Weimar Germany.[3]

Those who find it hard today to imagine the Germans as protector of Europe's Jews in the early twentieth century forget that the Third Reich was separated from pre–World War I Germany by a decade and a half of Weimar democracy. They also ignore the oldest rule of diplomacy: the enemy of my enemy is my friend. In their search for an alternative to British apathy and Bolshevik menace, many European national minorities bet on Germany to hold the League of Nations accountable for its promises of the protection and legal enforcement of rights. With millions of ethnic Germans spread across nine Eastern European countries, Berlin had a vested interest in supporting minority rights. And beyond that noble impulse was the attractive prospect of a German Empire reborn in virtual form, thanks to the law's reach across borders. Hoping to allay other countries' suspicions of its imperial ambitions, savvy German diplomats tapped Jewish leaders to be the public face of the European minorities movement. Men like Robinson in turn wagered that liberal internationalism braced by law would restrain the darker side of German nationalism.

This forgotten episode in the history of human rights offers another reminder of how well interwar Jewish rights defenders understood that idealism required power. They hoped the Law of Nations would ultimately transcend the politics of nationalism, but that was a goal, not the present reality. In the meantime, Jews needed allies. While Lauterpacht and his comrades held fast to their faith in British liberal imperialism, Robinson captained a second cohort in Eastern Europe who sought opportunity in the continent's messy geopolitics. Skeptical of British imperial caprice and fearful of Soviet repression, they hoped to leverage the common needs of European nation-states and national minorities alike to force the League of Nations forward in its march toward international justice.

Robinson's path from German POW camp to the Lithuanian parliament to the League of Nations encapsulates the strange logic of that period. During the decade of the 1920s, he took part in three crucial episodes that shaped the possibilities for international minority rights: the birth of the minorities bloc in the Lithuanian parliament in 1923, the launch of the pan-European minorities movement in 1925, and the creation of the World Jewish Congress in 1927. The first event involved a rapprochement between Jews and Lithuanians at the expense of Poles; the latter two embodied the complicated alliance between Jews and Germans. Together they represented the dramatic rise and staggering fall of international minority rights between the wars.

The Jews may have invented minority rights, went the joke in 1930s Geneva, but it was the Germans who used them. By 1933, German diplomats at the League had already filed hundreds of petitions on behalf of their German brethren in Poland and Lithuania. Contrast this activism to that of Jews, who submitted a total of three such petitions in the entire interwar period. To understand why, we need to turn back to the immediate postwar moment in Poland and look north to the country that best exemplified the intertwined promise and peril of minority rights in modern Eastern Europe.

Jerusalem in Lithuania

The man who would become known as the "Jewish People's Lawyer" and "legal counsel to the world" began his journey into Jewish politics in the small town of Saray (Suwalki), in the northwestern corner of the

Russian Empire. Born in 1889 and descended from the distinguished seventeenth-century Lithuanian talmudist Rabbi Yom-Tov Lipman Heller, Jacob Robinson received a traditional rabbinic education taught in a mixture of Hebrew and Yiddish. Throughout his life he would retain the marks of his Litvak heritage: a keen analytical mind, a prodigious memory, and a sharp tongue. For high school, Robinson attended a local gymnasium filled with Jewish, Russian, Polish, Lithuanian, and German students. The local language was Polish, yet all courses were taught in Russian. In 1905, as the first spasm of revolution shook Russia, Polish nationalists ordered a boycott of the town's Russian government-run schools. The local Jews were divided on whether to join in solidarity. Abstaining from the boycott would imply that they backed the Lithuanians, the Poles' local rivals, a strategy that Robinson urged on his peers. Like other Russian Zionists, he sympathized with the Lithuanian people's struggle for national freedom against the wealthy Polish nobility who dominated the region. "And beyond this," he recalled later, "the antisemitism was much worse among the Poles than the Lithuanians." In the elections for the Russian Duma held that year, Lithuanian Jews reached the same calculus. From the Jewish vote for Lithuanian candidates was born, in Robinson's words, "the first entente between Jews and Lithuanians."[4]

Just as it would do for Lauterpacht in 1918, the anti-Jewish violence during the Russian Revolution of 1905 prompted Robinson to search for new solutions. His generation found their guide in the Russian Jewish historian Simon Dubnow's *Letters on Old and New Judaism*. Dubnow had begun publishing these essays in 1897, the same year Theodor Herzl convened the first World Zionist Congress in Geneva. Against Herzl's dramatic vision of mass emigration and statehood in Palestine, Dubnow proposed a creative solution to the problem of Jewish nationhood at home in Eastern Europe. Since ancient times, Jews had survived in diaspora via a unique political structure, the autonomous Jewish *kehillah* (pl. *kehillot*). Lacking a land of their own, they built—with the permission of premodern monarchs—their own courts, schools, system of taxation, and internal self-government. This model of portable nationhood served them well for almost two millennia. But in the aftermath of the French Revolution, European liberals insisted Jews must abandon the *kehillah* in order to reap the promise of emancipation

as modern citizens. Dubnow believed that, in this bargain, Jews had sacrificed too much. In a dialectical move of the kind so beloved by Russian intellectuals, he argued that the ideal solution lay in the synthesis of citizen
and *kehillah*, individual and nation. "National emancipation" would give
Jews legal recognition as a distinct modern ethnic nation and autonomous
entity in the inevitably multinational states of postrevolutionary Europe.
Far from creating an incendiary "state within a state," national-cultural autonomy would allow modern states to constrain the disruptive potential of
competing nationalisms.[5]

This idea, which Dubnow labeled "Autonomism" and others came to call
"Diaspora Nationalism," elicited strong reactions. Zionists such as the writer
Ahad Ha'am complained that Dubnow's plea for nationhood without territory amounted to "settling for half a loaf of bread." Jewish Marxists dismissed
him as a closet Zionist. Yet by 1905 both Zionists and Jewish Socialists had
embraced national minority rights for Jews within the Habsburg and Russian Empires. Some Zionists saw this demand as a short-term solution, a
strategic move to win support from the Jewish masses and protect them until
a comprehensive emigration plan had run its course. For others, like Lauterpacht and Robinson, minority rights offered a longer-term solution that
perfectly fit the new spirit of Zionist internationalism.

Across Europe, wrote Robinson in his first book, modern times gave rise
to two extremes: a vicious chauvinism threatening to tear countries apart
and an uncompromising cosmopolitanism that "denies in principle the
national as nothing more than prejudice." Against both camps, the Jews
followed the "Golden Mean," hoisting "the flag of internationalism." We
internationalists, he wrote, believe that nationalism is a positive, "natural
force" that "bequeaths to the world so many of its values and treasures," from
"the Jewish Torah, Indian Buddhism, [and] Greek philosophy and art" to the
Italian Renaissance, the German Reformation, and the French Revolution.
In each case, universal human values emerged from "national forces" nurtured in "the boundaries of the particular." Though he did not say so, he
might as well have been speaking of international law as well.[6]

Everywhere he turned, Robinson found this idea confirmed. Shut out of
most Russian universities by anti-Jewish enrollment quotas, he chose in
1910 to study at the University of Warsaw. But his real education came in

summers spent in Leipzig, attending law lectures at the German university. There he encountered a vibrant Russian colony of expatriate Georgians, Armenians, and Jews, all united in their loathing for tsarist repression. They shared the hope that modern Europe would see the end of feudal regimes and the dawn of political freedom for their peoples.[7]

In 1913, Vladimir Lenin arrived in Warsaw to give a lecture titled "Social Democracy and the National Question." The Bolsheviks were just then formulating their position on the nationality question. Together with his specialist on the subject, a Georgian ex-priest named Joseph Stalin, Lenin hoped to win over Russia's minorities to the revolutionary movement. The two men insisted that Marxist socialism could accommodate nationalism better than could Western liberalism. Their solution, borrowed from the Austrian Marxists, amounted to the same idea as Dubnow's: national-cultural autonomy as a way to balance competing nationalist movements in a future socialist state. But they went out of their way to deny one particular European people a place in this scheme. The Jews, Lenin and Stalin insisted, were not a real nation and did not deserve special consideration.[8]

Robinson's new friends begged him to debate the Bolshevik leader. They were skeptical of Russian revolutionary intentions toward non-Russian peoples. Who better than the brilliant Jewish lawyer and talented orator to challenge Lenin's paternalistic attitude toward the political aspirations of Russia's smaller nations? He demurred. For Jews and Zionists, he explained, Lenin's campaign "was not really our fight. This was an internal socialist war between Bolsheviks and Mensheviks." Still, he showed up to listen. Socialism had made major inroads into Jewish politics, challenging the primacy of Zionism with its messianic vision of a universalism shorn of all cultural and religious differences. What Robinson heard convinced him that socialism held no promise for the Jewish national minority. Lenin reminded him of "an old Russian Orthodox priest quoting scripture to serve his own purposes," he remembered, "twisting the words of Marx and Engels to his own interpretation." Most crucially, the Bolshevik leader offered nothing for Jewish nationalists: "What could he possibly say to us, the Jews, if he denied cultural autonomy in favor of Russian centralism?" The same was true of the Jewish Labor Bund, Lenin's longtime opponents, who attempted to combine socialism with Jewish national-cultural autonomy and who struck Robinson as "five minutes away from Bolshevism."⁹

One debate challenge Robinson did accept during his time in Leipzig came from the Diaspora Nationalist leader Chaim Zhitlovsky. In a public lecture shortly before World War I, Zhitlovsky championed national minority rights for the Jews, but added his own Marxist twist to Dubnow's Autonomism. The only viable Jewish future, he claimed, was as a secular, proletarian, Yiddish-speaking nation: Jews must shed their religion and their fantasies about a Jewish Palestine. This time Robinson went on the attack, shouting in the crowded lecture hall that socialist revolution would lead only to forced assimilation. Absent Hebrew, religion, and a homeland, the Yiddish language alone would never guarantee Jewish survival. Then the impulsive young Zionist turned personal: "You married a *shiksa* [non-Jewish woman]. You have two Russian Orthodox sons. Why do you suppose the rest of the Jews are not rushing to follow you down your path?" He later claimed regret over this "tactless" gesture unbefitting a future diplomat, yet it suggested just how strongly he felt about the matter. Neither Marxist socialism nor Diaspora Nationalism could protect Jews in the future. Zionism meant national and cultural autonomy in Eastern Europe linked with Hebrew revival and political rebirth in Palestine.¹⁰

Robinson earned his law degree, an LLD, in June 1914, just in time to be drafted into the Russian military. Shortly after marrying his high school sweetheart Klara, he was mobilized to the Eastern Front, where he joined a half-million other Jews conscripted into the doomed cause of holding together the tsar's fraying empire. In September 1915, the Germans captured him after invading Vilnius. His war had ended. He spent the next three years shuttling through eight different German POW camps. Even with the constant movement, internment came as a relief: it provided safety and an unexpected intellectual freedom. Because of his law degree, German officials accorded him the rank of officer, sparing him from physical labor and permitting him to order books and newspapers for personal delivery to the camp. He even launched his own Zionist newspaper for fellow prisoners.

Behind this generous treatment lay not only an exaggerated German deference to scholarship but also the German High Command's great hopes of winning the Jews to their side. They even commissioned Robinson's comrade-

Jacob Robinson (top right) with the leaders of the Comité
des Délégations Juives in the mid-1920s

Courtesy of the United States Holocaust Memorial Museum

in-arms, Nahum Goldmann, member of the Zionist Executive and future
head of the World Jewish Congress, to write Yiddish-language leaflets promoting the German cause that they air-dropped across the Eastern Front. It
was the beginning of a Jewish dalliance with German nationalism that
would make for strange bedfellows in interwar Eastern Europe.[11]

Love for Jerusalem, Joy for Lithuania

Robinson returned home to Lithuania from Germany at the beginning
of 1919, still dressed in the heavy Russian Army woolen overcoat he had
worn into battle five years earlier. In the streets of Kovno, he delivered fiery
Zionist speeches supporting the Balfour Declaration. He lavished praise on
the new, independent Lithuanian Republic, whose leaders seemed prepared
to grant its Jews real rights as a national minority. Unlike the antagonistic
Poles, who from the beginning resisted honoring the spirit and letter of the
Minorities Treaties, the Lithuanians announced their readiness to sign
months before the treaties were even finalized. Moreover, in the 1918 "Paris
Declaration," Lithuanian leader Augustinas Voldemaras went far beyond
the proposed protections to offer the Jews equal status in the legislature

and the executive branch, public recognition of their national language, and broad "national self-rule" in "matters of religion, charity, social welfare, education and culture." He boldly promised, "The Jewish national autonomous bodies will be considered state institutions," authorized to tax themselves and pass "decisions binding on all members of their nation."[12]

True to their word, the Lithuanians created the Jewish National Council, which Robinson joined in January 1920. A cabinet-level Ministry for Jewish Affairs soon followed. Over the next few years, Robinson helped lead the Jewish negotiations with the government about what "national self-rule" should look like. "How much national autonomy do you want?" the Lithuanians asked. "And little by little," he recalled, "they would give us all kinds of rights." Then, they would turn around to boast of their progressive policies to the rest of the world. "Look how we deal with minorities! Our Jewish minority has special privileges, and you think that we cannot build a state?"[13]

The Lithuanian motivations were eminently pragmatic. On the western border, they were locked in a bitter war with Poland for territory vital to a viable Lithuanian state. Robinson himself witnessed Polish troop skirmishes in the Memel region between Vilnius and Kovno. To the east, the Lithuanians faced Bolsheviks eager to retake former Russian lands as part of the new Soviet empire. Placating the Jews was a low-cost way to win friends in the West, where, the Lithuanians feverishly imagined, Jewish bankers exercised massive power. Most importantly, there was the politics of demography. With a large number of ethnic Germans and Poles residing within their borders, Lithuanians viewed Jews as a demographic asset whose presence would dilute the other troublesome minorities.[14]

No sentimentalist, Robinson was untroubled by this Lithuanian realpolitik. He was writing a textbook of Jewish demography, which would be published in 1922, and he knew that life as a national minority depended on the hard facts of population numbers. A Lithuanian-Jewish entente would serve both peoples well. More importantly, an opportunity lay waiting to be seized. The Jews of Lithuania set about building hundreds of new social and cultural organizations, even an extensive network of communal banks. It was, Robinson exclaimed, the dawn of a "golden era for Jewish national existence in Lithuania."[15]

The keystone of the whole venture was schooling. "For the first time in history," he wrote, all the Jewish schools in Lithuania were government funded; "the Jews didn't have to spend one cent for this." He had already placed his law career on hold to found a Hebrew-language gymnasium in the shtetl of Virbalis (Virbalen in Yiddish), which he ran from 1919 until 1922. Raising a generation of Jewish children with Hebrew as their first language was a political and moral imperative. A vibrant new national culture was being born in the Land of Israel, but without Hebrew the Jews of Lithuania could not access it. Robinson held no brief per se against Yiddish—he even co-founded and ran a Yiddish daily newspaper, *Di idishe shtime* (The Jewish Voice), in order to reach Lithuanian Jews in their common tongue. But the future of Jewish nationhood had to be based on a truly global language. "Hebrew is the key to freeing ourselves from the [spirit of] Exile," he explained, and to "building our own political life."[16]

For the same reason, he attacked Lithuanian Jewish socialists and Yiddishist Diaspora Nationalists for pseudo-internationalism. Only Zionists, he insisted, truly believed in "the principle of world-wide Jewish solidarity." Minority rights were not merely a protective device for life in the diaspora but also a mechanism for forging a strong connection among Jews the world over: "Minority rights in the deepest sense of the term," he declared in one speech, "means the right of spiritual belonging to all other parts of the nation across the whole world."[17]

In 1922, the Jewish National Council of Lithuania selected Robinson to run for the Sejm (parliament) on the General Zionist Party ticket. He won and took charge of the Jewish national bloc. His rapid rise into the leadership stemmed in part from his being one of the few Jewish parliamentarians who had actually taken the trouble to learn Lithuanian. Just as in Leipzig a decade earlier, Robinson soon found himself cast as the spokesman for all the national minorities. Not only Jews but also Poles and Germans exercised a measure of minority rights in independent Lithuania. They turned to Robinson to speak for them, since as a Jew he could hardly be accused of dual loyalties to either Germany or Poland.[18]

From 1922 to 1926, Robinson led the Minorities Bloc in the Sejm. During these years, he made himself an expert on the law of minority rights. He assiduously studied the related legal statutes of the region's various countries. Every new law was a vote for the reality of this experiment; every ruling by the Permanent Court of International Justice of the League of Nations improved the prospects for the protection of international minorities. Next door, the tiny Baltic Republics of Estonia and Latvia followed Lithuania's lead in granting national-cultural autonomy to their Jews. Even in Poland, where the problems were obvious, a similar Minorities Bloc of nationalities emerged in its parliament, led by Robinson's friend Yitzhak Grinboym. Both men served in the leadership of the Comité des Délégations Juives, directed by Leo Motzkin from a small office in Paris. Keenly aware of the need to build a network of minority rights advocates, they also pursued contacts with minority parliamentarians in other Baltic states, the League of Nations Societies, and the international Inter-Parliamentary Union.[19]

Robinson viewed these overlapping affiliations as fundamentally complementary. People were complex. Multiple identities were a normal feature of modernity. "Can one split oneself in two," he wrote, "and say: 'From here to there, Zionist, and from there onwards, Lithuanian citizen'? No. Nor is that necessary." Zionism, minority rights, Lithuanian independence, and European democracy—all went hand in hand. "Our love for Jerusalem hardly weakens our joy in working for Lithuania," he declared and posed the same rhetorical question that Louis Brandeis had asked of American Zionism: "Are we not better citizens of this country because of the fact that we are better Jews and vice versa? . . . Life's own logic confirms this truth."[20]

Even in the early 1920s, however, there were signs that this delicate situation might not last. One anecdote Robinson often repeated told the whole story. After they took power, the Lithuanian authorities banned the Russian language from government use on political grounds, even though many politicians spoke it better than Lithuanian. This placed Robinson's friend Shimson Rosenbaum, the first cabinet-level Minister of Jewish Affairs, in an awkward situation. Rosenbaum spoke German, French, and Russian fluently, but not Lithuanian. Every time he wished to address a session of the Sejm, he was required to use pigeon Yiddish, with Robinson as his Lithuanian translator. But at cabinet meetings, which Robinson could not attend, the Lithuanian officials still insisted that Rosenbaum speak only Yiddish. In the protocols, the recording secretary would simply note that the Jewish minister spoke in a foreign language, without bothering to report what he actually said. It was an absurd situation that suggested a larger truth: to the Lithuanians, the Jews mattered for their bodies, not their opinions.[21]

What demography gave it also took away. Robinson's heady early days in 1920s Lithuania came during a brief period when regional war and rampaging violence still engulfed Eastern Europe. Borders all along the Eastern Front remained contested. As the dust settled, however, the picture changed. The Lithuanians fought off the Bolsheviks for control of their capital, Vilnius, only to face a direct challenge from the Poles, who occupied the city in 1920 in open defiance of a League of Nations agreement and then annexed it in 1922. The resulting border changes altered the Lithuanian Republic's demographic makeup with dire political consequences for its Jews.

By 1923 it was clear that there were far fewer Jews than initially anticipated, at most 150,000 out of the total population of more than two million, or just over 7 percent (versus 80 percent Lithuanian, 4 percent German, 3 percent Polish, and 2–3 percent Russian and others). Lithuanian leaders began to revoke aspects of Jewish autonomy that had only just been granted. Even as Robinson's Minorities Bloc reached the height of its power, holding fourteen of seventy-eight seats in the parliament (seven Jews, four Poles, two Germans, and one Russian), the Christian Democratic majority voted to dismantle the Jewish school system, his personal "pride and joy." Next, the Jews lost the right to self-tax. "And one fine day," he recalled later, Jews awoke to "read in the newspaper that there was no more Ministry of Jewish Affairs. They destroyed everything we had built over the course of three or four years." The Jewish National Council was dissolved and its leaders accused of running an illegal organization. Worse was still to come.[22]

Chronic economic and political instability led to seven different governments in six years. In this chaotic atmosphere, Robinson continued to insist that minority rights remained in force in Lithuania, including the right to seek international recourse from the League of Nations. Some Lithuanian political leaders agreed. At the September 1925 session of the League of Nations, the Lithuanian representative proposed universalizing the Minorities Treaties, applying it to every member state in the League. His country had nothing to fear from the law, he said, so why should all the others? Britain openly blocked the move, with Polish complicity. Still, as Lithuania slipped deeper into political crisis, Robinson began to look elsewhere for support for the cause of minority rights. Just at that point, help arrived from a most unlikely source: Weimar Germany.[23]

"Le Cri des Peuples"

One day in 1925, an obese German man appeared on Robinson's doorstep in Kovno. He introduced himself as the son of a small-town doctor in Estonia and a graduate student at a German university. The odd-looking visitor explained that he was writing his dissertation on the topic of the "cultural autonomy of minorities." Then he announced his thesis: if only Europe's national minorities would unite in a "Congress of Minorities," they could serve as a "third power" between the Communist East and the capitalist West. Not only would this help stabilize international politics but it would also advance minorities' shared aim of protecting their peoples within the various states under the Minorities Treaties system. Surely Robinson could see the value in a large political organization of this kind?

Robinson was immediately skeptical. He consulted with Comité colleagues Motzkin and Grinboym. The trio soon saw through the ruse. The "doctoral student" was actually Ewald Ammende, a Baltic German political activist with ties to the German Foreign Ministry, dispatched to secure Jewish support for an audacious new foreign policy gambit. With Germany scheduled to join the League of Nations the following year, its diplomats were seeking to position the country as the leader of a pan-European bloc of minorities. "Germany," wrote German foreign minister Gustav Stresemann in 1925, must "be the protector of minorities in Europe." What he did not state was that defending all minorities would allow Germany to reassert its power in the heart of Europe.[24]

Robinson knew the German offer was a Faustian bargain. Jewish autonomy had all but expired in Lithuania. Next door, Polish Jewry was in perilous shape. Britain and France were disinclined to press Poland about its treatment of Jews for fear of driving it into the arms of the Bolsheviks. American Jews could not help because the United States was not a member of the League of Nations. The Jews of Eastern Europe needed powerful friends. Without the Germans, they were too weak to demand enforcement of minority rights at the League of Nations. With them, however, the Jews risked becoming a tool in that country's pursuit of a Greater Germany.

Worse still, the diasporic German minorities were the most chauvinist of all in their nationalism, fast becoming "famous for their antisemitism." Robinson had fond memories of his encounters with Germans in the POW camp during World War I and knew that the German military had even supported the creation of an independent Lithuanian state during World War I. But they were not the diaspora Germans. "Could we really partner with a pan-Germanism that, at the end of the day, consisted of these people?" asked Robinson. The answer turned out to be a cautious "yes."[25]

In October 1925, fifty delegates representing thirty million Europeans across the continent arrived in Geneva for the opening of the first Congress of European National Minorities. They listened as Robinson delivered a keynote address in support of the proposition that "each national group should be permitted to conserve and develop its national individuality in corporations of public law." He told the crowd, "Our opponents tell us 'what you seek has never existed.'" But this model of "national self-determination is nothing new." As proof, he offered the example of Jewish history, painting a picture of the *kehillah* as a tradition stretching from ancient Babylonia to postwar Lithuania. More important than the past, he continued, was the future. Minority rights represented a necessary and inevitable step in the evolution of the modern state toward greater decentralization. Its antagonists were foolishly trying to stop history, like "the coach-driver fighting the train and the craftsman protesting the mechanical loom." "Together we will wage the great struggle for the dawn of national self-determination," he concluded, shouting in Latin, "In hoc signo vinces! (In this we will conquer!)" The crowd cheered wildly.[26]

The Geneva speech made Robinson an international celebrity. National minority groups across Europe began to regard him as their champion. Here was the man who could turn international law into an instrument of national freedom. Inspired by his speech's reception, he began work on a massive study of minority rights and international law, designed to show how lawyers and diplomats might safely handle what he described tongue-in-cheek as the deadly "Bacillus minoriarius." His budding law practice, which he ran together with his brother Nehemiah, thrived as the demand grew for legal

MINORITIES

After the War, many countries signed Treaties, or made Declarations to the League, in regard to their racial, religious and linguistic minorities. The fulfilment of the obligations thus contracted was placed under the guarantee of the League.

States having international minority obligations.

Each member of the Council has the right to bring to the attention of the Council any infraction or danger of infraction of these obligations.

Differences of opinion as to questions of law or fact arising out of these treaties or declarations may be referred to the Permanent Court of International Justice.

THE PROCEDURE IN MINORITIES QUESTIONS

is laid down by the Council.

It includes :

(1) A preliminary examination of petitions by the Secretariat.

(2) The forwarding of a receivable petition to the interested Governments for observations and the circulation to Members of the Council, for information, of such a petition and the observations.

(3) The examination of the petition and observations by the President of the Council and two other Members nominated by him (" Committee of Three"). The Committee decides whe therthe question at issue : (a) shall give rise to no action; (b) can be settled by the Committee without formal decision ; or (c) shall be referred to the Council.

The League of Nations Minority Treaties system

Pictorial Survey of the League of Nations (1931),
courtesy of the United Nations Office at Geneva

expertise on borders and minorities. He acquired a reputation as one of Europe's leading international lawyers and one of the most important public personalities in the Baltics.[27]

Back at home, meanwhile, the political situation was growing more uncertain. In 1926 Voldemaras's nationalist party seized power in a military coup, dissolving the parliament and suspending the democratic constitution. Despite Jewish fears, the threat of violent antisemitism remained minimal. In fact, the new conservative dictatorship proved eager to accommodate its Jews, an economically significant minority, and favored retaining some vestiges of cultural autonomy. As prime minister of the junta-led government, Voldemaras even relied on Robinson for personal legal advice on Roman Catholic canon law in order to get his first marriage annulled by the Vatican. With his blessing, Robinson launched a secret organization to direct Jewish communal affairs and serve as a liaison with Lithuanian government officials. He also was given free rein to continue his international work with European national minorities and to relaunch the Jewish political mission at the League of Nations.[28]

For the first half of the 1920s, the Comité des Délégations Juives had struggled to function effectively as a loose international network of like-minded European Jewish activists. Robinson played an active role in this effort, along with several other East European Zionist leaders, notably the Paris-based Comité leader Leo Motzkin and Natan Feinberg, who would later become the founding dean of the Hebrew University Law School. Noticeably absent from this effort were influential American Jews, cut off from the League by their government's isolationist policies. British and French Jewish liberal anti-nationalists, meanwhile, continued to complicate matters by asserting their own claims to Jewish diplomacy at the League. Lucien Wolf established a one-man bureau in Geneva from which he unsuccessfully lobbied British officials while also conducting a personal crusade against Zionism. But the biggest challenge for the Comité group was structural: they were forced to practice freelance diplomacy without the clout of a kin-state behind them.[29]

In theory, any individual or group could petition the League via a special Minorities Bureau in Geneva. But the state-based membership system meant that petitions without a state sponsor were virtually guaranteed never to receive a formal hearing. "The League of Nations is a league of states," lamented Robinson, "and not a league of nations. Its members are only governments and not citizens." The Minorities Section lacked the legal power to enforce the rights of Jews or any other minority; it could only gather complaints and pass them on to other bureaucrats. And only state members of the League could bring actionable claims to the attention of its governing body, the Council of Nations. Absent the political consent of other states, no investigation of an alleged violation of the Minorities Treaties could proceed. The title of the League's 1920s journal of minority affairs perfectly captured this status: "Le cri des peuples." Cry as they might, the little peoples of Europe found no one to answer them.[30]

In August 1927, sixty-five Jewish leaders from thirteen countries convened in Zurich to try and change that situation. The first international Conference for the Rights of Jewish Minorities included six members of the Polish Sejm, the Chief Rabbi of Vienna, Simon Dubnow from Berlin, Zionist leader Menachem Ussishkin from Jerusalem, Rabbi Stephen S. Wise from New York, and Rabbi Maurice Perlzweig from London. The Polish Zionist leader Nahum Sokolow opened the conference with a declaration of purpose. "Our slogan is not fight, but defense," he announced. "We consider this conference a continuation of the work begun in 1919 when Jewish leaders rendered the historic service of formulating and securing rights not only for Jews but for all minorities whose number is not less than 40,000,000."[31]

Spirits ran high. Sokolow joked that the presence of American Jewish delegates made it the first League of Nations meeting at which the United States participated on an equal footing: "The bridge across the Atlantic has been built." Stephen Wise called the conference proof positive that "we Jews are one people . . . not merely a collection of Shma yisroel reciters," a dig at Zionism's political opponents who insisted that Jews were only a religious community, not a nation. By the meeting's end, the delegates had agreed to create a new international organization to be headquartered in Geneva. The Jewish rights group slowly took shape beginning later in 1927, with Sokolow as its president and Robinson as a member of its executive committee. In 1932, under the name World Jewish Congress, it began to meet annually as a kind of virtual Jewish parliament operating along a federalist model. Each country elected its own delegates, who convened periodically to set policy positions for the leadership to speak in the unified voice of all Jewry.[32]

Many of these same men showed up the following year in Geneva for the fourth annual Congress of European National Minorities. Once again Robinson again played a starring role. He stirred the crowd by predicting an international legal regime would soon replace the tyranny of a states-only system with a new model of "transnational nations" unbridled by the boundaries of politics and geography. Critics might "depict us as pan-Semites, pan-Germanists, and pan-Slavists," he said, but this was sheer lunacy, for "we always separate politics and culture." The crowd roared its approval. Their hopes for peace were buoyed by the announcement during the conference of the Kellogg-Briand Pact, a new international treaty renouncing war as "an instrument of national policy," signed first by Germany, France, and the United States. There was even talk of a new federation plan for Europe, a United States of Europe, to strengthen economic ties and bolster peace. Robinson's closing line expressed his faith in the revolutionary progress at hand: "We simply wish to live in the transnational nation as one lives in a city and we don't particularly care in which street of this city we live."[33]

The minorities' great backer carried forward their cause. At the beginning of 1929, German foreign minister Stresemann announced a "Year of Minorities" diplomatic campaign intended to pressure the League to expand its minority rights system, especially the right of petition for minority groups. In Robinson's eyes, this was an essential move. Without a real right of petition, he said, the League itself was "a pure illusion." He continued to support German-Jewish cooperation, teaming up that year with an eminent liberal German jurist, Herbert Kraus, to publish a book on Soviet international law. From Kovno he closely monitored the progress of the German minorities campaign in Geneva.[34]

When the terrible violence flared in Palestine later that summer, Robinson, Motzkin, and Comité leaders publicly called for the League to intervene. Mass rallies, telegrams, and impassioned editorials poured forth. In his own unofficial petition to the League, Robinson did not mince words. On behalf of five thousand Lithuanian Jews, he called for the League Permanent Mandates Commission to remove the "hypocritical and criminal" British officials who had allowed the violence to occur and to fulfill the mandate obligation to "the whole Jewish People, in all its parts and classes, who has proved within [sic] thousands of years its religious and national coherence with Palestine." No response came. Worse still, a month after the Congress of European National Minorities met, the shocking news came down that the Germans had suffered a bitter loss in their quest for reform. A coalition of League bureaucrats, with Czechoslovakian, French, and British support, had blocked their proposal to revamp the League's policies.[35]

The dual defeat left Robinson furious. In a speech to the 1930 Congress of European National Minorities, he lashed out at countries that assumed they could ensure peace in Europe without taking their minorities into account. There could be no true "Pan-Europa," the cherished international community of which diplomats always spoke, without addressing the "Minorities-Elephant" in the room. He chided those "governments who ask the national minorities to silence themselves," with an obvious nod to Paris and London, "out of a false belief that if one can hush something up, it will disappear." "Totschweigen" (hush up) was neither a viable plan nor a rational strategy for dealing with "the central challenge of European politics." Besides, the national minorities would never agree simply to fall on their swords and die. On the contrary, Robinson told the cheering crowd, "We will defend ourselves in the strongest possible way. We stand for the right of minorities to live in Pan-Europa."[36]

Robinson's impassioned speeches still earned rousing applause in 1930. But new and ominous voices had begun to appear among the Germans at that gathering. As one Sudeten German activist told the other delegates, "The character of a minority suits us no longer. We regard ourselves rather as one of the governing peoples and demand political equality beyond that guaranteed by the Minorities Treaties." It was akin to George Orwell's famous line, "All animals are equal but some animals are more equal than others." The demand for more equality would soon lead to tyranny.[37]

The Bernheim Petition

On Election Day, July 31, 1932, Robinson went for a stroll in downtown Frankfurt. When the news trickled in that the Nazis had won their first major elections, he collapsed on a park bench in shock. "I thought that the

world was coming to an end," he recalled. "The Germans immediately began to drop hints about what the German people and German minorities
required: not minorities protection but reintegration into the German
people." Just as he feared, Jews had bet against German irredentism and
lost, and now were paying the price. In protest, he pulled out of the 1933
Congress of European National Minorities. The event went ahead without
him: Jews were no longer required. Ironically, as Robinson mused later,
"the idea of *Judenrein* first found expression among the minorities movement of all places."[38]

On the last Monday in January 1933, German president Paul von Hinden-
burg appointed Adolf Hitler as Reich chancellor. The Nazi Party celebrated
that evening with a torchlight procession through downtown Berlin. It was
the first stage of a campaign of political intimidation to cow their opponents into submission. In March, following the Reichstag fire, Hitler sus-
pended civil liberties, leading world Jewish leaders to panic. "The frontiers
of civilization have been crossed," wrote Stephen Wise from New York.
"None of us is quite alive to the fact that this may be the beginning of a
world-wide movement against us, a world-wide conflagration, a world-wide
undertaking against the Jews." Seeking to awaken the world's conscience,
he led a rally of ninety thousand Jews at Madison Square Garden.[39]

Public rallies in New York City provided a measure of moral satisfaction, but back in Europe, real doubt existed as to whether such efforts
could check the steady drumbeat of anti-Jewish measures emanating from
Berlin. The Nazis openly defied the very idea of ethics or laws in international affairs. "When the nations on this planet fight for existence," Hitler
announced, "then all considerations of humanitarianism . . . crumble into
nothingness."[40]

Law was a special target for Nazi nihilism. Attacking legal liberalism as
a Jewish cancer on the body of the German nation, the Nazis promptly
expelled all Jews from the country's legal organizations. The entire profession emptied out as Jewish lawyers fled the country by the thousands.
They were replaced by the followers of the likes of Carl Schmitt, "the crown
jurist of the Third Reich," who asserted that law was conditional on the
will of the sovereign state. Any constitution might be justifiably abrogated
and replaced by a new law devised by the sovereign. Schmitt mocked the

liberal ideals of individual equality enshrined in the Weimar Constitution as the product of a "Jewish Legal State." "There are peoples," he wrote of Jewish lawyers, "that exist without land, without state, without church, but only in the Law," who propagate false ideas of individual rights and freedoms separate from political community. But now, he boasted, "Germanic thinking" would replace the parochial rules and "helpless formalism" of the "Judaized" German legal code with an organic German racial law uniquely suited to the Aryan race. It was but a short step from this "jurisprudence of lawlessness" to a rejection of what Schmitt called the false "universal humanity" of the League of Nations and international law. To many observers, it looked as if all the laborious efforts in the field of international law had amounted to naught.[41]

And yet tiny hopeful signs of international law's tenacity remained. In 1932, the Lithuanian government turned to Robinson for legal advice about the disputed Lithuanian-German border region of Memel. A 1924 treaty signed by the two countries gave Memel's German and Lithuanian populations autonomy in internal affairs while placing external sovereignty in Lithuanian hands. When tensions flared over possible violations, Robinson advised the Lithuanian government to invoke Article 11 of the League of Nations Covenant, which granted each member of the League the right to bring forth a case in a situation threatening "to disturb international peace." He successfully argued the Lithuanian case before the International Court at The Hague. The experience gave him faith that perhaps the League might still have legal legs on which to stand. If the Memel Lithuanians in 1932, why not the German Jews in 1933?[42]

There remained only one difficulty. On their own, the Jews lacked the legal standing to present their own claim: there was no Jewish state licensed to speak on their behalf. Which country, then, would test German ire by bringing forward the Jewish case? Robinson and his Comité colleagues turned to Germany's rival, Great Britain. In early April 1933, Motzkin traveled to London to request the British government's assistance. He was rudely rebuffed by Foreign Secretary Sir John Simon, famously described by colleagues as "a toad and a worm" for his icy manner and predilection for appeasing Japan and Germany at the League. Simon then made an odious speech to Parliament disavowing any British interest in pressing Germany on its anti-Jewish policies, on the ground that Germany was not a party to the Minorities Treaties. From Kovno, an irate Robinson wrote Motzkin, "I just read that Sir John Simon delivered a statement in the House of Commons in which he claims that the League of Nations has no authority to interfere with the 'internal affairs' of Germany." Simon was not only a coward, Robinson observed, but he was also a poor lawyer. While it was true that Germany was not party to the Minorities Treaties itself, there remained the matter of Upper Silesia, which provided a clear opening to make a legal claim against Germany's treatment of its Jewish population.[43]

Upper Silesia was the German-Polish equivalent of the Memel case. At Paris in 1919, Polish and German diplomats had clashed over this border territory, rich with coal and iron ore. With both claiming the population to be predominantly made up of their nationals, the dispute threatened to collapse the entire League of Nations before it even began. A March 1921 plebiscite intended to clarify its demographic makeup revealed the region to be too intermixed to draw clean ethnic borderlines. The solution was a 1922 bilateral treaty in which the two states divided the land in half and guaranteed all minorities equal civil and political rights for a period of fifteen years, at which point a further decision would be made on the territory's status. To address claims of treaty violations, the League maintained a special tribunal that, unlike the rest of the League system, permitted direct petitions by members of Upper Silesia's minority populations. Throughout the second half of the 1920s, Silesian Germans and Poles, aided by Berlin and Warsaw, had flooded the tribunal with requests for legal action. This drew the close attention of Jewish activists, as did the stipulation that in some cases petitions could be brought directly to the League's Council.[44]

Now Robinson suggested a plan of attack. He and Natan Feinberg should "immediately send a quick petition on the destruction of the German Upper Silesian Jewry, with proper documentation, to the League of Nations, with the request to convene at least one meeting of the Council of Three. Such a petition might trigger an international debate, which would make an impression—if not on Germany today, then at least on the still uninfected States, so they do not succumb" to the Nazi poison. To lodge a petition, however, it was necessary to find a Jewish plaintiff from Upper Silesia willing to go on record against the Nazis. The first volunteer got cold feet, as he worried about repercussions for his family. Then, by chance, a Jewish refugee named Franz Bernheim wandered into the Zionist movement's office in Prague seeking help. He had fled to Czechoslovakia after the Nazis took control of the Upper Silesian government and forced him out of his job in a local warehouse. Robinson and Feinberg had found their man.[45]

On May 17, 1933, Bernheim appeared in Geneva with a petition demanding immediate redress. He gave it to Pablo de Azcarate, the head of the League's Minorities Section. Accompanying him were Motzkin, Feinberg, and a third colleague, Emil Margulies, who delivered their own general petition in the name of various Jewish organizations from Eastern Europe, the United States, and Mandatory Palestine. The Zionist activists knew that their petition was legally worthless; they lacked standing to make a claim to the League. Still, an orphaned petition was, in its way, an eloquent statement about the larger injustice facing the Jews.[46]

Over the strenuous objections of the Germans, the League Council agreed to accept Bernheim's petition and place it on the following week's agenda. The topic of Nazi racial persecution of Jews was thus officially open for diplomatic consideration. The German Foreign Ministry panicked: this was a public relations nightmare. The ministry instructed its representative in Geneva, Friedrich von Keller, to avoid all debate. Von Keller tried every possible legal maneuver to stop any discussion. He claimed that Bernheim lacked legal standing because he had left Upper Silesia and was now safe in Prague. He suggested that Bernheim had been dismissed from his job not because he was Jewish but because he was a Communist and a poor worker. He insisted that the 1922 Convention applied only to public government offices and schools, not private companies. Finally, he played his trump card: Bernheim could not be classified as a victim because he was not a member of a national minority but only a racial group. In the Nazis' perverse logic, a minority race did not have the same rights as a national minority. As Robinson explained, the German delegation effectively tried to define the Jews out of existence: "They said, 'We are in favor of the famous work of the Assembly of 1922 that every country in the world should respect its minorities, but the Jews are not a minority and therefore we cannot respect their rights.'"[47]

None of the arguments convinced the League of Nations lawyers. The debate went ahead as scheduled. On May 30 and June 6, two public discussions took place at the League Council on the subject of the Nazi persecution of the Jews. Once the floodgates were opened, other countries rushed in to voice their indignation. The French diplomat Joseph Paul-Boncour called on those assembled to acknowledge that "this particular case is but one facet of a much larger and more pathetic problem," namely, the "rights of a race dispersed across all the lands" and the broader fate of "minority rights." Even the Polish delegate, Count Raczinski, chided Germany for its deprivation of "the minimum of rights that must be guaranteed to every human being, regardless of his race, religion, or his native tongue." He neglected to mention the Cold pogrom in Poland, which was then placing in peril the lives of three million Jews in his country.[48]

By a unanimous decision, with only Germany and Italy abstaining, the League Council adopted a resolution requiring Germany to produce more information about its official policies. That fall, the League met in full General Assembly on September 30 to take up the issue once again. Nazi propaganda minister Josef Goebbels himself attended the session. There, for the first and only time in its history, the General Assembly directly considered one of the thousands of petitions it received. Seeking a swift end to the prolonged embarrassment, the Nazi diplomats arrived with a solution in hand. They presented a letter in which they claimed to have restored all the rights of the Jews in Upper Silesia.

It was a stunning victory. The Nazis had backed down. From that moment until the 1922 treaty expired on July 15, 1937, the Nazi government punctiliously fulfilled its legal obligations. Even as racist, anti-Jewish laws went into effect in Germany proper, Upper Silesian Jews remained exempt. Speaking of the September 30 session, Paul-Boncour remarked, "If the League of Nations since its twelve years' existence was there only on account of those one and a half hours, it would still have been worth its creation."[49]

Or would it? Even as the Germans pledged to honor the Polish-German agreement, they followed their September 1933 letter with another startling announcement: they were withdrawing from the League. Von Keller stated publicly at the time that the Minorities Treaties system was broken beyond repair, because it did not protect the true rights of the "ethnic nationality" beyond states' borders. He meant, of course, the Germans with whom Robinson had worked in the Congress of European National Minorities. These were also the Germans on whose behalf Germany would demand first Austria and then the Sudetenland—the Germans in whose name the Nazi Reich would go to war.

Poland soon followed Germany in quitting the League. As a parting blow, Polish foreign minister Josef Beck pointedly challenged the British to either expand the minorities system into a universal system binding on all countries or admit their hypocrisy. He knew that, as a colonial power, Britain would never agree to expand the system. From Munich, Carl Schmitt issued an even more incisive critique: British colonialism exposed the lie of the liberal empire. "Does the British Empire rest on universal and equal voting rights for all its inhabitants?" he wrote. "The British Empire could not survive a week on this foundation; with their terrible majority, the coloureds would dominate the whites."[50]

Robinson may actually have agreed with Schmitt, to a point. Despite his faith in law, he recognized its limits. Even as the Bernheim plan took shape, he confessed privately that he viewed it primarily as a "moral condemnation" of the Reich, unlikely to achieve concrete results. The deeply satisfying sight of the Nazis retreating from "an act of persecution" could not compensate for their larger assault on the Jews and humanity. Moreover, the crisis threatened to envelop all of Europe, with vastly more threatening consequences for the Jewish people. This raised the disturbing prospect that international law was not only unable to protect minorities from racial nationalism; worse still, it was powerless to prevent Europe from plunging into a second world war within a generation.[51]

No Such Friend

At the core of the League of Nations Minorities Treaties, Robinson once observed, lay the principle of reciprocity: "I protect your minority, you protect my minority." The diplomats who mapped the borders of interwar Europe had assumed that these reciprocal obligations would serve as an implicit backstop to the formal treaties, adding a balance of power to the equation. Germans in Poland could rely on the fact that Germany also held Poles among its population. Each state would look out for its co-nationals and respect the other's diaspora. But the Jews had neither a kin-state to supervise their interests nor a non-Jewish minority to use as leverage in international relations. This asymmetry made their position vastly more vulnerable than that of any other national minority in Europe. It also emboldened idealists such as Robinson to double down on the idea of minority rights as a means to equalize the power relations between Jews and their neighbors, while also offering a new paradigm for European politics as a whole. After centuries of sufferance, the Jews of Europe had arrived at a historic moment when modern politics would finally accommodate difference in a new way. The indignities of tolerance would yield to the durable satisfactions of justice.

Unfortunately, the European reciprocity contract had an unwritten codicil, which Robinson summed up with a dark joke: "I hit my Jews, you hit your Jews." His gallows humor was a bitter acknowledgment that diplomatic skills and legal acumen could not overcome the raw force of politics. Nor could the proliferation of rights compensate for the asymmetries of power in interwar Europe. Those setbacks of the 1920s gave way to the agonies of the 1930s.[52]

In 1933, one of the first Nazi acts of state was to ban the word "minority." The Germans had spent a decade and half championing minority rights. Now, not only had the concept outlived its usefulness but also the term itself had become an ideological enemy. German law would henceforth recognize only a racial hierarchy of nations, announced the Munich Academy of German Law. As "Super-Humans," the Germans occupied the top level. Each nation below them was assigned a rung in the new order of the German Reich, except for one: there was no place in the Nazi future for the Jews. By decade's end, the man who all but invented the modern legal concept of "minority" would find himself chased out of Europe by a regime that denied both him and his idea the right to exist.[53]

3

Golden Shackles

ON THE EVENING OF November 9, 1938, a wave of terror broke out across Germany. In hundreds of cities and towns, Nazi-led mobs ransacked Jewish stores, synagogues, and homes. Crowds jubilantly ripped up Torah scrolls and set them on fire in the streets. The orgy of violence continued into the next day. The sounds of shattered glass bequeathed the terrible events a name: *Kristallnacht.* Far off in the calm oasis of Windsor, England, the young men of Eton woke up the next morning to reports of the rampage. Most considered the ugly events in Germany quite remote from their lives. Few Jews attended England's most prestigious boarding school, and those who did came from patrician Anglo-Jewish families, dubbed by Lewis Namier the "Order of Trembling Israelites," anxious elites loath to cause a stir among their Christian peers. But not all felt that way. One exception was sixteen-year-old Peter (Benenson) Solomon, the scion of an Anglo-Zionist family split between London and Jerusalem. Within days, the future founder of Amnesty International delivered a manifesto to the college provost. His "Appeal to Rescue Jewish Youth from Germany" mixed equal parts upper-crust sensibility and liberal idealism.

> Seeing that it is now impossible for the Jews in Germany to enjoy the rights of man—life, liberty, and the pursuit of happiness, and especially for the younger generation to rise to manhood unbowed by shame and abuse, we have determined to try to give lease of liberty and education to at least

one Jewish boy, of exceptional brilliance, by providing the funds for his education and maintenance in England, until he is old enough to use his brain and his talents to the benefit of either the Dominions or the Colonies.

Solomon went on to urge "members both of our own and other communities" to help rescue "one or more of these boys, who, if they are not rescued now, may sink forever into moral and material enslavement." He ended with a special plea directed specifically at the parents of his classmates: "May we trust that all who remember with gratitude their childhood, and especially who have children of their own, will not reject this call of a common humanity?"[1]

The phrase "a common humanity" fits nicely into our contemporary lexicon of human rights. We routinely assert that the inspiration—and the onus—for our notion of universal rights stems from a shared humanity that transcends race, religion, nationality, and, most importantly, politics. Human rights are supposed to be pre-political—intrinsic and not dependent on citizenship or political status. Yet on the eve of World War II, Peter Solomon could not conceive of rights separated from politics. He even conditioned the right to pursue happiness, lifted from the American Declaration of Independence, on service to the British Empire. His Jewish plea for the Rights of Man came firmly couched in the language of British imperial politics.

Solomon's "Appeal" spoke directly to the dilemma facing all defenders of Jewish rights in the late 1930s. The events of the previous decade had shown that new ideas about international law and minority rights could not transcend the basic structure of modern politics. In a world of sovereign states, international law counted for naught unless backstopped by surpassing political power. After the demise of the ill-fated entente with Weimar Germany, Jewish hopes again lay with Great Britain. The empire "on which the sun never set" remained the League's strongest power and the official custodian of Palestine. That made Britain the only country capable of simultaneously guaranteeing the Jews protection in Europe and refuge abroad.

The story of the world's response to the Holocaust is often told as a morality tale of Jewish desperation and Western indifference. Europe's Jews attempted to flee Nazi persecution only to be refused admission to country after country. Yet such a viewpoint ignores a deeper, even more tragic irony in the situation. What compounded the danger was the very design of the League of Nations system, which tied the Jews' fate in Europe directly to the question of Palestine. In the late 1930s, as Arab-Jewish relations in Palestine worsened in parallel with the deteriorating political situation in Europe, both the mandate system and Minorities Treaties reached the brink of collapse. These two inventions had together promised a normalization of Jewish status. Jews might live in European diaspora precisely because they had a territorial homeland in Palestine. Now their very interdependence increased Jewish vulnerability. The twin Jewish crises in Europe and Palestine acted as a vicious feedback loop, multiplying the risk to Jews everywhere.

Every move related to the Jewish Question of the late 1930s rippled across the entire chessboard of international politics. The situation led the British government to harsh calculations. To defend Jewish rights in Europe through the League of Nations, British diplomats concluded, only risked alienating states like Poland, Romania, and Hungary and provoking Nazi Germany. The obvious alternative, mass Jewish resettlement in Mandatory Palestine, would likely further destabilize the country and jeopardize the British imperial defense perimeter in the Middle East. The troops dispatched to quell the violence in Palestine were needed elsewhere. In the name of political expedience and military strategy, the guardians of the liberal empire chose to pacify the Arabs of Palestine and placate the antisemitic regimes of Europe. Thus, in a bitter twist of fate, the principal refuge for European Jewry lay safely in British hands, yet just out of Jewish reach.[2]

The man who best grasped this dilemma also served as the inspiration for Solomon's 1938 rescue campaign. Rabbi Maurice Perlzweig held many titles in 1930s Anglo-Jewish society: senior leader in the English Zionist movement and president of the World Union of Jewish Students, spokesman for Liberal Judaism and celebrity rabbi known for converting England's rich and famous, and chaplain and mentor to the Jewish princelings of Eton. But his most important role in the gathering storm was as the leader of the Jewish rights-and-rescue movement. As head of the British branch of the World Jewish Congress, between 1935 and 1940 he transformed the fledgling political organization into an international Jewish legal defense network. That effort required racing around the world to negotiate with antisemitic despots and insincere diplomats, while reckoning with the looming question of British foreign policy.

"The post-War settlement brought two great gifts to the Jewish people: the Jewish National Home, and emancipation in the countries of the Diaspora guaranteed by the Minorities Treaties," wrote Perlzweig in 1939. "Both were built ultimately on the same foundation of human and national rights, and it is perhaps not surprising that the attempt to undermine one is accompanied by the attempt to undermine the other." In response to this double assault, Jews had no choice but to reassert their commitment to internationalism. That meant claiming both "human and national rights" in Palestine and Europe. To fulfill the demands of justice, Perlzweig preached, the Jews must renew their partnership with the British, while His Majesty's Government must honor its twin pledges to the Jews and to the League of Nations.[3]

In his 1927 classic, *The Wandering Jews,* the Austrian Jewish writer Joseph Roth mocked the League of Nations as a helpless institution notable for "turgid bureaucracy and the golden shackles that its best-intentioned commissioners wear." Despite their fancy titles and new-fangled policies, League diplomats could not even issue basic papers to protect imperiled Jews. The European powers that had given birth to the League treated their offspring with cynical disrespect. The result, noted Roth, was a terrible irony: "Animal welfare groups enjoy more popularity in every country, and with every level of the people, than does the League of Nations."[4]

Much like the bureaucrats of interwar Geneva, Perlzweig, Solomon, and the other European Jewish rights-defenders also found themselves handcuffed, in their case by the shiny bonds of British imperial politics. No amount of skillful diplomacy could compensate for their fundamental dependence on British clout. No clever legal innovation could mask the cold realities of sovereignty, and no appeals to conscience could escape European realpolitik. Worse still, each step forward only brought further confirmation of a bitter truth: the more Jewish needs and British aims diverged, the tighter those golden shackles became.

A National Universalism

One Monday morning in late October 1923, a delegation of gray-haired dignitaries from the Cambridgeshire branch of the Labour Party ushered themselves into the rooms of a precocious university undergraduate whom they had heard much about. They came bearing an offer to put young Mr. Perlzweig up for a seat in the House of Commons. Politely but vigorously, he protested. The idea was plainly absurd. Both his age and his foreign background disqualified him. But it turned out that the party elders cared little about his objections. They had only one question: "You're not a Catholic, are you?" He responded, "No, I am not a Catholic, but I am a Jew." That prompted another set of questions: "What sort of Jew? Are you the same sort of Jew as in the Old Testament?" His response: "I am descended from them."

That was enough: he was their man. As Perlzweig realized, Cambridgeshire fell squarely within "old Cromwell country"—the Puritan heartland of the seventeenth-century English revolution, where anti-Catholic sentiments still ran strong, accompanied by a peculiar strain of English philosemitism. An Old Testament Jew suited the Cambridge Labourites just fine, a budding rabbi even better. It did not hurt that Perlzweig also possessed a formidable rhetorical talent that had twice won him the poll (presidency) of the Cambridge Union, the legendary debating society. Or that as a precocious youth activist he had befriended Labour Party luminaries such as H. G. Wells, George Bernard Shaw, and Ramsay MacDonald and had personally launched the Inter-University Labour Federation. Still, what counted most that day was his Jewishness. He soon learned that the idea of adopting him as a candidate had come from Colonel Josiah Wedgwood, a prominent Labour MP and Christian Zionist, who saw Zionism as a just solution to the outrages taking place in postwar Poland.[5]

In the end, despite two more approaches by the Labour Party, Perlzweig declined to run. But the incident taught him a valuable lesson about English philosemitism, which both marked the Jews as not quite English and elevated them into a religious symbol of England's national redemption. He concluded that the British insistence on Jewish difference was a good thing for the cause of Jewish rights. Rather than shy away from Jewishness, Jews would do better to "bring their Jewish heritage to the service of their citizenship." That interplay between Jewish identity and British politics would become a singular factor shaping two generations of Anglo-Jewish rights activism.[6]

Born in the same East Galician region of Poland as Lauterpacht, Perlzweig grew up in London's Finsbury Park neighborhood, the son of a noted Orthodox cantor. His father, a friend and early follower of Theodor Herzl, was reputed to have composed the melody for *Hatikvah,* later to be Israel's national anthem. Short and compact, with "a round face with Mongolian cheekbones," Maurice Perlzweig looked something like a handsome bulldog—charismatic and pugnacious, erudite and verbose. He was a natural-born leader with a staggering capacity to talk, a man who at the drop of a hat could launch into a soliloquy that ran on without end. As a teenager during World War I, that loquaciousness had earned Perlzweig a junior spot in the Zionist leadership. When the Balfour Declaration was issued in 1917, he shared the podium with Chaim Weizmann, Nahum Sokolow, and other Zionist speakers twice his age. Moving on to University College London, he took his first degree in history. Then the political wunderkind made the surprising decision to become a rabbi.[7]

Liberal Judaism, the British equivalent of American Reform Judaism, had gotten off to a slow start in England. In search of a fresh face to lead the movement, Claude Montefiore and other lay leaders approached Perlzweig, who had grown dissatisfied with his father's Orthodoxy. Since no non-Orthodox rabbinical seminary existed, they agreed to pay for him to enroll at Cambridge for a second bachelor's degree in Semitics, studying ancient Jewish languages under the great Hebraist Israel Abrahams. In a highly unusual arrangement, Perlzweig spent his weekends in London, where he led Sabbath services at the Liberal Synagogue in St. John's Wood in north London on Saturdays, taught Hebrew school on Sundays, and then returned to Cambridge in time for Monday morning classes.[8]

The arrangement suited everyone involved, except for one sticking point: Perlzweig's politics. "To me not merely the Zionist idea but the Zionist movement and the participation in it were like drugs," he recalled. "I just could not live without it." His Zionism infuriated Abrahams and

Maurice Perlzweig in a 1940s Canadian
promotional leaflet

Perlzweig Family Archive

Montefiore, both outspoken anti-Zionists who believed that Jewish nationalism threatened the dream of liberal emancipation. It also earned him
public censure in the pages of the *Jewish Chronicle,* the official mouthpiece of the Anglo-Jewish community. Yet he refused to budge. Jewish
freedom "at the price of dissolution" of the Jewish people was not freedom
at all. "You solve the problem of my life very easily if I commit suicide," he
noted, and insisted that "Jewish liberalism means Jewish loyalty. . . . Nationalism and internationalism, which are sometimes set in opposition to
one another, are in reality complementary conceptions. It is a false inter-

nationalism which attempts to deny the right of nations to independent life and growth; it is a mischievous nationalism which asserts the right of any nation to live and grow at the expense of another."[9]

The proof of this view was the Jewish return to Zion. "The great experiment of which we are engaged in Palestine is an experiment not only in nationalism, but in internationalism," he wrote time and again in editorials in the Jewish press. "The principle of trusteeship, one of the most fruitful internationalist ideas which emerged from the chaos of the Great War, has a conspicuously successful application to Palestine," a land being built both for Jews and for the "enrichment of humanity." Despite his rabbinic position, Perlzweig did not employ Jewish theology to argue his point. He did, however, cite the historical example of the biblical prophets as evidence for the Jewish approach to global justice, "Some 2,000 years ago, in the face of the atrocious military greed of the mighty empires that flourished at that time, Judaism gave to the world the fundamentals of religion." Now, in another dark age, Zionism offered a new vision of how to balance "universalism and particularism."[10]

Perlzweig's Zionist jeremiads throughout the late 1920s and early 1930s earned him a reputation as the "angry young man of English Zionism." But his academic bona fides, personal charisma, and staunch religious progressivism endeared him to the Anglo-Jewish grandees to whom he ministered full-time at the Liberal Jewish Synagogue of London after graduation from Cambridge. They demonstrated their esteem in the most elemental of ways—by hiring him to teach Judaism to their sons at Eton College. As the only Cambridge-educated, Hebrew-speaking, non-Orthodox rabbi in the entire United Kingdom, Perlzweig was the obvious candidate for the job. "No sense in sending a man into Eton to explain that it was wrong to eat pig," he recalled later, "and then the boy would have bacon for his breakfast, so clearly it had to be somebody for whom the ritual laws were no longer binding." So each Sunday morning in the mid-1930s, while the other young Etonians filed into the college chapel for a Church of England service, a motley crew of Jewish boys of all ages assembled elsewhere on campus to take instruction from the visiting Jewish Master. Instead of the principles of Jewish law, the students learned the gospel of modern Jewish politics. "Zionism is not an alternative to but the crown of Jewish emancipation,"

Perlzweig taught, and many of the boys listened. Of the hundreds he came
to know and mentor during those years, one stood out above all the others:
a gangly, red-haired teenager named Peter Solomon.[11]

A Hebrew-Speaking Etonian

Strictly speaking, Peter Solomon did not need lessons in Zionism: few
British Jewish families could boast as storied a Zionist pedigree as the
Solomon-Benenson clan. Support for the Jewish national cause had begun
with his great-grandfather, a Minsk timber merchant who attended the
first Russian Zionist conference in 1902, and continued with his grandfather, Grigorii Benenson, who made a fortune in Russia's oil, sugar, and
gold-mining industries before launching the Anglo-Russian Bank in
1910. On the heels of the tsar's visit to London in 1909 to see his "Uncle
Bertie" (King Edward VII), Benenson's bank quickly emerged as the main
facilitator of trade between Britain and Russia, which were eager to forge
an alliance against a rising Germany. At one point, Grigorii Benenson was
reportedly worth $100,000,000 (in 1920s dollars). The family lived on the
top floor of the Volkonsky Palace on St. Petersburg's Moika River embank-
ment, opposite the Hermitage, with a view of the Winter Palace. From
there, Grigorii Benenson funded the Russian Zionist movement and the
Russian liberals of the Kadet Party. He was close friends with Alexander
Kerensky and personally paid for the defense of Mendel Beilis, the young
Jewish man whose sensational blood libel trial in Kiev in 1913 rocked all of
Russia.[12]

When the war came, Benenson resettled his family in London. There his
three flamboyant daughters—Fira, Manya, and Flora, nicknamed the "Sisters
Karamazova"—all embraced Zionism. Fira married a Polish count and
eventually settled in New York, where she became a successful fashion
designer and Zionist fundraiser. Manya married into the Harari family, an
Egyptian Jewish dynasty, and spent years living on a kibbutz in Palestine.
She went on to fame as a Russian translator and publisher who introduced
Pasternak's *Doctor Zhivago* and other Soviet writers to the West. Flora
banded together with her best friend Vera Weizmann, wife of the Zionist

movement's leader Chaim Weizmann, as well the daughters of other leading Anglo-Jewish families such as the Sieffs and Sachers, to launch the Women's International Zionist Organization in 1920. Then she plunged into Zion directly after her marriage to Harold Solomon, British Palestine's first director for commerce and industry.[13]

Though he descended from a long line of British Chief Rabbis, Harold Solomon was in every other respect the quintessential Englishman. Friends noted his unfailing good cheer, endless thirst for physical exercise (commemorated in the Harold Solomon Tennis Tourney in Jerusalem), and unquestioning devotion to the British Empire. During World War I he served in France and Serbia, earning an Order of the British Empire, a Military Cross, and a Serbian Order of the White Eagle. Seeking a career in the colonial administration after the war, he grudgingly accepted, at the behest of Flora, a post under Sir Herbert Samuel, the Jewish British High Commissioner for Mandatory Palestine. Solomon's encounter with the Jewish homeland affected him deeply. "He had arrived in Palestine the unemotional, detached colonial servant," Flora noted, and "suddenly gloried in every sight of Zionist endeavor." In 1924, Solomon persuaded his colleagues back in London to include a Palestine pavilion in the famed British Empire Exhibition held at Wembley Stadium. Fostering the Anglo-Zionist partnership quickly became his life's goal.[14]

Flora, too, threw herself into idealistic pioneering work. She opened an infant welfare center for the Old City's poor and gave generously to the Haganah, the Jewish self-defense brigade. Still, old habits die hard, and their home in Jerusalem remained a small piece of Britannia. A case of champagne arrived at the couple's villa each week from London's Fortnum and Mason department store. When Flora became pregnant, she told her husband, "We shall have a baby talking Hebrew as his ancestors did on these very Judean Hills." "Yes," replied Harold, "but if he's a boy he's going to speak it in an Etonian accent." The very day his son was born in 1921, Harold rushed out to register him for a place at Eton, sponsored by Humphrey Bowman, the British director of education for Palestine.[15]

As a little boy, Peter Solomon played in the city streets of Jerusalem with the son of Norman Bentwich, the Jewish attorney-general of Mandatory

Peter Benenson (rear, smiling) on vacation in Italy in 1936
with (left to right) Chaim Weizmann, Vera Weizmann
(behind Chaim), Benjy Weizmann, and Flora Solomon

Courtesy of Yad Chaim Weizmann, the Weizmann
Archives, Rehovot, Israel

Palestine. He might have remained there ever after, but the happy idyll ended
when a freak riding accident left his father permanently paralyzed from
the waist down. The family returned to London, where his mother hired the
poet W. H. Auden as Peter's live-in personal tutor. "As I was a spoilt kid of the
rich," Peter recalled, "he decided that it would do me no harm (even a bit of
good) if I ate all of my food off the floor. He took great delight in taking the
grapes one by one, throwing them on the floor and telling me to pick them
up." The two also produced amateur theatricals together. The unconventional
lessons stopped when the butler informed Peter's parents that another writer,
Christopher Isherwood, had been sharing Auden's bed. "My father drummed
him out in true military fashion," Peter later recalled.[16]

Zionism remained a family mission throughout the 1920s. Harold built the Anglo-Palestinian Club into a major organization and served as vice president of the Jewish National Fund. In 1929 he ran unsuccessfully for Parliament in London's North Tottenham district on the Conservative Party ticket, campaigning on a platform of "Anglo-Palestinian unity." Flora became a gifted Zionist salonnière and continued her public work on behalf of the movement. Her father, meanwhile, gave colossal sums to the Jewish Agency to purchase land in Palestine.[17]

In the summer of 1929, as violence raged in Palestine, another personal tragedy struck the Solomon-Benenson clan. On Peter's ninth birthday, Harold Solomon died in a car crash while on a road tour of Europe. His death deprived Peter of a father with whom he had been extremely close. His mother promptly embarked on a torrid public affair with her own father's good friend, Aleksandr Kerensky, a married man. Peter was shipped off to Oxford to prep at Summer Fields boarding school. In January 1936 he arrived at Eton College. It was there that he found a new Jewish father figure and a life mission in social activism.[18]

"A Real Politics of Humanity"

In 1935, the Nazis passed the Nuremberg Laws, turning the law into a perverse instrument of racialist politics. German Jews were stripped of citizenship and rights and consigned to a legal limbo. The following year, the Italian Fascist regime invaded and annexed Ethiopia. Then Hitler announced the remilitarization of the Rhineland, in explicit violation of the Versailles Treaty and the 1925 Locarno Agreement. In both cases, the League members agreed that international law had been broken, but they failed to produce a response. As many observers recognized, the reason came down to British unwillingness to risk war with Germany—at least not yet.

In protest, a Czech Jewish journalist named Stephan Lux walked into a session of the League of Nations in Geneva that July and shot himself with a pistol. In a suicide note, he begged the British foreign secretary, Sir Anthony Eden, to do something to stop Germany's criminal regime. "The most terrible explosion in the world is imminent," he wrote, and only Eden, "the representative of the still mightiest empire of this world," had the capacity to stop Hitler and practice "a real politics of humanity." Eden never saw the letter: the British consul in Geneva refused to pass it on to him. Yet another Jewish petition went unanswered.[19]

Perlzweig agreed with Lux that Britain alone could save the Jews, and the world, from calamity. "We are living in an atmosphere created by the Italian victory over Ethiopia, a victory of violence over justice as interpreted by the League of Nations," he told a crowd in Manchester a few weeks later, "and the faith of the whole of the East in the rule of law in international affairs has been shaken." Meanwhile, the Jews in Central and Eastern Europe had been reduced to a "state of unspeakable economic misery" by "humiliating legislative discrimination and physical violence." These vulnerable Jews needed refuge that was possible only if the British allowed them entry into Palestine. Hence both international law and Jewish lives depended on Britain's maintaining its legal pledge to the Balfour Declaration. "A wise statesmanship working for the ideal of a stable and contented Europe could not afford to ignore the existence of a population reduced by prolonged misery and frustrated hope to a state of desperation." It was high time, he argued, for British Jews to abandon the "pusillanimous doctrine of splendid isolation" and raise their voices in chorus that they might convince the British government to secure the Jewish people's rights on the international plane. "We believe in Britain," he proclaimed; "we believe in Britain's loyalty to her pledges. We are so close to the essential spirit of Britain that there are times when we feel impelled to act the part of His Majesty's opposition to His Majesty's Government."[20]

Not everyone looked kindly on Perlzweig's ideological call to arms. Many in the Anglo-Jewish establishment feared that speaking out publicly against German antisemitism or challenging British foreign policy would harm the Jewish position in a country where anti-Jewish attitudes and political movements were on the rise. Perlzweig vigorously disagreed. With Hitler in power, he argued, Jews must dispense with the old "assimilationist" idea that there is "no difference between the Jew and the Gentile." Antisemitism, whether genteel or murderous, British, Polish, or German, required the same response:

Our people is becoming increasingly encircled by hosts of enemies: extermination in one country, de-Judaisation in another, economic annihilation
in a third, and a nervous tension, a feeling of insecurity, all the world over.
Since the world is shrinking as far as the Jew is concerned, the Zionist
ideal must expand.

Still, as Perlzweig knew well, that Zionist ideal could not expand without
space to grow. Evacuating Europe's endangered Jews to British Palestine,
however, was no simple matter.[21]

In the aftermath of the 1929 crisis, the British government had revised
its Palestine policy. The 1930 Passfield White Paper explained that, for His
Majesty's Government, "a double undertaking is involved, to the Jewish
people on the one hand and to the non-Jewish population of Palestine on
the other." Seeking a balanced approach, the British rejected the Palestinian
Arab demand for a constitution while also disappointing Jews by asserting
that a "Jewish National Home" was not central to the mandate mission: it
must take a back seat to maintaining equity and stability in the territory,
both of which were threatened by unfettered Jewish immigration.[22]

The Jews were not the only ones unhappy with British rule. In 1936, a
major Arab nationalist rebellion began, during which some Arab groups
launched terror attacks on Jewish communities. The scale of violence
dwarfed the events of 1929. As the revolt continued over the next three years,
it forced British officials to contemplate a more radical policy. The simplest
solution was limiting Jewish entry to Palestine. Meanwhile, Hitler's regime was beginning its physical assault on Jews. In October 1937, the Nazis
deported 12,000 Jews with Polish citizenship, who had lived in Germany
for decades, back to Poland, where the government refused to accept them
as citizens, choosing instead to intern them in camps on the German-
Polish border. The Jews of Europe had become truly homeless even as
their own national home became off-limits.

Back in England, there was a stark shift in public opinion on British foreign policy. A centrist consensus about the value of the League for collective security had by 1935 yielded to two extremes: an isolationist camp that
favored peace through appeasement regardless of the cost to international

justice, and a hawkish camp that called for rearmament and a strong military posture against German aggression. The former faction was willing to dispense with international law; the latter no longer believed in Britain's ability to prevent war. Both, however, agreed that something must be done about the Palestine problem.[23]

In 1937, the British Peel Commission issued a report about the status and future of Palestine, which concluded that Mandatory Palestine was no longer viable. In its place it proposed territorial partition into two states, one Jewish and one Arab. Both sides would get some but not all of what they sought: Jews would have their own state, but with severely restricted Jewish immigration, and Arabs would have independence, but only in a state annexed to Trans-Jordan. The proposal left both sides again furious. A decade and a half of life under the British mandate had left both Jews and Arabs viewing themselves as reluctant minors in urgent need of emancipation from the indignities of British paternalism.[24]

In the year following the announcement of the Peel plan, the violence in Palestine only worsened. The arrival of 25,000 additional soldiers and policemen, the arrest of almost 10,000 Arab prisoners, and liberal application of the death penalty could not restore law and order. Arab rebels pushed the country to the point of anarchy, leading to thousands of Arab deaths and hundreds of Jewish casualties. Amid the chaos, Zionist leaders struggled with whether to respond with force or remain in a defensive position. Some right-wing Zionists called for open war against British and Arabs alike. The Zionist left, though disappointed by British policies, held to its position of trusting the empire ultimately to do the right thing. In a speech in October 1938, Perlzweig reiterated his conviction that Jewish "hopes and prayers for order lie with the British government. . . . We Jews are not fighting the Arab people in Palestine." Behind the Arab High Command, he speculated, lay the long arm of Nazi Germany. Jews, British, and Arabs alike faced a "terrorist movement financed by foreign power [which] aims at the destruction, not only of Jews but of British power in the Middle East." Perlzweig pledged his willingness to accept a British partition of the Land of Israel. But he remained adamant on one demand: "Minority status is not only unacceptable; it is unthinkable in Palestine. Wherever Jews are, we are a minority. We live on the sufferance and tolerance of others. Now we have had

Peter Benenson at Eton in 1938

Reproduced by permission of the Provost and Fellows of Eton College

enough of it. In one place we shall be masters of our own destiny, and that place is Palestine."[25]

Two weeks after Perlzweig's speech, a desperate Polish Jewish teenager named Herschel Grynszpan walked into the German Embassy in Paris and shot the highest ranking official he could find. It was a crime of passionate revenge. Grynszpan's parents were among the 12,000 Polish Jews deported into no-man's land. On November 9, two days after the shooting, Goebbels told a Nazi Party gathering in Munich that the assassination was the work of "World Jewry" and, as such, required a proper response. That night, Nazi leaders, some dressed in civilian clothes, launched "spontaneous" attacks on Jewish sites all across Germany and Austria. With the *Kristallnacht* pogroms, the time for appealing to law in defense of Jewish rights reached its end. Petitions and memoranda yielded to plans for rescue and evacuation. Rather than stopping the Nazis, European Jewish leaders now turned their attention to saving the Jews.

From Rights to Rescue

Just days after *Kristallnacht*, a delegation composed of the Chief Rabbi of England, Chaim Weizmann, and Neville Laski, a judge and Anglo-Jewish leader, approached Prime Minister Neville Chamberlain with the idea for a Kindertransport. There had been small-scale resettlements of German Jews in England since 1933. With the government's blessing, Jewish leaders had successfully subsidized the emigration of several hundred individuals. Now, however, the urgency had skyrocketed, and they proposed the suspension of normal visa regulations to enable Jewish children to escape Nazi Germany. Ever mindful of a potential influx of undesirables, however, the delegation stressed that these Jewish youth would be simply granted refuge, not citizenship. The children would be technically classified as migrants passing through England. When possible, they were to be dispatched elsewhere abroad or else maintained in the United Kingdom at private communal expense strictly for the duration of the war. The government's approval of the arrangement inspired a flurry of activity among English Jews, including the Movement for the Care of Children from Germany, headed by Flora Solomon's close friend, Lola Hahn Warburg. Meanwhile, at Eton, a parallel effort got underway.[26]

As a restless, idealistic teenager, Peter Solomon had at first bristled at Eton's rigid hierarchy and clubby elitism. But surprisingly, he soon found his niche as a campus activist. Shortly after his arrival, he joined a student campaign to sponsor Spanish Civil War orphans (he was assigned a baby named Jesus, causing much amusement among his fellow Etonians). Then, following Perlzweig's lead, he turned his attention to the rising crisis in Germany. Immediately after *Kristallnacht*, he launched his emergency fundraising campaign, and within weeks he had raised roughly 4,000 pounds, enough to sponsor two children from Germany. But he also encountered resistance. Many of his parents' distinguished friends did not relish the attention focused on their Jewishness. When he approached Lionel Cohen, the future member of the House of Lords and father of two Eton students demurred. "I'm not keen on what your son is doing," he complained to Flora. "We ought not to be so conspicuous at Eton; people will not approve of such direct associations with Jews." In fact, many Gentile parents loved the idea. The Eton administration was also supportive to a point. However, the headmaster, already leery of the boy's "revolutionary tendencies," balked at the idea that the money might be spent to enroll the boys at Eton itself. "Surely you're not serious," he said. "We support the oppressed of many races, Chinese, Hottentots, without discrimination. We can't bring them all to Eton." In the end, Solomon secured places for the two boys at a London boarding school.[27]

The young activist was not satisfied with this achievement. He took Perlzweig's words to heart: "If the Jew went down, human liberty goes down with him." In a November 1938 communiqué, Solomon announced his intention to form a new organization, "what we are calling the Jewish Youth Movement," to unite "all Jewish boys throughout the country" in the pursuit of "various permanent aims" beyond rescue and resettlement. Precisely what other goals he had in mind we do not know. By year's end, he had opted to forego his last year at Eton to answer the pressing "call" of the world. He found work at the Refugee Children's Movement, a Jewish-sponsored relief campaign run by Norman Bentwich. For the next year, Solomon helped Jewish students his age from Germany adjust to England and secured visas to send some of these children to new homes abroad. That year he also legally changed his surname to Solomon-Benenson to honor the dying request of his grandfather Grigorii Benenson. During the war, he dropped the "Solomon" to become Peter Benenson.[28]

The extent to which any of this relief work had an explicit political connotation was a topic of great controversy within the Anglo-Jewish

community. Much of the wealthier Jewish establishment still vigorously opposed Zionism. Earlier in the 1930s, they had agreed to partner with Zionist
organizations for a coordinated refugee relief effort under the auspices of
the Central British Fund for German Jewry. The overwhelming pressure
of a massive wave of arrivals, the outbreak of war, the worsening situation
in Palestine, and British restrictions on Jewish immigration all put extreme
political pressure on this nonpartisan effort. Over the course of 1938 and
1939, the equilibrium finally collapsed. At that moment a newly emboldened
Zionist leadership led by Perlzweig and others took control of the British
Board of Jewish Deputies, an umbrella communal organization dating back
to 1760.[29]

Among those who applauded the Zionist takeover was Flora Solomon.
From the late 1930s onward, she had turned the family home in Mayfair into
a central meeting point for the international Zionist leadership. Her proté-
gés included the future publisher and lord, George Weidenfeld, then an
Austrian Jewish refugee who had arrived in London from Vienna in 1938.
"Flora was a port of call for Zionist leaders from all over the world," he later
recalled. "No figure relevant to the cause did not pass through her Mayfair
drawing room." One person no longer invited was her ex-lover Kerensky.
She broke with him over his refusal to denounce anti-Jewish persecution
in the wake of *Kristallnacht*. He in turn accused of her of putting Jewish
concerns above Russian ones: "You break your heart about Jews and you
don't care about Russians." The charge was true, she replied. Neither Russian antisemitism nor Jewish identity could be denied. "We are a small minority and my pride is always to support the weak. We may suffer but with
dignity." Like mother, like son.[30]

The One Condition

While Solomon worked on the ground in London resettling Jewish refugees, Perlzweig raced around the world—to Warsaw, New York, Johannes-
burg, and Geneva—raising funds and negotiating with foreign governments
over their treatment of their Jewish communities. As official head of the
World Jewish Congress relief mission, he also engaged directly with the
British Foreign Office, always promoting a harmonious fusion between

Jewish rights and British interests. "We need Britain and we are proud to admit it," he remarked, "but we are most deeply convinced that in the course of time Britain will acknowledge how greatly she needs a strong Jewish people in Palestine." Still, to his private chagrin, he came to realize that neither his rhetorical skills nor his old Labour Party ties counted for much. His final prewar adventure in Eastern Europe revealed to him that what he proudly regarded as the greatest Jewish political asset—an interconnected global diaspora—had turned into a sharp double-edged sword.[31]

In 1938, British diplomats grew alarmed by evidence of the spread of Fascist elements into Romanian politics. The pro-Nazi Iron Guard movement threatened to overthrow the monarchy and drag the country into the arms of Germany. The fate of Romania's 800,000 Jews took center stage as a political drama with grave implications for international politics. A spate of new laws and administrative edicts severely penalized these Jews in ways both substantial and humiliating. Thousands were stripped of their citizenship. Orthodox Jews were ordered by law to open their shops on Saturday in desecration of the Sabbath. All Jews were forbidden to sell alcohol or tobacco or to employ Gentile women under forty years of age. Octavian Goga, the antisemitic prime minister, openly spoke of a "Jewish leprosy [which] spreads like eczema over the whole country."[32]

The British consul in Bucharest, Sir Reginald Hoare, wrote his colleagues of the Romanian government's "terribly grave incitement to race-hatred." Yet he counseled against any public British statements of protest for fear of strengthening the Iron Guard's grip and tilting the country toward Germany. He assured the Romanian foreign minister that the Jews would not try to petition the League for redress. Even if they did, he promised, they would not receive British support. Meanwhile, King Carol II, who opposed the Iron Guard, requested that the British help solve all his problems by removing the country's Jews. The situation would have been much simpler, the king told Hoare, if the British had earlier possessed the foresight to build "an independent Jewish state" in Palestine where Europe could dump all of its Jews.[33]

A year later, the situation had only grown more volatile. Jews were now subject to violent attacks in the streets. In the name of saving democracy, King Carol II disbanded parliament and appointed himself dictator, installing Armand Calinescu as a puppet prime minister. Meanwhile, the king taunted the British by flirting openly with Nazi Germany. This was the context in which Perlzweig traveled to Geneva in early 1939 to deliver a petition to the League of Nations protesting Romania's violations of its commitments under the Minorities Treaties. Yet without British support, he found himself shut out "in the corridors of the League," unable to deliver his complaint to anyone for consideration. Determined to keep Romania on their side, the British and French had pledged to guarantee the country's independence. That meant not challenging its internal antisemitic policies.[34]

Back in London, Perzlweig turned in desperation to his old Cambridge friend R. A. Butler, now the parliamentary undersecretary for foreign affairs. Butler agreed to help, but on one condition. "We are doing everything we can to be helpful to you," he assured him, but "there is one thing you could do for us in return. Try and get them to stop the illegal immigration to Palestine." Perlzweig's reply was succinct: "You stop Hitler, and I'll stop the illegal immigration."[35]

The testy exchange reflected the mounting tensions between Britain and the Zionist movement. After years of floating different schemes to accommodate competing Jewish and Arab demands for land and autonomy, London had finally had enough. Though a counterterrorism campaign had succeeded in quelling the Arab Revolt, the British felt they could no longer afford to devote the manpower and expertise needed to pacify Palestine. The looming threat from Nazi Germany and Fascist Italy required a shift of focus from the Middle East to Europe. In addition, the prospect of another world war made Arab support more appealing. Prime Minister Neville Chamberlain told his cabinet, "If we must offend one side, let us offend the Jews rather than the Arabs."[36]

In May 1939, the British issued their infamous White Paper. Declaring the Balfour Declaration fulfilled, they called for very tight limits on Jewish immigration and a ten-year waiting period to be followed by creation of a joint Arab-Jewish state. At the very moment when Jews were frantically attempting to secure exit from Germany, the British government shuttered the gates of Palestine. A furious Perlzweig declared that the White Paper had cast Jews back into the ghetto under the thumb of a "corrupt and bloodstained oligarchy." Not only was it a deep betrayal of the Zionist movement but it was also a threat to the entirety of Jewish existence in Europe: "Indeed, it is scarcely a secret that the same forces which have destroyed Jewish citizen rights over a large area in Europe are playing their part in the attack on the Jewish National Home."[37]

Embittered and anxious, Perlzweig arrived in Bucharest in July 1939 to undertake what would be his last diplomatic mission of the decade. He came armed with an official British diplomatic decree requesting Consul Hoare to aid him in discussions with the Romanian government on the status of its Jews. Under cover of darkness, Perlzweig was whisked into a heavily guarded palace for an extraordinary face-to-face meeting with Prime Minister Calinescu. The antisemitic politician welcomed him warmly with arms outstretched, speaking in French, "Mon cher Rabbin! I have been waiting for you!" After the pleasantries, Perlzweig began enumerating a long list of anti-Jewish policies, only to be interrupted by Calinescu, who insisted that the allegations were merely propaganda. When Perlzweig protested that he had evidence of the Jews' ill treatment, the prime minister relented, but maintained that these excesses were unauthorized. He took out a notebook and began making notes. Rest assured, Calinescu explained, all who were guilty would be punished. "Now the joke was that he was the man who had himself been responsible for this order," Perlzweig recalled, and "he knew that I knew that he was lying, and nevertheless we went on talking like that." As a result of Perlzweig's trip, the government briefly tempered some of its anti-Jewish policies. Yet it was another pyrrhic victory for Jewish rights. Within two months, Calinescu had been assassinated, and the Iron Guard stepped up its vicious campaign of anti-Jewish violence.[38]

After Bucharest, Perlzweig traveled to Geneva, where the Twenty-First Zionist Congress opened in late August 1939. The agitated talk of the British White Paper was interrupted by the stunning news of the Molotov-Ribbentrop Pact: the Nazis and Soviets had agreed to invade and divide up Poland. War was at hand. Perlzweig spent the final days of August attempting to persuade the Polish Jewish delegates not to return to Poland. Despite his entreaties, nearly all chose to go home. Their returning home to their deaths was a final lesson from the interwar experiment in Jewish minority rights. As he said later, "We don't believe in reality unless it hits us in the face."[39]

"Where Is Ginevra?"

On September 1, 1939, Germany launched its invasion of Poland. Two weeks later, as Soviet forces entered the country from the east, Perlzweig was summoned to a meeting at the Foreign Office by his friend R. A. Butler. "The Government is considering that if the position should become very bad we should not surrender the fleet to Hitler but should take it to Canada, and should continue the war from Canada," he confided, and then made an even more secret request: "We are making a list of people who ought to be taken out of England if we have to leave. We want to take out the people who are most vulnerable, and we would like your advice about those in the Jewish community." Perlzweig squirmed at the prospect of determining "who shall live and who shall die." He consulted Chaim Weizmann, who told him, "I do not want to be on that list." But the captain did not want all his first mates to go down with the ship. Weizmann urged Perlzweig to flee Britain for the United States, the better to establish a strong European Jewish diplomatic presence there. Ever famous for his belief in the British, Weizmann had begun to anticipate that the future of Jewish rights lay with American power.

At the end of 1939, Perlzweig met World Jewish Congress president Nahum Goldmann in Paris, and the two took the train to the French border with Spain. There they presented their passports to a teenage Spanish border clerk for entry. Perlzweig traveled on a specially arranged British passport, which she reviewed without comment. Goldmann's passport was issued by the government of Honduras, which had appointed him Honduran consul to the League of Nations in Geneva. The girl paused, confused as he stared at the open passport in her hands. Then she asked, "Where is *Ginevra*?" She had never even heard of Geneva. To the two men, it was as if the headquarters of the League of Nations, on which they had rested so much of their hopes for justice, had never existed in the real world.[40]

"In 1921, on my first visit to Vienna after the war, I happened to engage in a discussion about Jewish Nationalism and Zionism with one of those high-minded, broad-minded, open-minded, shallow-minded Jews who prefer to call themselves anything rather than Jews," wrote Lewis Namier in a 1941 essay for the journal Perlzweig edited, the *Zionist Review*. Namier's Viennese friend dismissed Zionism on the grounds that his rights should not depend on his identity: "First and foremost, I am a human being." Namier replied sharply, "I, too, once thought so: but I have since discovered that all are agreed that I am a Jew, but not all that I am a human being. I have therefore come to consider myself first a Jew, and only in the second place a human being."

Two decades had passed, Namier continued, and the friend was now dead. His wife had disappeared into the clutches of the Nazis. Their two children had fled to England, where the British promptly imprisoned the son on suspicion of German nationalist sympathies. The daughter came to Namier complaining about the absurdity of his situation. She chastised the authorities for failing to see that her brother was no Nazi, but one of their victims. Namier disagreed. Having long ago disavowed their Jewishness, he told her, how could she and her brother expect the British then to tell the difference? "How much Jews complicate things for themselves by professing to be 'first and foremost human beings'! It is only through attaining full national status that the Jews can hope to secure equal rights as human beings."[41]

The post–World War I generation of British Jewish rights-defenders insisted that, in Perlzweig's words, "human and national rights" formed two sides of the same coin. The dignity of difference demanded that Jews enter the world *as Jews* to secure their rights, both individual and collective. Naked humanity was not only a utopian abstraction but also a willfully blind rejection of the realities of human experience. The Law of Nations could not exist in the absence of nations. If this reality constrained the Great Powers, how much more did it constrain peoples consigned by historical fate to live as minorities spread across the globe?

Nationalism fired the interwar Jewish imagination with intertwined ideas of minority rights and Zionism. But this Jewish internationalism, born of politics, ultimately could not overcome the force of politics. In the shifting terrain of the modern world, the realities of nationalism cut both ways. As the world entered a second global conflagration that threatened to destroy the heartland of Jewish life in Europe, questions remained. Could nationalism be salvaged along with minority rights? Or would the goal of restoring justice, both to the Jews and to the world at large, demand something altogether new?

PART TWO

CONVERGENCE

Zionist political thinking still remain[s] in the realm of pre-war political conceptions including that of national self-determination. This doctrine was the product of the First World War. . . . Instead of emphasis upon *national* self-determination, stress will have to be placed on *human* self-determination.

—Morris Waldman, "A Bill of Rights for All Nations," 1944

In seeking to establish beyond question the inalienable rights common to all men, we cannot ignore the Jew qua Jew, nor resolve an entire people out of existence by ignoring its presence. Consequently, our Resolution on an International Bill of Rights stresses the right of the Jew to be a Jew individually and collectively. The test of a democracy is to be found in its attitude not only to the individual but to the group. There can be cultural and spiritual totalitarianism, even within a political democracy.

—American Jewish Conference, Report of the
Post-War Committee, 1944

Remembering his six million martyred brethren, the Jew is not yet ready to accept this second attempt within one generation to set up an organized community of nations as the remedy for his sufferings and his continued persecution. . . . [T]he civilized world will certainly understand why the Jews, who have so fervently prayed for the firm establishment of the rule of law on both the domestic and international scene, are somewhat reluctant to believe that this Messianic era was ushered in at the Paris [UN] Assembly.

—Robert Marcus, "Human Rights: A Jewish View," 1949

The time has come for the formulation of a new concept of democratic nationalism, if nationalism is not to become a weapon in the hands of tyranny and the grossest reaction. Just as the liberty of every individual must in justice be limited by the equal right of other individuals, so the emancipation of a national group must be limited by the right of other groups, however small or feeble. It is not a legitimate exercise of national sovereignty to massacre minorities, and it is not a valid defense of the right to massacre that it is a matter of internal domestic concern of every government.

—Speech by Maurice Perlzweig, 1952

4

Jewish Human Rights

ON DECEMBER 15, 1944, THE 153RD anniversary of the Bill of Rights, Americans across the country awoke to read in their daily papers about a new "Declaration on Human Rights." To achieve world peace, this document informed them, the forthcoming UN must "guarantee for every man, woman and child, of every race and creed and in every country, the fundamental rights of life, liberty and the pursuit of happiness." It was signed by more than "1300 distinguished Americans of all faiths," including Vice President Henry Wallace, Republican presidential candidate Thomas Dewey, two Supreme Court justices, thirty-seven Catholic and Protestant bishops, and the leaders of the U.S. Chamber of Commerce, the American Federation of Labor, and the NAACP.

Such broad support did not spring out of nowhere. The Declaration of Human Rights formed the central plank of a large public relations campaign. Its authors came from the ranks of the American Jewish Committee (AJC), which, after mostly sitting out the interwar period of legal diplomacy, now took the lead in crafting the American creed of human rights. "The rights of Jews will only be secure," declared the AJC's incoming leader, Jacob Blaustein, "when the rights of people of all faiths are equally secure." Bald and bespectacled, medium in height, the Baltimore native had grown a one-wagon kerosene delivery service into the American Oil Company (AMOCO), a national oil and gasoline industrial giant. Among his inventions and innovations were the first high-octane motor fuel for car engines, the first metered gasoline pump, and the first drive-through filling station. He brought the same spirit of innovation to his work at the forefront of American human rights promotion.

The idea of crafting a declaration of human rights emerged from a peculiarly American Jewish mixture of pride and self-consciousness about political activism. To survive in the postwar world, Blaustein believed, Jews needed to define themselves as an apolitical religious faith rather than as a quarrelsome national minority. Minority rights had not only failed the Jews but also sealed their terrible fate in Nazi Europe by corrupting international justice to the point where vulnerable minorities were transformed into political combatants. An American Judeo-Christian vision of human rights would tame the fires of Old World nationalism and advance international democracy at one fell swoop. After centuries of division and hatred, it was time to create, in the words of the Declaration, "the first human world in history."[1]

A noble logic governed this vision. Remove ethnic, national, and religious politics from the equation, and international law would protect all equally, without prejudice. Yet the image of nationalism and human rights as opposites struck Jacob Robinson, Maurice Perlzweig, and other veteran European Jewish rights-defenders as profoundly naïve—if not disingenuous. "While this document, at first sight, appears to be an innocent expression of pious wishes in an elevated style (God is invoked at least three times)," Robinson wrote in a blistering critique, the AJC's Declaration actually represented an attack on Jewish nationhood: "Once more an attempt is being made to disguise Jewish demands under the mask of general ones. This is not only a self-deception but also shows a lack of dignity and self-respect." If nationalism was the poison and human rights the antidote, moreover, then where did that leave Zionism? He counseled fellow Zionists that they must "not only oppose plans of the Committee, but openly denounce them." Were the AJC vision of human rights to prevail, Jews and other minorities would face a dangerous retreat from the rule of law and an assault on minority identity itself. "The U.S.A., by means of extreme liberalism," Robinson bitterly observed, "killed the separatism of national minorities." Now it threatened to do the same for the rest of the world with the willing consent of "assimilated" American Jews.[2]

The radical difference of opinion between Blaustein and Robinson was not merely a case of intramural Jewish squabbling. It reflected a larger uncertainty about the sudden appearance of human rights in the middle years of World War II. Until that time, most Americans had never even heard the phrase. Nor had most politicians and policy experts. A nearly 700-page compendium of statements on war aims issued between 1939 and 1942 mentioned human rights only once. Now, as the idea of an international bill of rights bubbled up in postwar planning discussions, no one could quite agree on what it meant or whether it was a good thing.[3]

Many prominent liberal intellectuals praised the AJC document's broad-minded internationalism, while others detected a stealth prescription for American unilateralism. Conservatives too split on whether human rights were a weapon against Communism and New Deal "socialism" or posed a dangerous threat to American sovereignty. Where some Protestant and Catholic observers saw in the document an ecumenical "international bill of religious rights," African American leader W. E. B. DuBois saw it as Jewish special pleading. "[T]his is a very easily understood Declaration of Jewish Rights," he wrote, "but it has apparently no thought of the rights of Negroes, Indians, South Sea Islanders. Why then call it the Declaration of Human Rights?" All this even though the text did not contain the word "Jew."[4]

The story of the Jewish role in the rise of human rights in wartime America exposes a truth conveniently forgotten by contemporary lawyers, activists, and even most historians. Today we may imagine that the Holocaust shocked the American conscience into action, producing a reflexive moral embrace of human rights. We may likewise assume that Jews viewed the unfolding European nightmare as a cautionary tale about the dangers of racism and the need for international law to protect humanity. Yet, in reality, the rise of human rights in wartime America had surprisingly little to do with the Holocaust or Nazi antisemitism. The UN Universal Declaration of Human Rights, adopted in 1948, was in large measure the brainchild of American policy makers and intellectuals who replaced the delegitimized European model of minority rights with a new ideal of American-style civil liberties. The era of international minorities protection had ended. In its place arose a new vision of individual human rights etched ambiguously into the structure of an American-led global order.

Those Jewish leaders who flocked to this scheme saw in it the promise of a democratic liberalism that would protect fellow Jews abroad and secure their place at home. Those who resisted the new human rights vision feared that it would further imperil postwar minorities and unfairly malign Zionism in the process. What they all shared was an understanding that wartime human rights discussions were as much a referendum on America's role in the future world as a policy debate over the shape of international law.[5]

Jacob Blaustein was among the first to grasp the fundamental ambiguity in the American World War II-era discussions of human rights. He entered public life at a moment when skeptics were asking why the United States should embroil itself in European or Middle Eastern affairs after the messy collapse of the League of Nations. Early enthusiasm for the UN did not dispel a strain of anxiety about the implications for American society of any prospective changes to international law. Blaustein's America was one in which pious talk of defending freedom abroad awkwardly coexisted with persistent racism at home. It was also an America in which the war against the Nazis coincided with an *increase* in domestic antisemitism. In response to this paradox, Blaustein seized on the new idea of individual human rights as a cost-free, apolitical solution. With one clean stroke, American Jews could display their democratic loyalty at home and protect their brethren abroad. The 1944 Declaration of Human Rights campaign formed part of a Jewish quest to walk the fine line that, in the American political imagination, separated enlightened advocacy from nefarious ethnic influence.

Meanwhile, Robinson, fresh off the boat from Lithuania, fought tooth and nail to prevent the American experts from eviscerating minority rights. To gain a foothold and a platform for his ideas, he built the world's first Jewish think tank in wartime New York City. From there he promoted a Zionist policy prescription for human rights that blended individual and group protections bolstered by a strong international legal framework.

In between these two men and their respective wings of American Jewish human rights activism stood a third figure, Hersch Zvi Lauterpacht, who found an unlikely role as a diplomatic go-between for the American and British governments and a mediator between the Zionist and non-Zionist wings of the Jewish world. Even as he advised his fellow Zionists on legal strategy for Palestine, Lauterpacht accepted a commission from Blaustein to prepare a draft of an international bill of rights. His resulting book offered an influential blueprint for international human rights, yet it also reflected his keen awareness of the two cardinal facts that would define the Jewish fate in the postwar world more than anything else: the decline of the British Empire and the rise of American power.

In Defense of Minority Rights

In early February 1941, Perlzweig convened a press conference at Atlanta's Biltmore Hotel to announce a new weapon in the envisioned postwar "fight for Jewish rights." Henceforth the World Jewish Congress (WJC) would sponsor a Research Institute for Contemporary Jewish Affairs, populated by a team of experts who would conduct a full inventory of the contemporary Jewish world. "The institute is needed now," he told reporters, "to develop our own concept of the new world order as far as the Jews are concerned. If we wait until the war is over, even the democratic powers might harden their concept of the new world order into a shape which might be beyond human power to remodel. This would be disastrous." To direct the new institute, Perlzweig introduced his friend Robinson, recently arrived from Soviet-occupied Lithuania, as "the foremost living authority on questions of minority rights and the Jewish status."[6]

Even before the outbreak of World War II, Robinson had called on his WJC colleagues to establish what would become the world's first Jewish think tank. His rationale was simple: "Our enemies have their institutes," so Jews should have one too. Jews had relied for far too long on other governments to develop policy proposals and collect demographic data that directly affected Jewish political options. Robinson knew firsthand the value of statistics in making political claims on behalf of national minorities in interwar Europe. Now the time had come for Jews to conduct their own research unhampered by anyone else's agenda.

After the Soviet invasion of Lithuania in June 1940, Robinson made a desperate dash across Europe, moving illegally through Soviet territory to Romania, Yugoslavia, Italy, and Vichy France. By December, he and his wife and two daughters were on a ship to New York City. There, working

Jacob Robinson in the early 1940s after his arrival in the United States

Courtesy of the United States Holocaust Memorial Museum

out of the joint American Jewish Congress/World Jewish Congress offices at Columbus Circle in midtown Manhattan, Robinson began building up his new organization with a Who's Who of prominent Jewish intellectuals, including the former Russian revolutionary and international lawyer Mark Vishniak, Zionist Revisionist and political demographer Joseph Schechtman, and American social philosopher Horace Kallen. Throughout the war they issued a steady stream of working papers and reports, which collectively amounted to the first systematic, real-time research on the destruction of European Jewry, conducted through an international network of scholars and informants.[7]

In addition to generating documentation and analysis, the Institute's other core mission was to help shape the policy planning discussions then underway in the United States. Throughout the early 1940s, Robinson himself made the rounds of conferences sponsored by such groups as the American Society for International Law, the American Bar Association, and the Commission to Study the Organization of Peace. There, he joined veteran Wilsonian diplomats, lawyers, and political scientists in discussing the future of international politics, economics, security, and global governance. At each of these events, he puzzled over two words he heard intoned over and over: "human rights."

In two decades of legal work in Europe, Robinson had rarely if ever encountered this term. Nor was he alone. Between 1800 and 1940, "human rights" was all but absent from international legal parlance. That did not mean it lacked any prehistory. Philosophers and theologians spoke of natural rights. Politicians invoked the Rights of Man in the late eighteenth-century context of the French and American Revolutions. But to lawyers, the term "human rights" was an archaic phrase with no place in international law. The early years of the war did little to change that perception. Not until January 1942, in the joint American-British-Soviet Declaration of the United Nations, did "human rights" enter the modern diplomatic lexicon, and even then only in passing. Later that same year, Winston Churchill proclaimed in a message to a London protest rally on behalf of German Jews that the "world struggle" against Fascism would "end with the enthronement of human rights." It was likely a throwaway line, yet it sparked a number of expansive visions of dignity and justice. From there, the phrase steadily gained currency in Anglo-American policy circles. In search of a new approach to replace the discredited minority rights ideal, American and British policy makers and intellectuals began to speak of an international bill of rights.[8]

As human rights became a buzzword, Robinson struck a sharp note of skepticism. People talked constantly about "the desirability and absolute necessity of an International Bill of Rights," he wrote to a British colleague after the 1941 American Society for International Law conference, yet none of the American experts had a clue how to formulate "either the content or form of this idea." "I also have the gravest doubts," he added, "as to the feasibility and practical use of a universal Bill of Rights." Without a larger conception of the global legal and political order, it made no sense to outline a wish list of individual rights. Lofty pronouncements came cheap. When the distinguished American international relations scholar Quincy Wright, in a 1942 letter to Robinson, cited the Atlantic Charter as a human rights manifesto, Robinson did not mince words in reply: "The attempt to read human rights into the Atlantic Charter is condemned to failure, not only because the Atlantic Charter is not at all concerned with human rights, but because Article 3 of the Atlantic Charter establishing the unqualified right of every state to have its own regime implies the right of the states to create totalitarian regimes which may not recognize any human rights at all." The proliferation of plans, proposals, and schemes for human rights left Robinson worried that the experts had lost touch with reality: was there no danger that "because of so many nurses the baby may remain without a nose?"[9]

He was troubled most of all by American lawyers' profound ignorance of international law. Without law, talk of rights was nonsensical. Yet America's failure to join the League of Nations had left a generation of U.S. lawyers oblivious to how it had tried to deal with legal matters, and Robinson's attempts to enlighten them in his eloquent if accented English fell on deaf ears. Things reached a critical point in late February 1942, when he spoke to the annual meeting of the Carnegie Conference on International Law. With considerable effort, he had persuaded the group to devote a session to the legal ramifications of an International Bill of Rights. Yet during the discussion, he found to his dismay that the lawyers blithely assumed that any such bill would essentially copy the American Bill of Rights; they gave little thought to enforcement or jurisdiction. When it was his turn to speak, he urged his colleagues to review the interwar European legal corpus: "If international law is going to be a law of all the world," he said, they needed "a study which would give us all the developments through these twenty-five years and would teach us what we have to avoid in the future and what may be advisable to do." The meeting's chairman interrupted him mid-sentence: "We have attempted that, Mr. Robinson, in twenty-three volumes of the *American Journal of International Law*. To which we have an excellent index." The room broke out in laughter. Robinson failed to see the humor.[10]

Robinson's colleagues at the World Jewish Congress shared his reservations about the human rights rage in American postwar planning. "I read your note on the meeting of the American Law Institute with disquiet but without surprise," Perlzweig wrote him in May 1943, for "even the best American opinion is intellectually very remote from the kind of thinking about the future of Europe which is commonplace among European liberals." These ignorant human rights schemes threatened to put Jewish plans for postwar Europe in "grave peril." Stephen Wise concurred: "I am not the least surprised by what you write about the American Law Institute," he told Robinson. "It has always been more or less dead. You find it completely dead. I never had the slightest confidence in its value or significance."[11]

The problem was not just utopianism, the three men agreed, but an excessive reliance on a parochial model of constitutional rights undergirded by a deep faith in American exceptionalism. American lawyers loved the idea of an international bill of human rights because it would be radically new, ostensibly cost free, and American inspired. Yet they completely ignored the situation of national minorities in the rest of the world. Robinson diagnosed this enthusiasm as based on the most specious reasoning: minority rights had failed in Europe because of the evils of nationalism. Hence America, the postnational nation, should remake the world in its image via the Bill of Rights. Yet the United States had its own racial minority problem, he observed archly, which a beautiful Bill of Rights had done nothing to resolve.

The hypocrisy troubled Robinson less, however, than the assumption that European group rights represented the opposite of American-style individual liberties. There was no logical contradiction between the two, he argued, since minority rights included basic civil liberties. The real choice was not "between a bill of rights and Minority Rights," but between *constitutional* and *international* guarantees. To correct these misconceptions, he spent much of 1942 co-authoring a major study titled *Were the Minorities Treaties a Failure?* His conclusion, poorly articulated in a dry legal volume, was that any failure lay not in the novel laws themselves but in the collapse of European democracy—a necessary precondition for the success of any international rights scheme. Speaking at Columbia University at the time, he was still more bullish, declaring, "Minorities protection by the League of Nations was possibly the greatest legal innovation of modern times." Though it suffered from problems in implementation, "it was in the final analysis a successful experiment." Even as some states refused to abide by League decisions, the overall "deterrent effect of the machinery for international protection was considerable." Thanks to the Minorities Treaties, "thousands of cases never arose and were never brought before the League." In their absence, the violence would have been still worse and begun earlier.[12]

Robinson's vigorous defense of minority rights was a departure from his ambivalent position of a few years before. While the change certainly owed somewhat to wounded pride, it also reflected a savvy awareness of the present opportunity. The very inchoate nature of the emerging human rights ideal allowed the possibility of preserving some of the better features of the interwar minority rights model. During 1942 and 1943, Robinson and his colleagues set to work on their own version of an "International Bill of Rights" that would provide essential "instruments for the maintenance of our Jewish group" after the war. That effort formed just one part of their larger research and planning agenda for the postwar period, which also included problems of migration, restitution, criminal justice, and the disposition of Palestine. All of this took on a new urgency as political conflict erupted within Jewish America over who should speak for the Jews in the coming postwar peace settlement. That fight would bring Robinson into confrontation with a man who had his own, very different human rights vision.[13]

"A Most Unusual Oil Man"

"He's not a Texan; he comes from Baltimore and has lived there all his life," *Forbes* magazine once noted in a profile of Jacob Blaustein. "He's not big, burly and boisterous, but slender and soft-spoken. He dresses quietly as a bank president, drinks sparingly, raises orchids, collects paintings—Gaugin, Derain, Utrillo—enjoys listening to classical music and used to play the piano." Yet even if Blaustein defied the stereotype of an oil tycoon, Soviet diplomats, Washington politicos, and fellow industrialists all quickly learned that America's top "part-time diplomat" was a tough negotiator with a long track record of deal making.[14]

The son of a penniless Lithuanian Jewish immigrant to Baltimore, Blaustein studied chemistry at Lehigh University before dropping out to join his father's fledgling heating oil delivery business. Over several decades, father and son combined scientific advances with marketing chutzpah to develop the company into an international conglomerate. Wealth brought political entrée. An ardent New Dealer, Blaustein emerged in the 1930s as a major donor to the Democratic Party. During the war he served

Jacob Blaustein in the late 1940s

on various advisory policy committees connected to the petroleum industry and volunteered his company's tanker fleet to transport government oil
for the war effort.

At the same time, Blaustein rose steadily to national prominence in
American Jewish affairs. He headed major philanthropic appeals and chaired
the board of the Jewish Telegraph Agency, an international news service.
In January 1943 he was named chairman of the AJC's executive committee,
a leadership role that instantly positioned him to speak broadly on American
foreign policy. It came, however, at a particularly fraught juncture in
American Jewish politics. Throughout the 1930s, even as Zionist leaders

fought publicly to secure Jewish immigration to Palestine, they maintained a strategic silence regarding their political endgame. That pattern ended in May 1942, when delegates from nineteen countries converged at the Biltmore Hotel in New York City to issue a formal demand for the immediate creation of a Jewish Commonwealth in Palestine at war's end. From that point onward, the Great Powers were on notice that the question of Zionism could not be shunted aside for the sake of the war effort.

That demand was followed a year later by a less dramatic but equally consequential development: the launch of the American Jewish Conference. Modeled after the World War I-era congresses, it was intended to be an umbrella Jewish political organization. In the summer of 1943, a coalition of nearly every major American Jewish group, including the American Jewish Congress, B'nai Brith, and the Reform movement, held nationwide elections for a kind of voluntary Jewish parliament. Twenty-five hundred electors from across the country, representing 1.5 million Jews, voted for delegates to the new political body that some likened to a Jewish Continental Congress. Just as did the wartime congress movement a generation earlier, the American Jewish Conference advanced a program for Jewish rights in the postwar world in Europe and Palestine. It also prompted a fresh debate about Jewish nationalism and minority rights, at home and abroad.[15]

Blaustein attended the first meeting of the American Jewish Conference, held in Pittsburgh in September 1943, and came away alarmed by what he perceived as a conspiracy to nationalize American Jewry. Relief for Europe's Jews was perfectly appropriate. Jewish resettlement in Palestine he readily accepted. But for *American* Jews, he felt the ideological thrust of Jewish nationalism went too far. The American Jewish Conference must be stopped. "The 'Zion' in Zionism we have always favored, always striven to aid; it is the special 'ism' in Zionism that we do not accept," he would later write. "That 'ism' has no faith in Emancipation; it preaches the inevitability of a murderous anti-Semitism, almost as much a fact of nature as the law of gravity. This we reject totally. We have faith in Emancipation, in liberalism, and in the ultimate power of education."[16]

At Blaustein's urging, the AJC withdrew from the Conference and refused to cooperate with it. Still, the situation left him in a quandary. The subtlety of the AJC's position—supporting a Jewish national home in Palestine while opposing Jewish nationalism—proved increasingly hard to explain to an American Jewish public that overwhelmingly viewed Zionism as a just response to both the Jewish devastation unfolding in Europe and the larger logic of democratic self-determination promoted in the Atlantic Charter. "[W]e have permitted the Committee to be jockeyed into the position of being the opposing group to the Zionists," wrote executive director Morris Waldman in the fall of 1943. Instead of fighting over Palestine— "the battleground chosen by the Zionists"—the AJC needed to put forth its own positive foreign policy vision, authentically Jewish yet unsullied by nationalism.[17]

Adding to the sense of urgency were the results of the AJC's first foray into public opinion polling. Blaustein's researchers reported to him that antisemitism had dramatically increased in American society during the war years. Most Americans viewed Jews as a greater threat than German Americans or Japanese Americans; one-third of respondents indicated that they would "join or sympathize with an antisemitic political campaign." That number soon rose to a whopping 57 percent of the public. Yet at the same time, 59 percent of Americans favored the creation of a Jewish state in Palestine. Even a majority of self-professed antisemites supported such a state. This presented a confounding situation for Jewish leaders: Americans liked the Zionist idea of a Jewish state even as they feared Jewish influence in domestic politics.[18]

Faced with this set of dilemmas, Blaustein announced in October 1943 that the AJC must do more than simply oppose Zionism: it "must proclaim its positive program and state in as definite terms as possible what it aims to do in behalf of the Jews of the world, including those of this country, and including Palestine." The solution came in the form of human rights. It offered a vision of American liberalism that resonated deeply with American Jews: freedom from discrimination, an end to divisive group identities, and a victory for American democracy over both Nazi and Soviet tyranny. It was also a political response to antisemitism and Zionism alike. Jews would be treated as individuals, with no special minority rights. Zionism would be reduced to a philanthropic refugee resettlement plan for Palestine, its political links to American Jews severed. The messy middle ground of Jewish minority identity and nationalism in America and Europe would disappear. Jews would be able to exercise benign moral leadership in American foreign policy without the taint of ethnic parochialism. "We do not go out to slay the dragon" of Jewish nationalism head on, Blaustein aide John Slawson told the AJC staff at one meeting, yet "everything we do is anti-nationalist. If we did not have that kind of Jewish philosophy, we wouldn't be concerned with human rights." All that was needed was a specific blueprint, a Bill of Rights for the world, to broadcast this vision. When it came to deciding who would define the details of that vision, Blaustein and his colleagues made a surprising choice. To spread their anti-nationalist gospel of human rights, they reached across the Atlantic to a devoted Zionist, Hersch Lauterpacht.[19]

"A Silly Book"

Lauterpacht was an odd choice, and not only because of his politics. Strikingly, until the middle of World War II, he had scarcely given any thought to the topic of human rights per se. Even as he presented bold arguments for the existence of international law in the 1920s and 1930s, he made no attempt to imagine individual rights outside the framework of conventional citizenship. The phrase "human rights" did not appear in the 1937 edition of *Oppenheim's Digest of International Law,* which he edited. This was not an oversight. Lauterpacht believed that chasing utopian schemes of international law would not only backfire but would also undermine the British support needed to sustain any international law.[20]

In April 1942, an invitation came to reconsider his views. That month an old friend from Poland, Simon Segal, now ensconced at the AJC's own in-house research institute, wrote him with an offer to prepare an "international bill of Rights of the individual (or something) with special application to the Jewish question." Lauterpacht grasped the moral imperative for Jews to speak up on this issue. "No people in history has suffered more cruelly from a denial of elementary human rights," he would later write. Yet he accepted the commission in 1942 with deep reservations. He was not troubled by the AJC's opposition to Zionism, but he worried that a laundry list of rights would be meaningless without legal force behind it. "We could cram into that Bill of Rights all kinds of things including the so called social and economic rights like the right to work, to social security, to equal opportunity in education, and so on," he wrote his son Eli, "but the Bill of Rights, if it is to be effective, must be enforced not only by the authorities of the State, but also by international actors if necessary." That required a keen attention to the realities of international relations: "[W]ould states agree to entrust to a foreign tribunal such questions touching the most essential aspects of their sovereignty?" Surveying the coming postwar world, he grasped that the question would be decided by the disposition of two states: the declining British Empire and the rising United States.[21]

Lauterpacht knew this because he had a front-row seat—and a bit part—in this global changing of the guard. In 1940–41, the Carnegie Endowment sponsored a speaking tour across the United States for him to rally support for the war effort. Midway through his trip, in January 1941, he received an invitation from Attorney-General Robert H. Jackson to assist in responding to a legal challenge to the proposed Lend-Lease Act. This law was designed to give the U.S. government a channel through which to provide material support to Great Britain while preserving official neutrality. Isolationists opposed to American participation in the war had served notice to the Roosevelt administration that this legal maneuver would not stand. Lauterpacht composed a memo for Jackson on "Qualified Neutrality" offering an original, compelling defense of the Lend-Lease Act's legality. The attorney-general used the text as the basis for a major speech at the New York Bar Association that March, where, as he put it, Lauterpacht played "the discreet first fiddle."[22]

Lauterpacht visited the United States twice more during World War II and even moved his family there for the duration of hostilities. Without American power, he realized, Britain had no hope of winning the war. By the same token, any future for international law would have to take account of the domestic political realities within American society. The assignment from the AJC was thus an opportunity to test out his ideas about how to reform international law in a way that would appeal to the rising liberal superpower, which was unencumbered by colonies but skeptical of European national minorities. Still, the effort was not easy. He nursed the project along over the next three years, complaining in letters to his family of the "dull business" of writing this "silly book." None of his many wartime commitments, including revising the British code of military justice, planning for future war crimes trials, and advising on the laws of war, "give me as much of a headache as the Rights of Man." The challenge lay in satisfying both cynics and idealists. Any draft would need to inspire Western liberals without scaring off hard-minded statesmen or Communist and non-Western leaders.[23]

In the preface to the eventual completed volume, *An International Bill of the Rights of Man,* Lauterpacht dismissed utopian schemes for world citizenship or ungrounded cosmopolitan pronouncements. "The law of nature and natural rights," he argued, "can never be a true substitute for the positive enactments of the law of the society of States. When so treated they are inefficacious, deceptive, and, in the long run, a brake upon progress." The true "Achilles heel of the natural rights of man" is that "in the last resort such rights are subject to the will of the State." And in the international system, what force could trump state power? Twenty years earlier, he had argued that the League of Nations, with its Covenant and International Court, reflected "a legal source superior to that of the State." Yet the League lay in tatters, and the UN was only an uncertain promise. Now he claimed that the "ultimate" safeguard for human rights, the "power superior to the supreme power of the State," was "international law" itself, which he defined as "the body of rules, voluntarily accepted or imposed by the existence of international society." Discarding theological or metaphysical justifications for human rights, Lauterpacht stressed a humanist, historically minded realism. Men made law real through their acceptance of it. This was not an act of faith or a philosopher's fiction; it was a natural historical process in all human societies that was now expanding to the international level. If law was premised on global human consensus, however, that made the details of *which* rights to incorporate into an international bill all the more crucial.[24]

In the second and third sections of the book, Lauterpacht sketched out a proposed international Bill of Rights along with procedures for its enforcement. The Bill's text consisted of a preamble and twenty articles to be included in the future UN Charter and written into the constitutions of the world's states. The rights he enumerated fell into two clusters:

(a) Personal civil liberties, such as freedom of religion, speech, association, and privacy, along with bans on unlawful detention, inhumane punishment, and slavery;

(b) Collective political and economic rights, such as self-government, secret ballot, public welfare, and the right to preservation of cultural entity.

This division of rights was deliberate. He deemed certain rights more important than others. Only the first cluster of rights should be written into the "domestic law and constitution" of every state. For these laws, the backstop would be the UN, with final authority residing in the Security Council, authorized by a three-fourths vote to pursue "such political, economic, or military action" as it considered necessary in response to a state's "refusal to remedy the situation." Tactical considerations also led to some curious omissions and moral compromises. He left out the rights to property, freedom of immigration, and full gender equality on the practical ground that they were as yet too contested. Remarkable as it may seem to us today, the father of international human rights law was willing to forego these fundamental rights to secure the international consensus he viewed as essential for the project's success.[25]

Even more striking, Lauterpacht insisted on including minority rights in substance if not in name. He had told Robinson late in 1944 that "it is of the greatest importance that the idea of an International Bill of Rights of Man should not be permitted to be used for the purpose of or with the effect of whittling down the existing protection of Jewish rights." Therefore in his draft Bill of Rights, he now proposed to extend to all "ethnic, linguistic or religious minorities" the right to protection from discrimination, the right to state-funded "schools and cultural and religious institutions," and the right "to use their own language before the courts and other authorities and organs of the State." These measures, intended to ensure "their cultural needs as an ethnic entity," were in substance minority rights. This group autonomy was not intended to substitute for democratic equality, he noted with reference to the status of colonized peoples and minorities such as blacks and Asians in South Africa. On these issues, he predicted confidently that "public opinion and the watchful eye of courts—both strengthened by the residuary powers of international concern in the matter" would bring about "gradual" change.[26]

With these compromises, Lauterpacht aimed to tread a careful path through the political thickets within British and American governmental circles of the early 1940s. Despite lofty rhetoric about freedom and justice in the Atlantic Charter, human rights were slow to emerge as a priority of either country's postwar planning. On the British side, any stirring image of freedom's defeat of Nazi racial imperialism had to contend with the realities of British imperialism, decolonization, and various political intrigues scarcely interrupted by the war. American officials confronted the awkward disjunction between the campaign for liberty abroad and the persistence of legal racism at home. Secretary of State Cordell Hull gave several wartime speeches about human rights, yet refrained from contemplating any substantive policy in that area. The State Department's policy planning team did take up human rights in a limited fashion, but focused on building a collective security framework. The wartime Roosevelt State Department was wholly uninterested in reforming international law or changing the nature of state sovereignty.[27]

To both British and American diplomats, Lauterpacht offered a reassuring image of international human rights law as a solid, sensible compact between state and society. "In the hands of governments with a statesman-like conception of realism," he suggested, human rights offered a chance to avoid a radical step into the chaos of the coming postwar world by instead advancing freedom in an orderly way. This moderate human rights template would eventually appeal most to Europeans. But the 1945 book arrived too late for the Great Powers' opening discussions about human rights in the postwar international order. Those conversations had already begun in 1944, as battlefield victories shifted attention toward the concrete questions of what kind of global organization would replace the discredited League of Nations. Impatient with Lauterpacht's slow pace and doubtless uneasy about his inclusion of minority rights, the AJC leaders looked for something more immediate, more American, and less legalistic to express their vision of human rights.[28]

"The Human Rights of Jews"

In late March 1944, Blaustein was summoned out of an AMOCO board meeting to take an urgent phone call from an AJC staffer. President Roosevelt had just agreed to a get-together to discuss Jewish affairs. The timing was purposeful. The White House was hard at work attempting to secure the Jewish vote in that year's election. Jews had earlier flocked to Roosevelt's New Deal Democratic Party, beginning a long-standing pattern of Jewish Democratic voting. But now a challenge had appeared from the right. Zionist leader Rabbi Abba Hillel Silver, a lifelong Republican, had engineered a set of congressional resolutions in support of a Jewish commonwealth in Palestine. Although they failed to pass the House, the resulting publicity suggested a way for Republicans to pry Jewish voters away from Roosevelt's coalition.[29]

In response, Roosevelt directed his staff to call in the Jewish Democrats. First came Stephen Wise and his cohort of Zionist liberals, who pressed hard for a public statement of support for a Jewish state. Roosevelt responded to them in his typical fashion, encouraging yet noncommittal. Next he summoned the AJC leaders, who were also staunch Democrats. It was the moment Blaustein had been waiting for. In a statement prepared in anticipation of his White House visit, he outlined the rationale for human rights. "We believe, Mr. President, that the future peace of the world depends upon a world order that will guarantee individual liberties and rights to all men, regardless of race, color or creed," and "the post-war World must be reconstituted on the basis of individual rights of man, rather than on the basis of 'minorities rights.'" To achieve this end, "the nations of the world must accept an 'international bill of rights' just as the American people have accepted the American Bill of Rights." Tucked at the end was a brief mention of Palestine. Blaustein called for an immediate end to the policies outlined in the British White Paper and the resumption of unimpeded Jewish immigration to Palestine, but he insisted that "questions on the permanent political structure of Palestine . . . should be deferred until after the war."[30]

It was a fine statement, but Blaustein never got the chance to deliver it. The day before the scheduled meeting, the White House called abruptly to cancel it. Repeated attempts to reschedule over the next few months came to naught. The snub was personal, but it was not directed at Blaustein, then a fast-rising star in Democratic donor circles. Instead, the White House feared a scene with Blaustein's predecessor and mentor at the AJC, Judge Joseph Proskauer. A retired New York State Court of Appeals judge and veteran of Democratic politics and civil liberties causes, the egotistical Proskauer, whom Felix Frankfurter once termed the vainest man he had ever met, refused to slip quietly into figurehead status. He had long ago earned Roosevelt's ire by backing FDR's rival, Governor Al Smith, for the Democratic presidential nomination in the 1928 election. Proskauer continued to make brash, melodramatic public statements denouncing Zionism as a threat to American Jewish acceptance. The White House knew that, if Roosevelt met with his successor, Proskauer would insist on a clarification of the president's position on Zionism—an unnecessary risk in an election year.[31]

Shut out, Blaustein and Proskauer both watched with alarm as their Jewish rivals began upstaging them on both Zionism and human rights. In June and July, the Republican and Democratic Party conventions each issued platforms calling for "a free and democratic Jewish commonwealth" in Palestine. Then the other shoe fell. In early July, the U.S. State Department announced that the Four Powers—the United States, Great Britain, Nationalist China, and Soviet Russia—would convene in August for the Dumbarton Oaks Conference in Washington, DC, to map out the UN Charter. The time had come to convert all the various schemes for rights and law from theory into action. In response, the American Jewish Conference launched a public campaign for an "International Bill of Rights."

"The problem of peace is monopolized by church organizations and liberals," Robinson concluded at one 1944 meeting of the WJC's Institute for Jewish Affairs, and "liberals are dreaming of forgetting and forgiving." Responsible Jewish leaders must try "to win over some [of them]" to their program. He proposed hiring Lauterpacht to draft a Jewish Bill of Rights. In the end, though, time was short and his colleague was otherwise engaged. Instead, that summer a committee comprised of Robinson, Perlzweig, Yiddishist scholar Max Weinreich, Latvian Jewish lawyer Max Laserson, future Israeli cabinet minister Zerach Warhaftig, Rabbi Mordechai Kaplan, and other leading Zionist intellectuals set about drafting their text. The document, completed that June, salvaged the nucleus of the old minority rights idea as part of an expansive vision of safeguarding "the human rights of Jews on an equal basis with those of all other human beings":

1. Full and complete protection of life and liberty for the inhabitants of all countries without distinction of birth, nationality, language, race or religion.
2. Unequivocal equality of rights in law and in fact for all the citizens of every country.
3. The inalienable right of all religious, ethnic and cultural groups to maintain and foster their respective group identities on the basis of equality.
4. The establishment of appropriate and adequate national and international machinery to secure the enforcement of these rights.

For Robinson, the third provision, calling for protection of group identity, was the most significant. It must be "made clear right away," he declared, in any such International Bill of Rights "that these rights should deal not only with the atomistic individual but also with ethnic and religious groups entitled not only to maintain their identity but also to foster it." His colleagues readily agreed. "The Jews have the privilege of combining national with humanitarian issues," remarked another member of the group; now it was their duty to remind the world what national minorities really needed.[32]

In the first two weeks of July, Robinson's Zionist Bill of Rights was presented in person to top State Department officials. Printed copies were sent to the embassies of every member of the UN alliance, to the offices of every U.S. congressman, and to more than twenty postwar planning organizations. A copy was included in the study kits issued by the National Peace Conference, whose secretary, Jane Evans, was a veteran Zionist leader in her own right. Robinson and Perlzweig even began batting around the idea of creating "a propaganda agency" to more directly influence "the field of peace planning."[33]

This publicity effort set off alarm bells at the AJC. With the Zionists invading their terrain, Blaustein and Proskauer sensed a mortal threat. Far from complementing one another, they believed, the national and the humanitarian were separate spheres that must not be confused. Human rights must be linked to democracy, not nationalism. The moment called for action: it presented not only risk but also opportunity. There was no time to wait for Lauterpacht's treatise—nor any guarantee it would serve the AJC's purposes. Instead the AJC decided to launch its own public relations operation to take its message to the wider American public. The result would be the Declaration of Human Rights and the largest media campaign up to that time ever conducted on behalf of human rights in American society.

"The First Human World in History"

The AJC was hardly a neophyte when it came to public relations. Its publicity department included several former Madison Avenue ad men, who leapt at the chance to develop a human rights campaign. First came the task of selecting a first-rank writer with an appropriately cosmopolitan political bent to write the text. Carl Sandburg, Pearl Buck, John Steinbeck, Howard Fast, Walter Lippmann, and several others were all considered before they settled on novelist and essayist Waldo Frank. A self-described "Jew without Judaism and an American without America," Frank had a strong reputation as a progressive, left-wing writer on foreign affairs and Latin America who had only recently turned his attention to Jewish matters. He could be presented as an impartial observer of the Jewish condition untainted by parochial loyalties.[34]

Frank's draft passed through many hands, acquiring in the process a religious tinge and a patriotic gloss. The final result was a curious document: a distinctly American Judeo-Christian appeal for human rights that made no explicit reference to either Jews or America.

> With the inevitable end of Hitler, the struggle begins, not of tank and plane, but of heart and soul and brain to forge a world in which humanity may live in peace. This new world must be based on the recognition that the individual human being is the cornerstone of our culture and our civilization. All that we cherish must rest on the dignity and inviolability, of the person, of his sacred right to live and to develop under God, in whose image he was created.

With this creed as our foundation, we declare:

1. That an international Bill of Human Rights must be promulgated to guarantee for every man, woman and child, of every race and creed and in every country, the fundamental rights of life, liberty and the pursuit of happiness.
2. No plea of sovereignty shall ever again be allowed to permit any nation to deprive those within its borders of these fundamental rights on the claim that these matters are of internal concern.
3. Hitlerism has demonstrated that bigotry and persecution by a barbarous nation throws upon the peace-loving nations the burden of relief and redress. Therefore it is a matter of international concern to stamp out infractions of basic human rights.
4. To those who have suffered under the Hitler regime because of race or creed or national origin, there shall be given fair redress.
5. To those who have been driven from the land of their birth there shall be given the opportunity to return, unaffected in their rights by the Nazi despotism.
6. To those who wander the earth unable or unwilling to return to scenes of unforgettable horror shall be given aid and comfort to find new homes and begin new lives in other parts of the world. This must be made possible by international agreement.

Thus, anew, may we justify the ways of God to man. Thus we may take a vital step forward, on the long road to which civilization seeks to create a world based upon the common fatherhood of God and the common brotherhood of man.[35]

The AJC's jumbled imagery reflected a deliberate attempt to appeal to the various constituencies in the nascent American human rights movement. The political reference ("life, liberty and the pursuit of happiness") nodded in the direction of American politicians and lawyers, while the ecumenical religious references appealed to Christian thinkers, many of whom spoke the language of human dignity against godless state power. This religious theme was bolstered by two literary allusions: a direct quotation from Genesis on man's creation in the divine image and a paraphrase of a line from John Milton's *Paradise Lost* ("justify the ways of God to men"). These images were meant to deflect attention from the ethnic and political aspects of Jewish advocacy and toward an enlightened Judeo-Christian moral ideal.

The same cautious downplaying of the Jewish dimension marked the elaborate public relations campaign. An early plan to launch the Declaration on Rosh Hashanah ("The New Year will be the Year of Liberation") was scrapped in favor of starting it on December 15, the anniversary of the Bill of Rights. On that day, a fifteen-minute radio play, "Answer to Tyranny," aired in several cities. The script presented human rights as a "truly American" initiative to provide "a universal guarantee of freedom" against the triple assault of German Nazism, Italian Fascism, and Japanese imperialism. Hitler's victims were described as "Christians and Jews from every part of Europe." Thus, not Jews as a people, but all religion, had come under totalitarian attack. Alongside the radio program, the AJC staff prepared special press releases for cities, states, and regions across the country, targeting specific groups such as women, sports fans, labor, and business. The biggest publicity element of all was a signature drive to advertise the support of "1326 distinguished Americans" for the Declaration.[36]

Week by week over the fall of 1944, the AJC staff carefully tallied the growing list of signatories. The final roster included an impressive cross-section of American elites: 348 Jewish, Protestant, and Catholic clergy; 172 public officials; and scores of prominent artists and intellectuals such as Leonard Bernstein, Kurt Weill, and Langston Hughes. But breadth did not equal depth—or unanimity. Even as Blaustein and his colleagues proudly pointed to the campaign as a sign of American Jewish acceptance, they worried about the critical letters that arrived by the bundle at AJC headquarters during the campaign. That correspondence testified to the radically different ways in which the wartime American public interpreted the message of human rights.[37]

The divided reactions began with self-professed liberals themselves. Veteran Wilsonian internationalists such as James Shotwell and Clark Eichelberger lauded the Declaration as a needed affirmation of multilateralism. Yet many other Roosevelt confidantes resisted the project. "Who is to guarantee to every man, woman and child the fundamental rights of life, liberty and the pursuit of happiness?" worried New York banker and Roosevelt advisor Thomas Lamont in his response to the invitation to sign. "Is this a job for the new League of Nations and its police force? If so the United Nations will be pretty busy from the start waging crusades against each other for the relief of the oppressed, a pretty bloody future." Journalist Edgar Mowrer had personally covered the Nazi rise to power. His reporting from Berlin included some of the earliest warnings of the grave danger to the Jews and the world at large. Yet he too declined to sign the "very respectable statement," noting that "there are at present too many more important issues before the American people." Even Eleanor Roosevelt, soon to become the chief American booster of human rights, offered only the blandest of endorsements in her newspaper column.[38]

If American liberals were divided, progressives and leftist thinkers dismissed the AJC human rights campaign in more aggressive, often cynical terms. Methodist missionary and pioneering sinologist John Calvin Ferguson was one of many who objected to the narrow fixation on "Hitler and the Nazis" instead of a more "universal" focus. Reverend Russell Stafford of Boston's Old South Church dismissed talk of human rights as little more than a "moral excuse . . . [for] sheer selfish imperialism." Nobel laureate Robert Millikan, president of the California Institute of Technology, protested that the document would force "our particular group of ideas down the throats of all peoples of the world; that means that we adopt the philosophy of Hitler at the start."[39]

Reactions on the right mirrored those of the divided American left. Many Southern Democrats balked at signing out of concerns for what the statement implied about America's racial policies. Midwestern Republicans such as Robert Taft stood by their prewar isolationist positions. Others challenged the very idea of human rights. Texas journalist Wright Patterson wrote that "for the vast majority of the American people, human rights" means one thing and one thing only: "protection for their property rights." Yet a striking number of conservatives embraced the AJC Declaration as a weapon against New Deal liberalism. To Senator Charles Tobey of New Hampshire, an "America First" advocate who had loudly opposed U.S. entry into the war, the Declaration reasserted "the inalienable rights" of the individual against New Deal interventionism at home and abroad. New York Herald Tribune columnist Mark Sullivan hailed it as an important Christmas gift "for some in our own country who miscall themselves 'liberals,' but follow doctrines which increase the power of the government to put compulsion upon the individual." In the name of human rights, he opposed cooperation with

the Soviet totalitarian regime in the war effort *and* federal and state civil
rights policies. North Dakota congressman William Langer denounced the
UN as an "international dope dream," but favored the AJC human rights vision as part of a "spiritual revival" in world politics. These men viewed
human rights as a bulwark of Christian values and individual freedoms
against Roosevelt's march toward godless Communism.[40]

For every respondent who saw the Declaration as a pro-Christian, anti-
totalitarian statement, another dismissed it as a Jewish capitulation to Soviet
tyranny. Some Catholic bishops complained that the absence of any mention of Christian persecution in Communist Russia and Hungary was an
inexcusable error on the part of the Jews. On Christmas Day, the National
Committee of Americans of Polish Descent ran a full-page advertisement
in the *Washington Post* under the title, "The Poles Are Also People with
Human Rights." The very day the Declaration was issued, it observed,
Winston Churchill acquiesced in the Soviet takeover of Poland. "[Don't]
exclude the Polish people from the International Bill of Human Rights,"
the ad pleaded. "It is impossible to speak of human ideals of freedom and
liberty through one corner of the mouth and at the same time aid and abet
human bondage of a whole nation through the other corner by silence, indifference or tacit approval of 'spheres of influence' and similar enslavement devices." These early reactions pointed to a phenomenon familiar
from the recent history of human rights: the competitive politics of victimhood. Far from being a pristine moment of American wartime unity, the
rocky reception showed just how contested human rights were right from
their entrance into the American political imagination.[41]

The angriest reaction of all came from the Zionist wing of Jewish America.
"[C]ouched in universal terms, without mentioning the Jews at all," wrote
Brooklyn rabbi Abraham Heller, the Declaration "fails to express the desire
of the vast majority of Jews, as well as of other minority groups, to maintain and foster their group identity." Guided by Robinson's analysis, the
American Jewish Conference blasted the AJC proposal as not only "inadequate and misleading," but actually "detrimental . . . to the grave problems
faced by the Jews of Europe." Others focused more on the connection to
self-determination. "Where is Palestine?" asked several respondents. Yiddish
journalist Gedaliah Bublick summarized this line of thinking in a column

in New York's *Morgn-zhurnal* newspaper. "The true meaning of the 'Bill of Rights' can only be realized through a homeland in the Land of Israel," he wrote, and the present document is but a "sneak attack" by "Jewish assimilationists" against Zionism.[42]

Taken as a whole, the sharply divergent reactions to the Declaration suggested a larger truth about human rights in the American imagination. The document that was supposed to secure a new consensus functioned as a palimpsest on which Americans of the early 1940s overlaid their hopes and fears for the postwar world. Staring into the uncertain future, they asked themselves time and again whether liberal internationalism could realize the promise of rights for all without the burden of national politics or costs to American sovereignty. For Zionists, human rights could not be separated from self-determination. For many other Americans, the ambiguous link between Jews and human rights only highlighted American liberalism's uncertain position on race, justice, and law. How much was American society willing to change at home to promote a foreign policy of freedom around the world? In interwar Europe, Jews had come to symbolize both the risk and reward of minority rights in the minds of Poles, Lithuanians, and Germans. Now a similar trope appeared in the American mind. The otherwise disparate reactions to the AJC's Declaration were united by a common pattern of elevating the Jews into an emblem of ambivalence.

Blaustein and Proskauer learned the truth of this ambivalence firsthand. After the initial burst of attention, the Declaration faded quickly from view. The summertime Dumbarton Oaks meetings had done little to advance a concrete agenda for international human rights. After years of internal debate, State Department policy planners included a modest expression of support for the encouragement of "human rights and fundamental freedoms" as part of the draft mandate of the UN. But despite repeated overtures to the State Department in November and December of 1944, the AJC leaders found themselves quietly brushed aside by government officials. Undeterred, the two activists continued to press publicly for a Commission on Human Rights endowed with "special standing" before national and international courts and legal powers of subpoena to investigate "violations of human rights" within sovereign states. "International machinery is needed," read one AJC policy pamphlet, "because the two other methods of coping with the problem—intervention by one state and international agreement by treaty—have been tried and found unsuccessful."[43]

Soon they would get their chance to make this argument on a world stage. In early February 1945, with the war's end in sight, the State Department announced that the UN Conference on International Organization would take place in two months' time in San Francisco. Then, in late March, Blaustein and Proskauer finally got their long-sought meeting with President Roosevelt. Both men were eager to direct the president's attention to their human rights proposal. "Mr. President, I didn't come here to talk Palestine today," Proskauer began. "Our mission is to enlist your interest and support of the movement to put human rights provisions into the UN Charter." Roosevelt, however, turned out to be completely uninterested in that subject. He wanted only to discuss Zionism. One week earlier, he told them, Rabbi Stephen S. Wise had sat in the very same spot and urged him to continue his support for Jewish Palestine at the upcoming UN conference. "I went out on a limb with these Goddamn Zionists and I've been to Yalta and I've talked to Ibn Saud," Roosevelt complained. Now he felt he had made a mistake. "You can't get a Jewish state in a country that's two-thirds Arab," he said, without starting a "third world war" or "a pogrom in Palestine." But he had publicly promised his support and now was stuck. Could they help him rein in American Zionist expectations? If human rights would help do that, the president told them, by all means pursue them. It was another decidedly ambivalent endorsement. Still, Blaustein and Proskauer left the White House all smiles: they finally had the American president on their side on both human rights and Jewish politics. Yet by the time the two men arrived in San Francisco a month later, Roosevelt would be dead, his oval office promise forgotten, and a new, uncertain era in American foreign policy just beginning.[44]

5

Unfinished Victory

AT 4:32 P.M. ON APRIL 25, 1945, Edward Stettinius Jr. rapped a silver-trimmed gavel three times on the wooden podium at San Francisco's War Memorial Opera House. Eight hundred diplomats from forty-six nations sat up in their plush, red velvet seats to take in the dashing new American secretary of state's film-star looks and shock of prematurely white hair. He was flanked by a row of national flags against a blue curtain backdrop and four huge square columns draped in garish golden-orange velvet meant to symbolize Roosevelt's Four Freedoms. After a minute of silence, Stettinius announced, "Ladies and Gentlemen, the President of the United States." The warm, flat voice of Harry Truman filled the room, piped in from Washington via a live radio link. "You members of the conference are to be architects of the better world," the invisible president calmly told the audience. "If we do not want to die together in war, we must learn to live together in peace." His words earned polite applause. Brief remarks followed from the stage. Barely twenty minutes later, the bewildered delegates found themselves herded toward the exits. The largest diplomatic gathering in history had begun not with a bang but a whimper.[1]

There was a reason for the rushed, perfunctory opening of the San Francisco conference. Outside the hall, history had hardly paused to accommodate diplomatic niceties. Combat still raged in both Europe and the Pacific. The Allies had liberated Buchenwald and Bergen-Belsen just days earlier, and Hitler's whereabouts remained a mystery. Roosevelt had died suddenly, casting the fate of the entire conference briefly into doubt. For a public long accustomed to the late president's stentorian tones, Truman's disembodied, unfamiliar voice proved startling. His emphasis on harmony and justice struck many as disingenuous, given that it was common knowledge that behind the scenes the Americans and Soviets were fiercely deadlocked over the fate of Poland. Skeptical observers joked that the host city ought to be renamed "San Fiasco."[2]

All this confusion left Robinson in a foul mood. He had arrived in San Francisco with his head full of thoughts about the failed League of Nations. There were obvious blank spots in the new international organization's mission and architecture. The campaign for human rights was a disaster in the making. "It is obvious," he told colleagues, "that the Big Powers will not commit themselves to an International Bill of Rights." The United States and Great Britain might respect the idea of human rights in principle, but their racial and colonial policies, respectively, would hold them back from any real commitments. Still less could be expected of the Soviets and the Chinese nationalists, both of whom he dubbed "totalitarian."[3]

Not everyone shared his verdict. Speaking at San Francisco's Temple Emanu-El on the eve of the conference, Blaustein told the audience that the UN project presented a unique opportunity for Jews and for all Americans. If we join together with our own government, we might forge "a moral and spiritual basis for the United Nations Organization" and "a new concept of the relationship between nations and their own citizens." The world stood on the cusp of a bright era, in which all nations would follow the American lead in recognizing "the rights of the individual human being, irrespective of race, creed or nationality."[4]

Given their wartime clashes over the meaning of human rights, the sharp contrast between Blaustein's New World optimism and Robinson's Old World pessimism was not unexpected. Yet their ideological divide masked a deeper shared conviction. Operating from divergent vantage points within the Jewish political landscape, each man nevertheless drew the same lesson from the Jewish experience at the League of Nations: rights without power were meaningless. Global governance and Jewish survival both depended on Great Power leadership. Only the world's strongest superpower could enact and sustain a muscular international rights regime at the UN.

Only the preeminent Western democracy could secure justice for Hitler's Jewish victims in Europe. And when it came to Palestine, despite their differences, both believed that only the United States could replace Britain's sorry intransigence with a fair-minded approach to the Jewish future there. Ultimately, all these issues depended on the willingness of American government to rekindle the flame of Wilsonian idealism for a second time.

At three key moments in 1945 and 1946, this shared Jewish faith in American leadership was put directly to the test. In San Francisco in the spring of 1945, Blaustein bested Robinson in a contest to steer his preferred vision of human rights into the UN Charter. But doing so required him to partner with U.S. diplomat Isaiah Bowman, the worst antisemite in the State Department, and to accept a neutered version of his cherished international bill of rights. At the opening of the Nuremberg Trials later that year, Robinson scored his own coup when he and Lauterpacht teamed up with Justice Robert H. Jackson to write the concept of "crimes against humanity" into the world's legal lexicon. The effort represented a breakthrough for international justice, accompanied by a painful reminder of the perils of Jewish statelessness. Then, in 1946, Blaustein, Robinson, Perlzweig, and Lauterpacht converged on the Paris Peace Conference to lobby for Jewish rights in the Peace Treaties. That time, however, both sides got their first taste of European postwar antisemitism and American diplomatic vacillation.

On her first day in San Francisco, the activist Jane Evans recorded in her diary that the "No Parking" signs issued by the city's Police Department read "Peace Conference." A few days later, those placards were gone, replaced by new ones that read "S. F. Conference." Someone had belatedly pointed out the obvious: the war was not over, and hence technically there could be no peace negotiations. The switch testified to more than bureaucratic incompetence; it reflected the ambiguity of the moment when international human rights first took flight. In the brief interval between San Francisco in spring 1945 and Paris in fall 1946, Jewish rights-defenders passed through three key way stations of postwar internationalism: the writing of the UN Charter, the prosecution of Nazi war criminals, and the negotiation of European peace treaties. At each juncture, they clamored for a seat at the diplomatic table. In each moment, they glimpsed the enormous potential of grafting their visions of Jewish internationalism onto American power. But each time, they were only able to log uncertain victories that served to remind them just how difficult was the task of making space for Jews in the postwar world. As the Cold War dawned, Jews found themselves wedged at the hinge of ethics and power in American foreign policy. In theory, it was the perfect place from which to exercise influence, as long as the mighty vise of American statecraft did not crush them in the process.[5]

"The Worst Place to Shout"

The San Francisco conference opened in an atmosphere of blaring publicity. Some 2,500 journalists attended, making it easily the largest media event the world had yet seen. That first day, reporters crammed the San Francisco Opera House balcony to the point of overflowing. Photographers aggressively prowled the aisles below, brazenly leaning in to flash their bulbs in the faces of dignitaries such as Soviet foreign minister Viacheslav Molotov and British foreign minister Anthony Eden. Despite this onslaught, many a newspaperman in search of a grand headline that first day went home disappointed. The mood in the hall was grim and sober, "dramatically undramatic," reported the *New York Times*. The ceremony set a "new record for brevity and celerity," observed the *Chicago Daily Tribune*.[6]

The real action, it turned out, took place offstage, where intrigues abounded. With the Cold War already in full swing, the FBI clandestinely eavesdropped on the Soviets. The underlying purpose of the conference, one Canadian diplomat observed, was to establish a means of "keeping peace between the Soviet Union on the one hand and the U.S. and the U.K. on the other for the next thirty years." But that emerging rivalry did little to deter the rest of the world from pressing their own claims. Despite the efforts of State Department organizers to screen out "importunate minorities" and "pure crackpots," hundreds of smaller groups from every corner of the globe massed on the conference sidelines: Polish anti-Communists, Indian anti-colonialists, rival Croatian American and Serbian American parties, even the Iroquois Confederation. Of all of these it was the Arab delegations who commanded the most attention. It was a depressing sight, wrote one Jewish journalist, to see Saudi Arabians parading around San Francisco "always accompanied by a State Department representative on one side and by a representative of American oil companies on the other." The exotic sheikhs "in their fancy burnooses and flowing robes" exerted a magnetic pull on the public, drawing crowds of gawkers and autograph seekers everywhere they went.[7]

Into this crowded field came the decidedly less glamorous Robinson and Perlzweig at the head of a fifty-strong coalition of Zionist leaders from around the world. Concerned about Arab assassination plots, World Jewish Congress benefactor Samuel Bronfman insisted on assigning Perlzweig a personal bodyguard. For the entire duration of the conference, he was shadowed by General "Two-Gun" Cohen, aka Morris Abraham, the Polish-born Jewish adventurer and legendary gunrunner for China's Sun Yat Sen. The biggest danger at San Francisco, however, turned out to be Western indifference, not Arab terror. The Soviets and the West might wrangle over whether to admit Poland or Argentina to the UN, but they easily agreed that it was states, not peoples, that belonged in the club of nations. The Dutch foreign minister put it to Perlzweig most baldly: "Your people have no land, no government, no parliament, no congress, no legislative body, none of the characteristics or trappings that constitute the basis for recognition at a conference of this character." Perlzweig ruefully concurred: "We cannot even add our voice to the formal proceedings because we are not a state, because we are a *sui generis* group, a unique collectivity." No amount of lobbying from the sidelines could make up for their distance from the main action. "San Francisco," lamented Nahum Goldmann, is "the worst place to shout."[8]

The only hope for Jewish entrée lay with an experimental State Department public diplomacy initiative. The official U.S. mission to San Francisco comprised two parts: the formal negotiating team of Secretary of State Stettinius and his veteran State Department policy advisors, including Leo Pasvolsky, Isaiah Bowman, John Foster Dulles, and Archibald MacLeish; and an official bipartisan delegation of congressmen and other carefully screened foreign policy elites. The former led actual diplomatic talks, while the latter were charged with drafting and approving U.S. policy positions and, no less important, ensuring congressional support for the UN project. Their presence reflected Roosevelt's canny determination to avoid an embarrassing repetition of Wilson's failure a generation earlier, when a signature foreign policy achievement collapsed at home thanks to an isolationist rebuff by Congress. In addition to these two groups, the White House and State Department dreamed up the idea of a third unofficial group to accompany the official U.S. delegation to San Francisco: an advisory board of twenty-five or so informal public "consultants." These civic leaders would help sell the UN to the broader American public. Stettinius also saw a more personal upside to the public consultants. New to the job, assuming the position in late 1944 when he replaced the ailing Cordell Hull, he had struggled with a Washington press corps that questioned his diplomatic acumen. The right press-friendly faces at his side might boost his political fortunes.

Of course, the challenge lay in choosing the right "special interest groups" to invite. In the weeks before San Francisco, Stettinius's team and the official delegation batted around a long list of leaders from different segments of American society: labor, business, education, clergy, veterans, black America, as well as a "tolerable representation of the fairer sex." The question on everyone's lips was how best to showcase American democracy to the world without exposing awkward domestic questions of race, ethnicity, and politics. When it came to the Jews, Stettinius preferred to invite only Blaustein's AJC because, as he told Truman, he thought the Zionists would hijack American foreign policy. Other delegation members agreed, including Barnard College president Virginia Gildersleeve and even the group's sole Jewish member, Congressman Sol Bloom, famous for his obsequious declarations of American Jewish patriotism. But the darkest views on Jewish participation belonged to senior Stettinius aide Isaiah Bowman, Roosevelt's influential political geographer, whose antisemitism colored his entire conception of American foreign policy.[9]

An avowed anti-black racist and aggressive antisemite, Bowman in the late 1930s devised a top-secret State Department plan to solve the European Jewish question by removing Jews en masse to underpopulated countries such as Angola, British Guiana, and the Dominican Republic while preventing them from settling in the United States or Palestine. The M-Project, as it was known, was shot through with racism and intended both to appease Europeans and insulate Americans from a new Jewish problem. As president of the Johns Hopkins University in the spring of 1945, Bowman launched an anti-Jewish admissions quota even as other elite American universities were moving to discard such measures. There were "already too many Jews at Johns Hopkins," he said at the time, and they risked ruining the school: "Jews don't come to Hopkins to make the world better or anything like that. They come for two things: to make money and to marry a non-Jewish woman." In Washington, meanwhile, Bowman fairly seethed about the "Zionist lobby" and the horde of pushy "Jewish newspaper men" who kept thrusting the Jewish Question into the foreground. He accused columnist Walter Lippmann and *Washington Post* publisher Eugene Meyer of conspiring to derail Stettinius, writing in an aide-memoire,

> The professional agitators and leaders, [Rabbi Stephen] Wise and all of the rest, are learning how powerful they are in Congress. . . . Thus the Jews have tasted blood and are going to push in every possible way for preferment. This will manifest itself not only in Jewish organizations but in Communist organizations and in their position with respect to the negro. The whole picture is extremely bad and the situation a dangerous one since it means our introduction into Near East policies with Congress bludgeoned into an active participation on the side of the Jew.[10]

But every antisemite has his exceptional Jew. For Bowman it was Blaustein. A local Baltimore boy, self-made and safely married to a Jewish woman, Blaustein represented a non-Zionist organization committed to harmonizing Jewish aims with larger U.S. foreign policy. Even better, he promoted an image of American society as a Judeo-Christian nation rather than as a European welter of ethnic and racial factions. Yet after weeks of discussion, Bowman and other officials concluded that it was politically impossible to invite only Blaustein's group and exclude the Zionists. So the American Jewish Conference delegation was also included, led by B'nai Brith president Henry Monsky, Rabbi Israel Goldstein, and Louis Lipsky. It was through these men that Robinson and his European Zionist rights-defenders would, at least in theory, have access to the American delegation. A war of words promptly erupted. Both sides claimed to represent the only legitimate Jewish voice in American foreign policy. Panicked at the prospect of an unseemly Jewish showdown in San Francisco, State Department officials went so far as to arrange to house the opposing Jewish consultants in different hotels.[11]

The May 2 Parley

The Jewish rivalry surfaced on the conference's opening day. After concluding the formal ceremonies, Stettinius swept into the first meeting of the consultants in the Blue Room of San Francisco's luxurious Fairmont Hotel. "The real battlefield of the peace," he explained to them, "is going to be American public opinion," and the consultants were the administration's vital partners in that struggle. After flattery came bluntness: he gave the floor to Bowman. Comments and suggestions were welcome at any time, Bowman explained, but official policy deliberations and diplomatic negotiations remained off-limits. Most consultants felt relegated to a passive, marginal role. American Jewish Conference staffer Isaiah "Si" Kenen, future founder of the American-Israel Public Affairs Committee (AIPAC), lamented that the consultants were simply props in the State Department's "public relations operation." NAACP president Walter White bitterly called their role "window dressing." Blaustein, in contrast, was thrilled. This collaboration with the official delegation was not only "democracy in action" but also a political victory for his team. The Zionists were "stewing," he boasted in a letter home, that he and Proskauer had "old, established relationships with many of the non-Jews in high places at San Francisco." He was right. His strange bond with Bowman would prove crucial when human rights surfaced on the conference agenda one week later.[12]

The American delegation entered San Francisco prepared to support the addition of human rights language to the UN Charter without insisting on binding legal enforcement. The United States would endorse the inclusion of "a statement on the promotion of respect for human rights and fundamental freedoms," Stettinius wrote to President Truman on April 19, while waiting to declare a final position "until we learn the views of other governments." This strategic hedge was born of realpolitik. Each of the Great Powers stood to lose more than it gained by subjecting itself to the scrutiny of international law—the Americans with their racial segregation, the French and British with their colonies, and the Soviet Union with its slave labor and national minorities. "The State Department never talks about 'minorities,'" noted Assistant Secretary of State Charles Dunn, so why embrace an international legal system that would invite deep scrutiny of America's treatment of its large racial minority?[13]

This issue drew to a head on May 2. Rumors had slipped out that the United States would drop all references to human rights in the final Charter text and completely table the International Bill of Rights. This was not quite true: there had been no substantial change from the pre-conference government position. Still, the consultants reacted with alarm, fueled by pent-up frustration over their exclusion from the policy deliberations. A meeting with Stettinius was called for 5 p.m. that day. In the hours leading up to it, Blaustein and Proskauer gathered a group of consultants to draft a short statement urging U.S. support for retaining human rights language and a provision for a UN Commission on Human Rights in the Charter. Then, in the session with Stettinius, Proskauer made a long, emotional plea. Let not the United States abandon its support for human rights. Even a noble failure would only redound to the moral credit of American leadership. The secretary of state responded enthusiastically, pledging to do his utmost.[14]

In later years, Proskauer's May 2 speech became the stuff of legend. Here was a courageous Jewish leader, in the shadow of the Holocaust, demanding that his own government live up to its ideals to promote freedom around the world. The AJC eagerly promoted this narrative, beginning with Proskauer, who boasted that he had saved human rights in the UN Charter and defeated his Zionist rivals. "I stole the show at San Francisco," he declared of his speech. That image has become enshrined in both scholarly accounts and the AJC's own promotional literature. Yet it amounts to a misleading myth. The real human rights drama was not the public face off between Stettinius and Proskauer, but instead took place offstage, in a private rapprochement between Blaustein and Bowman. May 2 was actually the day that American antisemitism ushered human rights into U.S. foreign policy.[15]

When the question of human rights first surfaced, Blaustein went straight to his fellow Baltimorean. Ignoring Bowman's prejudices, he urged him to view human rights not as a dangerous concession to minority privileges, but as a practical way to defeat Soviet talk of group rights for national minorities. The argument resonated. Bowman had already insisted on striking the words "Jew," "Negro," and "minority" from State Department statements on human rights. Using these words, he told colleagues, did "the greatest possible disservice to these groups." It was "general equality and not favored treatment that was basic to the new world organization and national unity as well as international cooperation." In their meeting on May 2, Blaustein confirmed that this message of individual equality and blind justice was just what the American public needed to hear—and what the Soviets feared—on human rights. Furthermore, foregrounding human rights would blunt the Zionists' political cachet, which both men feared, albeit for different reasons. Bowman was delighted. Of all the clamoring by special interests about human rights, only you, he told Blaustein, have "hit the nail on the head." The other utopians (including Proskauer) had lost him with their exaggerated oratory.[16]

After this conversation, Bowman kept to his word, pushing hard for amendments in his closed-session negotiations with his Soviet, Chinese, and British counterparts. Specific clauses urging the protection of human rights and authorizing the formation of a UN Commission on Human Rights entered the Charter. Still, there were decided limits to his enthusiasm. Unbeknownst to Blaustein, Bowman and other State Department officials slipped a clause, known as Article 2(7), into the Charter proscribing international "intervention in matters which are essentially within the domestic jurisdiction of the State concerned." This brief phrase provided a legal escape hatch for states worried that international human rights law might reach into their internal affairs. States could freely invoke this clause to protect their sovereignty, just as they had done in the past. By the same token, the Commission on Human Rights mentioned in the Charter was granted no legal powers whatsoever. Adding insult to injury, when it was all said and done, Bowman refused to give the Jews public credit for human rights. He actively discouraged Blaustein from lobbying other delegations in San Francisco in support of the U.S. position. Linking human rights too closely to the Jews, he warned, would only turn countries against the idea. The exchange drove home the strange partnership between antisemite and Jew in the making of American human rights policy.[17]

Ever the pragmatist, Blaustein remained unfazed by this mixture of scorn and hypocrisy. Nor did he heed Bowman's admonition not to preach the Jewish gospel of human rights too loudly. Before the conference was even over, the AJC issued a press release proudly announcing its achievement. Working hand in glove, American civic groups and their government leaders had secured "an extension of the whole area of international law by the recognition that no plea of sovereignty shall ever again be allowed to permit a nation to deprive those within its borders of fundamental rights." Then the AJC launched a national media campaign emphasizing that it was the Jews who had saved Roosevelt's vision of liberal American foreign policy—and redeemed Wilson's dream. If "Versailles was a Peace Conference," Blaustein declared in a speech a few weeks later, San Francisco amounted to "a constitutional convention of the world."[18]

Others were not so easily swayed. When word reached Robinson of Blaustein's back-channel lobbying, he tried to mount a last-ditch lobbying and press offensive of his own. But it was too late. The Bowman-Blaustein product prevailed in the UN Charter. The results were pitiful, Robinson complained privately to his colleagues right after San Francisco: "We see no enactment of human rights, no supervision of human rights and no enforcement of human rights. No procedure, no jurisdiction; all these things don't exist." Far from a step forward in human affairs, the UN Charter represented "the greatest deterioration, in my opinion, of international law in 100 years."[19]

Robinson blamed this step backward not on the duplicity of American officials but on the calamitous amateurism of Blaustein and the AJC. Those people anointed themselves experts on human rights, he grumbled, without knowing anything about the subject: "You know the specialist of the left nostril. He doesn't care about anything else, about the throat or rest of the nose. He doesn't care for the face and he doesn't care for the nose, but he cares [only] for the left nostril." Blaustein and company blathered on about human rights as law—yet cheered when legal enforcement was blatantly stripped from the Charter. They mistook diplomatic verbiage for legal principles. The result, Robinson fumed, was a document that included "the words of human rights and fundamental freedoms without any power."[20]

Robinson premised his bitter critique not only on a lawyer's respect for law but also on a diplomat's keen awareness of political context. "The basic guarantee of Jewish freedom," he explained, "is the democracy of the country where the Jews live." The five million Jews then living in America secured their freedom with the Bill of Rights, not international law: "I would like to see a single Jew among these five million live in safety when Washington will cease to be his shield and when some court in The Hague will be his shield," he said. By the same token, no "court outside the Soviet Union can give the Jews protection when the Soviet Union refuses to give such protection." As for the Middle East, "here you have an area where human rights and fundamental freedoms didn't exist and don't exist and certainly I cannot believe that these 750,000 Jews and their future will be in the slightest degree affected by this phrase of human rights and fundamental freedoms in this Charter."[21]

Robinson and Blaustein's divergent interpretations each contained a measure of truth. It was never likely that the United States, the Soviets, or the British would risk exposure of their internal moral and political weaknesses by agreeing to sweeping changes to international law that would allow the UN human rights program to overcome the bar of sovereignty. But that did not make all such efforts equally hopeless. Blaustein understood that saving American internationalism was an achievable goal for the UN. In enshrining the language of human rights in the UN Charter, he won a major symbolic victory. In sacrificing a probably unattainable reform of international law, he helped advance norms and ideals. No less important in his mind, he promoted a positive Jewish partnership with a magnanimous if fickle American power.

Robinson, in contrast, recognized that human rights not backed by binding law and compelling force would continue to provide states a free pass. Given the grave challenges Jews now faced, having rights without power was a political risk they could no longer afford. Platitudes about international liberalism and world peace were no substitute for Jewish sovereignty and Great Power support. However, even Robinson glimpsed two silver linings in the defeat in San Francisco. Thanks to the Zionists' strategic advocacy, the United States had rejected an Arab diplomatic effort to use discussions over the fate of UN trusteeships to torpedo Jewish claims to Palestine. And the essential project of organizing international society with American leadership had begun: "Whatever the future of the United Nations may be, we are satisfied that if there is any hope at all for international cooperation, this hope is today embodied in the United Nations. If

FDR hadn't gotten the UN under way before the end of the war, we would never have had a UN." Ultimately, then, both men grasped the necessity of working with American power. Each would go on to grapple with the consequences of that dependence as they traveled to Europe in search of justice and security for Jews in the aftermath of the Holocaust.[22]

"The Conscience of Humanity"

In late fall 1945 Robinson could be found wandering the streets of Nuremberg. The city struck him like a surreal dreamscape.

> The rubble and ruins [are] wherever you go, on every street, even within the buildings. Amidst these ruins, exists a tremendous court building, the jail beneath, [and] a grand hotel in which live many people connected with the trial, complete with night club. . . . You realize that you're living on a no-man's land, an island of Little America, isolated from reality. Coming down to the court, many people are more interested in the American PX [military commissary] than in the proceedings of the court.

The image of an island of American justice amidst European ruin and depravity had an element of truth to it. Robinson tactfully did not mention that the grand hotel also featured a brothel. Beyond the seedy underbelly of postwar Nuremberg, Robinson believed that only the Americans had both the moral commitment and political clout to ensure that justice would be served. He had reached that conclusion after an unsuccessful three-year effort to join in the European planning discussions about war crimes trials for the Nazis.[23]

The road to Nuremberg began in London in 1942, when ministers from nine exiled governments quietly convened the St. James Conference. The absence of Jewish representatives was not by accident: the European diplomats refused to acknowledge the Jews as separate victims of the Nazi Holocaust. Jewish groups were not even informed of the gathering, nor were they allowed to attend subsequent meetings. "The race or religion of the victim ought not" to matter, declared Polish prime minister-in-exile Wladislaw Sikorski. Singling out Jewish suffering would only endorse "the racial theories which we all reject." Robinson was livid about this snub. "The

Nazis waged an actual war against the Jews," he wrote, "an open, declared war, the first in the series of Nazi wars" that began with "the weakest of their alleged enemies." World leaders were pouring salt on the wounds by denying that the victims died as Jews: global justice must begin with an acknowledgment of Jewish nationhood. "The World Jewish Congress has made it its goal from its very inception to struggle unflinchingly for the public recognition of the oneness of the Jewish people and against the conspiracy of silence which condemned our people to live and to suffer in the shadow of anonymity." Denying Jews their peoplehood had earlier set back the cause of international law; recognizing "the gravity of this crime against the Jews for all humanity" would advance it.[24]

Throughout 1943 and 1944, Robinson directed his research staff to compile evidence of anti-Jewish crimes from across Europe: they read through smuggled Nazi policy documents, eyewitness reports of deportations and killings, official statements and speeches by Nazi leaders, and lists of the names of individual victims. Meanwhile, he drafted a series of legal memos outlining options for prosecution. If the logic of the St. James Conference held, there might be no way to try the Nazis and their allies for crimes against Jews qua Jews. That curious legal loophole would mean that the greatest crime of all, the attempted mass murder of an entire people, might escape punishment. Killing an individual in peacetime was obviously a grievous crime. Yet the existing laws of war did not address a state massacring its own population or the state-sponsored mass murder of other states' civilians. "Our conscience is revolted," he wrote, "at the idea that a crime, when multiplied by millions, should cease to be a crime." The only way to prosecute such a novel offense was by naming a new kind of victim: not the individual or the state but the group. Hence Jews were uniquely positioned to push this important legal claim: "[U]nless we come up with some constructive ideas of a general character, nobody else will. We have specific Jewish interests to take care of, but it is impossible to divorce these from the general problems of war crimes." The aims of securing universal justice "in the name of humanity as a whole" and restoring Jewish national dignity were thus interrelated "moral imperatives." The challenge, however, was to find a powerful ally willing to listen to this argument.[25]

Hersch Zvi Lauterpacht and
his wife Rachel (Steinberg) Lauterpacht

Reproduced with permission of the Estate of Sir Elihu Lauterpacht

Across the Atlantic, Lauterpacht had reached a similar conclusion. In 1940, he had begun contributing legal opinions to the British Foreign Office on questions of warfare and criminal law. This led to his appointment to the newly created UN War Crimes Commission in October 1942, an Anglo-American-Soviet initiative that replaced the St. James Conference. But brushing up against the diplomatic inner circle did not give Lauterpacht any more of a free platform from which to air his views. The genteel diplomats of the Foreign Office were not shy about their clubby antisemitism. Even after two decades in England and despite his endowed Cambridge chair, Lauterpacht was still, in their eyes, a Polish Jewish immigrant and a Zionist, and hence not entirely to be trusted. Insult to injury, his work on the War Crimes Committee also brought Lauterpacht face to face with the same Polish government officials who so readily denounced Jews for their special pleading. These men even held a certain power over him, because his parents and siblings remained trapped in occupied Poland. Desperate to help his family, he had sought Polish diplomatic assistance to send them food parcels.[26]

Lauterpacht's solution to this dilemma was to hide his Jewish politics behind a cloak of anonymity provided by the World Jewish Congress. In May 1944 he prepared a singularly important memo, unknown even to legal scholars today, in which he made the first crucial link between "crimes committed against Jews" and what he would soon call "crimes against humanity." Something uniquely awful, he argued, had occurred in this war.

> It is an unchallenged fact that numerically—both relatively and absolutely—the Jews have been the greatest victims of the war crimes committed by Germany in occupied territories. Moreover, as the avowed object of the war crimes committed against Jews has been the total extermination of the Jewish race on the continent of Europe, the resulting character of these crimes is such as to put them in a category of their own. . . . In the case of other races the reason given for deprivation of life has been an allegation of direct guilt or, in the case of hostages, of a kind of vicarious responsibility. In the case of Jews it has been membership of the Jewish race. . . . There is no true comparison between this slow torture of extermination accompanied by a denial, most savage of all time, of the dignity of man, and the mass massacres in the past which have soiled the pages of history.

Like Robinson, Lauterpacht believed it was necessary for the general cause of justice to identify suffering as Jewish. "[F]or the sake of the Jewish race and, we believe, of the conscience of humanity, the design to murder an entire people must be branded and penalized as such." Doing so might provide "a deterrent as potent as retribution itself."[27]

A revised version of Lauterpacht's memo—without his name attached—was submitted in late July 1944 to the very same UN War Crimes Commission on which he sat. It formed part of a steady flow of ideas and petitions delivered by Robinson and his colleagues to American and British officials over that year and into the next. Meanwhile, in his role as advisor to the British Foreign Office, Lauterpacht proved much more circumspect in doling out his legal advice. He called for war crimes trials without reference to Jewish victimhood or future deterrence. Such trials were necessary, he maintained, to reaffirm the authority of the rule of law in international affairs. The explicit leap to a charge of "crimes against humanity" he did not yet make. That development emerged only through private conversations between Robinson, Lauterpacht, and the American lawyer leading the war crimes trials, Justice Robert H. Jackson.[28]

In May 1945, at the request of President Truman, Jackson stepped down from the U.S. Supreme Court in order to set up the International Military Tribunal. Designing a new international criminal legal system from scratch was no easy task. There was little obvious legal precedent. Many senior British officials remained unconvinced that any such trials would bring little more than victors' justice. Equally vexing was the task of collecting the proper evidence to prove just how the Nazis had perpetrated their crimes. In search of expert advice on both fronts, Jackson turned to Robinson and Lauterpacht.

Fresh from San Francisco, Robinson sat down with Jackson for the first time in June 1945 at the Federal Court House in Lower Manhattan. He came armed with a raft of documents and a promise of many more. Since 1943 his team of researchers at the Institute of Jewish Affairs had collected more than two thousand German government memos and legal codes. Together they amounted to a compelling portrait of a massive, deliberate plan to terrorize and murder civilians far beyond the battlefield and well before the formal outbreak of war in 1939. Echoing Lauterpacht's 1944 memo, Robinson again stressed the Jewish dimension of the crimes. The entire Jewish people, he told Jackson, "is the greatest sufferer of this war" and the target of "a well-conceived, deliberately plotted and meticulously carried out con-spiracy." As such, Robinson urged Jackson to include a novel charge of criminal conspiracy—a deliberate plan with conscious intent, encompass-ing not only governmental officials and military leaders but also Nazi Party members and collaborators in German industry and finance—to murder European Jewry. Robinson's search for justice for Jews prompted him to make two other requests of Jackson. Let there be appointed a Jew-ish chief prosecutor to represent the Jewish people formally in the Allied Powers prosecution team and let Chaim Weizmann, president of the World Zionist Organization, provide expert testimony on behalf of the Jewish nation. Jackson readily embraced the idea of a military trial with criminal conspiracy charges, but he hesitated to assign Jews a specific legal role in the prosecution. He worried that any emphasis on the Jewish dimensions of the crimes might risk alienating other key European allies. For the same reason, he resisted the idea of presenting Weizmann as an expert witness. It was a pattern that would appear throughout the Nurem-berg process. Jewish help was welcome, but only in its most discreet, sotto voce form.[29]

A few weeks after the June conversation with Robinson in New York, Jack-son traveled to London to meet his British and Soviet counterparts and pre-pare the International Military Tribunal's charter and indictments. While there, he spent a day in Cambridge for a friendly reunion with Lauterpacht. Over a pleasant luncheon at his home, Lauterpacht recommended to Jack-son that he add yet another novel charge to the court's legal charter: "crimes against humanity." Building on Robinson's arguments, Lauterpacht insisted that neither of the two main charges planned for the indictment, war crimes and crimes against the peace (aggressive war itself), sufficiently covered the atrocities that the Nazis had directed against Jews and other civilians. A new kind of crime required a new kind of law. Jackson was convinced. "Crimes against humanity" soon entered the legal lexicon as Article 6(c) of the Nuremberg Charter, defined as

> murder, extermination, enslavement, deportation and other inhuman acts committed against any civilian population before or during the war; or per-secution on political, racial or religious grounds in execution of, or in con-

nection with, any crimes within the jurisdiction of the Tribunal, whether or not in violation of the domestic law of the country where perpetrated.[30]

Ironically, Lauterpacht felt more at liberty to speak openly with a visiting American official than with his own government. In their July conversation, he, like Robinson, stressed the Jewish dimension of the tragedy. Let Weizmann be allowed to testify as part of the prosecution's case as a meaningful moral gesture, he urged. This time, Jackson agreed. Yet when Lauterpacht went to raise the same Jewish issues with the British team of prosecutors, he took a decidedly more circumspect approach. Years of working with an impassive British establishment had taught him to avoid any pleadings that might be judged as indecorous parochialism. In a mid-August letter to the British Foreign Office's assistant legal advisor, Patrick Dean, he argued that the British should approve the charge of "crimes against humanity," but made no mention of Jews. Instead, he urged Dean to accept the innovation in the spirit of "the outraged conscience of the world and an enlightened conception of the true purposes of the law of nations." Likewise, he declined to ask Dean directly to let Weizmann testify. Instead, he quietly recruited two other prominent Anglo-Jewish figures, Lewis Namier and Leonard Stein, to deliver the request. In the end, the effort came to naught. The British Foreign Office quashed the idea of Weizmann's appearance for fear that it might inadvertently tip the scales toward a Jewish state in Palestine. It was once more sign of the double-edged sword of Jewish politics in the making of international law.[31]

"Always the Same Struggle"

The Nuremberg Trials began in October 1945 and continued on through the following summer. Both Lauterpacht and Robinson remained heavily involved throughout. Even as the size of Jackson's official staff ballooned into the hundreds, he continued to rely closely on Robinson for technical and legal assistance. It was Robinson, for instance, who prepared the charge sheet used for the twenty-four highest-ranking German leaders and redrafted several indictments. He initially declined to help unless Jackson agreed to seat him in the prosecution as an official representative of the

Jewish people. In the end, though, he bowed to the American prosecutor's personal pleas for assistance. In addition to writing and advising, Robinson conducted some of the interrogations and prepared an affidavit on the Jewish death toll of 5.7 million. He was also the first person to identify Adolf Eichmann as the architect of the Final Solution.[32]

Lauterpacht's fingerprints could also be found all over Nuremberg. At the request of the British, he redrafted the opening and closing statements for British prosecutor Hartley Shawcross, which dealt particularly with "aggressive war." Some of his language surfaced nearly verbatim in the court's judgments. The famous statement declaring that international law must be seen as applying "not upon impersonal [state] entities, but upon human beings" came directly from his pen. Yet in articulating the British case against the Nazis, Lauterpacht again felt compelled to strip out Jewish themes. The official statements he wrote are models of restraint, devoid of emotion. He left to Robinson the task of laying out the Jewish case more plainly via the American prosecution team. Lauterpacht even drew more satisfaction from listening to Jackson's opening statement than the sound of his own words in the mouth of Shawcross. Hearing the American lawyer relate "the story of the Jewish atrocities," he wrote to his wife from Nuremberg, was an "unforgettable experience" that confirmed his faith in the law. He passed over the British speeches he had written in silence.[33]

Robinson shared Lauterpacht's view that American leadership was solely responsible for the legal "revolution" at Nuremberg. "If there is any group which took the Jewish case seriously," Robinson wrote afterward, "it is only the Americans." This development held profound consequences for the future of global justice. "It is the self-assertion of American leadership in world affairs on the moral plane which has proved of tremendous importance. The others missed the bus." Yet his satisfaction had limits. The achievement at Nuremberg had to be weighed against the painful fact that Jewish victimhood was still strikingly absent from the legal proceedings. Contrary to popular perception, the trials did not emphasize the Holocaust or the mass murder of Jews. The law was applied, Robinson complained afterward, so that no count in any indictment singled out Nazi mass murder of Jews as a crime against humanity. Instead, Jews were subsumed into a general category of all civilian victims of criminal warfare. They were nowhere recognized "as the chosen victim of Nazi persecution." For this outcome, however, he blamed not Jackson, but another Jewish lawyer on the American staff: Raphael Lemkin, the inventor of the term "genocide."[34]

Lemkin sprang from the same East European soil as his slightly older Jewish colleagues. Like Lauterpacht, he grew up in the Polish Zionist movement and graduated a few years behind him from Lviv University. From the mid-1920s onward he practiced law in Warsaw, where he also offered Jewish legal advice and Zionist political commentary through columns in the Yiddish- and Hebrew-language press. Like Lauterpacht and Robinson, Lemkin believed that minority rights were an essential tool of international justice. As Polish Jews confronted rising antisemitism in the late 1920s, he argued for the need to change international law to protect national cultures from the dangers of "criminal barbarism" directed at groups and their identities. His outspoken legal activism was labeled a Jewish provocation by Polish nationalists in the early 1930s. Undeterred, Lemkin continued to advocate his ideas throughout the decade. After the German and Soviet invasions, he escaped Poland and eventually made his way to the United States. There he renamed "criminal barbarism" as "genocide" in a 1944 legal study, *Axis Rule in Occupied Europe*. Joining Jackson's staff as a mid-level attorney, he insistently promoted "genocide" and succeeded in having it included in the final version of the Nuremberg Indictment as part of the "war crimes" count: the "extermination of racial and national groups, against the civilian populations of certain occupied territories in order to destroy particular races and classes of people and national, racial or religious groups, particularly Jews, Poles, and Gypsies and others."[35]

Given all that they had in common as Zionist legal activists, it would have made sense for Lemkin, Lauterpacht, and Robinson to see eye to eye. Yet the two veteran lawyers dismissed Lemkin as a utopian amateur. Once the trial began, Robinson was shocked to see that Lemkin had managed to slip the word "genocide" into the indictment, but had defined it in terms of the broad destruction of Jews, Gypsies, and Poles. The move infuriated him chiefly because it lumped Jews together with the Poles who had murdered their own Jewish neighbors. "It is always the same struggle for the recognition necessary to call a Jew a Jew," he complained. For Robinson, Lemkin's "genocide" term was at best a distraction from the main thrust of "crimes against humanity," and at worst a self-inflicted assault on Jewish collective identity. In truth, Lemkin had really done little more than promote his own overlapping legal vision of international justice. It was Jackson who ultimately determined how to treat Jews and Jewish legal proposals at Nuremberg. Yet, caught between his faith in American benevolence and the realities of Jewish political anonymity, even in the court of law, Robinson chose to blame a fellow émigré Jewish lawyer rather than his American patron.[36]

In the years to come, Lemkin would go on to wage his own political battle to win American support for a separate international genocide convention. Meanwhile Robinson faced a more immediate challenge to his faith in American benevolence. Even as the Nuremberg proceedings continued, Jewish rights-defenders turned their attention to the third major arena of postwar internationalism: the Paris Peace Conference. There once again the Jewish drive for international legal recognition and protection would clash with the realities of American statecraft in a Cold War world.

"Minority-Phobia"

On the last Saturday in September 1945, Blaustein and Proskauer visited the White House for their first official meeting with Harry Truman. The president knew Blaustein as a major Democratic donor, whom party leaders had leaned on to pay off Roosevelt's leftover campaign debt. But the agenda that day was Jewish politics. The duo told the president they had not come to add to his headaches. The AJC neither endorsed nor rejected the idea of a future Jewish state in Palestine. It insisted only that America persuade the British to admit more Jewish refugees from Europe as an "absolutely essential [step] in order to save human lives." Truman liked what he heard. Rabbi Wise and his ilk, he complained, were "acting like fanatics" who would lead the country straight into "World War III." Truman possessed a natural sympathy for the Zionist cause. Irked by the intense pressure from Zionist lobbying, however, he had settled into the position he would hold for the next three years: a focus on Jewish refugee relief combined with steadfast avoidance of longer-term American entanglements in the Middle East.[37]

Harry Truman and Jacob Blaustein in the early 1950s

MS 400, Personal and Business Papers of Louis and Jacob Blaustein,
Special Collections, Sheridan Libraries, Johns Hopkins University

After stating his non-Zionist position, Blaustein then outlined his human rights vision, which aligned perfectly with Truman's own agenda—politically neutral, resolutely individualist, and thus a safe alternative to the hard questions then emerging around nationalism, state-building, and decolonization. The future of the Jews, Truman told his visitors, would "depend not only on Palestine, but instead, as with all minorities and people, upon the recognition by all countries of the individual rights of each human being regardless of race, religion or nationality." The goal must be that Jews "as all people could live in Poland, Romania, Hungary, or any place else, as they do in this country."[38]

Truman's words were music to Blaustein's ears. No more would one speak of minorities at all. Instead, Jews formed part of a "triple melting pot," coexisting with Catholics and Protestants as an American religious group, linked to a universal struggle for religious freedom as opposed to national liberation. For the same reason, under Blaustein the AJC joined the struggle for civil rights, strongly supporting the NAACP in its legal campaign in the courts that led to the 1954 *Brown v. Board of Education* Supreme Court decision. A color-blind society in which only individual faith separated citizen from citizen would benefit Jews and African Americans alike. Justice meant ending all formal legal discrimination. By the same token, the AJC did not pause to consider the institutional legacies of seg-regation or other economic, social, or cultural rights claims by African Americans and other minorities. They identified these concerns with the discredited minority rights ideas of prewar Europe. The tribal differences of the Old World must be left behind.

Yet Europe would not retreat so easily. A year after the war's end, several hundred thousand Jews remained in Displaced Persons camps across Ger-many, Italy, and Austria. Low-level violence continued to ripple across the region. Then on July 4, 1946, a vicious pogrom broke out in the Polish city of Kielce. In a repetition of a thousand-year-old anti-Jewish libel, local Poles accused Holocaust survivors who had only just returned home of kidnap-ping and murdering a local Christian boy for his blood. By day's end, civil-ians, police, and soldiers had killed forty-two Jews and injured forty others. The Kielce massacre served as a devastating reminder that antisemitism did not begin or end with the Nazi regime. Shocked, Blaustein dispatched a let-ter to Truman, urging the president to call on the Vatican to denounce the crimes. What troubled him most, he explained, was a Polish cardinal's suggestion that the crimes were justified because of political conflicts be-tween Jewish Bolsheviks and freedom-loving Poles. Our "democratic faith," Blaustein wrote, teaches us that "exposing to persecution and terror an entire group, because of the politics of some individual acting entirely on their own, is contrary to all principles of humanity and religion." Two weeks later, Blaustein flew to Paris to press this vision at the Paris Peace Conference.[39]

After World War I, the nations of the world had gathered in Paris to negotiate the peace terms and the new League of Nations simultaneously. This time, the Allies waited a year after the United Nation's founding conference to turn to the drafting of the European peace treaties. In the aftermath of the United Nation's creation, plans were floated for general human rights protections to be built into the constitutional template for the central European states. But by the time the nations finally gathered in Paris, in July 1946, Winston Churchill had already delivered his famous "Iron Curtain" speech. Europe was split into Soviet and Western spheres of influence, and minority affairs reemerged as a sensitive topic. Millions of ethnic Germans, Poles, and others had begun to be forcibly displaced across the new borders to create more homogenous nation-states. Having been down the road of postwar European diplomacy a generation earlier, many Jews wondered whether the new talk of human rights could survive a divided Europe any better than had the first experiment with international governance, the League of Nations. The test of the much-discussed idea of human rights, wrote one American Yiddish journalist, would be whether the world translated the phrase from "a pious wish" into real "law in every country." Some took quite pessimistic positions. The American Labor Zionist leader Aron Alperin put it most stringently: "How misguided are all those who proclaim loudly that with the general formulas bearing beautiful-sounding names—like an international 'bill of rights' and others—they'll heal the awful wounds of the Jews in Europe, who still bleed profusely . . . when we request to separate out the special question of the remaining Jews, this is absolutely not a request for privileges, 'privileges' that Hitler awarded us in the Maidenaks and Auschwitzes."[40]

As in San Francisco, all of the major Jewish organizations dispatched delegates to Paris. Heading the list of leaders were Blaustein and Robinson, along with Lauterpacht, Perlzweig, Proskauer, Wise, and Goldmann. From Jerusalem came David Ben-Gurion, Yitzhak Ben-Zvi, and Jacob Talmon—the future prime minister, president, and leading Israeli historian, respectively. As before, the tangle of personalities and groups boiled down to a Zionist coalition versus an AJC-led band of liberal, non-Zionist Jewish organizations.[41]

Based on his San Francisco experience and his growing rapport with Truman, Blaustein entered Paris confident that he had the upper hand in representing Jewish interests. In July he wrote to the new secretary of state, James Byrnes, to announce his hope that the partnership effected between American diplomats and NGOs at the San Francisco conference would be repeated. This time, however, it was not to be: the State Department politely shot him down. San Francisco, he was informed, had been a "unique" event where public opinion had mattered more. Now the technical questions and logistical constraints made it impractical to include "private American organizations."[42]

The Zionist team fared no better in breaching the "wall of indifference" separating them from the Luxembourg Palace where the Council of Foreign Ministers met. Just as in San Francisco, stateless peoples were denied a seat at the table. Once again, like San Francisco, complained Si Kenen, "our work will be confined to lobbies at hotels." Frustrated Zionist leaders compensated with a flood of paper. From his temporary office overlooking the Champs-Élysées, Robinson groused about the new Jewish disease of "memorandumania"—the indiscriminate and futile dispatching of reports, letters, and entreaties to official diplomatic negotiations seeking redress for Jewish claims.[43]

Desperation made for strange bedfellows. A few weeks into the Paris Peace Conference, all the Jewish parties joined forces in hopes of presenting a united front. Yet deep divisions remained. The Zionists led by Perlzweig and Robinson continued to speak of minority rights as essential for Jewish life. In their official position statement, they called for "the inalienable right of Jewish communities to maintain and foster their collective ethnic, religious, linguistic, and cultural identity and institutions with legal protection in the exercise of this right, and, with assistance from the state, where such is granted to any other ethnic or religious group." They criticized the abundance of "well-worn clichés bearing upon human rights and fundamental freedoms." Blaustein and his team, in contrast, insisted on capitalizing on the newly minted idea of international human rights.[44]

The joining of these factions led to nasty fights. The AJC remained convinced that the Zionists were pushing Palestine in through the back door. To win what it called "the media war in Paris," Blaustein's team insisted on issuing its own press releases. The Zionist spokesmen, meanwhile, derided the AJC and their French and British allies as deracinated "prophets of universalism." It fell to Robinson, as the undisputed senior legal diplomat in the room, to oversee this fractious drafting process. He, in turn, leaned heavily on Lauterpacht, the one man whom all sides considered a neutral voice, because of his work across the Zionist divide in the Jewish world. Together the two men distilled Jewish demands into a 10,000-word memorandum calling for equal human rights for the Jews and special annexes to the Peace Treaties to guarantee those rights, including automatic citizenship for Jewish refugees and economic rights of local Jewish communities to restitution for Jewish property seized during the war. It was an attempt to bridge the two different strains of Jewish human rights thinking—the older European group rights model and the newer American individual rights model—through a shaky compromise that balanced concrete Jewish demands with general principles.[45]

Reaching this compromise was not easy. When all the leaders gathered at the city's luxury Hotel Royal Monceau on the Avenue Hoche near the Arc de Triomphe to approve the final version of the memo on the evening of August 18, another bruising fight occurred. The normally mild-mannered Blaustein got into a screaming match with Perlzweig over how to credit the Jewish sponsorship of the memorandum. Blaustein accused the World Jewish Congress leaders of a naked power grab and a transparent attack on the AJC's "non-nationalistic principles." Perlzweig shot back that a handful of American plutocrats could not speak for the Jewish world. The debate lasted four hours and at points even threatened to turn violent.[46]

Robinson watched this childish brawling with disgust. The fight was all the more pathetic, he wrote, because the stakes were so embarrassingly low. Weeks spent canvassing the twenty-one national delegations at Paris had failed to yield a single country willing to introduce the Jewish memorandum into the official deliberations. Expressions of sympathy could not disguise a simple truth. Not only minority rights but minorities themselves had been written out of the postwar international order.

> The word "minority" is taboo—nothing can be said in its favor. . . . The moral standards at Paris are the lowest I have ever witnessed or read about. The Russians believe that only they should receive reparations, and only these reparations do not adversely affect the economy of the defeated country, while the elementary right of restitution is cited as "exploitation." Declarations of love were voiced by the Rumanian delegation to the Jewish delegation, while fighting "Jewish clauses" by every means.[47]

Self-interest ruled the day. The draft peace treaties for Romania and Hungary had included a section labeled "Human Rights for Jews." Inside the Council of Foreign Ministers, however, even mention of Jews proved objectionable. No country was willing to accept anything remotely close to the Minorities Treaties of 1919. In the end, the treaties established only that the Big Three—the Soviets, Americans, and British—would supervise their enactment for eighteen months, including the "clauses affecting Jews and human rights." After that, "normal diplomatic channels" would become the main forum for dispute resolution. If the diplomats could not agree, the International Court of Justice theoretically had the authority to arbitrate, but only between states. In its memorandum, the combined Jewish delegation had sought the right of individual direct appeal to the UN in case of violations. That, too, did not come to pass. Enforcement remained dependent on Great Power support.[48]

Still confident in American power, Blaustein came away from Paris optimistic about Jewish prospects. "We have achieved great success," he wrote in December 1946, for they had secured rights for Jews like everyone else, without singling them out for second-class citizenship. Despite the setbacks, the plan provided a clear path forward. Vigilant supervision by international Jewish groups, backed by U.S. diplomatic support, would ensure the future of Jewish life in Europe. When problems arose, the "ultimate jurisdiction of the International Court of Justice" provided the legal forum of last resort that had been absent in the Minorities Treaties. Unlike after World War I, the United States remained firmly involved in the new international institutions. So Jews would always have a powerful friend to make sure their cases reached the court.[49]

Once more, Robinson vigorously disagreed. Having lived through the same system at the League of Nations, he knew that promises of jurisdiction meant little on their own without explicit mechanisms to bring claims forward. "Arbitration" translated into state-to-state political negotiation, leaving a stateless minority like the Jews once again voiceless. Reliance on American diplomatic intervention on behalf of vulnerable Jews was not a substitute for real, positive law. American support was essential, but it was not a permanent strategy for Jewish diplomacy. Now even our friends "are allergic to the word 'Jews,'" he observed, and East and West alike obsessed over "minority-phobia." In the new climate of the Cold War, national minorities had emerged as political liabilities.[50]

Unfinished Victory

A divided Europe was not the only place where "minority-phobia" prevailed. Underlying all the debates about rights, justice, and recognition for postwar European Jewry lurked the unresolved question of Palestine. The 1946 Peace Conference coincided with the first postwar meeting of the Jewish Agency, also held in Paris at the Hotel Royal Morceau, where the Jewish peace conference debates took place. With the war concluded, Zionist leaders renewed their push to secure Jewish title to Palestine, but they faced a new political hurdle. Determined to rid themselves of the festering problem, the British had invited the Americans to help them solve the question of how to dispose of Palestine. Months before Paris, the Anglo-American Commission of Inquiry issued a report calling for the country to become "neither a Jewish state nor an Arab state." Instead, as set out in the July 1946 Morrison-Grady Plan, Palestine was to be administered as a unitary federal trusteeship, with Jewish and Arab provinces enjoying self-government under British supervision.

Reactions from both Jewish and Arab leaders were swift and negative. After decades of violence and mistrust, neither side considered the British an honest broker, let alone a proper legal custodian. The time for complicated power-sharing arrangements had passed. Having witnessed the genocidal violence of two world wars, neither Jews nor Arabs wished to become a minority in their own land. As Max Laserson, Robinson's close colleague from Eastern Europe and the World Jewish Congress, wrote, "Even the best federation cannot protect us from our inferior minority political status, from being a national minority." Officially, Palestine was off the table for discussion at Paris. In reality, the "idiotic cantonization plan," as Stephen Wise called it, hovered behind the peace conference proceedings. Just as in the interwar period, the Jewish pursuit of rights in Eastern Europe was shaped by the question of Palestine—and dependent on the largesse of the Great Powers.[51]

While still in Paris, Robinson wrote a short pamphlet called "Unfinished Victory." The war was over, the Nazis punished, and a measure of justice secured. Yet Jews remained in a most uncertain state. "Despite the

changes of regimes," he wrote, "anti-Semitism is stronger than it was before and during the war not only in the traditional anti-Semitic countries
like Poland, Slovakia, Hungary, and Romania, but in Western Europe." Relief,
rehabilitation, and restitution efforts, all vital to Jewish life, were stymied
by "the failure, or sheer unwillingness, of governments to see . . . Jews as
Jews." As a result, the vast majority of Jewish survivors in Europe "look to
emigration as their one hope of survival," with Palestine as their destination. All the partial successes over the course of the years 1945 and 1946
could not disguise the fact that a crucial phase of struggle remained unfinished. To complete the victory, Jews would need to trade minority status for
a place in the international order as a sovereign nation. What that meant for
relations between Jews and Arabs in Palestine he did not say.[52]

After stops in San Francisco, Nuremberg, and Paris, the postwar path of
internationalism wound its way to the new UN headquarters in its temporary
location in Queens, New York. There, in 1948, the intertwined fates of
Zionism and human rights reached a critical juncture with the creation of
the State of Israel and the Universal Declaration of Human Rights. Both
developments would inspire new confidence in postwar internationalism.
Both would promise new hope for Jewish rebirth in the ashes of the Holocaust. Yet the subsequent rise of Israel and the UN rights regime would also
force Jewish rights-defenders to confront the question of whether human
rights and Jewish sovereignty were two sides of the same coin—or paths
leading in opposite directions.

6

The Failed Partitions

ON SEPTEMBER 16, 1949, Maurice Perlzweig received the welcome of his life. Ten thousand Libyan Jews mobbed him at the entrance to Tripoli's ancient ghetto. As they ushered him through the city's winding narrow streets toward its largest synagogue, perfumed water rained down from the roofs and balconies above; joyful ululations pierced the air. The Jews of Libya greeted the English rabbi-diplomat as a political savior. After the Italian colonial government fled invading British forces in February 1943, the North African Muslim country had plunged into a four-year cycle of antisemitic violence. In November 1945, 130 Jews had been murdered in a vicious pogrom. Since then smaller-scale attacks had plagued the British-controlled territory about to be reborn as an independent Arab state. Yet while Perlzweig came bearing a message of international human rights for the Jews, the roaring crowds chanted one word over and over: "Aliyah! Aliyah! Aliyah!"[1]

This disconnect between messenger and audience neatly encapsulated the paradoxical situation in the years right after 1948. In the eyes of the urbane British visitor, the newly minted Universal Declaration of Human Rights, soon to be made into binding international law, offered robust protection for vulnerable Jews throughout the diaspora. Although still firmly a Zionist, Perlzweig hoped the UN's fledgling human rights program might insulate Middle Eastern Jewry from the Arab-Israeli conflict enough to provide a choice between continued life in the diaspora or relocation to Israel. To the 30,000 Jews of Libya, however, the distinction between human rights and politics was meaningless. Arab nationalism had placed their lives in jeopardy; Jewish nationalism would redeem them. In their eyes, there was no choice. The sole legitimate source of rights was citizenship in the new State of Israel, under a Jewish government with land and an army of its own.

The year 1948 marks the great turning point for both Jewish history and the history of human rights. After two thousand years in exile, with the establishment of the State of Israel, Jews returned home to reclaim their sovereignty. That same year, for the first time ever, the world promulgated a new kind of international human rights intended precisely to constrain sovereignty. The relationship between these events is conveniently encapsulated in a three-day sequence at the close of the year. On December 9, the UN General Assembly approved the idea of an international convention banning genocide. The next day, December 10, the same body adopted the Universal Declaration of Human Rights (UDHR). On December 11, in response to the ongoing Arab-Israeli war, it passed UN General Assembly Resolution 194, which offered a plan to resolve the outstanding legal and political questions of borders and refugees. From the quest for a new global order governed by high-minded principles of international law, the UN turned directly to a raging national conflict that had stubbornly resisted international attempts to tame it.

This sequence was more than an accident of timing. It was a logical consequence of the fact that the same dramatis personae populated both stories. Throughout 1947 and 1948, Robinson shuttled between roles as Israel's top lawyer at the UN and the first legal advisor to the nascent UN Commission on Human Rights. Lauterpacht wrote influential drafts of both the International Bill of Rights and Israel's Declaration of Independence, while secretly advising the newborn State of Israel on legal strategy in its conflict with the Arab world. Perlzweig worked closely with the UN's top human rights officials on the drafting and diplomacy of the UDHR and Genocide Convention—and was one of the first to try to use the laws that emerged. Twice in two years he charged Arab states with committing "genocide" in the treatment of their Jewish populations. Yet he insisted that the matter should be kept strictly separate from the political conflict in Palestine. Returning the favor, his colleague Charles Malik, the Lebanese vice chairman of the Commission on Human Rights and chief spokesman for the Arab League, accused Jews of perpetrating genocide in Palestine.

In the moment of the dual incarnation of human rights and Jewish sovereignty, Jewish rights-defenders believed the phenomena formed two sides of the same coin. A bifurcation of Palestine would produce two nation-states, one Jewish and one Arab. A strict partition between politics and law would allow the UN to supervise international human rights without partisanship. The sovereignty of self enshrined in individual human rights constituted the obverse of the sovereignty of the state. Perlzweig hailed the rise of Jewish sovereignty even as he called on all governments to acknowledge sovereignty's limits. "The state, like the individual," he argued, "loses nothing either of true self-respect or fundamental freedoms in acknowledging the sovereignty of a higher law." Left out of this idealistic formulation was the crucial materiel that linked individual and state, and divided Arab from Jew: the nation.[2]

In her 1951 magnum opus, *The Origins of Totalitarianism,* Hannah Arendt famously captured this paradox: "Not only did loss of national rights in all instances entail the loss of human rights, the restoration of human rights, as the recent example of the State of Israel proves, has been achieved so far only through the restoration or the establishment of national rights." The right to have rights began with membership in a political community. Rightly or wrongly, she observed, the sole form of community that could guarantee those rights was the nation-state. She criticized the Universal Declaration of Human Rights as a utopian venture disconnected from political reality. But Arendt also recognized the dangerous temptation for all forms of nationalism—including Zionism—to violently exclude others from the political community. Like the Jews of Libya, Arendt grasped that national sovereignty was both the best source of meaningful rights and the gravest challenge to those rights.[3]

The grand Jewish dream of 1948 was to dismantle Arendt's paradox by slicing the Gordian knot of politics and law. Doing so would shield the Jewish diaspora from dangerous entanglement in both the Arab-Israeli conflict and the deepening Cold War. History turned out to have other plans. The war in Palestine ended with the Jews in possession of their own country, but the Arab state next door remained unrealized. The Cold War

divide, along with questions about decolonization and domestic race relations, left the Great Powers unwilling to surrender a measure of their own
political sovereignty even as they urged smaller nations to do so. Once
again, Jews were forced to ask which power could make human rights a
reality. Only now, the rise of Israel meant that they also had to ask about
how to balance the pursuit of international Jewish rights with the practice
of sovereign Jewish power.

To be successful, partition required symmetry, both between Jews and
Arabs in the hot sand of the Middle East and between law and politics in
the frozen tundra of the Cold War. Yet in both cases, symmetry proved
elusive. Instead of two states rising in Palestine, only one appeared. Instead of insulating justice from geopolitics, the UN human rights program
squeezed the two further together. The story of Jewish politics and human
rights in 1948 is a tale of two failed partitions in one fateful year.

A Setback at Lake Success

Robinson returned from Paris to his Upper West Side New York apart-
ment in the late fall of 1946 to find a surprising invitation from the new UN
Commission on Human Rights. Would he temporarily put aside his work
with the World Jewish Congress to serve as its first legal advisor and help
design the International Bill of Rights? It was a unique opportunity that
pitted his roles as Zionist politician and international lawyer against each
other. Just months before, he had confided to Stephen Wise that he held
out little hope for the UN's human rights program.

> The very fact that 11,000,000 Jews alive throughout Europe, the Jewish
> communities of the U.S., U.S.S.R., and the British Commonwealth of Na-
> tions have no interest in such a bill is sufficient for us to assess the real
> value of it in the general framework of the Jewish situation. Nor are human
> rights denied to Jews in the danger zones of Europe and Latin America.
> Perhaps the only place where the problem of human rights may present
> some Jewish interest is the Near East. But we know very well that here
> again there are problems of greater interest than this.[4]

Yet Robinson was not yet ready to jettison the entire UN human rights
venture. Earlier that year, he had published a book-length commentary,

Human Rights and Fundamental Freedoms in the Charter of the United Nations, in which he argued that the 1945 UN Charter, despite its design flaws, had "effected the first breach in the formerly inaccessible citadel of domestic jurisdiction." By authorizing the organization to investigate violations of human rights inside member-states, the UN had made a significant advance in the rightful authority of international law. If properly pursued, "the internationalization of human rights" could create a new direct legal relationship "between the international community and the individual." But much depended on the "if."[5]

The man seeking Robinson's help largely shared his mixture of skepticism and hope. As the newly appointed director of the UN Division of Human Rights, Canadian law professor John Humphrey was charged with inventing his job on the fly. That meant corralling an unruly herd of international diplomats with competing agendas into a cohesive multilateral team that would define the first universal law code of its kind. Who better to start the process than the world expert on the last attempt to legalize international rights at the League of Nations? Despite his misgivings, Robinson agreed to a two-and-a-half-month stint at the Commission on Human Rights. Better to try to fix the conceptual flaws and screen out the politics from the UN's human rights law, he reasoned, then to give up prematurely. At the temporary UN headquarters in the Long Island town of Lake Success, the two men assembled a core of legal proposals on human rights, heavily influenced by Lauterpacht's work. Out of this mass of materials, Humphrey wove together a 400-page draft of what would eventually become the Universal Declaration of Human Rights.[6]

When the first official session of the new Commission on Human Rights opened in January 1947, Humphrey asked Robinson to stay on as a consultant. He did so for a short time, only to find himself disappointed by the puerile squabbling and political pretense. Like the UN itself, the Commission fell victim to its impressive diversity. The initial roster of members included just nine delegates: former U.S. First Lady Eleanor Roosevelt served as chairwoman, Peng-Chun Chang (Nationalist China) as vice chairman, and Charles Habib Malik (Lebanon) as rapporteur, along with René Cassin (France), Alexandre Bogomolov (Soviet Union), Charles Dukes (United Kingdom), Herman Santa Cruz (Chile), Col. William Roy Hodgson

(Australia), and Carlos Romulo (Philippines). That group soon expanded to eighteen members, including five spots permanently assigned to the Security Council's permanent members. This sundry cast of strong personalities guaranteed large-scale debates about the meaning and scope of the International Bill of Rights.

The pragmatic Humphrey sought to focus the work by convening a drafting subcommittee comprised of Roosevelt, Cassin, Malik, and Chang. Yet even in this more intimate format, he found it almost impossible to make headway. Chang, a scholar, urged the quartet to begin their work with a study session devoted to Confucianism. This irked Malik, a Lebanese Christian philosopher, who preferred to cite Thomas Aquinas. Malik, meanwhile, clashed over the question of Zionism with Cassin, a distinguished French Jewish jurist, hero of Charles de Gaulle's French government in exile, and head of the Alliance Israélite Universelle. Malik had by this time emerged as spokesman for the Arab League, which advocated the total rejection of Jewish claims to Palestine, at times spiced with calls to eradicate Jews from Palestine and the equation of Zionists with Nazis. Cassin had emerged from World War II newly convinced of the justness and necessity of a Jewish state. The quartet's presiding matron, Eleanor Roosevelt, vainly tried to broker a truce. She had beaten out an eager Blaustein for the U.S. seat and commanded authority because of her popularity with the American public and status as FDR's widow. Yet she immediately found herself fighting her State Department handlers over her desire to operate independently of the Truman White House.[7]

As these grandees spent the opening weeks of 1947 arguing back and forth about the philosophical meaning of rights, Robinson kept an eye trained on the first major human rights controversy to surface at the UN General Assembly. In 1945, while still British colonies, India and South Africa had each been granted member seats in the UN. A year later, on the cusp of independence, the Indian government filed an official complaint over South Africa's racial discrimination policies. The closing net of apartheid had drawn South Africa's large Indian population into the restrictive legal category of "coloureds." It was a crucial early test of human rights in the postwar world. To his disappointment, Robinson detected stunning hypocrisy on all sides. In its grievance, India condemned South Africa for legal classification regimes, yet retained its own equally unseemly caste system. The South Africans bristled defiantly at international meddling in their internal affairs, but offered an ominous brief that, in Robinson's estimation, read less like a principled defense of sovereignty than "a Polish or Czechoslovak reply to the complaints made by German Minorities" at the League of Nations.[8]

Other countries' reactions were worse. The Communist countries cynically sided with India for plainly political reasons and in spite of their own obvious sins. "[It is] very easy for the Slav bloc to object to the South African methods," Robinson groused to Perlzweig, "when they themselves solved their minority problems . . . by the method of the Assyrian Kings, i.e. wholesale expulsion (on a racial basis)" of millions of Germans and Poles after 1945. "With such a method of removing the minorities," Robinson asked, "where is the moral legitimacy for supporting the Indian complaint?"[9]

From the outset, then, Robinson found his worst fears confirmed. There was a real danger, he wrote Quincy Wright, that the states would "use the legal phraseology of the Charter for the political decisions of individual members." The only way around this dilemma was to insist that, on questions of human rights, law and politics be kept separate. International law must be applied consistently and equally to all states. Doing so required two crucial elements conspicuously lacking in the postwar world: a global consensus about which rights were worth protecting and a binding legal mechanism for enforcement. Yet given what he witnessed at the UN in 1946, achieving either of these objectives was highly unlikely, let alone both. The intense political turmoil of the intertwined dramas of Cold War and decolonization playing out over much of the world further lessened the likelihood of success.[10]

Dismayed, Robinson left his post at the UN in March 1947 to answer an urgent call from Tel Aviv. He would spend the next seven months as legal counsel to the Jewish Agency, the main foreign relations arm of the Palestine-based Zionist movement, helping resolve questions of partition and independence. The time had clearly come to move on from human rights to "problems of greater interest."[11]

"The Problem of Palestine"

By the end of 1946, relations in Palestine between Jews, Arabs, and British had deteriorated so much that the British government despaired of finding any policy solution. After both Arabs and Jews decisively rejected the Morrison-Grady plan, President Truman shifted to a tentative position in favor of territorial partition with side-by-side Jewish and Arab states. But a fed-up British cabinet had no appetite for overseeing any more policy experiments. In February 1947 it declared a pox on both the Jewish and Arab houses and handed over responsibility for Palestine to the UN. This was accompanied by the announcement that the British planned to withdraw all of its military and civilian forces the following year. The news only sparked an uptick in violence among all parties.

At the UN in New York, the first Special Assembly on the Palestine question was held that April. Robinson tangled directly with Malik over the ties between human rights and the Arab-Jewish conflict. Malik was quick to link the Commission on Human Rights' work to the live political question in the Middle East: "Justice, equality, the dignity and sanctity of man, the freedom of the spirit of man—these things are in truth Palestinian in origin." Territorial partition, he argued, was but a parochial concession to nationalism. Since Palestine "is holy for all humanity, the solution of the problem of Palestine [must] be therefore truly Palestinian." By that he meant one state where Arab Muslims and Christians would care for their Jewish brethren, since "those Jews who inhabit our country, speak our language, and share our sentiments . . . are all Arabs."[12]

Robinson found Malik offensive. His universalist language barely concealed an Arab nationalist attack on Zionism. Malik spoke of human rights while helping plan an Arab League boycott of "Zionist goods" and a massive regional invasion in defiance of the UN partition resolution. He condoned his own country's massacre of its Lebanese Jewish population. It was abundantly clear that the Arabs were playing a hypocritical game, propagating belligerent anti-Jewish rhetoric and incitement alongside appeals to self-determination and peace. In the rise of the Arab League, an explicitly "racial unit," Robinson argued, "we are witnessing the transfer of the Hitlerian pan-Germanic idea into the Middle East." "The real friend of the UN cannot but ask himself, why should this young organization ruin itself in the eyes of the world by actions which betray the very principles of the UN?"[13]

Still, Robinson's indignation masked a complicated reality on the Jewish side. In a joint memo to his colleagues at the World Jewish Congress and Jewish Agency, he admitted that "the Palestine problem is now more a political problem than a legal one. But it would be irresponsible on our part not to use legal arguments whenever and wherever they strengthen our position." The desire to preserve the law's purity clashed with the expediency of its practical use. Robinson addressed this issue in a rapidly written book published in 1947 and titled *Palestine and the United Nations*, which documented that spring's UN debates on Palestine and outlined the Jewish diplomatic and legal case. It was published just before the opening of the UN's autumn session, which had the Palestine question at the top of its agenda. As the debates continued, Robinson watched "nearly all the Arab speakers" denounce the partition plan on the grounds that "any solution of the Palestine problem acceptable to the Jews would mean the beginning of the Third World War." Behind the scenes, he worked feverishly to secure the necessary votes from friendly countries, including the United States, to advance the partition plan.[14]

That November, the UN General Assembly adopted Resolution 181, a plan to create two independent states in Palestine, one Jewish and one Arab, the following year. Thirty-three countries voted in favor of the resolution, including both the United States and the USSR, and thirteen opposed it, chiefly Arab and Muslim states. Another ten countries, led by the United Kingdom and China, abstained. The news of the vote was greeted with jubilation by Jews around the world and defiant rejection by the Arab states. Those mirror-opposite attitudes would persist for decades.

To Robinson, the partition resolution "definitively solved the problem of Palestine" by legally creating separate Jewish and Arab states. Ugly as partition might be in practice, it would deliver justice to both peoples. Perzlweig concurred. "I am certain that the problem will be brought to an end," he told a Toronto audience at the time, "when the Jewish and Arab States complete their machinery" under the firm tutelage of the UN. Even Blaustein concluded that partition was the best option. "There comes a time when

Maurice Perlzweig (left) with Stephen S. Wise (right) in the 1940s

Perlzweig Family Archive

practical people realize that endless debate on what should have been, should cease," he said in a January 1948 speech. Partition was the only road forward: "As Americans and Jews, it is our clear duty to do everything we can to have the decision implemented." He added that they should do it quickly, too. On the ground in Palestine, violence between the two sides had begun to escalate. "There is genocidal strife going on in Palestine which has undermined the security of the entire Yishuv," Blaustein warned, "While the Arabs are clearly the aggressors, the Jews are rallying in kind, and the result is a war of mutual extermination on racial grounds."[15]

"A Juridical Heresy"

The turmoil in the Middle East was only one of many reasons for the slow pace of work on the International Bill of Human Rights in 1947 and

1948. Cultural and religious differences, large egos, and the sheer novelty of the concept all created huge challenges. The largest obstacle, however, was the clash between the West and the Soviet Union. Hoping for a compromise, Eleanor Roosevelt proposed in July 1947 that the Bill of Rights be split into two parts: a nonbinding Declaration, enunciating rights but without legal force, and a Covenant (or Treaty) that would be formally ratified by each country. The Commission would begin with the Declaration. Only after support for that document was secured would it turn to the more difficult Covenant.

Over the rest of 1947 and into 1948, the Declaration draft ballooned into a massive text comprising forty-eight sections, with four hundred pages of official commentary. Each new version only brought more ideological clashes. Adding to the complexity was the presence of numerous NGOs, including the AJC and the WJC, along with many other American and international groups. All had ideas on which rights should be given priority: the right to life for Christians, freedom of nonreligion for Communists, and so on and so forth.[16]

The man who would have most liked to be present at these sessions was not invited. After the publication in 1945 of his *International Bill of the Rights of Man*, Lauterpacht had ample reason to assume he would be named the UK delegate to the Commission on Human Rights. Even the Americans hoped he would get the position. But the Foreign Office's chief legal advisor, Eric Beckett, advised his colleagues that such an appointment would be "disastrous."

> Professor Lauterpacht, although a distinguished and industrious international lawyer, is, when all said and done, a Jew fairly recently come from Vienna. Emphatically, I think that the representative of Her Majesty's Government on human rights must be a very English Englishman imbued throughout his life and hereditary to the real meaning of human rights as we understand them in this country.

This sabotage was all the more egregious given that Beckett relied heavily on Lauterpacht for all manner of legal advice regarding Britain's position on UN affairs. He knew full well that the Jewish lawyer had lived in England for twenty-three years by then (and been naturalized for fifteen).

Yet three damning strikes counted against Lauterpacht: his overt Jewish-ness, his semi-covert Zionism, and his steadfast liberal internationalism. Despite Lauterpacht's discretion about his Jewish politics and his determination to place legal questions ahead of partisan loyalties, many British diplomats were alarmed by his deep ties to Israel and his insistence on the creation of a binding legal framework before specifying the content of human rights. The Foreign Office, nervous about anticolonialism, much preferred to see what rights were to be recognized before committing Britain to any new international law. So they quietly dropped Lauterpacht from the list of candidates. Adding insult to injury, the "very English Englishman" sent instead turned out to be a trade unionist named Charles Dukes, wholly ignorant of law, international or otherwise.[17]

Shut out of the formal process, Lauterpacht offered his commentary gratis, via the press. In a scorching letter to the *Times of London* published in July 1947, he attacked the practice of holding elaborate discussions about rights before establishing the proper legal machinery. Doing so risked "a mere statement of generalities" that would have no purchase on real political affairs "in this period of uncertainty and turmoil." In a BBC radio address to the British public, he went further:

> To a lawyer the enunciation of a right without the provision of a remedy is a juridical heresy. . . . What is required at this juncture of history is not the recognition and not even the formulation of inalienable human rights but their effective protection, by an instrumentality higher than the state itself, against the arbitrariness of willful men and against the complacent or selfish indolence of entrenched interests.

Build the legal system first, Lauterpacht argued, and then specify the rights to be protected. Otherwise, human rights risked becoming "the object of diplomatic bargaining and of political maneuvers." "An effective and enforceable international Bill of Rights," he added, will "open a new chapter in the constitutional law of mankind and in the relationship of man and state. . . . That contribution cannot be achieved by verbal incantations and by elegant devices of diplomatic language."[18]

With Lauterpacht and Robinson both absent, Humphrey and Cassin took the lead in fashioning the raw mass of ideas and rights into what we now recognize as the Universal Declaration. As finally published in 1948, the document comprised thirty articles. Cassin's impact earned him world acclaim and a Nobel Peace Prize in 1968. But to Lauterpacht and most other international lawyers, Jewish and otherwise, Cassin was an amateur mandarin, seeking to burnish his reputation as an activist without losing the support of his handlers at the French Foreign Ministry. Lauterpacht continued to criticize the UN plan. When Cassin and company announced in May 1948 that they would issue a Declaration of Rights and postpone the work on the legal covenant, Lauterpacht again professed gloom: "It is clear to me that the Declaration does not carry things further and that in some important respects has put the clock back. We shall have to make a new start." He did so by writing another book that year, *International Law and Human Rights* (published in 1950), that offered a template for what human rights might look like if law came before principles. The book served as the model for the European Covenant on Human Rights, then just beginning to take shape.[19]

Those at the Commission on Human Rights took Lauterpacht's critique seriously, but remained focused on achieving some kind of positive result in the face of deepening ideological rifts. Humphrey protested that Lauterpacht's charges were unfair: "He has no idea whatsoever of the political difficulties involved, nor does he want to know about them." The observation was apt. Lauterpacht shared with Robinson a deep wish that politics and law could be strictly separated into autonomous spheres. Better to pursue human rights region by region than to chase after a faux universalism. But as events would soon make clear, untangling law from politics proved as difficult as partitioning Jews and Arabs.[20]

"The Natural Right of the Jewish People"

In the spring of 1948, as the Universal Declaration inched toward a final draft, Palestine hurtled toward war. Technically, the UN Partition Plan had set a date of August 1, 1948, for the official expiration of the British Mandate and the transfer of power to Jewish and Arab leaders of the two states. Yet tit-for-tat violence flared steadily from November 1947 onward, prompting the fed-up British government to advance the timetable for withdrawal to the middle of May. Both Jewish and Arab leaders launched small-scale military campaigns even as they readied for an all-out conflagration. But while a divided local Palestinian leadership postponed political planning, hoping that a quick rout of the ragtag, outnumbered Jewish forces would lead to the establishment of a single Arab state covering the whole territory, Jewish authorities devoted equal attention to military preparations and to assembling the political institutions necessary to sustain an independent functioning government. Acting prime minister David Ben-Gurion was determined to announce statehood on May 14, the day on which the British Mandate terminated, so as to provide a seamless transition in authority on the Jewish side of the partition line. Doing so required an actual Declaration of Independence. In New York that March, Abba Eban, the Jewish Agency's top man in New York and the husband of Lauterpacht's niece, asked him to draft the document.[21]

Throughout the 1940s Lauterpacht had advised the Zionist movement on various questions about the legal recognition of Jewish claims to statehood, the legality of territorial partition, and related matters. In 1947, he also published a book on the recognition of new states in international law, in which he argued that the existing community of nations had a positive obligation to recognize newly declared states automatically, regardless of politics. Now a chance arrived for him to write the new state into existence. For the Declaration of Independence, Lauterpacht quickly produced two different documents, a six-page "Act of Independence" and a fifteen-page "Declaration on the Assumption of Power by the Provisional Government of the Jewish Republic." In the first, he offered a basic Zionist argument for Jewish statehood in the language of natural law:

> [The] natural right of the Jewish people to national existence has received repeated recognition on the part of the nations of the world. . . . Justice requires that the Jewish people should be enabled, through an independent State in its ancient home, to preserve the life and the culture of the Jewish race, to carry on the torch of its contribution to the spiritual values and to the welfare of mankind, and to provide for the survival and the happiness of the anguished remnants of the most cruel massacre in history.[22]

History had already issued its verdict: Jews deserved a state as a matter of natural right. To be sure, this right was confirmed through the recognition offered by the UN resolution, for "Resolution [181] of the General Assembly is and will remain a great and beneficent act of international distributive justice." Nonetheless, he insisted, the justness and legality of Jewish title to their territorial state did not depend on the political will of other sovereigns.

> The inherent right of the Jewish people to national self-determination through statehood is independent of any express confirmation by an outside authority. . . . The basic legal and moral features which underlie it cannot be affected or altered by changes to the political constellation in the relations of states. . . . [The Jewish people possess the] supreme right of self-defense and self-preservation.

Despite his stated belief that law was made by states, in the "Act of Independence" Lauterpacht asserted that a higher law governed the situation. Moving seamlessly from that bold claim to the larger realm, Lauterpacht asserted that the new Jewish state would bolster the entire project of international law.

> It will be the duty of the Provisional Government . . . to [ensure] that the law of the Jewish State and its international conduct shall be subordinated to the generally recognized rules of the law of nations, that the obligations of the Charter of the UN and of any international treaty or Bill of Rights adopted in pursuance thereof shall form part of the organic law of the Republic; and that the Republic shall adhere permanently and on the sole condition of reciprocity to international instruments conferring compulsory jurisdiction upon the International Court of Justice.

In effect, Lauterpacht promised that in exchange for sovereignty, the Jewish state would become a model of how *all* states should approach the new ideals of human rights.[23]

Eban sent Lauterpacht's texts on to Acting Justice Minister Pinhas Rozenbluth in Tel Aviv. The document arrived on the morning of May 12, just in time for the final rush to the scheduled moment of independence. Yet unbeknownst to the New York group, a team of Jewish Provisional Government attorneys in Tel Aviv had been hard at work on their own draft. In the end, Ben-Gurion shelved Lauterpacht's version in favor of the local text. The final version of the Israeli Declaration issued on May 14 echoed certain features of Lauterpacht's text, including the insistence on "the natural right of the Jewish people to national rebirth in its own country" and a pledge to Arab inhabitants of "full and equal citizenship and due representation." Conspicuously absent, however, was any mention of international law or bills of rights.[24]

There was little time to reconsider. The Israeli Declaration of Independence triggered a quick descent into an all-out regional war between the Jewish state and its Arab population and neighboring states. The Arab forces—consisting of the Syrian, Iraqi, Lebanese, Egyptian, and Jordanian armies; the Palestinian Holy War Army; and the Arab Liberation Army— rushed in from all sides. Fierce fighting continued until June 11, when a UN-brokered truce went into effect. A month later, that truce expired and the war resumed. At that point, in early July, Robinson urgently wrote to Lauterpacht, who was then in the middle of a summer lecture tour across the western United States. The Israeli government now faced a new challenge on the battlefield of law. The Syrians had sought a ruling from the International Court of Justice invalidating the legal basis for the Jewish state's Declaration of Independence. How, asked Robinson, should Israel proceed?[25]

"There is little doubt that the real purpose of the Syrian proposal is an attempt to challenge the entire jurisdiction of the United Nations on the issue of Palestine," Lauterpacht responded, in a confidential legal brief prepared at Robinson's request. "It is an attempt to overthrow a political and legislative decision of the General Assembly." Just as he had voiced faith in the League of Nations mandate over Palestine three decades before, he now expressed confidence in the UN's partition plan as a product of international law. Yet in a break with his own earlier position, he cautioned against proceeding to the International Court for resolution of the dispute. We always wish to empower that court by giving it as much business as possible, Lauterpacht wrote, but such a move in this instance would serve neither the cause of UN nor Jewish statehood, because the Arab-Israeli conflict "lies so conspicuously on the borderline of law and a most intractable problem of politics."[26]

In the end, the Syrian legal challenge led nowhere. Eban used Lauterpacht's brief in a July UN speech, but the legal issue was soon moot. The war resumed after a few weeks. Facts on the ground shifted once more. Still Lauterpacht held on to a copy of his work, carrying the memo back to Cambridge to deposit it in his personal archive. It remained there, untouched and unmentioned, for the next half-century, a small, painful reminder of how difficult it was to elevate law into a neutral juridical science above the grubbier realm of politics. As he now recognized, the Jewish national cause fell precisely on the messy boundary between the two. The partition had failed. Worse still, its erasure had imperiled the lives of hundreds of thousands of Jews across the broader Middle East and a roughly equal number of Palestinian Arabs.[27]

"The Total Destruction of the Jews"

"Acts of violence already perpetrated together with those contemplated, being clearly aimed at the total destruction of the Jews, constitute genocide which, under the resolutions of the General Assembly, is a crime under international law." The January 1948 WJC press release by Perlzweig did not mince words. From Pakistan to Iraq, Egypt to Tunisia, he wrote, the Jews of the Middle East faced the "danger of annihilation." "Murder, mass arrests, imprisonment in concentration camps, confiscation of property, boycott of Jewish goods and business" in each Arab country "followed precisely the Hitlerian-Fascist model of terror and persecution against the Jews." Perlzweig harbored few doubts that Amin al-Husseini, the Grand Mufti of Jerusalem, now in Egypt after fleeing Berlin at war's end, had conspired with the Arab League to transplant Nazi-style racial antisemitism to the Middle East. But what could be done about it?[28]

The events of 1948 revealed both the crying need for an international justice system and the growing gap between ideal and reality. Despite two-and-a half years of drafting and discussion at the Commission on Human Rights, no actual laws yet existed. The Commission was handicapped by its refusal to empower itself to undertake independent investigations. Meanwhile, Perlzweig received daily reports of worsening conditions across the Middle East. In search of a creative solution, he considered various ideas based on the UN Charter itself: an appeal to the UN General Assembly for a new law banning jihad as a threat to international peace and a violation of state sovereignty, or a demand that all member states affirm their obligation to "fulfill the promise of equality . . . without distinction of race, sex, religion, or language." But these ideas felt at once too far-fetched and too modest for the violations at hand. Instead, Perlzweig pinned his hopes on a parallel project making its way through different channels at the UN: the draft Genocide Convention.[29]

Despite the absence of a formal anti-genocide law, the UN General Assembly had issued resolutions in 1946 and 1947 declaring genocide "a crime under international law." Perlzweig and his colleagues had taken the lead in shaping the emerging convention, both in drafting its contents and lobbying on its behalf. This meant putting aside prior differences with Raphael Lemkin to work closely with him to secure the necessary votes. From Nuremberg, Lemkin had made a beeline for the UN, where he pushed forward his idea of a formal convention banning genocide. Though a popular image has persisted of Lemkin as a solitary crusader, in fact he relied extensively on the WJC's support. It was Perlzweig, for instance, who lobbied the Soviet Union to approve the convention, Lemkin having disqualified himself with his vocal anticommunism.[30]

Across the first few months of 1948, Perlzweig deployed all of his diplomatic talents to persuade various country delegations to agree to address the Middle Eastern situation. It was imperative to treat "anti-Jewish persecution and discrimination in the Arab countries as a matter not directly concerned with the fight about Palestine, but as a matter involving the safeguard of human rights." In April he scored a key victory. The UN's Economic and Social Council (ECOSOC) approved a UN Ad Hoc Committee on Genocide. The sole NGO invited to testify was the WJC. But once the session began, Perlzweig found himself strongly opposed by his friend Charles Malik, spokesman for the Arab League and ECOSOC chairman. Where Perlzweig blamed the Arab League for the terrible fate of the Arab and Jewish refugees alike, Malik laid blame exclusively at the feet of the

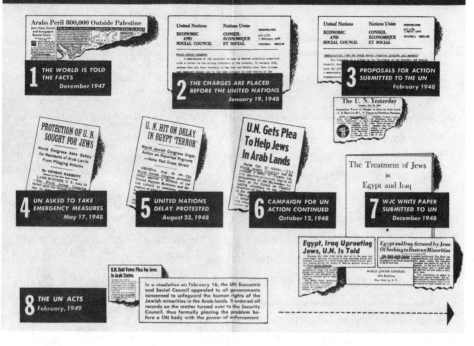

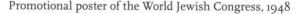

Promotional poster of the World Jewish Congress, 1948

Courtesy of the Jacob Rader Marcus Center of the American Jewish Archives,
Cincinnati, Ohio, americanjewisharchives.org

Zionists. In the eyes of an Arab nationalist, the link between the rise of
political Zionism and the decline of Jewish security was self-evident. So
too was the solution. A draft Arab League model law at the time proposed
to treat all Jews as Zionists and citizens of the illegitimate Jewish state
unless they pledged their anti-Zionism and willingness to serve in an Arab
army. Arab countries would respect Jewish rights "so long as these nationals
remain loyal to their own mother-land, and so long as they scrupulously
refrain from entering into any relations with the Zionists of Palestine." At
the ECOSOC session, Malik heaped public praise on Perlzweig and the
Jewish role in promoting human rights while burying every petition and
document he submitted for consideration.[31]

Malik's duplicity led Robinson and others to dismiss Perlzweig's quest
for a UN remedy for Middle Eastern Jews as a fool's errand. But Perlzweig

was convinced that Malik and others like him could be reasoned with. Surely "some Arabs were against massacre, if even on anti-Zionist grounds. . . . There is at least the possibility that we could so handle the situation as to confine the battle to the frontiers of Palestine," he wrote to Robinson's brother Nehemiah, "and I am sure you will agree that if even one life can be saved, we must explore this possibility." He counseled against succumbing to Jewish "hysteria" regarding the Arabs and Palestine: "We must face every possibility with cold-blooded realism, [rather than] the unreasoning prejudice which sometimes moves us, and which is the death of effective diplomacy."[32]

The same month as the contentious ECOSOC hearing, Perlzweig hopped a plane to North Africa to investigate conditions firsthand. What he saw there convinced him that the dangers to Jewish communities were very real. On his return, he set about working the UN corridors in the hopes of advancing the claim of anti-Jewish genocide to either the General Assembly or the Security Council, where it might find a better reception. To his surprise, he found the Chinese and the Soviets quite agreeable to the proposition. Both pledged in principle to treat the Jewish genocide initiative as a human rights problem, not a political issue. Western powers, by contrast, resisted his entreaties. The Dutch warned him not to push the issue too strongly lest he sink human rights as a whole. British representatives told Perlzweig that the status of Middle Eastern Jews was of a "highly political (not legal) nature." The Americans were hardly much better. "In spite of the fact that Mrs. Roosevelt appears from outside to be an enthusiastic defender of human rights," a WJC colleague complained to Perlzweig, the American delegation is "thoroughly opposed to any extension of human rights." They feared its exploitation by the Russians—and they frequently resisted allowing the WJC to speak.[33]

The Clock Set Back

As Perlzweig lobbied in the halls of the UN into the fall of 1948, drafts of both the Universal Declaration of Human Rights and the Genocide Convention wound through various vetting committees to the General Assembly. A total of 110 separate meetings were held that autumn to debate the final UDHR text. During drafting debates in the General Assembly's Third

Committee that October, the meeting paused to hear a report about the Arab refugees from wartorn Palestine. After a long debate, it was decided not to formally discuss the Arab refugee question. The absurdly slow pace and endless pontification drove even core UN staff members nearly to the point of insanity.[34]

Finally, the matter came to a vote. On December 9, 1948, the General Assembly took up a resolution to draft a Genocide Convention. When ratified, the law would require states to prevent and punish genocide. The motion passed unanimously with no debate. Immediately after the vote, at 8:30 p.m., Malik introduced the next item on the agenda: the Universal Declaration of Human Rights. Speeches began and spilled over onto the next day. The debate, recalled Humphrey, was "long but uninspired." He personally found it hard to listen. Before the final floor vote, Eleanor Roosevelt took the floor to declare:

> This Declaration may well become the international Magna Carta of all men everywhere. We hope its proclamation by the General Assembly will be an event comparable to the proclamation of the Declaration of the Rights of Man by the French people in 1789, the adoption of the Bill of Rights by the people of the United States, and the adoption of comparable declarations at different times in other countries.

Roosevelt's words were stirring. Yet it cost nothing to accede to a nonbinding declaration that postponed dealing with the harder questions of law. Even then, voting reflected consensus without unanimity. Forty-eight nations voted "yes," and none opposed. But there were eight significant abstentions: the six Soviet bloc countries, South Africa, and Saudi Arabia. The Saudi representative, Jameel Baroody, a colorful diplomat who would dominate UN debates on both human rights and Middle Eastern politics for decades to come, denounced the Universal Declaration as a forcible imposition of "Western civilization" on the Islamic world. The ideas of freedom of marriage and freedom of religion, he protested, were colonialist attacks on fourteen centuries of Islamic law. The right to change one's religion, in particular, he found incompatible with Islam—even though the Pakistani representative thought the opposite. Behind his posturing, Baroody feared that human rights would make Saudi Arabia a prime target because of the well-known persistence of slavery in the kingdom.[35]

The very next day, the General Assembly debated the Arab-Israeli conflict. The result was GA Resolution 194, designed to outline principles for a negotiated end to the 1948 war and a resettlement of the Palestinian Arab refugees who had been displaced. That year, roughly 750,000 Arabs had fled Palestine for neighboring countries. Some left to escape the war, many others in panic, fearing massacre by Jews. A smaller number were expelled by Jewish forces. In the end, the circumstances of their departure mattered less than its permanence. Most uprooted Palestinian Arabs thought their exile would last only until the war's end. But they became a new permanent diaspora of stateless refugees.[36]

Article 11 of GA Resolution 194, whose meaning remains contested even to this day, was designed to resolve this crisis by asserting that "refugees wishing to return to their homes and live at peace with their neighbours should be permitted to do so at the earliest practicable date," with compensation for their economic losses. Yet in spite of this focus on the plight of Arab refugees—and with no mention made of Jews displaced from Arab lands—the Arab states unanimously rejected it. Acceptance implied normalization of relations with the Jewish state, something to which the Arab League was ideologically opposed. Even though Egypt, Syria, and Jordan came to control significant portions of historic Palestine—the Gaza Strip, the West Bank, the Golan Heights, and the eastern half of Jerusalem— none of their governments made any move to create the promised Palestinian Arab state. Holding these lands and the human masses in legal limbo, they chose to await the eventual defeat of Israel on the battlefield. It was another sign of the failed partition.[37]

Perlzweig had spent those three December days in Toronto, thousands of miles away from Paris. With the prospects for human rights and Zionism apparently secure, he had decided to leave the World Jewish Congress that fall and return to the pulpit. After ten years of virtually nonstop travel around the world, it was time to settle into a more sedate lifestyle, suitable for a family man with a wife and two young boys. December 10 fell on a Friday, and he delivered a sermon at synagogue that night on the events of the past few days. His remarks were a trademark mixture of lofty idealism and political pragmatism. What had happened in Paris was an "important milestone in the march of human progress," for which Jews should feel justly proud of their contributions and hard sacrifices. The UDHR would establish "an international recognized standard to which all those subject to discrimination could appeal, and it would help to undermine the barbaric concept that persecution was a domestic matter in which humanity was not interested." Yet one disturbing detail had caught his eye. In the aftermath of the vote on the Declaration, there was a second procedural vote directing the Commission on Human Rights to draft a legal treaty to turn the Declaration into real positive law. Canada suddenly switched its vote to oppose such a move out of fear that its French-speaking Quebecois minority might invoke the law in support of their separatist aims. Perlzweig deplored the Canadian vote switching: "The greatness of the conception of a universal Bill of Rights should certainly have been priority over provincial prejudice and technical timidity."[38]

He contrasted Canada's diffidence with the inspiring example of Israel. The proposed constitution of the new Jewish state, "the most advanced and progressive of its kind in the world," he said in another sermon a few weeks later, "will mark a turning point in the history of constitutional law." Perlzweig spoke most proudly of Israel's treatment of the Arab minority, which went beyond its commitment to human rights and bans on hate speech and torture: "It is safe to say that in no country anywhere in the world will the rights of minorities, racial or religious, be so effectively fostered and safeguarded." Whatever happened outside its borders, he believed, Israel would not reciprocate Arab violence by denying rights to its own minority population.[39]

"Only a Tactical Instrument?"

The moment of optimism did not last. The anticipated Israeli constitution never materialized. Nor did Resolution 194 end the Arab-Israeli war. Instead, the two sides fought to a draw. Armistice agreements were signed in 1949 between Israel and various Arab states, but a peace treaty failed to emerge. The crisis of both Jewish and Arab refugees only expanded. Frustrated by the unresolved situation, Perlzweig quit his new job after only a few months and returned to New York. The comfortable confines of the synagogue could not compete with the urgent thrill of the diplomatic chamber. His first order of business back at the UN was to delineate the borderline between diaspora Jewish organizations and the Arab-Israeli conflict. The Jewish Agency and World Jewish Congress brokered a loose division of labor by which the WJC would serve as the "international legal defense agency of Jewish people" in the diaspora, while Israel would focus on immigration and its own governmental affairs. Perlzweig would lead the WJC at the UN as its International Affairs Representative, while Robinson would serve as the Israeli UN Legation's legal counsel.[40]

Next, Perlzweig turned back to the ECOSOC, seeking a formal statement that might help insulate Middle Eastern Jews from the spillover effects of the war in Palestine. For his troubles, he was rewarded on February 16, 1949, with a resolution noting that "the unsettled conditions in Palestine may have affected the observance of fundamental human rights in Palestine and some other areas," and calling on "governments and authorities concerned . . . to safeguard the fundamental human rights of individuals and groups of different faiths." The ECOSOC formally placed the WJC petition in the hands of the UN Security Council in charge of enforcement for this issue. Still, the move did little, and the situation on the ground deteriorated. The governments of Egypt and Iraq began to implement policies designed to expel hundreds of thousands of Jews.[41]

Libya was one of the places where Jews were most endangered. After passing from Italian Fascist hands into British military control after the war, the territories were now preparing for Arab independence. Perlzweig's visit in September 1949 confirmed to him that something must be done. Despite the cries of "Aliyah," he maintained that the only moral and practical solution was a dual approach allowing for protection and selective emigration. The Jews of Libya, he wrote, deserved both "the recognition of the right to emigrate with transfers of property, and the international recognition of safeguarding of human rights of all those who elect to stay." Yet they would get neither without international legal supervision. He flew home to New York determined to once again press the case up the ladder at the UN.[42]

Back at UN headquarters, he found himself blocked at every turn by Western and Arab diplomats disinclined to let him address the General

Assembly. Arab foreign ministers demanded to know his nationality and in which government's name he spoke. Any talk of antisemitism in Libya, they insisted, was only "Zionist agitation." "Israel is denying the natural, legal and human rights of the Arabs to their country which they have inhabited for thousands of years," declared the Iraqi representative. *That* was what the UN must address. When he finally won the right to speak on the floor of the General Assembly, Perlzweig chose his words carefully. In a fiery speech, he denounced not Arab intransigence but Great Power apathy. Despite all the negotiations among the Western leaders about the future of Libya, he declared, there was no evidence that "any thought has been given to the problem of human rights or to the protection of minorities. . . . The Great Powers seem to be concerned only with questions of sovereignty and strategy," while willfully avoiding the plight of minorities: "The question now being asked in these colonies, and not by Jews alone, is whether the Western advocacy of human rights is only a tactical instrument in the 'Cold War.'" There was no question of special pleading, he hastened to add. "The faith of many minorities in the UN will stand or fall with fulfillment or denial of this claim."[43]

Perlzweig's decision to blame Great Power intrigues for the faltering start of postwar human rights was not merely tactical. He was convinced that Cold War politics was the greatest culprit in both the Middle East conflict and the UN human rights drama. He drew encouragement from the fact that the WJC was the first NGO to win official recognition as a UN-affiliated group. That feat and his personal closeness with the UN Secretariat encouraged him to hope the UN might be just the place to pursue a Jewish political philosophy of neutralism. In time the WJC might grow into an important force "bridging the gulf between East and West." Despite plain evidence of the failed partitions of Jewish and Arab Palestine and of law and politics, he remained confident that the Jewish state too could play a role in this process.[44]

"You and I know that it is not impossible for the small nations to defeat a coalition of the Western Powers," he told a colleague at the time. But to do so these countries must be convinced that international jurisdiction is not "a punishment to be suffered under duress," but "a high responsibility to be discharged with pride." An NGO could hardly make the case as well as a fellow sovereign state. Who better to lead this effort than a Jewish country founded on the very ideals of international justice and freedom? The final threat from 1948, however, was that Jews would focus solely on Israel's security at the expense of their historic mission.

> One of the dangers which confronts us externally no less than internally, is that the Messianic passion of the Jewish centuries may seem to have found fulfillment in the establishment of a small Levantine state. I would like to show that the state is not yet what it will be and that we are still at the stage of promise rather than fulfillments. Moreover, the state is not an end but an instrument. Otherwise instead of a great tragic drama moving toward a heroic climax, we should be left with a conception of a mere melodrama ending in bathos.

Even as he experienced firsthand the new political difficulties Israel posed for diaspora Jewish rights-defense, Perlzweig retained his faith in the larger project of Zionist internationalism. The question was whether he was alone in this vision. Would other Jewish rights-defenders, inside and outside of Israel, share his internationalist faith? Or would the exigencies of statehood and the vicissitudes of Cold War politics in the Middle East turn Israel into a fortress of realpolitik?[45]

PART THREE

DIVERGENCE

You have taken a truly humane interest in the work in favour of wounded soldiers, of which I am the founder. . . . At present, sir, I am engaged in another work . . . [that] concerns Palestine, the country made over by God to the glorious people of which you have the honour of being a member. . . . [I seek the] moral and econom-ical re-constitution of the ancient patrimony of the Hebrews . . . whose rights to Palestine are superior to all others.
   —Letter from Jean Henri Dunant, founder of the International
      Committees of the Red Cross, to the editors of the London
      Jewish Chronicle, 1867

The law is distinctly not at its best when it is confronted with such a movement as anti-semitism.
   —Max Radin, "What Can the Law Do about Anti-Semitism," 1944

We shall have to wait, I hope for not too long, and not with the resignation with which we have waited for the Messiah, before the time for a rational discussion begins. . . . Moreover, when the time for discussion comes we shall have to deal not only with moral values and juridical principles but the grim fact of international interests and military power.
   —Letter from Maurice Perlzweig to Julius Stone, June 26, 1967

7

The Limits of Neutrality

ON AUGUST 15, 1951, a proud, relieved Jacob Robinson walked into a dining room full of diplomats at Geneva's famed Vieux-Bois restaurant across the street from the UN headquarters. The group had just completed a marathon conference to draft the UN International Refugee Convention. A month earlier, the law seemed to stand little chance of success, and few countries even bothered to send representatives to the meeting. The *New York Times* reported an embarrassing UN failure in the making. Yet through savvy diplomacy and hard work, Robinson had secured the treaty text. Buoyed by the success, he suggested to the UN staff that they host a luncheon to mark the moment of triumph.

As the delegates filtered in, however, an ugly scene erupted. The Egyptian envoy, Abdel Monein Mustafa Bey, refused to take an open seat next to Robinson. The two men had crossed paths before at the UN, where Bey had served in the Egyptian delegation and discussed Palestinian refugee questions with his Israeli counterparts. Yet he now angrily accused Robinson of staging a Zionist plot on the seating arrangements, even though the places were unassigned. To the great annoyance of the hungry delegates, the mortified UN official in charge began rearranging the seats to accommodate his concerns. Only after an excruciating thirty minutes was the matter finally resolved to the Egyptian diplomat's satisfaction.[1]

Robinson refused to make an issue of this "ridiculous" slight. He often criticized his fellow Jews for their "morbid super-sensitiveness to antisemitism."

Compared to the Holocaust, an infantile public insult amounted to very
little. But something else troubled him about the Egyptian envoy's gauche
disregard for diplomatic protocol. It symbolized the plague of politics at work
at the UN. Both the other diplomats' acquiescence and the UN official's
feckless response testified to the organization's susceptibility to cynical exploitation. "Neither in letter, nor in spirit, nor in substance is the United
Nations what it was supposed to become at the San Francisco Conference,"
he would soon observe. From a "community of purpose," the organization
had become "a battle-ground of particular interests" where the rule of law
is sacrificed "on the altar of political expediency."[2]

Given this disappointing reality, what was to be done about human rights?
From 1948 onward, Robinson counseled Israel to take a cautious, selective
approach. Deft Jewish diplomacy might still salvage some valuable ideas
for international law where blind fealty to the UN human rights program
would not. Every engagement had to be carefully weighed against political
realities. This strategic hedging was the beginning of a long pattern of Israeli human rights diplomacy that alternated bold creativity with defiant
unilateralism. It also triggered an immediate debate in 1950 between Robinson and Lauterpacht over a crucial question. Just how much risk and responsibility should a Jewish state shoulder in promoting human rights at
the UN?

The answer to that question depended on many factors, ranging from the
Palestinian refugee question to the shaky Arab-Israeli armistice to the abor-
tive Israeli constitution. Most of all, however, it depended on the nascent
geopolitics of the Cold War. The first internal Jewish debate over Israeli and
human rights took place in the fluid moment before Israel and its Arab
enemies had firmly settled into their respective Western and Communist
camps. As Israel hovered uncertainly between the two sides, Robinson was
one of many Israeli diplomats who courted African and Asian countries to
win Israel a place in the emerging Non-Aligned Movement. Perhaps, he
reasoned, there was just enough space outside the Cold War and inside the
Third World for a scrappy new state to maneuver its way into diplomatic
neutrality.

Given the febrile atmosphere of postwar American anti-Communism,
nonalignment was not an option for American Jewish activists after 1948.

Yet in his own way Blaustein pursued a different version of Jewish neutralism. Throughout the first half of the decade he shuttled between Egypt and Israel, and between the White House and the State Department, as a self-appointed mediator in the Arab-Israeli conflict. In his mind, a larger enemy threatened Israel, the Arabs, and the United States alike: Soviet totalitarianism. Muscular Cold War liberalism was the only way to defeat Soviet Communism, and the best weapon in liberty's arsenal was human rights. This was the message he brought to Truman, then Eisenhower, and to Israel and the Arab states.

"Don't beat me and don't lick me," says the Yiddish proverb (*Shlog mikh nit, un lek mikh nit*). Political neutrality was an old Jewish dream revived and reinvented for the new era of Israeli sovereignty. Theodor Herzl imagined a Jewish Switzerland on the shores of the Mediterranean. Both Blaustein and Robinson epitomized modern-day versions of this reverie. Yet each was destined to suffer a piercing series of wake-up calls in the first decade of Jewish statehood and the Universal Declaration of Human Rights. The first alarm bell rang in 1953, when the incoming Republican Eisenhower administration flatly rejected Blaustein's views on human rights. In 1954 came a shocking Egyptian antisemitic show trial that exposed the brutal underbelly of Middle Eastern politics and the disappointing limits of human rights. The Suez War of 1956 delivered the final rude awakening. That brief, explosive episode crystallized the geopolitical realignment at work in the Middle East. Israel fell into the Western camp, while Egypt found a new benefactor in the Soviet Union. It also raised the question of whether human rights as a whole could survive the Cold War.

From Zion Shall Go Forth the Law

In May 1950, Jerusalem played host to a celebration of the Hebrew University's twenty-fifth anniversary. It was a heady but confusing time. Each day, Jordanian snipers shot across the divided city. The university itself had been exiled from its home on Mt. Scopus, now in Jordanian hands, to Terra Sancta, a Catholic seminary in West Jerusalem. The newly opened law school held its classes in the nearby Ratisbonne Monastery, which had only just stopped serving as the refuge for Jewish women and children evacuated from the Gush Etzion kibbutz during the 1948 war. It was into this fraught climate that Lauterpacht arrived as a distinguished foreign guest to deliver two lectures during the official ceremonies.[3]

"I was present twenty-five years ago at the opening ceremony" of this university, Lauterpacht told an audience filled with old friends and colleagues, and now "I can pay my tribute to an inspiring achievement of a quarter of a century." He found it especially gratifying that the law faculty was led by his former comrade, the great international lawyer Natan Feinberg. "What can be more proper," Lauterpacht asked, "than that the discipline of the rule of law among nations should be taught in the City of Prophets who first proclaimed, in resounding language which will stir mankind even after the Federation of the World has become reality, the ideals of international peace and brotherhood among the nations of the earth?" In time, he predicted, the UN would produce a "civitas maximas" or universal society united by law. As heirs to the ancient prophets and lawgivers, modern Israeli lawyers would build the bridge from the distant past to that bright future.[4]

To be sure, he quickly conceded, this was no easy task. The rule of law in world affairs had declined precipitously since the end of World War II. The anarchic depravity of the Nazis had been suppressed only at tremendous cost: "The very part which power played in conquering lawlessness has tended to enthrone power as an end in itself." As evidence, he pointed to the UN Security Council, where the Big Five zealously guarded their super-veto. Making matters worse, the "division of the world into two opposing groups of States" had produced an "ideological cleavage" that threatened to tear humanity apart.[5]

Still, Lauterpacht insisted, there was cause for optimism. The principle of human rights lay at the core of the new international organization. Even with the recent debacle of the UDHR, the member-states of the UN had recognized that the "sovereignty of the individual" was a check on the "unbridled sovereignty of the omnipotent State." Though the development of the legal framework of a covenant still lagged, the human rights idea found concrete expression in one crucial new initiative: the right of petition.[6]

From the first announcement of the Commission on Human Rights, thousands of letters began arriving at the UN building in New York from around the globe. Each one outlined a personal grievance or tale of gross rights violations. The avalanche of mail powerfully testified to the need for an international human rights system. It also raised the question of how to handle these complaints in the absence of any formal laws or procedures. Unfortunately, the answer that appeared was the very opposite of what those letter writers hoped. In the fall of 1947 the Commission enacted the "Self-Denying Rule." Absent a specific legal mandate from the UN members, the state members concluded, the Commission lacked the authority even to publicize the contents of the complaints, let alone investigate them. It could not even divulge the names of the countries from which complaints had been received, for fear of causing political embarrassment or legal controversy. Instead, the letters were read, shelved, and effectively dumped into "the world's largest wastepaper basket." "For once the great powers, and most of the smaller ones seem to be in complete agreement: to do nothing," observed Humphrey bitterly.[7]

By the time of Lauterpacht's Jerusalem lectures, the Commission was getting more than two thousand petitions a month. Perlzweig and Blaustein were among a number of activists, joined by a handful of sympathetic delegates, who insisted that the right of petition was the key to the entire future of human rights. Lauterpacht vigorously concurred. In his second Hebrew University lecture, he made a prediction: "There is no prospect of the fulfillment of the purpose of the Charter in the matter of human rights and freedoms unless an effective right of petition is accepted as being of the essence of the system." Someone would have to exercise moral leadership. But who might convince sovereign states, large and small, of the necessity and virtue of accepting the right of petition? Practically pointing at the lawyers and politicians in attendance, Lauterpacht made plain his preference. It was up to the State of Israel to lead the way in the international arena.[8]

From the Comité des Délégations Juives at Paris in 1919 to the World Jewish Congress's Bernheim Petition in Geneva in 1933, Lauterpacht reminded his listeners, it was Jewish lawyers who created the legal precedent for petition. Now the Jewish state should take that tradition one step further. "Law is primarily the function and the result of the will of States," he explained, and hence the efforts of NGOs and activists would always remain secondary to the actions of governments: "International law is not the product of writings of publicists. It exists effectively to the extent which sovereign States submit to its rule." If Israel would jump first into the sea of human rights law, other states would follow. He closed his second lecture by reiterating his opening image from the first talk: "I have thought it fit that this call should come, at this time, from Jerusalem, the city in which Isaiah proclaimed the message of eternal peace."[9]

After his lecture, one of the first reactions came from an audience member, who remarked within earshot: "What good Hebrew he speaks for a Goy!" The Polish Zionist youth activist was hardly visible inside the staid Cambridge professor. Lauterpacht laughed off the mistake, but in truth he was more the outsider in Israel than he cared to admit. Despite decades of service to Zionism, his idealistic vision of Jewish internationalism was at odds with the tough-minded statecraft being practiced in Israel. That became evident right after his lectures, when he clashed over the right of petition with Robinson and another former Zionist comrade-turned-Israeli official, Shabtai Rosenne, the Foreign Ministry's legal advisor.[10]

While Lauterpacht was visiting Jerusalem, Israel had submitted its response to a UN questionnaire on the future of the human rights program. On Robinson's advice, the Foreign Ministry rejected the idea of an individual right of petition for fear of overwhelming the system with a tsunami of competing claims. "The idea that there will be 2,500,000 potential petitioners is horrifying for the international community, for the UN, for Israel, for world Jewry and above all for the future of Human Rights," Robinson wrote to Rosenne. A better design was necessary. Upset by the news of Israel's position, Lauterpacht wrote Rosenne in protest:

> Israel's answers are likely dictated by the special circumstances of Israel and its own problems of minorities. For that reason I must not be critical of it, although I regret that that method of reproach should have become necessary. If these special circumstances did not exist—I do not know to what extent they do in fact exist—I would not consider your contribution as either helpful or progressive. The right of petition by individuals is, in my view, of the essence of an international protection of human rights. . . . I would have preferred the Israeli approach to the subject to be more in accordance with Jewish ideals and with Jewish experience.[11]

Rosenne relayed the contents of the letter to Robinson, who bristled at the rebuke. Lauterpacht might survey the UN from the Cantabrigian heights of academic detachment, but he ignored the very basic fact that Israel was in the "negligible liberal minority" in the world on human rights. The Middle East was full of antidemocratic regimes, many of which wanted to wipe out the Jews along with their "Jewish ideals." Israel had no reason to be "ashamed" of its cautious position on the right of petition, Robinson answered. Idealism was no excuse for naiveté. Surely Jewish history taught that lesson as well.[12]

Rosenne followed Robinson's tack in his reply to Lauterpacht: "I would have thought given the problems of the UN in 1950 this was a smart move and consistent with Jewish ideals and experience." Then he added a telling comment:

> On this vital matter which is of direct concern to Jewry as a whole, we felt that it would be a mistake to tie the implementation of the human rights provisions too closely to the UN chariot. On the contrary, we regard human rights as something so fundamental to the international order that proposals for their implementation should be framed in such a way that they could exist independently of the continued existence of the UN.[13]

This rejoinder offered a clue to an alternative Israeli human rights vision already emerging shortly after 1948. International law was a given. So too was the Israeli commitment to international human rights. But perhaps there were better ways to realize these ideals in law, separate or apart from the problematic developments at the UN.

The rift with Lauterpacht soon healed. Before long Robinson was sending Purim gifts and showing up for visits to the Lauterpacht family home in Cambridge. As it turned out, he needed his old friend's help. In 1951 Robinson was asked by the Israeli government to draft the nearly one billion dollar war reparations agreement with West Germany. He went on to help lead the bilateral negotiations on the deal. From behind the scenes, Lauterpacht discretely supplied advice on the finer points of legal strategy. Given this easy collaboration, what, then, separated the two men? On its face, the brief 1950 contretemps reflected the divergent paths of two veteran

Jewish activists, one a diaspora international lawyer of prominence and the other a legal diplomat working in service of a sovereign Jewish state. Yet the debate was not actually a clash between diasporic idealism and Zionist realpolitik. Like many British Jews of his day, Lauterpacht deeply identified with Israel, routinely vacationed there, and even planned to make aliyah in his retirement. Natan Feinberg recalled an incident in Cambridge when Lauterpacht refused to shake hands with a Polish Jewish émigré who had converted to Christianity. Such an act, he told Feinberg, was a betrayal of the Jewish people. And while Robinson devoted the second half of his career to Israeli legal diplomacy, he never moved permanently to Israel nor took out Israeli citizenship. However much he worked on Israel's behalf, his life remained anchored in New York. It was thus not Zionism that divided the two men.[14]

Where Lauterpacht and Robinson differed was in their views on the relationship between law and politics. Lauterpacht still fervently wished to see law remain insulated from politics. Without some politics, of course, there could be no law or human rights—but *too* much politics could undermine the entire enterprise. When Roger Baldwin, founder of the American Civil Liberties Union, invited Lauterpacht in 1951 to serve on the board of the International League for the Rights of Man, he politely declined: "I have made it a rule not to be associated formally with political movements, however praiseworthy and lofty." A few years later, when the Israeli state archivist uncovered documents about his legal work on behalf of Zionism in the 1940s, Lauterpacht wrote to Rosenne, begging him to help bury the documents "among secret files and to forget all about it."[15]

Robinson saw such a response as an evasion and a luxury that an Israeli diplomat could ill afford. On a deeper level, it was also an unnecessary overreaction. If states made law, then national interest could hardly be ignored. Nor should it be. By definition, human rights represented a moral *and* a political matter. A young state poor in geography but rich in legal experience must approach the UN in the spirit of strategic pragmatism. For that reason, Robinson advised his Foreign Ministry colleagues in the early 1950s not to waste time and effort seeking membership in the Commission on Human Rights or a sizable role in drafting the human rights covenants. Better to seek out only those projects that could serve their values and interests at the same time. This is precisely what Robinson proceeded to do throughout the first half of the decade through his involvement in three key projects: the Genocide Convention, the International Refugee Convention, and the International Criminal Court.

The Elusive Balance

Lauterpacht was not the only voice urging Israel to set a global example on human rights in the early 1950s. Senior officials from the UN Secretariat repeatedly requested that Israel take the lead in championing various human rights treaties. Robinson was the first point of contact for these discussions, and in each case he was receptive but wary. Regarding the Genocide Convention, he told colleagues that Israel could hardly delay

Jacob Robinson signing the International Refugee Convention
on behalf of Israel in 1954

United Nations Photo Library

signing a Convention "inspired primarily by the mass slaughter of European Jewry." Yet the text of the law was so vague and broad that it might easily be used "to drag us into the Court" over unfavorable treatment of Israel's sizable Arab minority. Why should we be the guinea pig for a law whose "practical value is nil?" A preemptive law to stop genocide without an enforcement mechanism was unlikely to prevent further atrocities. He reluctantly concluded Israel should sign it, yet found the widespread "enthusiasm" for the law incomprehensible.[16]

Robinson felt very differently about the 1951 International Refugee Convention. Proud of his role as one of its chief architects, he saw the law as a moral imperative for Israel and a useful tool to protect vulnerable Jews around the world. When other colleagues at the Ministry of Foreign Affairs hesitated to sign the completed convention, worried that it might be used on behalf of Palestinian Arab refugees, Robinson pushed back. The Arab refugee question was not a legal problem, but a political question, he told Foreign Minister Moshe Sharett in 1951. It had resulted from the failure of Arab states to follow the UN partition plan and create an Arab state on their allocated portion of partitioned Palestine. Eventually, the Palestinian Arab refugees would be resettled elsewhere (the idea of their return to Israel was something even he was not willing to entertain). Israel's remaining ethical (but not legal) responsibility for uprooted Arabs could be discharged via a compensation fund. Assuming this settlement brought peace with its neighbors, he speculated, Israel might even one day become "a country of refuge for various types of religious, racial, and political refugees from this troubled area."[17]

Not everyone in Tel Aviv or New York agreed with this rosy scenario. For a full three years, Robinson lobbied his superiors at the Foreign Ministry, even as UN officials anxiously pressed him for Israel's commitment. Only in 1954 did he succeed in securing the official Israeli signature on the convention, after stressing both that "there are still many Jews in the world requiring this protection" and that the Jewish state's "moral" reputation was on the line.[18]

The time and trouble it took Robinson to steer the Refugee Convention into law showed just how narrow a bridge he walked in the 1950s. In the face of ambivalence from his superiors, skepticism from his diaspora colleagues, pressure from UN officials, and hostility from Arab diplomats, he struggled mightily to balance idealism with realism. What gave him confidence and energy was the actual experience of legal diplomacy at the UN conferences in Geneva and New York. As he sat around the table with fellow international lawyers and UN officials, many of whom he had known since before the war, he found a reassuring, invigorating momentum in the work of drafting treaties. History was moving forward, and law with it.

So too was the practice of diplomacy. Times had changed, he told an audience of international lawyers at The Hague. Diplomacy used to be all about deceit and propaganda. As the wags had it, "Diplomacy is the art of making your counterpart believe you do not realize that he wants to deceive you." Now, however, the ancient art of courtly obfuscation had been replaced by a new model: "the quiet diplomacy of the smoke-filled room." While politicians postured in "public meetings with their loudspeakers and microphones, artificial light and air," professional diplomats gathered "in the private meetings in the lobbies, lounges, and restaurants in order to work out more acceptable and sometimes innocuous compromises."[19]

This conviction impelled Robinson to devote much of his time in the early 1950s to another project, the ill-fated attempt to create an International Criminal Court. The idea had emerged in earlier discussions about the UN human rights program. The existing International Court of Justice could only adjudicate claims between states and had no power to hear petitions from individual victims or censure perpetrators for human rights violations. Advocates believed that a global court with such powers would bolster the fortunes of the new UN human rights system, adding an authoritative legal body to backstop the system. Here again, Robinson acknowledged Israel's dilemma. An International Criminal Court represented an obvious challenge for a young state "without peace with any of its neighbors and burdened by such problems as an uneasy armistice, Arab refugees, and the unsettled question of Jerusalem." In the end, however, he insisted that the benefits outweighed the risks. The more Israel took a hand in crafting this legal institution, the better the odds that a responsible instrument of justice would emerge. By leading the UN effort, Israel could ensure that "nothing in the new statute could be used later by the enemies of Nuremberg."[20]

Unlike the Genocide and Refugee Conventions, the International Criminal Court went nowhere. The reasons had little to do with Arab intransigence or Israeli vacillation, however. None of the Great Powers expressed the slightest willingness to support it. Not even the United States, whose role at Nuremberg had so impressed Robinson, could be persuaded to submit its sovereign power to such a court's authority. No amount of dexterous Israeli diplomacy could alter the calculus of American interest in the Cold War. That would have to come from elsewhere. Ironically, the best hope for changing the United States' stance on human rights—and building an American-Israeli strategic alliance—emerged in the form of one of Robinson's old political rivals. After a decade spent fighting Zionism, the leader of the AJC transformed overnight into Israel's best American friend.

"Freedom's War"

"You and Averill Harriman are the only two persons of large wealth whom I know to be sound and sensible," President Truman told Jacob Blaustein in 1952 during one of their frequent White House chats. After their first encounter at the end of World War II, Truman had quickly warmed to Blaustein as more than a large donor. The modest businessman proved a trusted advisor and discreet, loyal intercessor in a range of affairs—energy, the Middle East, and the UN. Best of all, he asked for nothing in return. Truman repeatedly offered Blaustein jobs in his administration, but each time, Blaustein declined. Divesting his assets would be impossible, and more importantly, he harbored no appetite for politics. I only want "to be useful in getting across to the President from time to time the views of industry and of certain groups, like the Jewish group, and getting industry and these groups to see the President's point of view," he told Truman.[21]

Blaustein's pitch to Truman reflected one of the oldest principles of Jewish political philosophy. In an uncertain, dangerous world, stirring ideals and broad alliances might prove attractive to a small minority living in diaspora, but it was always safest for Jews to stick closest to the highest authority in the land. The best way to do so was to disavow any self-interest and pledge absolute loyalty to the monarch. Of course, that strategy had emerged at a time when neither a Jewish state nor the UN existed. What would the vertical alliance look like now, in the era of a sovereign Israel and international human rights?[22]

Blaustein had long recoiled from what he called Zionism's message of "political world Jewish nationalism" because he feared it could politicize the identities of diaspora Jews. In 1948, however, as Zionism reached its goal of a conventional nation-state, he began to consider the possibility that Jewish sovereignty might actually neutralize the danger of dual loyalty. At a January AJC board meeting, he told his colleagues that the new Jewish state would mark the end of diaspora Zionism. "The former divisions" among American Jews "into Zionists, non-Zionists and anti-Zionists" were bound to disappear, and in their place would arise "a non-political agency with activities limited to securing material and moral support for the newly created state." All American Jews—Zionist and non-Zionist—could now support and advocate for Israel on "spiritual and humanitarian" grounds rather than national-political ones.[23]

Convinced by his own analysis, Blaustein moved quickly to position himself ahead of veteran Zionists as America's chief Israel booster. In March 1949 he toured the new country, ignoring both live border skirmishes and a painfully debilitating back condition to make the trip. On his return, he delivered a national radio address in which he compared Israel to the United States. "Like America" in 1776, Blaustein told the NBC network audience, Israel was a young democracy fighting for its freedom and a "humanitarian haven for the persecuted and the oppressed." He went on to describe the stirring sights he had seen during his trip: colorfully dressed Yemenite Jews arriving in airplanes, reminding him of biblical prophesies that Jews would return home "on wings of eagles"; gaunt Holocaust survivors overcome by emotion as their ships reached Haifa harbor; and brave farmers at Kibbutz Negba in the Negev Desert who had just "miraculously" repelled a large Egyptian tank attack with light weapons and limited ammunition: "All the while the battle raged, they also managed to tend their orange groves, [and] protected them as they protected life."[24]

In Washington, Blaustein took the image of those fighting farmers directly into his pursuit of foreign aid for Israel. In the fall of 1949, Great Britain agreed to an arms deal with the Arab states to repair its reputation after acquiescing to the Palestine partition. The British pointedly refused to provide the same military aid to Israel. Blaustein now worried Israel might seek aid from the Soviets, who had provided arms indirectly via Czechoslovakia in 1948.

At the time, Israel remained officially nonaligned. Two schools of thought prevailed in its foreign policy. Prime Minister Ben-Gurion prized the ideal of an independent, sovereign Jewish state as master of its own fate, but saw Israel's destiny as inevitably linked to the West. Foreign Minister Moshe Sharett favored a conscious effort to cultivate a permanent neutral position in between the East and West. Following Sharett's lead, Robinson went so far as to identify Israel as "an Asiatic country" in UN meetings and pursue overtures to India, Pakistan, and other members of the Afro-Asian bloc of countries. Blaustein, by contrast, thought it a dangerous folly to imagine that the Jewish state would remain "permanently neutral like Switzerland." Its future lay exclusively with the West, he told both Ben-Gurion and Truman. The country's socialistic elements notwithstanding, Israel was clearly destined to join in the free world's struggle against Communism. Ben-Gurion grudgingly acknowledged the point. Truman readily agreed with Blaustein, telling him in one conversation that "a Jew cannot live up to the tenets of his religion and be a Communist. They are incompatible."[25]

If international neutrality was impossible for Israel, however, it was an imperative for American Jews. Blaustein made a point of telling Truman in every meeting that he spoke on Israel's behalf not as a Zionist or an anti-Zionist, but as the head of "a non-Zionist organization with an objective but sympathetic approach to Israel." It was from that vantage point, he stressed, that he advocated U.S. military aid to Israel. Peace remained the ultimate goal for the Middle East, yet if the United States did not support Israel with weaponry, it would jeopardize the young state's security and create a regional imbalance that would guarantee war. This would put at risk a country that was undoubtedly "the best friend America ever had in the Middle East."[26]

Blaustein's lobbying annoyed many on all ends of the political spectrum. His AJC deputy John Slawson complained that he had become Israel's top cheerleader while neglecting the rest of American Jewish life. Perlzweig registered the shared exasperation of Zionist leaders at the sight of Blaustein securing a monopoly on American Jewish access to the White House. It was infuriating to watch as someone who did not even support the basic

David Ben-Gurion and Jacob Blaustein in the early 1950s

MS 400, Personal and Business Papers of Louis and Jacob Blaustein,
Special Collections, Sheridan Libraries, Johns Hopkins University

tenets of Zionism could cultivate a "special relationship" with the Israeli
government. Most of all, Truman's own State Department officials grumbled loudly that Blaustein's constant whispering in Truman's ear risked
distorting U.S. foreign policy in the Middle East. Some sympathized in-
stinctively with the Arab refugees and were distrustful about Jewish ties to
Communism, in both Israel and the United States. Others worried that
the United States might alienate the large roster of Arab-rich oil states by
siding with their enemy. With his oil wealth and expertise, Blaustein pushed
back on these analyses: "The Arab countries need the U.S. interests as

much as the U.S. needs the Arabs' oil. While the Arabs have the oil under-
ground, the Americans have the technique, equipment, world transporation
facilities, markets and dollars." Yet Blaustein's oilman expertise carried
only limited clout. He struck out on securing military aid in 1949. Undeterred, he switched to another track, asking Truman to approve a $100
million development loan to Israel via the U.S. Export-Import Bank, which
the president did the same year.[27]

Few were aware at the time that requesting development aid was not his
idea, but the Israeli government's. Blaustein and Ben-Gurion often clashed
publicly over the latter's provocative calls for young American Jews to leave
exile and return home. Blaustein found Israeli rhetoric endlessly irritating,
but he also saw the deeper ties that linked the two communities. So too did
the Israelis. Privately, the Israeli prime minister and his top diplomats
Sharett and Abba Eban relied heavily on Blaustein's entrée to the White
House. They understood that, as a non-Zionist, he was the perfect messenger for their aid requests, especially because he agreed with the basic Israeli
narrative of the Arab-Israeli conflict. When State Department officials caught
wind of the $100 million Export-Import loan deal, they threatened to with-
hold the money unless Israel agreed to accept back in 200,000 Arab refugees. In their eyes, this action would go far toward conciliating the Arab
states and might even lead to a lasting peace. Blaustein countered by offering a partial repatriation. "It would be unrealistic to expect the young state to
repatriate all of them," he told Truman, "especially since it was Arab aggression that had put them into their present plight." In the end, the aid package
was approved without mention of the refugees, to the annoyance of State
Department officials who muttered darkly about Blaustein's meddling.[28]

Whatever the Arabists at Foggy Bottom might say, Blaustein viewed
himself as an honest broker more than willing to challenge all sides. Starting in 1950, he began trekking to Jerusalem every few years to seek a public statement from Ben-Gurion clarifying the Israel-diaspora relationship
and disavowing any Israeli claims to speak on behalf of world Jewry. He
positioned himself as an unofficial go-between for Israel, the Arab states,
and the Truman administration, a role happily accepted by all sides. In
the fall of 1950 he tried to arrange a meeting in Washington between State
Department officials, Eban, and the Egyptian foreign minister. He made

similar efforts over the next several years, always with the approval of the Israelis, who viewed him as a useful backdoor channel to both the State Department and Arab diplomats. Each time he would begin the conversation with his Arab interlocutors by explaining himself to be "neither a Zionist nor an anti-Zionist, but a non-Zionist."[29]

In Blaustein's estimation, the pathway to peace lay in the recognition that America, Israel, and the Arabs all faced a common larger enemy. "The dominant problem in the world today is totalitarianism," he repeated again and again. "The totalitarianism of the Communists . . . has replaced the totalitarianism of the Nazis. If there is any substantial difference between these two tyrannies, we in the AJC have been unable to detect it." It was but a short step from this conclusion to a view of human rights as a weapon in "freedom's war."[30]

This conviction led Blaustein into a vocal role in American life as a prominent advocate for international human rights. As in the Wilsonian era, liberal internationalism represented an answer to the ominous spread of Communism. But he embarked on this advocacy effort just as a new Republican administration in Washington declared human rights a threat to American foreign policy. This would force on Blaustein a pair of hard questions. Was he willing to break with this own government in defense of international human rights? And how would his doing so affect Israeli-American relations—and American Jews?

The Pink Paper

In May 1948, the new president of the American Bar Association (ABA), Seattle lawyer Frank Holman, came to Boston to slay the dragon of human rights. You might think the Genocide Convention is a benign and well-intentioned law, he told three hundred of the city's leading lawyers in a speech at the Copley Plaza Hotel. But imagine the following scenario: "What if you had an auto accident and seriously injured someone of another race?" Under the Genocide Convention, this accident might count as attempted murder of a racial minority, he argued speciously. Charged with genocide, you could be dragged out of the United States to face trial in an international court meeting in some foreign country without any access to the constitutional protections Americans possessed at home.

It was plain as day to Holman that the new international human rights laws threatened American citizens. Why, then, had all the Boston lawyers in attendance been seduced by this "fraudulent instrument"? He thought he knew the answer. "Many were Jews who had been propagandized into believing that the Genocide Convention was a great new charter of human freedom to prevent any further persecution of Jews anywhere in the world," he wrote in his memoirs. Do not be fooled, he warned them, the UDHR is actually a dangerous manifesto on "pink paper" that would "promote state socialism, if not communism, throughout the world." American participation in the UN's human rights treaties would not only hand the Soviets an easy propaganda win but also usher in "a dangerous, far-reaching and revolutionary change in the process of [our own] constitutional government."[31]

Holman's campaign was part of a conservative backlash against human rights among American lawyers and politicians after 1948. At times this rhetoric blurred the line between hysterical anti-Communism and anti-semitism. Blaustein responded forcefully. In 1950, the AJC wrote its membership, urging the lawyers among them to resist Holman's campaign at the annual ABA meeting. That same year he went before Congress to testify in favor of U.S. ratification of the Genocide Convention. Determined to win the battle of public opinion, the AJC turned extensively to television and radio, producing a number of cartoons, documentaries, and promotional spots that aired nationally. Many of these were done in partnership with other liberal religious and civic organizations, among them the Association of Americans for the United Nations, for which Blaustein served as a main donor. To ensure the AJC's access to the NGO community at the UN, he also had the AJC partner with its British and French sister organizations, the Anglo-Jewish Association and the Alliance Israélite Universelle, to form an international coalition, the Consultative Council of Jewish Organizations.[32]

Blaustein's best ally in all of this early 1950s activism was Eleanor Roosevelt. The two shared a warm working relationship dating back to the middle of the previous decade. After 1948 Blaustein fed the former First Lady a steady stream of proposals for her consideration as American delegate to the UN and chairperson of the Commission on Human Rights. But Roosevelt found herself continuously hamstrung by her State Department handlers, who feared that an unfettered UN human rights program would get in the way of Washington's Cold War policies. When Blaustein raised the issue of the right of petition in 1950, for instance, he was curtly shut down by State Department legal advisor James Simsarian. Blaustein and his colleagues hoped that Simsarian, as an Armenian American, would support a right of petition, but he firmly explained to them that moral considerations could not trump the politics of "East-West conflict." While the United States might eventually sign a human rights covenant, he told them, the Soviets most likely would not. A right of petition, therefore, would allow the Soviets to flood the Commission's inbox with politically motivated complaints at no cost to themselves.[33]

The situation only worsened in 1951. That July, Senator John Bricker of Ohio, a conservative Republican who had been Governor Thomas Dewey's 1944 running mate, called for a constitutional amendment to restrict American treaty-making. Alarmed about Communist infiltration at the UN, Bricker wished to shut down American participation in UN human rights treaties by stripping the presidency of its diplomatic powers. In the face of this kind of opposition from the United States, as well as from other Great Powers, that fall the UN General Assembly tried to save the human rights covenant by splitting it in half. Henceforth instead of one covenant featuring all the rights declared in the UDHR, there would be two separate covenants. The first would encompass political and civil rights, followed by a second for economic and social rights. The diplomats hoped this piecemeal approach would reduce ideological conflict and encourage more states to support the effort.[34]

Faced with these setbacks, Blaustein doubled down on his faith in executive power. He urged Truman to run for a third term in 1952. "I shudder to think what will happen to the country if the Republicans get in," he told the president. Not only would it jeopardize the gains Truman had "succeeded in making vis-à-vis civil rights and civil liberties" but also "Republican Isolationism with respect to foreign affairs might get us into a war." In the end, Truman declined to run, bowing to political reality. The Korean War had driven down his approval ratings to the low twenties. His replacement on the Democratic ticket, Illinois governor Adlai Stevenson, fared no better. Former general Dwight Eisenhower won the 1952 presidential election in a landslide victory. Soon after he took office in January 1953, his secretary of state, John Foster Dulles, announced that the United States would no longer consider signing any human rights treaty because such treaties might introduce "socialistic conceptions" into the nation while offering no guarantee of the "general acceptance of human rights." Instead, the U.S. government favored a UN approach focused on cultivating a "human rights conscience" throughout the world through educational efforts.[35]

A stubborn optimist, Blaustein quickly switched gears. In February 1953 he organized the "Committee of 100 against Community Inhumanity" to protest Soviet antisemitism and suppression of religious freedom. If it was Communism the Republicans feared, Blaustein was determined to show them that human rights constituted a potent "all-American" weapon against the Reds. He also offered his services to Eisenhower as an oilman and head of a "non-Zionist" organization "with an objective but sympathetic approach to Israel." "I have for a long time maintained close contacts with our State Department; with Prime Minister Sharett, former Prime Minister Ben-Gurion and other Israeli officials," he wrote in a letter to the president, "and have had talks with the Arabs—all, of course within the framework of our American interests."[36]

Blaustein brought the same message to Dulles, along with a special appeal on behalf of his liberal anti-Communist vision of human rights: "Not only would the Covenant not impose upon us alien concepts, but it would strengthen our country by spreading our American ideals of freedom throughout the world, which is a basic objective of American foreign policy." As for the Genocide Convention, there was no reason to oppose it: "Our people could never commit the heinous crime of genocide."[37]

Blaustein's efforts fell on deaf ears. Worse, he found himself staring down a revolt within his own organization. That threat came from Philip Halpern, a Republican judge on the New York State Supreme Court and fellow AJC senior leader, who was tapped to serve as legal advisor to Mrs. Oswald Lord, the wealthy Republican socialite who in 1953 replaced Eleanor Roosevelt as U.S. delegate to the Commission on Human Rights. Described by Perlzweig as "several miles to the right of Secretary Dulles,"

Halpern delivered a series of public speeches that year urging the Jewish community to drop its support of the human rights treaties. Alarmed, Blaustein invited him for an "in the family" conversation at the AJC executive committee meeting in Chicago that October. Halpern used the occasion to attack his fellow Jews for clinging to the "false hopes" of international covenants.

> A premature adoption of a system of paper guarantees in utopian terms would not magically transform a world of police states and slave labor into a world of freedom and good will. Guarantees of human rights cannot be made truly effective in the world of today merely by the fiat of international law—forces are at large in the world today as sinister, as ruthless and as wanton in their disregard of human rights as any that have been known to history.

Americans, warned Halpern, should realize that the rest of world did not see "eye to eye with us as to what human rights are and as to their order of precedence in the scale of virtues." It was time for the AJC to stop pushing for ratification and embrace the Eisenhower-Dulles policy of using "the spotlight of publicity, the mobilization of public opinion, and the force of moral condemnation to deter violations of human rights."[38]

Blaustein was furious at Halpern for hijacking the meeting and then leaking remarks intended as private to the press. But he faced a bigger problem: other senior AJC leaders had rallied to Halpern's position. Among them was Caroline Simon, a trailblazing New York lawyer, famous for her slogan, "There are four things a woman needs to know. She needs to know how to look like a girl, act like a lady, think like a man, and work like a dog." A Republican allied with Nelson Rockefeller, Simon was one of several rising conservative Jewish voices that challenged the easy equation of American Jews with liberal internationalism. Later in 1958 she would join Halpern as a legal advisor to the Eisenhower administration's UN delegation.[39]

Throughout 1954 Blaustein responded aggressively to Halpern's provocations. He decried the shameful "pussyfooting" on international human rights laws at a time when the AJC was fighting for civil rights at home. The group had just filed an amicus brief in the *Brown v. Board of Education* case then being argued before the Supreme Court. Under Blaustein, it had also sponsored much of the psychological research on the harmful effects of segregated classrooms that was presented in court by the NAACP's expert witnesses. One could not fight for legal freedom at home, Blaustein argued, and then abandon the cause abroad. In a January 1954 speech concluding his formal tenure as president of the AJC, he reiterated his stance on liberal internationalism.

> Whatever the reasons may be which induced our Government to abandon its leadership in this field, we are convinced that in the long run human rights must and will be implemented. A stable, peaceful society of free men can never be established as long as nations cannot be prevented from robbing whole groups of political rights, civil rights, property, and life itself, on the basis that such monstrous acts are internal affairs immune from interference of any kind.[40]

The spring of 1954 brought him a double validation. The Supreme Court issued its landmark ruling banning "separate, but equal" education, and he won the internal battle within his organization over human rights. The AJC leadership reaffirmed its commitment to Blaustein's position in favor of international human rights law. But the respite proved short-lived. His attention was soon snapped back from domestic politicking to a terrifyingly "monstrous" legal drama erupting in the Middle East.

A Shocking Deception

On July 2, 1954, a bomb exploded in a post office in the Egyptian port city of Alexandria. Ten days later, three more explosions rocked U.S. Information Agency buildings there and in Cairo, as well as a British movie house. The first signs pointed to domestic terror. Colonel Gamal Nasser, who had overthrown the monarchy in a military coup in 1952, faced opposition from an array of groups, including the Muslim Brotherhood and Communist elements. It soon became apparent, however, that the terror campaign was a rogue Israeli spy operation gone awry. Without notifying the new prime minister, Moshe Sharett, Israeli agents had recruited local Egyptian Jews to plant the bombs. They were not intended to injure Egyptians, but to send a clear signal to the Americans and British: a chaotic, unstable Egypt could not be left in Nasser's hands. The Israelis especially feared that a British military withdrawal following the coup would lead to a breakdown in the delicate status quo with its southern neighbor.

The Egyptian authorities quickly identified the Israeli hand in the attacks. But in seeking the culprits they cast an alarmingly wide net. Scores of Egyptian Jews were arrested and charged with treason, espionage, and sabotage punishable by death. The principal intelligence agents had escaped back to Israel, leaving behind a scattering of local Jews who had little if any involvement in the crime. Yet Nasser saw an opportunity to suppress internal dissent and improve his standing by attacking the putative Zionist threat lurking inside the Egyptian Jewish community. Soon, reports of prison torture and forced confessions began to emerge, prompting an international outcry.[41]

The Israelis found themselves in a terrible position. Sharett had initially denied all involvement, only to be forced into an embarrassing volte-face once the truth came out. After it was revealed that Defense Minister Pinhas Lavon had misled him, a massive political scandal erupted that led eventually to both men's resignations. Meanwhile, the accused languished in Egyptian prison with potential death sentences hanging over their heads. In Washington, Eban asked Blaustein to intercede quietly on behalf of the Jewish prisoners. The Eisenhower State Department seconded the idea. Perhaps he could defuse the situation through a personal visit to Cairo.[42]

In October 1954, Blaustein approached Mahmoud Riad, a member of the Egyptian UN delegation and a veteran of Egyptian-Israeli armistice negotiations, to secure a face-to-face audience with Nasser. For security and discretion, the State Department arranged for Blaustein to stay at the U.S. Embassy in Cairo rather than at a hotel. Yet on November 6, while en route to Egypt, he received word that Nasser had changed his mind: there would be no meeting. Aware of Blaustein's stature with the Americans, the Egyptian leader took pains to mollify him. He assured Blaustein that there was nothing to fear. The trial would be fair and any sentences proportional.[43]

Yet once the trial began, disturbing reports emerged of legal irregularities and rights violations. One prisoner was found dead in his cell under suspicious circumstances; another defendant, Marcelle Nino, whom the

Egyptian press nicknamed the "Zionist Ingrid Bergman" for her beauty, attempted suicide after allegedly being tortured. The international press began to speak of the events as an egregious show trial. Increasingly alarmed, in mid-December the Israelis asked Blaustein to go again to Egypt and attend the trial. But the time for quiet diplomacy had passed. Instead, he and his advisors took a different tack: "[We must] consider this whole problem from a human rights rather than a political point of view." Someone else would have to go in his stead.[44]

Blaustein quickly settled on Roger Baldwin, the president of the American Civil Liberties Union and the International League for Human Rights. In addition to his "international prestige as a champion of human rights," Baldwin could claim a neutrality beyond even that of Blaustein, because he was well known in the Middle East as "a fighter against colonialism and is considered by the Arabs as a friend of their cause." Having caught wind of the plan, Perlzweig hastened to make sure his staff also briefed Baldwin so as to coordinate efforts. Baldwin agreed to go provided he could also visit Israel and look into recent political trials of Arabs there.[45]

Baldwin reached Cairo in the first week of January 1955. The trial had ended, but the judges had yet to render their verdict. He met with Nasser and various senior officials, all of whom assured him that justice would be served fairly and humanely. Whatever the outcome, no death penalty would be applied. Their government, after all, was completely committed to human rights. As proof, they pointed to the fact that Egypt had just assumed the chairmanship of the UN's Commission on Human Rights.[46]

Baldwin found troubling signs that government meddling and "vindictive judgment" had plagued the trial. Yet he left Egypt reasonably convinced that justice had been administered impartially. The ideals of international human rights were spreading out across the decolonizing world, or so he thought. It was not until the end of the month, after he had returned home, that he realized how callously he had been deceived. When the verdicts came down, two young defendants with only marginal involvement in the affair were sentenced to death by hanging. The others received long prison sentences. Outraged, Baldwin sent Nasser an open letter, stating, "Your approval of the savage sentences . . . compromises Egypt's role as a champion of human rights in the United Nations." He begged him to reconsider:

"To carry out death sentences would shock world humanitarian opinion."
Privately, Baldwin confessed his despair to Blaustein: "I am both shocked
and heart-broken over the deception to which both I and the U.S. Embassy
were subjected. . . . I gave the Egyptians undue credit for the moderation
they professed."[47]

The announcement of the death penalty verdicts sparked a new round of
outrage in capitals around the world. The French, American, and British
governments registered official complaints with Egypt, followed by appeals
for clemency. The Grand Rabbi of Egypt did the same. All fell on deaf ears.
On January 31, 1955, the two young men were hanged. Sensitive to world
opinion, the Egyptian Embassy in Washington issued a pamphlet that February titled "The Story of the Zionist Espionage in Egypt." "Zionism and
Communism are two distinctive forces with one political objective—world
domination," read the text. "Both powers cooperate secretly and in public
without friction since the power in the end will eventually go to Zionism."
At home in Egypt, the trial marked a turning point in a campaign of persecution that would eventually lead to the forced emigration of nearly the
entire Egyptian Jewish population of 80,000. The decisive factor would be
the intrusion of the Cold War directly into the Middle East.[48]

In the fall of 1955, the Soviets and Egyptians announced a new arms
deal. Now sliding increasingly into the Soviet sphere of influence, Cairo
would no longer issue verbal attacks on Communism. Blaustein urged
Dulles and Eisenhower to respond by lifting the American embargo on
arms to Israel, but they were reluctant to do so for fear of driving Nasser
further into the Soviet fold. Blaustein, feeling the Egyptians had played the
Soviets against the Americans, complained, "It seemed like the Arabs were
shaping U.S. policy." It did not help matters that the White House appointed as the new U.S. ambassador to Egypt a career official, Henry Byroade, who had enraged American Jews in 1954 with a provocative speech
denouncing Zionism and Israel in terms widely viewed as antisemitic. Byroade's clever idea of proving he was no antisemite was to tell Ben-Gurion
that, if the Israelis made peace, "your people are so capable, they'll be
running every bank in the Middle East in 50 years."[49]

Eisenhower sought to placate Blaustein by making him a member of the
U.S. delegation to the 1955 UN General Assembly. It was a shrewd move.

Jacob Blaustein as member
of the U.S. UN delegation, 1955

Blaustein had long dreamt of an official diplomatic role, but by assuming this position, he was forced to toe the U.S. line and tone down his vocal support of human rights. "The pursuit of equality," he conceded in a speech at the fiftieth anniversary AJC celebration banquet at the Waldorf-Astoria Hotel, "is a timeless pursuit, a never-ending endeavor to shape for mankind a happier future." Echoing the Dulles-Eisenhower line on human rights that he had recently fought so hard against, he called for psychological, moral, and political struggle grounded in the "Judeo-Christian heritage." Ten years after hailing legal machinery as the key step forward for human rights, he now blithely asserted, "No mechanisms, no inventions can construct the spirit of the brotherhood of man." The moment instead demanded an urgent effort to defeat Communism and secure a "global victory for democracy."[50]

This neutered message reflected Blaustein's heightened anxiety that Jews would appear to be out of step with American interests. When news broke of his appointment to the UN delegation, the Boston *Jewish Advocate* hailed the "historic" appointment of the first "Jew who lives his Jewishness." This sent a clear signal, the editors wrote, that President Eisenhower "wants to see Israel's sovereignty safeguarded." The truth was that the appointment placed Blaustein in a political bind. With Arab-Israeli tensions steadily increasing after the Cairo trial, he worried about how his own image might affect American attitudes toward Jews. Arab diplomats in Washington lobbied hard to undo his appointment. He grew testy with his senior staff, berating them for not ensuring proper media coverage of his activities. He scoured newspapers to compare coverage of his speeches with those of other Jewish leaders. To many at the AJC, it seemed like an exercise in vanity. In reality, it reflected the frustration of a man who had reached the limits of his neutrality. His Israeli counterpart was about to discover the same limits.[51]

"A Democratic Island in an Autocratic Sea"

Jacob Robinson watched the tragic events in Cairo play out just as he began his first stint as the Israeli delegate to the Commission on Human Rights. The Egyptian episode left him sickened by the world's hypocrisy. Neither UN statements nor Great Power warnings had deterred Nasser. Roger Baldwin had willingly played the fool, Robinson wrote, flying all the way to Cairo only to let himself be "distracted" by Nasser's empty promises—"and what were the results?" When a colleague suggested Israel issue a booklet on human rights in the Arab states to expose "the contradiction between the Arab appearance at the UN and their statements on

human rights and the ugly reality," Robinson dismissed the idea as not
even worth the trouble.

> There is no doubt that they don't honor human rights in Arab countries
> and no doubt that the whole world knows it. Furthermore, mature democ-
> racies in this region [acquiesce to] authoritarian regimes with clear knowl-
> edge that these regimes repress human rights. And who in general worries
> today about human rights? It is only necessary to see Egypt chairing the
> Commission on Human Rights in order to be convinced that in the whole
> business at the UN they lie and deceive thoroughly.[52]

It was time to face the facts, Robinson argued. Israel was simply "a
democratic island in an autocratic sea." Looking across the Middle East,

> we find at this moment, in addition to the two despotic monarchies, one
> military dictatorship, one monarchy with a strong tendency toward mili-
> tary rule (Iraq), a second monarchy submerged in a permanent conflict
> between the interest of two elements of the population (Jordan), and, fi-
> nally, a republic (Lebanon) with an uneasy denominational balance and a
> consequent sense of permanent crisis, particularly in its relationship with
> its closest neighbor, Syria, itself in a state of political chaos.

At a UN increasingly dominated by Arab states, human rights were a pipe
dream.[53]

A further blow arrived in April 1955 when several African, Asian, and
Middle Eastern countries convened in Bandung, Indonesia, to mark the
start of the Non-Aligned Movement. Here was precisely the alternative
geopolitical path of neutrality between Soviets and Americans that Robinson had hoped might materialize. Israeli diplomats had lobbied to attend
the conference, but Nasser threatened to boycott the event if the Israelis
were invited. With the convening of the conference, it became official:
there was no space for Israel in the Third World.[54]

While the weeklong Bandung Conference was being held, Robinson received a letter from Yaakov Tzur, the Israeli ambassador to France. He had
been contacted by Daniel Mayer, head of the Foreign Committee of the
French House of Representatives and a friend of Israel, who had convened
a meeting of politicians to discuss a new approach to breaking the international deadlock over human rights. If the UN could not move forward,

Mayer suggested, perhaps it was time to create a new "international organization to protect the individual from persecution and crimes against humanity."[55]

Mayer's idea had come from an op-ed in *Le Monde* published by Eugene Aroneanu, a Romanian Jewish lawyer, who had served as a French legal advisor to the Nuremberg Trials. Since states zealously guarded their sovereignty, a fresh approach should forego law and rely instead on the pressure of world public opinion. A new organization like the Red Cross could act with moral authority outside of politics *and* law. French readers were not particularly excited by the idea, Tzur reported, but it was hard to oppose such an idealistic venture. He asked Robinson, "What should we do in response?"[56]

Robinson was unconvinced: "There are already enough international organizations active for the defense of human rights and the results of their activities are nothing." The issue ran much deeper.

We've never been prepared to deal with the problems of human rights as in the period after the Second World War and there's never been the results like in the meetings in that era. The reasons are two: there is no global consensus but rather at least two or three views, that did not exist twenty years ago. Second, human rights are like a check on the function of authoritative regimes and precisely these authoritarian regimes are not prepared to enroll themselves in organized norms like democratic states.[57]

Robinson's dim view of international law extended even to the International Court of Justice. In 1955, Hersch Lauterpacht replaced his mentor, Lord Arnold McNair, as the British judge on the world court. It was the fulfillment of a lifetime dream. After the humiliation of having his Britishness questioned, Lauterpacht would now become the first Jew to sit on the bench in the British seat alongside the leading lawyers of the world. With all due respect to our friend, Robinson wrote Rosenne, his fellow newly elected judges revealed a disturbing pattern. The Pakistani and Mexican judges were legal amateurs, while the Argentinian was "an ultra-nationalist if not [a] negator of international law." The politics behind these other appointments made plain that "the decline of the Court is in full swing."[58]

As depressing as the world looked to Robinson in 1955, the following year proved worse. In the last week of October 1956, two events took place, half a

Hersch Zvi Lauterpacht (second from right) as a judge on the
International Court of Justice in the mid-1950s

Reproduced with permission of the Estate of Sir Elihu Lauterpacht

world apart, that decisively sealed the postwar realignment of the Cold War
and decolonization. On October 24, Soviet troops rolled into Hungary to
quash a democratic uprising against Communist rule. Five days later,
Israeli forces crossed the Sinai Peninsula and bore down on the Suez Canal.
This action came in response to Nasser's decision to nationalize the water-

way and cut off Israeli access, in violation of the 1949 Egyptian-Israeli Armistice agreement. In a coordinated response, British and French parachute battalions landed soon after, planning to seize the Suez Canal under the pretense of establishing an Anglo-French buffer between Israel and Egypt. In the guise of peacemakers, the two European powers actually hoped to nullify if not topple Nasser. It was what many in the Israeli political establishment wished to see, but the military adventure backfired spectacularly.

These Suez military operations ended in less than a week. Intense political pressure from the United States forced England and France to retreat from their secret gambit. With the Soviets occupying Hungary, Eisenhower was in no mood to allow his Western allies to pursue a similar neocolonial intervention. By the time the diplomatic dust had settled, the Tory government under Prime Minister Anthony Eden had fallen, the French Fourth Republic was on its way to collapse, and the United States and the UN had together confirmed Egypt's sovereignty over the canal. Nasser had secured his power at home and won a new reputation abroad as a key leader in the anticolonial world. Israel was humiliated into a public withdrawal, which Robinson helped to negotiate behind the scenes at the UN. Worse still, Israel still found itself dependent on an ambivalent American government and bracing for what many assumed would be another war with an emboldened Egypt.[59]

Still, the greatest casualty of Suez was the ideal of Jewish neutrality. With Israeli tanks fighting alongside British and French paratroopers against Egyptian soldiers armed with Soviet military equipment, the Arab-Israeli conflict had intersected directly with the Cold War. The events in 1956 marked the final end of Blaustein's dreams of an Arab-Jewish peace founded on a joint alliance with the West against Communism. Lauterpacht's hopes for bold Israeli leadership on the UN human rights front also died in the sands of Sinai. Even Robinson's seasoned diplomatic pragmatism seemed little match for the political thickets now engulfing Israel and international human rights alike. Yet few would have predicted that the next chapter in the story of human rights would actually begin in Suez, when another Jewish lawyer arrived in the Middle East in search of a path beyond the political limits of Jewish neutrality.

8

The Road to the Kingdom

THE 1956 WAR IN SUEZ ENDED so fast that Peter Benenson, *The Spectator's* reporter, never made it into the battle zone. Instead, he found himself, absurdly enough, caught in a different war, next door on the island of Cyprus. The violent three-way standoff there among Greeks, Turks, and British struck the young barrister-turned-war-correspondent as painfully familiar. Cyprus, he wrote, is Palestine all over again, a place where "the fires of ethnic nationalism" and "interracial jealousy" flared dangerously under the heavy hand of a declining empire. Alongside the clear blue waters of the Mediterranean Sea, the rule of law dissolved in a bath of blood. The island, he concluded, was "running down like an unwound gramophone."[1]

Like many British Jews of his generation, Benenson knew Cyprus well for two entirely different reasons: in the final years of the Mandate, the island had served as the site of British detention camps for Jews caught sneaking into Palestine, and since the end of World War II it had blossomed into a popular retirement destination for British pensioners. Now both images were overshadowed by a third, much darker one. In 1955 the EOKA, a Greek ultranationalist group, had launched a terror campaign to expel the British military authorities through indiscriminate violence. British soldiers, British civilians, and ethnic Turks all fell victim to a deadly wave of shootings and bombings. Journalists were picked off in the street. The two weeks of the Suez crisis in November 1956 coincided with the "blackest period in the emergency." "Taken on average one human being is killed every other day in Cyprus," Benenson wrote, "and every day at least one person is wounded."[2]

The British authorities responded with martial law and a "shoot first, talk later" policy. It did little good: 25,000 troops, 5,000 police, and 20,000 emergency detentions failed to subdue a small guerilla force that the British Chief of Staff conceded was "not more than 50 to 100 men." Meanwhile, the RAF continued to parachute battalions into the Sinai even though, thanks to the diplomatic fiction in play, the army spokesman could not name the actual enemy they were fighting. As he sat sweltering in the bar of the Ledra Palace hotel, "Cyprus's equivalent of the ill-fated King David in Jerusalem," Benenson described a situation that had plainly turned absurd:

> There is no more succinct summary of the mixture of Ruritarian farce and Draconian terror prevailing in Cyprus since the first bombers took off for Egypt than the censorship arrangements at the airport. Under a new regulation outgoing travelers have to surrender every single written or printed word in their possession. Classical books, novels, love letters, hotel bills, are all seized by the RAF police. The Archbishop of Canterbury may perhaps get some reassurance about the essentially Christian nature of Sir Anthony Eden's "police action" when he hears that there is a special exemption in favour of the Bible, while a copy of the Sacred Books of the East was seized.[3]

As a child, Benenson had played in the streets of Jerusalem; as a teenager, he quit Eton to rescue Jewish children from Nazi Germany. Now he returned to the Middle East to make sense of a collapsing British Empire, the second Arab-Israeli war in less than a decade, and a stillborn international human rights movement. He harbored no doubt that all these events were connected. The twilight of European empire and the emergence of the Cold War had unleashed violent chaos in the Middle East and beyond. The eerie sense of déjà vu in Cyprus highlighted the futility of relying on law and diplomacy to heal a divided world. A new way forward must be found, and it would begin with a radically new kind of human rights organization: Amnesty International.

"To everything there is a season, and a time for every purpose under the heaven," Benenson wrote years later, quoting Ecclesiastes. "There was only one time when Amnesty could have been born, and that was in the exhilarating, brief springtime in the early Sixties, when after rebuilding the cities we set about reshaping the world." In his frequent retellings, the story began not in Nicosia or Jerusalem but in London. One day in the fall of 1960, as he rode the Tube, just another bourgeois barrister casually thumbing through his newspaper, a foreign news item caught his eye. Two young Portuguese students had been imprisoned for toasting freedom and criticizing the country's dictator. Outraged, he thought first of rushing in person to the Portuguese Embassy to protest. Instead, he dashed off an open letter, which was published in *The Observer* newspaper in May 1961. The "Appeal for Amnesty" called on governments East and West to release eight people unjustly imprisoned around the world for their political ideas. Within months, a global movement had sprung up. Thousands of volunteers across the world embraced the mission of an apolitical letter-writing campaign appealing to foreign governments for legal amnesty for "prisoners of conscience." Human rights would never be the same.[4]

This story of Amnesty's origins is compelling in its pristine moral simplicity, but it is largely a myth. To begin with, Benenson was no ordinary Englishman. He was a study in contradictions: a proud Zionist who sympathized deeply with the Palestinian Arab refugees, a secular Jew who dabbled in Catholic mysticism, a loyal Labour politician who chafed at party labels, and a practicing lawyer disenchanted with the law. In addition, Amnesty owed its origins less to the idealistic springtime of the 1960s than to the wintry deadlock of the late 1950s. In 1958 the tenth anniversary of the Universal Declaration of Human Rights came and went with little prospect of forward progress at the UN. The freedom fighters of the rising Third World showed little interest in civil liberties as compared to the intoxicating force of violent struggle. The intensifying Cold War split the West itself in half, leaving Jewish human rights activists caught in the middle. "What is to be done?" wrote Maurice Perlzweig in 1958 as he reflected on the widespread "frustration and disillusionment" among veteran Jewish rights-defenders. To his surprise, the answer came from his former student.[5]

Before he launched his Amnesty campaign, Benenson tracked down his mentor to seek his advice. Their forgotten reunion forms one piece of the hidden Jewish backstory to the emergence of Amnesty. It is complicated by the fact that Benenson approached his former rabbi as a new convert to Catholicism. His passage out of Judaism and into Christianity was at once a personal journey of spiritual rebirth and a public act of tribal renunciation. The old religion, with its clannish ways and law-centered justice, yielded to an embrace of all humanity via the universal church. Like a latter-day Paul, Benenson rejected law itself as an obstacle to human freedom. Again like Paul, he expressed deep ambivalence about his Jewish roots. These Jewish-Christian underpinnings of Amnesty guaranteed that Jews and Israel would play a special role in the organization's religiously inflected search for universalism.

Amnesty marked a radical new chapter in the history of human rights. Instead of another passel of laws or a clever diplomatic gambit, Benenson proposed a global grassroots movement based only on the power of public opinion. Using the now-familiar tools of modern politics—mass media, celebrity endorsements, public lobbying, even a bit of stunt publicity—he forged a conscious *anti*-politics. From the pulpit of his religion-less church, he preached the gospel of human rights as unalloyed universalism. Most of all, he reinvented human rights activism. Amnesty's army of volunteers would not only free the unjustly imprisoned, one individual at a time; they would also redeem themselves in the process.[6]

Human rights activists before Amnesty spoke exclusively in the language of international justice. They aspired to realize legal rights, whether for individuals or groups. In contrast, Benenson insisted on the primacy of the *human* over that of *rights*. Where law and politics divided humanity into competing claimants, he aimed to unite through religion. "To me the whole purpose of Amnesty," he stressed, "is to re-kindle a fire in the minds of men. It is to give him who feels cut off from God, a sense of belonging to something much greater than himself, of being a small part of the entire human race." Yet uniting humanity proved an even greater challenge than internationalizing law. Over ten years, between 1956 and 1966, as he nurtured Amnesty from a fanciful idea to a global movement, Benenson came face to face with the limits of universalism. Just as his own Jewish past

stubbornly persisted into the new Christian present, the politics of the
Cold War Middle East reappeared at every turn. By the mid-1960s, as war
loomed again between Israel and the Arabs, these political forces even
threatened to consume not only Amnesty but also Benenson's sanity.[7]

A Trial in Cyprus

In early January 1957, Charles Foley, the editor of the *Times of Cyprus,* went
to court to keep his newspaper open. Unable to defeat the Greek nationalists' terror campaign, the British had decided to punish the press. Foley
was charged with and convicted at trial of violating a new law that effectively banned negative coverage of the British counterterrorism operations.
He was no stranger to controversy, having previously run the foreign desk
of the tabloid *Daily Express,* but he returned to his lawyer's hotel deflated
after losing at the trial. There he was unexpectedly accosted in the lobby by
a tall, red-haired man with a thrusting, flat-footed walk. I've just "dropped
in from Syria to see the fun," Benenson cheerfully explained. You've lost,
he said, "Isn't it wonderful? Now you can take it to the Privy Counsel!" An
appeal was sure to succeed. Not to worry, he would take it on himself.[8]

Benenson had followed a long and winding road from Eton to Cyprus.
After spending 1938 and 1939 doing Jewish refugee work in London, he
had taken a quick three-term degree at Balliol College, Oxford, before entering the military in 1940 to work as a code breaker at the famed Bletchley
Park. He spent his war years there alongside the likes of British mathema-
tician Alan Turing and Walter Eytan, the future Israeli diplomat, decoding
German ciphers. In 1941 he met and married Margaret Anderson, a math-
ematician and the Gentile daughter of a British civil servant. They would
go on to have two children. He entered the bar after the war and in 1954
won a city council seat as a Labour Party alderman from the Bethnal Green
area of London, a heavily Jewish neighborhood that had been plagued with
antisemitism during the war. In Bethnal he reconnected with an old Eton
friend, Hallam Tennyson, a BBC radio journalist married to a Jewish woman
Benenson had helped rescue from Germany. In 1953 the two families
moved into a sixteenth-century farmhouse in Hertfordshire, which they
shared for the next four years.[9]

As a practicing lawyer, Benenson's actual career was limited to defense attorney work on minor criminal defense and immigration cases. But what he lacked in domestic courtroom experience, he made up for with his passion for international political trials. Beginning in 1949 he had traveled to Spain, Hungary, Yugoslavia, and the Mediterranean basin observing show trials with a group of Labour Party-affiliated lawyers. He followed the Cairo espionage trial in 1954 and the same year set up the Labour Party and Trade Union fund for political prisoners. By December 1956 Benenson had grown convinced that a Labour Party legal organization was too narrow. So he dreamed up the idea of Justice, "a nonparty, all-party body supported by all lawyers enthusiastic for Civil Liberties" at home and abroad. These lawyers would pledge to work equally in Communist and non-Communist countries and to devote especial attention to "the Rule of Law in the territories for which the British Parliament is directly or ultimately responsible: in particular, to assist in the administration of justice and in the preservation of the fundamental liberties of the individual."[10]

The Justice organization continued to grow over the late 1950s. Eager to extend its reach, Benenson took the further step of affiliating the British organization with the International Commission of Jurists, a like-minded European group based in Geneva. Still, the work of Justice was primarily to observe trials, and Benenson hungered for more. Rather than merely watch, he wanted to act. In Cyprus he found his first opportunity to do so.

Despite his breezy confidence, the January 1957 appeal hearing proved a disaster. Benenson chose the unusual tactic of filing a mandamus order, alleging impropriety on the part of the previous judge. Bucking decorum, he aggressively fired off quotation after quotation from obscure legal precedents. The Chief Justice grew irritated, interrupting the young lawyer every other minute to question his sources. At one point, Benenson shot back with a quip about "whether this was a hearing or an obstacle race," then raced on before the judge could respond. He rested his case by citing Jeremy Bentham: "Publicity is the very soul of justice, the surest of guards against improbity—it keeps the judge himself, while trying, on trial." Not surprisingly, the Chief Justice was not pleased to be thus rebuked. He rejected the appeal and admonished Benenson for rude behavior.[11]

Benenson took the loss in stride. If anything, it emboldened him to think more broadly about the meaning of justice. Judicial impartiality was elusive. Politics constantly intruded into the British colonial courtroom. Worse still, the legal profession itself had become a casualty of the crisis in Cyprus. Following the trial, British authorities arrested several local lawyers on charges of abetting terror. Countercharges surfaced of government torture of suspects in custody. The situation was no better in the newly independent states that had emerged from the collapse of European empires. Benenson's travels around the Middle Eastern region—in Syria, Turkey, Lebanon, and Yemen—only confirmed this sense of justice as everywhere compromised. The more he traveled, the more hypocrisy he found on all sides.[12]

Nor did international law offer a way out. To those who cited UN treaties and the International Court of Justice rulings as a cause of hope, Benenson answered with skepticism. The British government condemned the Soviet invasion of Hungary in 1956 as a violation of international law, he noted in a letter to *The Times* of London, yet the British navy had blatantly violated the political sovereignty of Oman the same year by interfering with its shipping lanes. Her Majesty's Government should stop talking out of both sides of its mouth: "Britain, which gave to the world the concept of rule of law, should be the first to respect it." Selective respect for international law only exposed its abiding weakness. Benenson published his critiques in a series of reports in the British press. Every country he visited received a withering review. Every country, that is, save one. He remained silent on the one Mediterranean country to which he had the deepest personal ties: Israel.[13]

Laboring for Israel

For the Solomon-Benenson clan throughout the 1940s and 1950s, Zionism remained very much a family affair. Peter's mother, Flora Solomon, made it her personal mission to secure British support for the State of Israel. She spent the war years lobbying senior officials in the Churchill government and mentoring rising Labour Party stars such as Frank Pakenham and Richard Crossman. Her clout derived partly from sheer chutzpah, partly from a talent for cultivating high-placed friends. She maintained close personal connections to such prominent Anglo-Jewish families as the Sieffs and the Warburgs. But her influence also stemmed from her social activism. In the late 1930s she embarked on a path-breaking career as the first social welfare advisor at the legendary Marks & Spencer department store. Under her tutelage, the company pioneered progressive policies to accommodate its female workforce, including paid vacations, private staff rest rooms, and maternal benefits. During the war she had earned the national nickname "Lady of the Ladle" and an MBE (Member of the British Empire) for her welfare work, which included the establishment of a national restaurant system to feed the poor. This was one of the projects that led to the creation, in 1948, of the British National Health Service.[14]

That same year, Solomon arrived in Israel just after the first round of fighting ended. She docked at the port in Haifa, disembarking with her own Ford automobile brought from London. She came at the invitation of Labor Minister Golda Meir to help devise welfare policies for the masses of new immigrants and stayed through much of the early 1950s, working on housing and related absorption issues. Activism blended seamlessly with family ties. Both Peter and Flora remained personally close with Vera and Chaim Weizmann, now the first president of Israel, and their son and daughter-in-law, Benjy and Maidie Weizmann. At Solomon's insistence, Weizmann hired as his chef d'affaires her protégé George Weidenfeld, an ambitious young man who had been rescued in the Kindertransport ten years before.[15]

Just about the only political career Flora could not fix was her son's. Benenson tried four times to win a seat in the House of Commons, once from Streatham in South London in 1950 and then from Hitchin (Hertfordshire) in 1951, 1955, and 1959. He was one of several young Jewish Labourites seeking to break into British politics. Like his mother, he was committed to building out the British welfare state in a Fabian model of democratic socialism while remaining staunchly anti-Communist. He was also part of the Labour Party's pro-Israel wing. But he could make no headway against the Conservative-dominated British electoral politics of the 1950s.[16]

It certainly did not help that he displayed a conspicuous lack of interest in the normal conventions of electoral politics. In his 1955 campaign, for instance, Benenson skipped all public campaign events and instead tried to personally visit every possible voter at home. In two weeks, he called on some 4,076 homes and spoke directly to more than three thousand voters. This impressive feat made no difference in his final electoral result. But it did leave him with a strong impression of the average voter's "almost complete lack of interest in current political questions." Even with the growth of television, he observed, postwar Britons seemed to be glumly incurious about national affairs, let alone events abroad. For this he blamed not the public but the political class and their unholy alliance with the media.

> If democracy becomes a whore, then the press will be her pimp. Increasingly today, on both sides of the Atlantic, elected representatives are transferring their allegiance away from the sovereign power to which they have sworn loyalty, to the fickle favours of the Public Opinion Polls. These sinuous curves, crawling over the magnified graph-paper, influence the words and actions of politicians. So long as there are 50.1% of the electors prepared to support their policy, then it matters not to them whether that policy is morally right or wrong, empirically successful or disastrous, historically far-sighted or blind. Their constitutional obligations go by the board, debates in Parliament are brushed off like sticky burrs; what counts is favour of the press or television baron, who alone can manipulate the bends in the graph curve of popularity.[17]

The lesson about the power of public opinion—and its susceptibility to manipulation—would directly inform Benenson's emerging vision of a new kind of human rights activism.[18]

His iconoclasm extended as well to Zionism. Mother and son shared the same politics, but not the same sensibilities. In 1948, she burst into tears at the very sight of an Israeli flag. Meanwhile he deplored the way in which the "patriotic struggle" in Palestine turned progressive-minded Jews into political zealots. When the Suez War began, Peter rushed to the Middle East to cover the crisis as a neutral journalist; Flora flew to New York to attend Golda Meir's UN speech defending Israel's actions. Benenson rejected his mother's "us versus them" mentality regarding the Arab-Israeli conflict. No solution would come from demonizing the Arabs or turning a blind eye to Jewish faults. A balanced approach should recognize culpability on all sides—including the British. There is no question that "the Arabs have a case," he wrote in a March 1957 article, "and until it is properly understood by the world, there is little hope for any permanent settlement of the Arab-Israeli conflict." Yet he criticized those who adopted crudely pro-Arab, anti-Israeli positions. "A burning conviction in the rightness of the Arabs' cause" was no substitute for historical understanding.

> This conflict is not one of numbers; nor does it depend on the statistical balance of armaments between the two sides. Fundamentally, it is a problem of the interrelations of two Semitic peoples, whose history and religions, have been inextricably bound for over 2,000 years. . . . How the fierce suspicions of two peoples with so much common history and ancestry can be allayed is the most intriguing and important problem of the world today—and the lessons to be learned do not only apply to the Middle East.[19]

In a world riven by intractable conflicts, neither law nor politics held much promise in Benenson's eyes as ways to a permanent solution. Men of good will, including his late father, had tried and failed to solve the Middle East question. In the mid-1950s, in search of a different answer, he began to read deeply in Catholic social and mystical thought. One line in an essay by the Christian writer Julia de Beausobre, Russian-born wife of Lewis Namier, stood out to him: "And we may perhaps conclude that the right way to outgrow one's nationality can only be found along the path of sanctity." This remark reminded him of Cyprus and, by extension, Palestine. "There must be a spiritual union transcending national barriers." The path of sanctity, he began to think, would come through a new kind of universal human rights organization: a religious group with no ties to any church, implementing a global justice campaign that dispensed with law as an international movement that transcended politics. The crucial act that brought him one step closer to Amnesty was his conversion to Catholicism in 1958.[20]

The Road to the Kingdom

"Why I find ever greater inspiration in the Catholic Church is because of increasing understanding of St. Francis's mission," Benenson wrote to his

friend Eric Baker, a Quaker academic and Justice colleague, at the beginning of 1960. He had just lost his fourth election race a few months earlier,
a devastating upset in a contest he was expected to win. After falling ill
around the same time with what would eventually be diagnosed as celiac
disease, he retired from the bar and renounced politics. Recuperating at his
vacation house in Lago d'Orta in northern Italy, he turned for inspiration to
his new faith. He had become more and more convinced, he explained to
Baker, that "the quest for an outward and visible Kingdom is mistaken."

> The attempt to construct a just society by altering the external framework
> is, I am sure, doomed to failure. Look on the Socialist Parties the world
> over, ye mighty, and despair. When each citizen is individually on the road
> to the Kingdom, then I believe that there will be a just society on earth with-
> out the need for the intervention of Parliament. And if only a few of our
> leading citizens trod that path, then I believe we would be nearer the goal
> than if 51% of the electors voted for laws designed to promote social jus-
> tice. . . . All this may seem heresy from one, who, as you point out, was re-
> cently a Labour Candidate. But, before you burn me and my works, let me
> say this in defence; I still seek the same ends, but by different methods.[21]

This passage aside, Benenson never wrote about his actual decision to
convert to Christianity. Certainly, he was well aware that throughout Jewish history, converts were typically regarded as opportunists at best, trai-
tors at worst. His own mother termed conversion a force that "crumbled
our nation within a nation at the edges." Yet her attitude was tempered by
family history. Her sister Manya married a Jew, converted to Catholicism
in 1932, but still identified as Jewish. Fira, in contrast, married a Polish
Catholic count, but remained Jewish. Flora herself spoke of her "personal
trinity—Russian soul, Jewish heart, British passport" and allowed that all
three sisters stood "as regards their ancestral heritage, half in and half out.
We puzzled our friends by our complicated characters and conflicting loyalties."[22]

Family precedent aside, the choice of Catholicism was a lonely one. Practicing Catholics in postwar England made up less than 5 percent of the
population (as opposed to 1 percent who were Jewish), and even among his
new Catholic brethren, Benenson cut an unusual profile. From the outset,

he broke with many core Catholic tenets and called for a new "reasoned Christianity" in place of the old "superstitious Christianity." He was skeptical of Jesus's divinity and the power of baptism. Most crucially, he also rejected the ideas of influential neo-Thomist Catholic thinkers like French theologian Jacques Maritain, who saw in human rights advocacy a vehicle for the reassertion of natural law. Benenson scornfully dismissed the traditional Catholic view of natural law as "divinely-inspired ordinances of an immutable character." "The true concept of natural law," he told a group of Catholic lawyers in 1963, finds expression in man's creation of "ever-widening communities. From this it follows that anything which is conducive to the stability and ultimate growth of a community until it encompasses the whole earth is in accordance with natural law."[23]

Benenson's iconoclastic reinterpretation of Catholic theology was not just a novice's ignorance. Nor was it an attempt to fashion a European strain of liberation theology. He rejected Catholic human rights thought out of a deeper antipathy to law itself. "Law was never a subject that intrigued me," he recalled later. "I was a historian by training and now a Labour Party enthusiast by conviction." The postwar mania for international law failed to impress him: "The whole of this outpouring of law" was an artificial system "imposed from above" and "a feature of the fragmentation of the world into mutually exclusive sovereign States." "One day there can and will be a system of World Law," he allowed, "but it cannot exist until there is a world ideology. Catholic lawyers believe that the first task in this direction is in the creation of a single Christian ideology." Until that day, law remained a stumbling block to human freedom: "It has always seemed to me that a humanitarian movement should decide its actions from the heart not from the book of law."[24]

In rejecting law as a sterile set of shackles that cut people off from each other, Benenson resembled no one more than the ancient apostle Saint Paul. History's most famous Jewish convert, Saul of Tarsus left behind his Jewish roots to preach a transcendent vision of Christian universalism. "There is neither Greek nor Jew, male nor female, slave nor free, for you are all one in Christ Jesus," taught Paul in Galatians 3:28. Once humanity came together as Christians (and only Christians) to accept the Kingdom of Heaven through Jesus, true universalism would prevail. The other side of

Paul's theology was an unremitting critique of Judaism as the mirror opposite of Christianity. The former Jew painted a caricature of his previous religion as embodying a slavish, parochial devotion to fossilized law and a clannish particularism that stood in the way of true redemption. This twin legacy of stirring universalism and obsessive anti-Judaism was Paul's contribution to Christian thought. It suggested an animus to his former self paralleling Christianity's intolerance toward its Jewish antecedents.[25]

This dualism passed directly into Benenson's complex Jewish-Christian identity. Yet he proved more ambivalent than hostile toward his Jewish origins. In the 1950s he was involved in both the Jewish Society for Legal Study and the Pax Romana society of Catholic lawyers. Moreover, the two religions remained linked in his mind. In an early Amnesty interfaith liturgical service, he paired Old and New Testament readings so as to segue directly from the Book of Isaiah ("He sent me to proclaim freedom for the captives and release from darkness the prisoners") to the Sermon on the Mount ("You are the light of the world. . . . Let your light shine before others, that they may see your good deeds and glorify your Father in heaven"). The two texts fused in a vision of human rights that nodded to the Jewish past yet culminated in Jesus. The message was clear: "Jewish compassion" deserved respect, yet the world would be redeemed not through Jewish justice but Christian salvation. Beyond merely imitating Jesus's ideal of self-sacrifice, he told Eric Baker, "the good man is he who tries to reach an even higher goal: to be Christ reborn."[26]

More than a few of Benenson's close friends observed that this Christian ethos existed alongside a peculiar attitude toward Jews and Judaism. "I always told Peter," recalled Amnesty co-founder Tom Sargant, that "he should have really been christened 'Paul.'" Yet despite years of debate, Sargant added, "I could never get him to admit that his passion for justice came from his Jewish heritage. . . . So that I found, that was a very strange quirk, that he put it all down to Christianity. . . . He seems to deny that his sense of justice comes from his Jewish heritage. . . . He thinks the salvation of the world is entirely Christianity's role." In his own interviews years later, Benenson displayed a conspicuous aversion to attributing his activism to his Jewish upbringing and downplayed his wartime Jewish rescue work. He had been born Jewish, to be sure, and never denied it. His moral calling, however, emerged solely through the spiritual imprint of Christianity.[27] The best evidence of Benenson's effort to Christianize human rights without completely severing his Jewish roots comes from an episode that he later omitted from his accounts of Amnesty's origins. When he returned from Italy to England in 1960, the first person he sought out for advice on his idea for Amnesty was neither a fellow Catholic nor a Labour colleague. Instead, he tracked down the rabbi who had first inspired him to think about human rights and religion.

A Call from the Past

One day in the fall of 1960, the phone rang in Maurice Perlzweig's room at the Mount Royal Hotel in London. It was a call from one of his Jewish pupils from his days at Eton. The former student wished to meet while Perlzweig was in London to talk about human rights. Perlzweig happily obliged, but he confessed he did not recognize the student's last name. That was because I changed it in the army due to antisemitism, Benenson explained. "Being Solomon was such [a burden] that it was not worth fighting for." Something else, however, was worth the fight. In Cyprus and Turkey, he had seen innocent prisoners tortured while courts looked the other way. The work of international human rights law had devolved into fruitless debate while a million people around the world lay "rotting in prison because their ideas or religion are unacceptable to their government." Now he proposed an "Appeal for Amnesty," a global campaign to free political prisoners all around the world. What did Perlzweig think of his idea?[28]

Whether or not he realized it, Benenson had reached the right man. Perlzweig himself had begun calling publicly for "a new beginning" in human rights. The tenth anniversary of the UDHR had come and gone. It was painfully obvious, he told colleagues, that "the UN has so far failed to fulfill its promise in the field of human rights, and that there is no prospect in sight that it will create protective machinery." Something else had to be done. Any solution would need to begin by avoiding the trap of politics: human rights must not become "a battlefield for the Cold War." As a leader of a transnational Jewish organization less beholden to Israel on the one hand and American Jewish communal life on the other, Perlzweig still carried the torch of Jewish neutralism in the late 1950s. Jewish activists must avoid being exploited by either the Soviets or the West.[29]

Perlzweig was flattered that his former student turned to him for counsel. Benenson's new Catholicism hardly bothered him. As a liberal rabbi who dispensed with Orthodox Jewish law, he took a decidedly tolerant view of conversion both to and from Judaism and was comfortable with the interfaith dialogue at the heart of the postwar ecumenical movement. Catholic internationalism even offered a useful model to Jews for navigating the Cold War. "It is one of my heresies that the Jews do not have a monopoly of all the wisdom and virtue in the world, and certainly in diplomacy, in which we are less than perfect, we can learn from others," Perlzweig advised his WJC colleagues. The Vatican acted with "more flexibility and intelligence than Jews tend to display" in dealing with the Communist world. In light of shared concerns and methods, he wrote in 1960, now might be just the time for a cautious Catholic-Jewish rapprochement. In a series of clandestine visits to Rome, he and WJC president Nahum Goldmann began laying the groundwork for the Jewish-Catholic dialogue that would eventually produce Vatican II and a new era of Catholic-Jewish relations.[30]

Perlzweig easily warmed to Benenson's ecumenical vision of Amnesty as "an impartial organization as regards religion and politics, uniting groups in different countries working towards the same end—the freedom and dignity of the human mind." He liked the idea of a wholly independent organization that would "seek to influence government representatives and international opinion [rather] than artificially . . . manufacture evidence of pseudo-activity for the edification of welfare funds." In later years, he would express delight at the thought "that it was I who planted the seed that ended up in Amnesty International."[31]

Why did Benenson seek out Perlzweig's approval before launching Amnesty? At the time, Perlzweig's World Jewish Congress represented one of the few truly international NGOs in existence. Unlike, say, the International Commission of Jurists, the WJC had an impressively global footprint stretching across not only the Iron Curtain but also Asia, Africa, Latin America, and the Middle East. No doubt Perlzweig's determination to preserve the independence of human rights lest it "be exploited by either side in the Cold War" also appealed greatly to Benenson. Still, there were other organizations he might have consulted. Indeed, to locate Perlzweig, Benenson went through a mutual contact at the venerable British Anti-Slavery Society, which traced its roots to another Christian moral crusade begun by nineteenth-century British abolitionists. Though he left no account of the conversation from his side, it could hardly have been incidental that Benenson chose to seek the blessing of his old Jewish teacher.[32]

On a deeper level, Perlzweig's early mentorship had provided Benenson with something missing from his life in his difficult teenage years following the sudden, tragic death of his father. Perlzweig was a charismatic Jewish male role model and, like Benenson's father, a passionate yet iconoclastic Zionist. Finally, Perlzweig remained a rabbi who could offer what amounted to a personal Jewish *hekhsher*—a kosher seal of approval—on Benenson's ecumenical venture. That very year, Perlzweig spoke publicly in London several times about the need to renew Western religion. "It is one of the appalling aspects of our contemporary civilization that both the Old and the New Testaments are reduced to the status of texts to be read ceremonially but not to be applied to life." *Both* religions could stand to relearn the lesson, Perlzweig said at the time, that (quoting Paul) "in the sight of God there is neither Jew nor Greek." The meeting with Benenson showed the importance of his Jewish ties even at the moment of his incipient universalism. With Perlzweig's rabbinic blessing secured, Benenson spent the next few months preparing for the launch of his new movement to redeem humanity.[33]

Amnesty's Launch

On May 28, 1961, a full-page advertisement appeared in the London *Observer*. Titled "Forgotten Prisoners," it profiled eight political prisoners, one each from Romania, Angola, Czechoslovakia, Greece, Hungary, South Africa, Spain, and the United States. The text read:

> On both sides of the Iron Curtain, 1000s of men and women are being held in gaol without trial because their political or religious views differ from those of their governments. Peter Benenson, a London lawyer, conceived the idea of a world campaign, Appeal for Amnesty, 1961, to urge

governments to release these people or at least give them a fair trial. The campaign opens today, and "The Observer" is glad to offer it a platform.[34]

Benenson had reached out to David Astor, the newspaper's publisher, with the help of Eric Baker and of another colleague from Justice, the prominent Jewish lawyer Louis Blom-Cooper. The prisoners had been carefully chosen to represent East, West, and the rest of the world. They included the Romanian philosopher Constantin Noica, Archbishop Josef Beran of Prague, the African American pastor Ashton Jones of Louisiana, and Angolan poet Agostino Neto. The crucial defining feature of the list was that none had committed violence. All were dubbed "prisoners of conscience," individuals imprisoned solely for expressing opinions, who did not "advocate or condone personal violence" or conspire "with a foreign government to overthrow their own." Amnesty's strategy was straightforward:

> Experience shows . . . that governments are prepared to follow only where public opinion leads. Pressure of opinion a hundred years ago brought about the emancipation of the slaves. It is now for man to insist upon the same freedom for his mind as he has won for his body.

Or, as Benenson told a British tabloid, Amnesty simply aimed to "make bloody nuisances of ourselves" until governments agreed to release political and religious prisoners.[35]

Not all were convinced by the idea. In an article in *The Spectator,* the journalist Bernard Levin lampooned the Amnesty launch party at the Charing Cross Hotel. "There was tea, there was cake," he observed, and "there was any amount of goodwill." But while the idea of a neutral, apolitical enterprise was sound in theory, its impartiality was potentially both its greatest strength and greatest weakness. By advocating on behalf of both Communist and non-Communist prisoners, he predicted, "it will inevitably become suspect" to various parties. Labour Party leader Hugh Gaitskill picked up the same line of critique. "Perhaps it is only in a relatively free world that the concept of prisoners of conscience has much reality," Gaitskill told Benenson, whose eagerness to criticize every country with prisoners of conscience seemed "deliberately to blur the differences between them."

Yet, I am sure you would agree that the mere balancing of one case from a Communist country against one from a Fascist country, one from America and one from the British Commonwealth, really does not adequately reflect the true world situation. . . . To put France alongside the Soviet Union without further explanation is surely a little grotesque.[36]

The critics were soon quieted by the sheer scale of popular response. Benenson claimed a thousand inquiries by the end of the month. Operating out of his law chambers at Mitre Court, he quickly assembled a volunteer team to collect donations and names of prisoners. Individual prisoners were then assigned to local chapters around the country, which in turn undertook their own letter-writing campaigns on their behalf. To ensure neutrality, Benenson devised the "Rule of Three." Each chapter would sponsor one prisoner each from the West, the Communist world, and the nonaligned countries. By the end of 1961 forty such groups had formed in Great Britain. Within three years the number had risen to 360 across Europe, the Middle East, Africa, and North America. In May 1964, an internal report noted 1,357 prisoners of conscience adopted, 329 of whom had been released.[37]

Amnesty's rapid growth was not only a spontaneous response to Benenson's idea. It owed just as much to his experience as a jaded ex-politician who had learned how to leverage media "to catch the public imagination." The May 1961 appeal coincided with the publication of a short book by Penguin Press, *Persecution 1961*, in which Benenson profiled nine prisoners. He evidently waited until 1961 to launch Amnesty in order to link it to the 100th anniversary of the American Civil War and Russia's emancipation of its serfs. As for the precise day, he initially chose Armistice Day in November, marking the end of World War I, but then he decided on May 28 as Trinity Sunday, the church holiday celebrating the Father, Son, and Holy Spirit.[38]

Religious themes continued to mark the early Amnesty public events. Benenson arranged a number of candle-lighting ceremonies and concerts in London cathedrals with the likes of musicians Yehudi Menuhin and Jacqueline du Pré. At one of these events, he premiered the new logo, a candle in a barbed wire as a symbol of hope. Nor was he was above staging pure spectacle. Since the idea of prisoners in the abstract was too boring,

Peter Benenson re-creating the 1961 lighting of the Amnesty
International candle twenty years later

Simon Dack/Getty Images

Benenson recalled later, "I got a friend to mock up one of those wretched
machines that gives you electric shocks in the genitals" for a public dem-
onstration, and the story went viral in the British media.

> I realized that if you want to get a story across, you want to get a young, at-
> tractive female prisoner tortured or allegedly tortured. . . . Although I'm as

opposed to torture as anybody, I do think there's a danger in this [public fascination with gore] because there are a great number of prisoners who actually suffer worse without that type of physical, electrical torture. I mean, for a sensitive person simply to be locked up away from any writing material can be just as great a torture as for a taxi-driver to have his balls pricked. All imprisonment is torture really.[39]

This chillingly elitist attitude notwithstanding, Benenson's comment did reflect a deeper conviction that human rights were about more than injustice. He sought "the release of the enchained spirit of Man." Physical confinement was merely the vehicle; spiritual freedom was the goal. Not surprisingly, nearly a third of the sponsored prisoners in Amnesty's first three years were "practicing ministers of religion." Among them was the first Jewish prisoner of conscience, Gedalia Pechersky, a Soviet Jew from Leningrad. Yet Pechersky was not imprisoned for his religious beliefs but for another crime: Zionism.[40]

A Fake Spy and a Real One

In October 1961, a secret Soviet court sentenced three senior members of Leningrad's main synagogue to harsh prison terms for "cavorting with foreign agents," "espionage," and "crimes against the state." The longest sentence, twelve years, went to sixty-year-old Gedalia Pechersky, a dentist and Orthodox religious lay leader. Pechersky also had been a Zionist cultural activist since before the Russian Revolution. In recent years, he had sought permission to teach Hebrew and tried to contact Israeli diplomats. The authorities had hesitated to arrest him on any grounds that might suggest religious persecution, but by 1961 a Soviet diplomatic charm offensive in the Arab world had led to an internal campaign against anything remotely related to Israel. Pechersky was convicted of passing "anti-Soviet literature" and forbidden materials—handwritten Hebrew poetry—to the diplomats ("Israeli spies") for money.[41]

At his trial, the prosecutor directly accused him of being a Zionist. Pechersky answered that of course he was: Zionism was part of his religious faith. As an Orthodox Jew, he prayed three times a day for the restoration of Zion. When news of the trial reached the West, an outcry emerged.

Among the first to condemn the harsh verdict was the World Jewish Congress. Soviet spokesmen responded by denouncing Nahum Goldmann, Perlzweig's boss, along with U.S. Secretary of Labor Arthur Goldberg as Zionist stooges and "knights of the Cold War" who had "sunk into the morass of anti-Soviet slander." The pairing touched a nerve for Perlzweig. "We can't influence the Soviets as long as they associate us with one side in the Cold War," he told his colleagues. Yet, not to seek to aid Pechersky and other Jewish political prisoners would be an abdication of responsibility. It was at this point that Benenson decided to adopt Pechersky as a "prisoner of conscience."[42]

A month later, Pechersky's case was assigned to Amnesty's Oxford branch. A young woman from Lady Margaret Hall College, Oxford, wrote to Perzlweig early in 1962 for advice and background on the case, leaving him slightly flummoxed. He liked the idea of "a non-Jewish intervention," he confided to a colleague, but worried that the broader political overtones of the case required the WJC to consult privately with the Israeli government. Benenson, unencumbered by these concerns, pushed on exuberantly. He dispatched letters that spring to the Chief Rabbis of Great Britain and Israel with news of the Amnesty advocacy and an invitation to participate in a World Day of Prayer for the Persecuted. The Very Reverend Dr. Israel Brodie of London responded enthusiastically, devoting his April pre-Passover address on the BBC Home Service to the plight of Soviet Jews and the noble effort of Amnesty.

> Our prayers should not be exclusively directed to heaven on behalf of our own people. We think of others, created in the image of God, like ourselves, people of other faiths and nations and colours, wherever they may be, east and west, who are not free from want or oppression; men and woman who are prisoners of conscience, held in gaols without trial because of their political and religious views. The international movement known as Amnesty which had its initiative in this country, has drawn particular attention to the plight of the prisoners of conscience in different countries. That it has aroused public interest everywhere is a tribute to humanity and [its] sense of justice.[43]

Benenson responded by asking the rabbi to join Amnesty's advisory board. Brodie recommended in his place the eminent Orthodox rabbi and religious court judge, Dayan Isidor Grunfeld, a Holocaust survivor who had ministered to Jews detained in pre-1948 British camps on Cyprus. Grunfeld was soon joined by family friend George Weidenfeld and prominent Israeli philosopher Martin Buber. Benenson also reached out to Haim Cohn, former attorney general of Israel and newly appointed Supreme Court justice, to help start Amnesty in his country. As a result, the first branch in a Middle Eastern country opened in Israel in 1964, with a team of volunteers split between Haifa, Jerusalem, and Tel Aviv. These close ties were further nurtured by the first official secretary-general of Amnesty hired by Benenson, a young Jewish veteran of the 1948 Arab-Israeli War, Jack Halpern. Under his leadership, Amnesty even briefly pursued a joint fundraising campaign with the British branch of the World Jewish Congress.[44]

These early warm relations between Amnesty and the Jewish world did little to help Pechersky. He ended up in a Siberian prison camp, where he served a full twelve-year term, after which he emigrated to Israel. Meanwhile, within the Amnesty leadership circle, other voices had begun to take notice of the organization's coziness with the Jews. Among them was Ian Gilmour, a fellow Etonian, former publisher of *The Spectator,* and Tory politician, who publicly denounced Zionism as a "pathological condition," "a racial myth similar to Hitler's vicious non-Aryan nonsense," and "an extreme example of colonialism." He criticized his fellow Amnesty leaders for not aggressively adopting the Palestinian refugee cause as their own. Benenson rejected this caustic approach and instead sought "the right balance" between Jews and Arabs, and the three Abrahamic faiths. But he worried less about the Middle East conflict than the East-West split. "Amnesty is facing its toughest test," he wrote in the summer of 1962. "It is one thing to organize activities to prevent Africans being flogged—sometimes to death—on Transvaal penal farms; this work is warmed by public approval all over the world. It is another thing to go out as individuals, without backing, into the icy blasts of the Cold War."[45]

Soon enough, however, the Cold War returned to the Middle East. A peculiar early warning sign arrived later the same summer, when Flora Solomon stumbled into an international spy controversy involving Palestinian refugees, MI-6, and the KGB. For decades, the infamous double agent Kim Philby, one of the Cambridge Five, had eluded detection by his

British Intelligence colleagues while he worked as a Soviet spy. By 1962, MI-6 had assigned him to Beirut, with a cover as a journalist for *The Observer*. There he dutifully composed articles lionizing Nasser's achievements and highlighting the unresolved Palestinian refugee crisis.[46]

Sitting in Tel Aviv that summer, where she sponsored an exchange program for British and Israeli youth, Solomon grew incensed at Philby's pro-Arab writings, which she felt were blatantly tilted against Israel. She approached an old friend, Sir Victor Rothschild, at an August cocktail party to complain. "How is it the *Observer* uses a man like Philby? Didn't they know he was a Communist?" Philby's anti-Israel jeremiads perfectly reflected the "Soviet view of Middle Eastern politics." She added that he had once even tried to recruit her to the Communist Party.

Rothschild relayed her allegations back to London, triggering a panicked internal investigation. MI-6 sent a team to interview Flora. There the plot thickened. The investigator suspected her of an affair with Philby and perhaps even a dalliance with Communism herself. Claiming fear of KGB reprisal, she refused to speak on the record. Nevertheless, the inquiry exposed Philby as a spy. After confessing to the agent sent to arrest him in Beirut, he fled to safety in Moscow. Flora pronounced herself satisfied with the outcome. In her mind, the spy who jeopardized Anglo-British solidarity and fomented antisemitism had been neutralized. Some measure of balance in the British media's Middle East coverage would now return. Yet the strange episode only prefigured a whole new round of Cold War intrigues that would soon engulf her son and his organization.[47]

Cold War Challenges

From the outset, Benenson vowed that Amnesty would remain strictly apolitical. Neutrality was its magical calling card in a world riven by ideological divisions. Yet old instincts died hard. Throughout the early 1960s he turned time and again to his network of upper-crust political contacts for help with Amnesty's affairs. He enjoyed cutting through red tape with a quick phone call or a friendly, discreet letter to another Old Etonian. The roster of men recruited to serve as early patrons and leaders of Amnesty included many with whom he shared school ties, both Conservatives and

Liberals, such as Ludovic Kennedy, Ian Gilmour, Jeremy Thorpe, and John Foster. Most of all, he relied on his long-time Labour friends, including the likes of Christopher Mayhew and Gerald Gardiner, with whom he had worked in Justice. With the advent of Prime Minister Harold Wilson's Labour administration in 1964, Benenson saw a government full of old friends who shared his values. The men in the Foreign Office and Colonial Office in turn saw Amnesty as a responsible organization led by a reliable if eccentric old chum: a non-Communist humanitarian group that "on balance hurt[s] our enemies more than ourselves."[48]

The 1964 change in government coincided with a reorganization of Amnesty. In its first two years of existence, Benenson had run the organization as a free-wheeling collective dominated by his charismatic, impulsive leadership. The effort began to take a toll on his health. Reluctantly, he consented to a more formal professional structure. It was at that point that Jack Halpern came on board as the director of day-to-day operations. To chair a new International Executive Committee, Benenson chose Sean MacBride, an Irish lawyer and politician and the son of a legendary nationalist hero killed by the British after the 1916 Easter Uprising. MacBride had served as the Irish Republican Army's intelligence chief before turning to mainstream political work in the Irish government, after which he worked in the UN and at the International Commission of Jurists. With this team in place, Benenson was free to continue in his roles as chief evangelist and roving crusader while leaving the more routine administration to others. Soon, however, the new organizational strictures began to irk him. Worse still, Benenson began to show signs of paranoia. He told friends that MI-5 was following him and cautioned that Amnesty might have been compromised by spies. His behavior became increasingly erratic, alarming his colleagues. All of these issues came to a head in 1965, as a human rights controversy in the Middle East led Amnesty and Benenson into a tailspin that nearly sank the movement.[49]

Following the ignominious British retreat from Egypt after the 1956 war, the seaport city of Aden on the southern tip of Yemen remained the principal British colony in the Arab Middle East. In 1964 an anticolonial uprising began there, backed by Nasser, the regional strongman. Determined to quash the rebellion, British forces once again applied a heavy hand. After allegations of British torture of prisoners surfaced, the Swedish branch of Amnesty dispatched Dr. Salahadin Rastgeldi, an Arabic-speaking Kurdish physician, to investigate. Late in 1966 he issued a report that found evidence of torture. The British authorities shot back with a flat denial—and a charge that Amnesty had violated its own principles. "There are no political detainees in Aden," declared a British official. "All of these people are either terrorists or associated with terrorism as couriers, suppliers of weapons etc., or they are educated and prepared as terrorists." As for Rastgeldi, he was known to have stopped in Cairo en route to Aden where he had met with expatriate Yemenite political groups under the auspices of the Arab League. An official Foreign Office investigation reported no evidence to confirm the "somewhat wild allegations made in the name of Amnesty." The gullible activists had simply been played by pan-Arabist politics.[50]

Benenson fiercely defended the report, stating that Rastgeldi was above reproach. He stood by Amnesty's investigation. Yet his public remarks began to take on a disturbing edge. Benenson grew convinced that his colleagues in the Amnesty leadership were not truly loyal to the cause. He had already fired Jack Halpern after less than a year on the job, and replaced him with a fellow Etonian, Robert Swann. Now he decided that Swann was a British intelligence operative tasked with infiltrating Amnesty. MacBride he accused of being a CIA plant. As 1966 drew to a close, Benenson's charges sent Amnesty into a full-blown crisis. An internal report concluded that Swann had in fact worked for MI-5 in the past, but that there was no present plot to infiltrate Amnesty. On the other hand, MacBride had unknowingly accepted CIA funds in his capacity at Justice. The twin scandals rocked the organization, generating embarrassing headlines around the world. It was not clear whether the organization or its founder could weather the storm.[51]

Exhausted, ill, and on the verge of a mental breakdown, Benenson announced his resignation in December 1966. He retreated into the bosom of the Catholic Church, cloistering himself in a Trappist monastery in France for the next two months. His colleagues were left in charge of the organization. In February 1967, however, he reappeared in London, determined to vindicate himself and retake control of Amnesty. The move set off a vicious internal power struggle with his old friends. Then in March the British media dealt him a further blow. A young former Amnesty volunteer, Polly Toynbee, handed over letters she claimed to have found in the organization's Rhodesia office that proved Benenson himself had taken British government money for relief work conducted there in 1966. Mortified, Benenson dispatched an impassioned letter to the Foreign Office, in which he announced his intention to repay out of his own pocket all the monies the government had given Amnesty to relay to Rhodesia:

> It may be asked why I ever accepted these payments if I now wish to return them. The answer is that at the advent of the Labour Administration I believed on the evidence of my friends' record and their public declarations that they would set an example to the world in the matter of human rights.

Instead, they had let him down in Rhodesia and in Aden. He had been physically sickened by what he personally saw the British government doing in Yemen. "During many years spent in the personal investigation of repression, voyaging to many faraway and rigidly-guarded places, I never came upon an uglier picture." Compounding matters, he insisted, without evidence, that Amnesty's phones had been tapped. He pledged to start a new organization, Courage, to stop the wiretapping and government infiltration of voluntary organizations. Disgusted by his own government, he announced his intention to quit England and resettle permanently in France:

> It is a hard thing to have to decide to uproot oneself from one's country, but so long as British Intelligence are uncontrolled by Parliament I do not intend to return, except on visits. . . . It has not been an easy decision to make, but I am fortified as always by St. Thomas More who, at his trial, said "I am not bound, my lord, to conform my conscience to the counsel of one realm against the general counsel of Christendom."[52]

Alarmed, the British attorney-general and solicitor-general insisted on meeting with Benenson. They found him dangerously excited, even delusional, and determined to go through with his plan of repayment even at the risk of pauperizing himself. As they tried to sort out fact from fiction with him, he laid out a series of dark conspiracy theories about the Security Services' covert takeover of Amnesty, "talking absolute rubbish."[53]

While the fallout from the British government's entanglements with its founder continued to grab headlines, Amnesty struggled to correct its course. On March 11 and 12, 1967, a secret two-day meeting was held at the Hamlet Hotel in Elsinore, Denmark, to resolve the crisis of trust. A compromise measure was implemented, with new internal policies for official travel, acceptance of government money, and investigation oversight. Also announced, after some frantic backroom negotiations, was Benenson's departure. He retreated to a monastery in France, seeking refuge in religion from the worldly pain of politics.[54]

The Amnesty crisis of 1966–1967 occurred precisely at the moment when the Middle East had begun to convulse with tensions related to the second stage of decolonization and the rise of pan-Arab nationalism. All of the intrigues swirling around the affair—clandestine British funding of Amnesty mixed with allegations of government spying, an official British cover-up on torture in Aden combined with Egyptian political meddling—suggested the growing collision between anticolonial politics and Western human rights activism in the 1960s. Benenson saw a volatile region in need of healing as European colonialism breathed its last gasps. But the tonic of human rights was not everyone's first choice for the proper medicine.

In 1964 in Cairo, the Arab League launched the Palestine Liberation Organization (PLO), committed to liberating historic Arab Palestine by waging "holy war" against "the forces of international Zionism and colonialism." The same year a young Palestinian veteran of the 1948 war, Yasser Arafat, began mounting cross-border guerilla attacks against Israel from Syria and Jordan, provoking reciprocal responses from Israeli commandos. In November 1966 Egypt and Syria signed a mutual defense pact that threatened Israel from both sides. Shortly thereafter, Israel deployed several thousand troops across the Jordanian border in an ill-fated operation that led to Israeli and Jordanian military casualties. Then, in the spring of 1967, as Soviet aircraft strafed the southern reaches of Israel, Nasser announced his intention to blockade Israeli ships from the Straits of Tiran. It was Suez all over again.[55]

Amnesty was an idea born of the flight from Jewish politics and the Cold War into a purer realm of Catholic religious universalism. But as Benenson discovered, neither the Cold War nor the Middle East would leave him alone. Time and again, Jewish questions surfaced at the nexus between human rights and Cold War geopolitics. During the same period of the early 1960s, other veteran Jewish rights-defenders discovered the same thing. Paralleling Amnesty's rise and crisis, two other key human rights dramas unfolded in the same years: an American Jewish campaign in the UN against Soviet antisemitism and an Israeli war crimes trial of the world's greatest Nazi fugitive, Adolf Eichmann. Each effort began with the question of what Jews could do to combat the enduring scourge of anti-semitism and retrieve the lost promise of human rights. Yet both revealed not only the limits of human rights as a tool for global justice but also the tight political confines of Jewish activism within the increasingly overlapping arenas of the Cold War and the Arab-Israeli conflict.

9

The Swastika Epidemic

THE FIRST REPORTS TRICKLED in during the opening days of January 1960. Late on Christmas Eve in 1959, someone in the city of Cologne had defaced the newly rededicated Roonstrasse Synagogue. The vandals doused the building with red, white, and black paint; on both sides of the entrance, they drew swastikas and scrawled an antisemitic slogan: "Juden Raus" (Out with the Jews). Over the next five days, swastikas appeared on synagogues and Jewish communal buildings throughout West Germany, alongside words that came straight out of the 1930s: "Death to the Jews," "Jews Go Home," and "Heil Hitler."

Over the New Year's holiday, the swastikas spread to the Notting Hill neighborhood in London and then to Antwerp, Vienna, Paris, and New York. On January 6 in Oslo, a statue of President Roosevelt was defaced with the painted caption, "Potsdam Jewish Shopkeeper." That day, swastikas appeared in East Germany and Latin America, and the next day in Australia. They soon surfaced in Hong Kong, Algeria, and South Africa. Meanwhile, West Germany continued to see new swastikas for twenty days straight. By January 10, there had been five hundred antisemitic episodes in thirty-four countries. Two weeks later the number reached one thousand. The total for 1960 would eventually climb to 2,500 incidents across forty-one countries.[1]

The "Swastika Epidemic," as the press dubbed it, marked the first outburst of global antisemitism since World War II. It provoked an international crisis. British politicians reported an avalanche of mail—according to some reports, the most ever received from the public—demanding action. There were calls for an emergency international police force to intervene. In North Carolina, the gentle eighty-two-year-old American poet Carl Sandburg gave a fiery interview to the *New York Times*. Sandburg publicly opposed capital punishment, he said, but he favored a death sentence for any man caught painting a swastika on a synagogue. When the reporter asked if he was serious, Sandburg answered, "Yes. The swastika stands not for the murder of an individual or a few individuals, but for the death of a race. It is the symbol of race murder."[2]

Jewish rights-defenders shared Sandburg's outrage, but they also sensed an opportunity. If antisemitism had returned in a way not seen since World War II, perhaps the law might finally meet the challenge head-on. The Nuremberg Trials, Robinson once suggested, had served merely as a "substitute for a thing we dream about: the outlawry of antisemitism on an international plane." Now the time had come to make that dream a reality. The legal fight against antisemitism took the form of two different but parallel Jewish campaigns in 1960. At the UN that year, Jewish NGOs pushed forward a draft treaty banning international antisemitism. Meanwhile, from Jerusalem came news of the arrest of the world's most notorious Nazi fugitive, Adolf Eichmann. Before year's end, Robinson would be on a plane to Israel to join the prosecution team for one of the greatest trials of the century.[3]

After the disappointments of the 1950s, the new decade promised more fertile terrain in which the toughened root of Jewish particularism might sprout a sturdier version of universal justice. The spray of swastikas would act as a catalyst, Jewish rights-defenders hoped, loosening the soil of European memory and prompting a long-overdue global reckoning with the Holocaust. The Eichmann trial would yield a major advance in international criminal law, and the parallel UN campaign against antisemitism would mark the first step toward eradicating all forms of hateful discrimination.

Just five years later, however, the picture could not have been more different. To the surprise of many, the draft international law begun as a response to the Swastika Epidemic morphed into a larger legal convention on racism that did not even mention antisemitism. Worse still, the 1965

UN Convention on the Elimination of Racial Discrimination (CERD) introduced a new polemical catchphrase: "Zionism Is Racism." Over the next decade, this slur would appear with increasing frequency at the UN, culminating in the 1975 UN General Assembly Resolution 3379, which officially branded Zionism "a form of racism and racial discrimination." Meanwhile, in Jerusalem, the trial of the world's worst living antisemite turned into a referendum on the very legitimacy of Jewish justice. In the most extreme formulations, critics now alleged that Zionists were partly responsible both for causing the Holocaust and for abusing its memory. It was Eichmann whose human rights had been violated. The breakthrough moment for international criminal law triggered a still-unresolved debate about whether Jews can ever secure Holocaust justice untainted by politics.

Carl Sandburg was more right about the swastikas than he realized. In the Western moral imagination of the 1960s, the enormity of the Holocaust turned antisemitism into a special variety of human hatred that transcended mere racial prejudice or religious intolerance. The idea of antisemitism as somehow exceptional was precisely what led a death penalty opponent like Sandburg to urge execution for the minor crime of graffiti vandalism. There could be no worse kind of hatred than antisemitism, Sandburg suggested. Yet exceptionalism was a double-edged sword. The more unique the Jewish case, the less relevant it was to a human rights culture grasping for symbols of the universal in the era of anticolonialism. In a decolonizing world increasingly focused on the evils of apartheid and colonialism, antisemitism hovered awkwardly between the categories of racism and religious intolerance. Like the Jews themselves, antisemitism was just too sui generis to fit the dictates of the human rights imagination.

Still, the philosophical complexities of antisemitism alone cannot explain how Zionism came to be recast in the 1960s as an irreducible symbol of moral parochialism. Just as in previous decades, the Jewish struggle for international justice grew entangled in the web of global politics. In retrospect, the obvious explanation for the reimagining of Zionism is the 1967 Six-Day War. Yet well before 1967, Jewish rights-defenders made the disturbing discovery that Zionism was fast becoming identified as the singular enemy of international human rights. At the UN, Soviet and Arab diplomats flipped the idea of an antisemitism ban from a principled claim to minority self-defense into an expression of Jewish national chauvinism and racialism. Instead of avatars of moral universalism, Jewish rights-defenders were depicted as the ultimate partisans of the particular. Far from the moment of renewed promise many anticipated it might be, the 1960s marked the beginning of the end of the grand romance between Jews and human rights. The strange tale of how the legal struggles against antisemitism and for Holocaust justice led to the global demonization of Zionism starts with a deceptively simple question: Who was behind the Swastika Epidemic?

In Defense of Imaginary Groups

A pandemic of Judeophobia was the last thing on Perlzweig's mind at the start of the new decade. "Anti-semitism [has] now ceased to be the main problem of World Jewry," he wrote in late 1959. "The dangers to Jewish survival come now much more from within than from the outside world, they are the dangers of dis-integration and assimilation rather than anti-semitism and persecution." The Swastika Epidemic left him flummoxed— nor was he alone in this reaction. On January 5, a friendly Jewish CIA officer approached Perlzweig with a discreet request for help. The Agency suspected a Soviet hand might be involved in the antisemitic outbreaks. Could the World Jewish Congress's Institute for Jewish Affairs confirm this? Perlzweig balked at his friend's typically American "childish tendency to refer everything wrong back to Communist intrigue." At the same time, however, he too found it hard to believe that a spontaneous "psychological infection" or copycat pattern of "crackpots" could be responsible for the Swastika Epidemic: "Is it plausible to suggest that within the same 24 or 36 hours there would be people ready with paint and the same German symbols and slogans in half a dozen countries, if there had been no prior organization?"[4]

If not the Communists or the crazies, asked his CIA contact, then who? More than likely, Perlzweig explained to him, "what had happened was the result of an organized international effort directed by a small group of Nazis or Neo-Nazis in Germany." These "extreme nationalists want a united and independent Germany, like what Nasser has done" with pan-Arabism.

The swastika attack on the Cologne synagogue, 1960

picture-alliance/dpa

The antidote to this recrudescence of xenophobic nationalism was a renewed push for a ban on "incitement to hatred against racial and religious groups." It was time to focus the power of international law directly on the scourge of hate speech, beginning with antisemitism.[5]

Throughout the 1950s, the WJC had floated the idea of an international law outlawing all "racialism and antisemitism." Minorities faced a unique threat that demanded a specific kind of legal recognition, beyond the universal template of human rights. While work on the covenants dragged on

at the Commission on Human Rights, Perlzweig and his colleagues focused their attention on its subsidiary body, the Sub-Commission on the
Prevention of Discrimination and the Protection of Minorities. This body
had been created in 1947 to recommend legal and other measures relating
to bias and minority affairs. In the 1950s and 1960s it would become the
locus for the UN human rights community's attempts to think through
the meaning of antisemitism for the future of human rights.[6]

The Sub-Commission met each January and February in New York just
before the main commission held its spring session in Geneva. These
meetings took place in the spectacular ECOSOC chamber on the second
floor of the UN General Assembly building. The room's dramatic purpose
was built into its Swedish modernist architecture. A partially exposed pipe
ceiling symbolized the unfinished business of combating global conflict;
the rear wall consisted entirely of a massive glass window overlooking the
East River, representing the wide-open future that lay ahead. It was the
perfect setting in which to talk about human rights. Yet the overwhelming
sentiment of those seated around the room's elegant wooden horseshoe-
shaped table was that they faced an impasse. The reason was politics. Technically, the fourteen official members of the panel were supposed to function
not as national delegates but as independent "experts," more like legal
plumbers than official diplomats. In practice, they acted as surrogates for
their respective states.

That was certainly the case for the United States. Since 1956 the American
delegate had been none other than Judge Philip Halpern. The Eisenhower
appointee and senior AJC leader still railed against the dangers of human
rights and "world government." The Sub-Commission itself he cheekily re-
christened "SODOM." Yet the globalist den of iniquity served for him as
the perfect place to expose the most egregious example of discrimination
in the world: Soviet antisemitism. After the Supreme Court's *Brown v.
Board of Education* decision in 1954, Halpern insisted that America's problem
of racial injustice had been solved once and for all. The Soviets, meanwhile, kept their Jewish community locked in a discriminatory legal caste
system. Deprived of basic access to their religious and cultural life, terror-
ized by Stalin and his henchmen, and forbidden to emigrate, Soviet Jews
had for decades lived in a country that effectively made Jewishness itself a

crime. Even after Stalin's death in 1953, troubling reports emerged of new forms of anti-Jewish persecution, including the banning of Passover matzah and the arrest and execution of a large number of Jews for economic crimes such as currency trading. The trial of Pechersky offered still further proof of the Soviet anti-Jewish campaign at work.[7]

Halpern seized every chance to denounce the Soviets for their discriminatory laws and policies. Perlzweig would have none of it: he complained repeatedly to his colleagues that Halpern's blatantly ideological "denunciation, propaganda and public relations activity is difficult to distinguish from participation in the Cold War." Plus, the crowing about Soviet prejudice missed the point. The real scandal, Perlzweig insisted, was not Soviet anti-Jewish discrimination but the Soviet government's failure to provide protection to its Jewish national minority. "A man who is not free to be a Jew is not free at all," he maintained, and "wherever there is a Jewish community, it has the inalienable right to create the institutions for the preservation and development of its cultural and religious values." It was a violation of the Soviet Constitution that the Kremlin denied Jews the same "basic cultural rights" as other "national groups," such as the legal right to use their national languages (Hebrew and Yiddish) in schools, publishing, and the arts. Better to challenge the Soviets quietly to live up to their own laws than to confront them publicly with overheated political charges. American Cold War hawks should stop trying to pin the disturbing upsurge of global antisemitism on the Soviet Union.[8]

These tensions surfaced at the January 1960 session of the Sub-Commission. With the Swastika epidemic still in full swing, Perlzweig took the floor to make an impassioned plea for international action. For Jews around the world, these attacks signified "a matter of life and death." Roger Baldwin spoke up to second Perlzweig's call for a UN special investigation. A host of other Jewish NGOs also chimed in, including the Anti-Defamation League of B'nai Brith and the Orthodox Jewish Agudat Yisrael. Still, these NGO appeals did not carry the same weight as the votes of country "experts." As always at the UN, no campaign for action could be launched without the support of the state members.[9]

Fortunately for Perlzweig, Halpern agreed with him on the seriousness of the problem. Other delegates did as well. Together with the British, French,

Austrian, Finnish, and Uruguayan members, Halpern co-sponsored a resolution condemning "manifestations of anti-Semitism and other forms of
racial prejudice and religious intolerance of a similar nature" as "violations
of the human rights of the group against which they are directed and as a
threat to the human rights and fundamental freedoms of all peoples." The
resolution provided for a UN investigation of the "causes and motivations"
of the Swastika Epidemic in order to recommend a global response.[10]

Crucially, however, Halpern made one notable addition in his version of
the draft resolution. Tackling a global threat should not preclude punish-
ing the worst offenders. He urged that the UN concentrate its investigation on
those governments that use antisemitism "as a weapon against a racial or
religious group." Sensing an assault, the Soviet expert, Dr. Zoya Mironova,
responded immediately by insisting that the resolution include a reference
to Nazism, past and present. Most of the attacks, she noted, had taken place
in West Germany, the neo-Fascist counterpart to Communist East Germany
and a U.S. ally. "The spreading of antisemitism," she maintained, "could not
be explained only by the existence of prejudice." The UN must target the real
culprits: "organized groups of fascist elements." Today it might be Jews,
she added; tomorrow's victims might be the Slavs.[11]

The official Soviet explanation for the swastikas put Perlzweig in an awkward place in between East and West. He too suspected a neo-Nazi hand in
the antisemitic outbreak, but he had no desire to help the Soviets peddle
their anti-Western propaganda or play into the hands of American anti-
Communism. Alarmed by the implicit politicization on both sides, he
went to work behind the scenes to de-escalate the brewing conflict. "I persuaded the Soviet representatives to vote for this resolution," even without
"the words 'Nazi' or 'German' in the text," he explained, by leveraging Jewish neutrality in the Cold War to argue for an apolitical approach to antisemitism. The result was an initial success. The text of the 1960 resolution
left out both the American and Soviet language and won unanimous support. All the states present agreed to condemn antisemitism and call for an
official UN investigation. The list of countries, Perlzweig was pleased to
note, included Egypt, Lebanon, Sudan, Poland, and the USSR.[12]

The resolution passed swiftly through the Commission on Human Rights
and the General Assembly that spring. The result was a mid-1960 call by

the UN Secretary-General for all states and NGOs to submit evidence of antisemitism and other forms of hatred to the UN the following year. Perlzweig felt entirely vindicated by this turn of events. Here was a win for Jews and human rights outside the contexts of the Cold War and the Middle East conflict. Others were less convinced. "You have handed a victory to the Soviet Union," Moses Moskowitz, the AJC liaison at the UN, angrily told him. The Israeli ambassador to the UN, Uri Raanan, angrily lambasted Perlzweig and his colleagues for failing to help attack the Soviets more directly. After Suez the Israelis had no choice but to take a hard line against the Soviets. Then there was Halpern, who insisted that a "golden opportunity" was now at hand to highlight Soviet antisemitism. It was high time to put the pressure squarely on the USSR, he told an assemblage of Jewish NGOs that April. Most of the groups agreed. Only Perlzweig dissented. The Soviets had unequivocally condemned antisemitism, he argued, and "for us to turn this into an opportunity to suggest Soviet complicity in what they had condemned would be an outrage against good sense and a tactical error of major proportions." He prided himself on resisting the machinations of those "Americans and Israelis, who sometimes seem to me to be ready to pay almost any price in order to achieve some small propaganda advantage against the East."[13]

What neither Perlzweig nor Halpern knew at the time was that the CIA was correct in its initial assessment: the Soviets *had* launched the Swastika Epidemic. In 1959, the KGB created a disinformation section known as Department D, headed by General Ivan Ivanovich Agayants, a veteran agent who had previously worked in Tehran and Paris. One of his first assignments was to help discredit West Germany as a neo-Fascist state populated by former Nazis and the direct heir to Nazi Germany. Doing so would thwart Chancellor Konrad Adenauer's plans to reintegrate his country into the Western alliance and disrupt Bonn's negotiations with Israel over Holocaust reparations. It was an opportunistic antisemitism born of Soviet realpolitik.[14]

Late in 1959 Agayants dispatched a team of agents to West Germany to paint swastikas and antisemitic slogans. The Soviet mouthpiece *Pravda* was ready with an editorial denunciation: "These disgusting fascist provocations and manifestations of the swastika are directed toward the fanning of the Cold War and toward the poisoning of peoples against peoples." An article in the Soviet Writers Union's *Literaturnaya Gazeta* accused the Israeli government of a "fondness for Swastikas" and linked the campaign directly to Israel's growing coziness with West Germany.[15]

The secret KGB operation proved an instant success. Within six weeks, 833 such attacks had occurred in West Germany. To the Soviets' surprise, the swastikas spread like wildfire well beyond Germany. Local hooligans and neo-Nazis across Europe and beyond immediately launched copycat attacks. What had begun as a disinformation campaign in one European country turned into a global phenomenon. The pace and breadth of attacks dwarfed the intended effect of exacerbating conflict between the two Germanys and needling Israel. The KGB dialed back its efforts: its work was done. By the time the UN reconvened that September, however, events had taken yet another unanticipated turn. Starting that summer, a new slogan began to appear alongside the swastikas: "I love Eichmann."[16]

Israel on Trial

On the brutally hot afternoon of May 23, 1960, David Ben-Gurion walked into the Knesset building on King George Street in downtown Jerusalem and strode to the podium to address the parliament. Anticipation hung in the air. Rumors had slipped out earlier that day that the prime minister would make a major announcement. Yet none were prepared for what he said:

> I must inform the Knesset that a short while ago, the Israeli Security Services discovered the whereabouts of one of the Nazi arch-criminals, Adolf Eichmann, who was responsible, together with the Nazi leaders for . . . the annihilation of six million of Europe's Jews. Adolf Eichmann is currently under arrest in Israel and will stand trial soon, in accordance with the Nazi and Nazi Collaborators Punishment Law.

The normally raucous parliamentarians fell silent. Then, they erupted in applause. Ben-Gurion's remarks struck like "a sixty-two-word electric shock," wrote one journalist: "It is difficult—no, it is impossible, to describe what took place in the modest parliament building in the aftermath

of these two sentences, which carved their places in the history of this nation." The Israeli leaders and public had spent a decade and a half doing
their best to ignore the Holocaust as they busied themselves building a
new country. Now the past came flooding back.[17]

The rest of the world was also stunned by the news of Eichmann's capture. Yet while Israelis grappled with painful memories and long-buried
emotions, international observers were considerably less sentimental. A
week after Ben-Gurion's announcement, the *Washington Post* blasted Israel's actions as "Jungle Law."

> Everything connected with the proceedings against Eichmann is tainted
> with lawlessness. If, as reported, he was abducted from another country,
> international law was violated. The crimes with which he is to be charged
> were committed in Germany and Austria; Israel has no jurisdiction to try
> the case. In any event, Israel can try him only under *ex post facto* statues.
> To try him according to the forms of law is to make a mockery of law.
> All that the government of Israel can do in this case is to wreak vengeance;
> it cannot secure justice.[18]

From his perch on New York's Upper West Side, Jacob Robinson winced
at these comments. Both their ignorance and hypocrisy pained him. In a letter to the editor, he enumerated the *Post*'s gross inaccuracies one by one.
Eichmann's crimes were not committed only in Germany and Austria but
all over Europe. Contrary to these erroneous claims about jurisdiction, he
wrote, "there are no such rules of international law and it is left to the sovereign will of each individual state to decide the limits of its own criminal
jurisdiction." No other state had expressed a competing interest in trying
Eichmann—not even West Germany. Given the concentration of Holocaust
survivors, the presence of documentation, and Israel's "special Jewish
character," he wrote, "it is natural and proper for Israel to assume jurisdiction in a case involving the Nazi design to exterminate the Jewish people."[19]

Also justifiable was the charge of genocide based on a post–World War
II law. "Your criticism of the Israeli statute," he wrote, "strangely ignores
the revolution in international legal concepts which followed the defeat
of Nazi Germany." The Nuremberg Trials, the Genocide Convention, and
various national laws of which Israel's Nazi and Nazi Collaborators Pun-

ishment Law was but one example all formed a new body of legal precedents for precisely this kind of trial. That it was to be held in Israel and not
an international tribunal pointed to yet another instance of selective memory on the part of Israel's critics. Where were these American voices in the
mid-1950s, when Israel had vocally campaigned for an International Criminal
Court, only to be thwarted in large part by U.S. intransigence? Finally, how
could these critics so callously dismiss the "profound moral and historical
purpose to be served by the trial"?[20]

The sole issue Robinson sidestepped was that of Eichmann's capture. In
early June a furious Argentina took the matter to the UN Security Council,
claiming Israel had violated its sovereignty. In a July 1960 essay in *Commentary* magazine, Robinson responded by invoking the venerable legal
principle of "Male captus, bene detentus"—wrongly captured, properly detained. "There is nothing in international penal law which would deny
jurisdiction to a state because regular extradition procedures were not followed or because, in 'hot pursuit' of a wrongdoer, the domestic law of a
country was violated," he wrote. Moreover, he noted, Argentina had repeatedly and blatantly ignored "repeated UN appeals to all nations for the surrender of war criminals residing therein."[21]

It fell to Robinson's Israeli colleague, Shabtai Rosenne, to fly to Argentina
that August to quell the diplomatic furor. Some of the outrage was manufactured. Rocked by coup after coup, the Argentinian government worried
less about its sovereignty than about domestic politics. It had to appease
the angry rightist crowds gathered in the streets of Buenos Aires chanting
"Vive Eichmann, down with the Jews!" After a quiet negotiation, a joint
Israeli-Argentinian statement buried the affair. Argentina received a formal public apology, and Israel kept Eichmann.[22]

A week later, Rosenne touched down in New York to meet with Robinson. There the old friends discussed plans for Robinson to join the team
being assembled by Israeli chief prosecutor Gideon Hausner. It was an
easy decision for Robinson. Since retiring from the Israeli Foreign Ministry in 1957, he had devoted much of his energy to the fledgling field of
Holocaust history. He had written several reference works on the subject
and served as an advisor on the creation of Yad Vashem in Jerusalem and
similar scholarly efforts at the YIVO Institute in New York, London's

Weiner Library, and the Paris Centre de Documentation Juive Contemporaine. It was almost as if he had been unwittingly preparing for the trial
that would cap his career and define his legacy. Now, all that accumulated
historical knowledge would be put to use to alongside his legal skills. Robinson was given responsibility for handling all the international legal fac-
ets of the greatest international criminal trial since Nuremberg.

There were hundreds of potential witnesses to depose, endless legal arcana
to consider, and reams of evidence to process. There was also the defendant himself. The Israelis placed Eichmann in a secret location inside a
heavily fortified police station near Kibbutz Yagur on the outskirts of Haifa.
Robinson repeatedly joined the small team of police investigators known as
Bureau 06 who interviewed Eichmann there from dawn until dusk for nine
straight months. It was not easy to sit across a small wooden table from the
architect of the Final Solution. The man who personified evil incarnate
was a "thin, balding man of 55 who looked more like a bank clerk than a
butcher." He chain-smoked without pause, chattering incessantly like an
over-caffeinated Viennese café patron. His very eagerness to talk in his bi-
zarre, Nazified German language proved eerily disconcerting.[23]

Throughout, Robinson's curiosity trumped his anger. Eichmann was
both defendant and witness. As prosecutor, Robinson had the case of his
life to prepare; as a scholar, he had endless questions for the master criminal. Here was a man uniquely equipped to describe how the Nazis had
perpetrated the Final Solution. The trial was not only a forum for seeking
justice; it was also a historical inquiry into how the Nazis had perversely
twisted law itself into an instrument of illegality.

As Robinson and the prosecutorial team prepped for trial during the
winter of 1960–1961, they continued to face a volley of criticisms from
abroad. Roger Baldwin gave an interview in which he called the Israeli trial
a huge mistake and a clear case of "the ends justifying the means." Former
Nuremberg prosecutor Telford Taylor, who had relied extensively on Robinson's services in 1946, now accused Israel of acting in the spirit of "an
absolute nationalism which is irreconcilable with the very idea of international law." "To define a crime in terms of the religion or nationality of the
victim instead of the nature of the criminal act," Taylor wrote in a *New
York Times Magazine* article, "is wholly out of keeping with the needs of the

times and the trend of modern law." "As the Eichmann trial approaches," wrote Labour MP Richard Crossman in the *New Statesman*, "I feel more and more uneasy" about Israel's "tribal vengeance," which marks a "pattern of behavior more akin to the ideals of the white settler than to those of the Socialist pioneers who started the National Home." After an uproar from Jewish Labourites, including Flora Solomon, Crossman backtracked, clarifying that "Christian antisemitism has never been cured by an appeal to reason, an appeal to history, or even an appeal to justice. Zionism is the only cure I have ever believed in." This curious apology pointed to the growing symbolic entanglement of global antisemitism and the Jewish state.[24]

Even Israel's closest allies in the Jewish diaspora expressed concern in the run-up to the trial. Nahum Goldmann disappointed Robinson—and infuriated Ben-Gurion—by suggesting in late 1960 that the Israelis would do better to hold the trial with a mixed tribunal of judges from Israel and other Eastern European Communist countries affected by the Nazis. (In a rare break with his superior, Perlzweig told Israeli radio that he disagreed with Goldmann and favored an Israeli trial).[25]

Blaustein and his AJC colleagues, in contrast, worried more about the trial's impact on American Jews. "Since Eichmann committed unspeakable crimes against humanity not only against Jews," read an AJC board communique to the Israel Foreign Ministry, the Israeli emphasis on "crimes against the Jewish people" was not only illogical and unseemly but also "harmful to the interest of both of Israel and the Jewish communities throughout the world." The AJC had just gone through an internal debate over whether to drop the word "Jewish" from its name to avoid charges of parochialism. In another self-conscious gesture of broad-mindedness, its brand-new building at the corner of New York's Third Avenue and 56th Street, paid for in part thanks to a large donation from Blaustein, was dubbed the Institute for Human Relations. The last thing he and his fellow AJC leaders wanted to see in 1960 was an Israeli-sponsored war crimes trial that explicitly highlighted Jewish concerns rather than universal ones. When the Israelis showed no signs of abandoning course on Eichmann, the AJC mounted a last-ditch effort to sway them, convening a blue-ribbon panel of lawyers and judges who collectively proposed a solution: let Israel prepare the case against Eichmann while the trial itself could be conducted by an international tribunal.[26]

Robinson found these worries overblown and the suggestions wholly unrealistic. "Those who invoke against Israel various principles which are now obsolete in their rigidity are like Rip van Winkle waking from a centuries-long sleep," he fumed in a confidential memo. "They are unaware of the revolution of criminal law and criminal jurisdiction." With or without the support of American Jews, international lawyers, or the world community, Israel was well within its rights to try Eichmann. Such a trial did not represent a provincial step backward from humanity, but a large leap "closer to the universality [jurisdiction] principle."[27]

Ben-Gurion cared less for legal niceties than for the compelling display of Jewish justice. Israel's trial of Eichmann was not the cause of antisemitism, he told anyone who deigned to listen, but the solution. In an infamous speech in Jerusalem in December 1960, he pronounced all of world Jewry to be in peril. "In several totalitarian and Moslem countries, Judaism is in danger of death by strangulation," the Israeli prime minister told the World Zionist Congress, whereas "in the free and prosperous countries it faces death by a kiss—a slow and imperceptible decline into the abyss of assimilation." In the cases of both Eichmann and the Swastika Epidemic, Israel was the main line of defense against global antisemitism and the sole guarantor of Jewish collective survival. More than that, Ben-Gurion's intemperate remarks testified to an inconvenient truth: Jewish rights depended above all on Jewish sovereignty.[28]

The Human Rights of Adolf Eichmann

The Eichmann trial opened on April 11, 1961, in a heavily guarded temporary courtroom in Jerusalem's new cultural center, Bet Ha'am. As the audience watched that first day, Hausner, Robinson, and the other prosecutors purposefully filed in wearing their traditional black lawyers' robes. They were followed by Dr. Robert Servatius, the German attorney recruited by Eichmann's brother as his defense counsel. Then, seemingly out of nowhere, Eichmann himself suddenly materialized in a chair in an eerie, bullet-proof glass box, having entered from a discreet door in the wall. When the three judges were announced, he shot up from his seat. For the next forty-five minutes Eichmann stood ramrod straight at attention as he listened intently through headphones to the German translation of the proceedings.[29]

Some five hundred reporters and observers attended the trial's opening. They included Hannah Arendt, on assignment for the *New Yorker*; Telford Taylor, reporting for *The Spectator*; and Julius Stone, representing the International Commission of Jurists. At no point did they hear Robinson's voice in the courtroom. When Hausner asked him to conduct part of the cross-examination, he declined out of modesty. He also refused to testify as an expert witness on the history of Jews in Europe before the Shoah. That role went instead to Columbia University historian Salo Baron. Robinson, by contrast, sat quietly throughout the trial at the end of the prosecutor's table, occasionally leaning over to whisper in a colleague's ear. He focused on the finer points of law and left the theatrics to others.[30]

Jacob Blaustein arrived in Israel during the trial's second week. He avoided the Jerusalem courthouse and went instead to the prime minister's office. His mission was to patch up relations with Ben-Gurion in the aftermath of all the tensions about the trial's meaning. Emotions and ideologies aside, the two were old friends by then. Blaustein was one of the few people outside of Israel to address Ben-Gurion simply as "David." He in turn called Blaustein by his Hebrew name, "Yaakov," not Jacob. Both men were too intelligent as strategists and too savvy as deal makers to discard a useful relationship. Blaustein knew he served as a valuable port of contact between Ben-Gurion and the Kennedy White House and the UN Secretariat. During the late 1950s, Blaustein had developed a very close personal relationship with UN Secretary-General Dag Hammarskjöld. A liberal pragmatist and staunch anti-Communist, Hammarskjöld increasingly viewed human rights as a liberal check on Soviet malfeasance. Blaustein and Ben-Gurion had also worked together on a possible Arab-Israeli peace plan centered on solving the Palestinian refugee crisis. Finally, Blaustein's role as a key figure in the reparations negotiations with West German Chancellor Konrad Adenauer made him a main conduit at this time when Tel Aviv-Bonn relations were warming up. All of this was too useful to abandon just for the sake of Zionist rhetoric.[31]

For his part, Blaustein's negotiations with the Israeli prime minister gave him a chance to reassert his primacy among American Jews. He had retired from his formal role as head of the AJC, but he had no wish to let go of his role as the unofficial American Jewish leader on international affairs. In April 1961, Ben-Gurion and Blaustein issued a joint statement reaffirming their 1950 agreement. Ben-Gurion once again walked back his claim that Israel spoke for American Jewry. This was followed by a concession on the part of Blaustein. After decades of complicated ambivalence about Zionism, the AJC announced it would finally open a permanent office in the Jewish homeland. It was a telling gesture of the increasingly intertwined destinies of American Jews and Israel.[32]

If the Eichmann trial solidified a reluctant but vital partnership between American Jews and Israel, it marked a more ominous turning point in Soviet-Israeli relations. During the trial, the Soviets switched from the subterfuge of painted swastikas to overt propaganda attacks linking Zionism and antisemitism. A 1961 cartoon in the Ukrainian satirical magazine *Perets* presented the first image of a swastika embedded inside a Star of David. What began as crude rhetoric denouncing relations between Israel and West Germany as an unholy alliance turned into something much more sinister. The "Eichmann Affair," as the Soviets now called it, represented the larger struggle between the forces of human justice and "the forces of evil in the world." The latter were defined in just three words: "Zionism and Nazism."

None of the Soviet attacks in the 1950s, even during Stalin's last murderous campaign and the Suez War, had ever equated Jews with their antisemitic persecutors. Now, with the Swastika Epidemic and the Eichmann trial, the East-West Germany crisis brewing, and rising decolonization, the Soviets seized on the propaganda opportunity to argue that Zionism was *worse* than Nazism. The Nazis had perpetrated their crimes in the remote past, while Zionist outrages continued daily. Far from being a political response to hatred, Zionism increasingly symbolized hatred itself. This trope soon followed Jews back to the UN as they pursued the legal campaign against antisemitism there.[33]

Soviet antisemitic cartoon equating Zionism and Nazism, 1961

The Eichmann trial concluded in August 1961 with a swift guilty verdict and a death sentence. He was hanged at midnight on May 31, 1962. At the final appeal hearing, Servatius conceded Eichmann's guilt, but tried a novel legal strategy. Eichmann's human rights, he told the judges, had been grossly violated. The Israeli court should allow him to appeal his conviction to the UN Commission on Human Rights. The judges rejected this argument. Nazi defense counsels had tried the same tactic at the Nuremberg Trials, where it had also been shot down. The difference now was that it suggested a larger inversion of the moral order. Zionism itself was on trial in the symbolic court of international human rights.[34]

From "Antisemitism" to "Racial Prejudice"

By the fall of 1962, the Swastika Epidemic had receded from the headlines. The UN special investigation of the causes and culprits had solved only one-third of the cases. Despite reports submitted from some forty countries and twenty NGOs, the KGB's early guiding hand remained well hidden. The lack of evidence of an organized international conspiracy coupled with the decline in attacks dampened the sense of urgency. Some members of the Sub-Commission on the Prevention of Discrimination and the Protection of Minorities now claimed that Jewish groups had "over-dramatized" the whole problem. Perlzweig pushed back. The "epidemic" had not ended. Rather, it had become a "chronic disease" that might still flare up at a moment's notice. In search of a way forward on an anti-bias law, he turned to the UN's newest members for help in the battle for human rights. For in addition to being the year of the Swastika Epidemic and the Eichmann trial, 1960 was best known at the UN as the "Year of Africa."[35]

In 1945 nearly all of Africa remained under European colonial rule. The slow pace of decolonization in the 1950s suddenly gave way in 1960 to a wave of new states that transformed the demography and geopolitics of the UN. Contrary to later popular opinion, these postcolonial states at first registered little overt concern for international human rights. Most anticolonial movements sought the full reward of national sovereignty rather than the consolation prize of human rights. Like their former colonial overlords, they tended to view human rights schemes as an unwanted intrusion into their internal affairs.[36]

The Soviets were quick to recognize this view and capitalize on it. In September 1960, Soviet premier Nikita Khrushchev introduced Resolution 1514 (XV), "Declaration on the Granting of Independence to Colonial Countries and Peoples." The most frequently invoked resolution in the history of the UN, it redefined international human rights from being a check on state power to serving as a vehicle for anticolonial nationalism. "The subjection of peoples to alien subjugation, domination and exploitation constitutes a denial of fundamental human rights," read the text. The single most important human right is "the right to self-determination." The intent was to block the political threat of human rights and position the USSR as the leader of the global anticolonial movement.

Ever the optimist, Perlzweig hoped the new African and Afro-Caribbean states would see through this gambit. Fellow victims of racism, not yet committed to either side in the Cold War, these new nations might yet join Jews in a fight against the twin evils of racism and antisemitism. "Year by year, as new States become emancipated and colonial regimes come to an end," he confidently predicted, "public opinion will come to realize that independence is not an end in itself but must be made to serve the rights and interests of the citizens who have fought for it." Yet these hopes were soon dashed. True, some Third World states did take seriously the challenge to renew the promise of human rights. Jamaica led a coalition of countries that seized on the idea of banning international racism as an important mission to pursue at the UN. It was in large part thanks to their initiative that the proposed antiracism law remained alive in the first few years of the 1960s. But the emerging African/Afro-Caribbean alignment pointedly excluded Israel. That new reality was unmistakably revealed in November 1962 at the UN's Third Committee session where Perlzweig witnessed "an all-out assault on Israel based on the theme of anti-colonialism."[37]

The trouble began when the Israeli delegate, Michael Comay, delivered a speech complaining about the fact that antisemitism was not even mentioned in the current draft of the antiracism law. The entire effort to criminalize discrimination had begun with the Swastika Epidemic. Yet while the epidemic had ended, antisemitism had not. Reactions to Comay's speech were swift and harsh. The representative of Mauritania, a North African country that had only just won its independence from France in 1960, blasted "Zionist expansionism" as the very antithesis of human rights. He accused Jews of inventing the concept of racial superiority. Christians are "anti-racist as a matter of principle" and Muslims have "never practiced racial intolerance," he boasted, unembarrassed by the fact that his own officially Islamic country still permitted legal slavery and tolerated widespread racism against its black African population. The attacks continued through the next several days of debate as Mali, Nigeria, and other African and Arab nations echoed the same theme. Any talk of antisemitism was a Zionist plot. In a final twist, the United Arab Republic delegate accused Zionists of engineering the "so-called wave of anti-Semitism" by drawing the swastikas themselves.[38]

Perlzweig was pained and bewildered by the ideological animus against the idea of combating antisemitism. He had long prided himself on his friendly relations with even the most "anti-Israel" Arab diplomats. More-over, he saw in the map of the swastika attacks a telling fact: "Only a hand-ful [took place] in the Moslem world, and there only in places where there were European or Christian settlements." This fact proved that "antisemi-tism is a disease of Christian democracy," not Islam or Arab society. Strug-gling to understand the new current of blunt antagonism, he blamed his fellow Jews for their inept diplomacy. The Israelis failed to grasp that in-sisting on bringing up antisemitism in such a "sharp and conspicuous form" was bound to backfire: "It ensured the Communists and the Arabs would unite in assailing Israel, which certainly did no good; and the Afro-Asians, who not unnaturally regard what is happening in South Africa as infinitely worse than what is happening to the Jews in the Soviet Union, were, to put it mildly, not impressed."[39]

Alongside Israeli clumsiness, Perlzweig identified a second culprit: the new Kennedy administration's U.S. expert to the Sub-Commission, Morris Abram, who to Perlzweig's dismay proved just as hawkish as his Republican predecessor. A native of the American South, Abram had be-gun his career as a junior attorney at the Nuremberg Trials before becom-ing a well-known civil rights lawyer. He was also the incoming president of the AJC. Like Blaustein, with whom he closely identified, Abram was a Cold War liberal determined to protect Jews and defend American honor at the UN. Entering the UN in the fall of 1962, he lost no time zeroing in on Soviet antisemitism as a principal target for combined action by the United States, Israel, and the Jewish NGOs. Nor was he shy about put-ting his aggressive approach on display when dealing with his Soviet counterparts.

Abram's tactic of choice was to raise the issue of the Soviet passport system at every turn as a prime example of Soviet anti-Jewish discrimination. According to Soviet law, Jews were classified Jews as a separate ethnic nationality in their internal passports. Viewed through American liberal eyes, the so-called Line 5 was equivalent to the racial classification that the United States was then struggling to eliminate from its own society. Perlzweig strongly disagreed with this conclusion. Marking Jews as a separate nationality on their passports was not necessarily antisemitism—*all* Soviet citizens were classified by nationality, including ethnic Russians. Moreover, formal classification, even if it risked discrimination, had the benefit of preserving Jewish minority identity. "The last thing we need," he wrote, "is to persuade the Russians to promote assimilation further by suppressing this last tenuous link with the Jewish heritage." This disagreement spoke to the long-standing tension between human rights as a protective device for minority group identity versus an extension of individual civil liberties. Twenty years in to the UN, Perlzweig lamented, his American Jewish opponents still refused to acknowledge the necessity of minority rights.[40]

Abram's frequent "outbreaks of passion" horrified Perlzweig for another reason as well. Public attacks on Soviet antisemitism were "an inadequate and sterile device" given the stakes. The best hope for Soviet Jews—and for human rights—was to keep both on the sidelines of the Cold War. Quiet diplomacy and public consensus building would serve Jewish and Western interests much better than saber rattling. "We are not electing a member of the New York City Council," he wrote, "We are dealing with the rulers of a totalitarian state. . . . Let's avoid a dialogue of the deaf."[41]

Thanks largely to the raucous debates about antisemitism and Zionism, the entire discussion of an international antiracism law nearly collapsed in the fall of 1962. In the end, a compromise was reached. Two separate international treaties would be drafted: a Convention on the Elimination of All Forms of Racial Discrimination and a Convention on the Elimination of All Forms of Religious Intolerance. Neither mentioned antisemitism by name. The following spring, when the Sub-Commission took up the task of drafting the racial discrimination law, Abram aggressively pushed to put antisemitism back into the document. He continued to lambast the Soviets,

accusing them of "ethnic genocide" against Soviet Jews. The Soviet diplomats had no shortage of pointed rejoinders. Why did African Americans
attending white schools in the American South need federal troops to protect them from racial violence? Was that not the very definition of genocide? And by the way, the Soviet envoys also asked, why had the United
States still not ratified the Genocide Convention, when their government
had done it years before?[42]

Alongside these verbal darts, the Soviet authorities ratcheted up their
propaganda against Judaism and Zionism elsewhere. The pairing of the
Star of David and the swastika now proliferated across the Soviet press and
was accompanied by a sharp uptick in published diatribes against religious
Judaism and Zionism in official publications, often conflating the two. A
nadir came in 1963 with the publication in Kiev of "Judaism without Embellishment," a text by a Ukrainian "scholar" of Judaism who recycled the
lies of the Protocols of the Elders of Zion and other antisemitic motifs to
indict Jews as the enemies of all humankind.[43]

It was amid these clashes that Abram called again in January 1964 for a
separate amendment in the draft convention against racism requiring that
"State Parties condemn anti-semitism" and eliminate it from their juris-
dictions. The Soviet representative countered with a sly rhetorical strategy.
"[We can all] agree that antisemitism in all its manifestations, past and
present, is a repugnant form of racial discrimination," he announced in a
conciliatory tone. But *specific* instances of racism had no place in a general
legal document of this kind. Apartheid constituted a general form of racial
discrimination because it theoretically targeted anyone based on a universal physical attribute, skin color. Antisemitism, by contrast, was directed
only against one historic group. Still, he continued, if others desired to
name antisemitism explicitly, the Soviet Union would readily agree on one
condition. There ought to be a sub-amendment that also included "Nazism, neo-Nazism, and colonialism and other manifestations of atrocious
racist ideas and practices." It was a not-so-veiled attack on two American
allies: West Germany and Israel.[44]

After much debate and no resolution, the Sub-Commission concluded
its 1964–1965 session with a decision to forward the draft convention against
racism, with the proposed American amendment and the Soviet sub-

amendment, to the General Assembly for consideration at its fall 1965 session. There, to Perlzweig's chagrin, the situation rapidly slid out of control. In the larger forum of the General Assembly, the Soviets had even more allies. When the item came up for discussion, the Saudi delegate, for instance, complained that any mention of antisemitism would need to be matched by reference to all abhorrent "isms," including "anti-Arabism." A game of chicken ensued. Then the Soviets played their trump card. The Soviet delegate proposed a new formula:

> State Parties condemn antisemitism, Zionism, Nazism, neo-Nazism and all other forms of the policy and ideology of colonialism, national and race hatred and exclusiveness and shall take action as appropriate for the speedy eradication of those inhumane ideas and practices in the territories subject to their jurisdiction.

Zionism, declared the Soviet delegate, was as "dangerous" a form of racial discrimination as Nazism, fascism, and antisemitism.[45]

A ferocious daylong debate ensued, with the Soviets and the Americans at loggerheads. Comay, the Israeli representative, angrily blasted the "contemptible maneuver" as "tantamount to substituting the victims for the persecutors." Finally, Greece and Hungary proffered a compromise measure that removed mention of any specific "ism." Nazism was gone. Antisemitism was gone. Zionism was gone. Only apartheid remained. After a roll-call vote, the Convention on the Elimination of All Forms of Racial Discrimination was approved and opened for ratification.[46]

"A Devastating Defeat"

Abram believed he had won. The Soviets and Arabs had been forced to resort to an argument so specious and perverse that it could not be taken seriously by enlightened opinion. There still ought to be a law against antisemitism, but that would perhaps come with the draft Convention against Religious Intolerance. In the meantime, CERD could be used to pressure the Soviets for their antisemitism. American and Israeli interests had aligned together on the side of freedom. Once again, Perlzweig reached the completely opposite conclusion. We have just witnessed a "humiliating, devastating defeat for the United States and Israel," both of whom were again outmaneuvered by the Soviets. This was something far "worse than a crime; it was a blunder." By demanding antisemitism be named in CERD, Abram and his allies "just ignored basic political arithmetic. . . . There is only one Jewish state, but there are now fourteen Arab states."[47]

Perlzweig also mocked the "silly suggestion" that the CERD "will be a useful instrument in the struggle for Jewish equality in the Soviet Union." It strained credulity to think that "rapping the Soviets on the knuckles with this law" would stop anti-Jewish persecution or help the Jewish minority. He spoke caustically of Jewish popular protest: "marching rabbis with lighted candles" parading down Fifth Avenue "will obviously have no impact on the Russians."[48]

While Perlzweig and Abram offered their divergent assessments of the CERD episode, the Israeli legal team found itself internally divided. UN Israeli diplomat Meir Rosenne agreed with Abram that the Soviets had lost the debate. The controversy had drawn the world's attention to the fate of Soviet Jews, he wrote in a diplomatic cable, who no doubt would take comfort from the sight of a small, feisty Jewish state defending them. As for the Soviet authorities, they surely knew that the Arabs were fair-weather friends. Abram had been a natural partner and bridge to American interests, while Perlzweig he dismissed as a "fanatical Hasid of quiet diplomacy."[49]

Robinson, however, sided with Perlzweig. "Quiet diplomacy was precisely the way to improve the status of Soviet Jews," he wrote, "not public relations." Grandstanding at the UN stood no chance of ameliorating their condition. Nor did Robinson approve of Abram's hyperbolic interpretation of the Line 5 question. Though it might sometimes be abused, "this [passport] mark enables Jews who so wish to demonstrate their identity (whatever its intensity)."[50]

The conflicting ideas over how to handle Soviet antisemitism came down once again to a philosophical question about the meaning of human rights. Abram could not stomach a separate legal designation for Jews any more than he could tolerate racial classifications at home. Thinking in terms of groups violated the individualist character of his American liberalism. Ironically, the same reasoning would lead him in later years to oppose

Jacob Robinson sitting behind Abba Eban (front right),
Israel's ambassador to the UN, 1950s

United Nations Photo Library

affirmative action: the goal was to end all discrimination, he insisted, not to promote group differences. Perlzweig and Robinson, as veterans of the European minority rights movement, saw Jewish groupness as the starting point for pursuing universal justice. What all these Jewish activists now agreed on, however, was that Zionism's image had begun to change ominously. A pernicious caricature of the movement now complicated all efforts to combat antisemitism in the realm of international law.[51]

Further evidence of that change arrived during the denouement of the UN debate on antisemitism. It came in the form of a dramatic coda to the Eichmann trial. In 1964 and 1965, Robinson became enmeshed in a public polemic about the most incendiary Jewish text on antisemitism to emerge in English since the Holocaust: Hannah Arendt's *Eichmann in Jerusalem*.

The Formidable Dr. Robinson

In February 1963, the *New Yorker* began publishing in serial form Arendt's account of the Eichmann trial. After an earlier phase of Zionist activism during World War II, Arendt had largely distanced herself from the Jewish state. The trial was a chance for her to see Israel firsthand and make a new evaluation of its political character. From the very first page of her reportage, she registered her scorn. Amid brilliant philosophical meditations on the nature of evil, the causes of the Holocaust, and the meaning of historical justice, Arendt systematically disparaged the trial itself as an exercise in Zionist parochialism. Ben-Gurion, Hausner, and "almost everyone else in Israel" operated from a myopic belief that "only a Jewish court could render justice to Jews, and that it was the business of Jews to sit in judgment on their enemies." The Israelis, she charged, had pursued justice for Jewish victims at the expense of humankind: "Insofar as the victims were Jews, it was right and proper that a Jewish court should sit in judgment; but insofar as the crime was a crime against humanity, it needed an international tribunal to do justice to it." The implication was clear. When it came to international justice, Jews could not stand in for all of humanity. She further suggested that European Jewish leaders had been complicit in the Nazi destruction of their communities, while Zionists were only too willing to profit from Jewish death to further their political aims in Palestine.[52]

Arendt's polemic triggered an explosive reaction inside the American Jewish community. "Self-Hating Jewess Writes Pro-Eichmann Series for the New Yorker," read a headline in the *Jewish Spectator*. Gideon Hausner flew to New York to address a crowd numbering one thousand people in defense of the trial's legitimacy. Arendt's articles, published also that year as a book, *Eichmann in Jerusalem: A Report on the Banality of Evil*, sparked a "civil war" among American intellectuals. While Bruno Bettelheim and Hans Morgenthau heaped praise on Arendt's achievement, Marie Syrkin and Norman Podhoretz savaged her for reversing the roles of good and evil, Jew and antisemite. "In place of the monstrous Nazi," wrote Podhoretz in *Commentary*, "she has given us the 'banal' Nazi; in place of the Jew as virtuous martyr . . . the Jew as accomplice in evil." By far the most significant response came from Robinson. His first salvo was a pamphlet written at the request of the Anti-Defamation League, and his conclusions were damning: "To the extent that the book's research and its author's understanding are glib and trite, *Eichmann in Jerusalem* is a banal book," but "to the extent that it gains acceptance as a work of unquestioned authority—and undermines the realities of history—it is an evil book." He accused Arendt of approaching the trial and the Holocaust itself in supremely bad faith:

> Her book is a mine of misinformation, half-truths, suppression of evidence running against her thesis, and flatly contradictory statements on numerous points. . . . In her fault-finding mission, she attacks the panel of judges (subtly), the Attorney-General (vehemently), the defense counsel (contemptuously), the witnesses, Ben-Gurion, Israel, Zionism, Jews generally, [and] Germany (pre-Nazi, Nazi, post-Nazi). The only figure to escape her wrath is Adolf Eichmann.

Far from being a mass murderer, Arendt's Eichmann "emerges as a vaguely sympathetic object, a victim of the system, and somewhat to be pitied."[53]

Robinson did not actually dispute Arendt's core thesis on the ultimate cause of the Holocaust. In coining the phrase "the banality of evil" and depicting Eichmann as a careerist bureaucrat and something of a "clown," she had intended to show how Nazi totalitarianism as a political system inverted morality and deformed the human capacity to exercise the critical thought necessary for ethical conduct. Robinson concurred that it was not any one malevolent genius, but "the incredibly evil social system of the Nazis . . . that resulted in the destruction of European Jewry." What troubled him about her argument were two corollaries of it: the accusation that the Jews, especially Zionist leaders, were complicit in Jewish self-destruction by aiding the Nazis, and the charge of Jewish moral parochialism in the Israeli prosecution of the crime. In Arendt's version of history, he complained, "there was factually no difference between the victims and the criminals, all of them being equally in a state of moral collapse."

> If a hold-up man enters a store and at pistol point forces the storekeeper to open the register and deliver him the cash and the storekeeper obeys, did he cooperate with the criminal? Did he become his own accomplice? If in an era of general lawlessness and military rule a gigantic mass-murder organization imprisons the Jews and then forces them to do what the mass-murderers wish, and they do so, do they cooperate? Are they accomplices? From the comfort of the Manhattan apartment, armed with a code of ethics destined for free men in a free society, not burdened by any knowledge of the realities of life under the Nazi regime and devoid of a sympathetic understanding of conditions in which millions of people lived, the author condemns each and every member of the Jewish Councils.[54]

Robinson reserved his second line of critique for a book-length riposte he published in 1965 under the title *And the Crooked Shall Be Made Straight*. The book made instant headlines. His dense litany of her book's faults—a tally of some six hundred egregious errors of historical fact and legal reasoning—served as an angry yet pedantic prosecutorial brief. But he also called her out for libeling the Jewish pursuit of universal justice: "She has no clear idea of the way in which new law emerges, or of the function of law in national and international society." Thus instead of recognizing the moral and legal necessity of an Israeli trial, she blamed Israel for the very act of "advancing the rule of law and the principles of justice in the international community."[55]

Arendt's reply took the form of a long letter to the *New York Review of Books*. She mocked Robinson's "eminent authority" and turned his legal acumen and historical focus against him. The "formidable Dr. Robinson," she wrote, was "psychologically color blind" and had written a "non-book," which engaged in "super-quibbling" and revealed "a truly dazzling display of sheer inability to read." After attacking his credentials and his nit-picking focus on small-bore factual questions, she went on to assert Robinson's role at the center of a vast, powerful conspiracy of Jewish organizations and the Israeli government, all of which were engaged in a "war" to paint her as an "evil person" for the crime of courageously telling the truth.[56]

Robinson resisted the temptation to do battle in the pages of the *New York Review of Books*. His only public rejoinder came in the conclusion to the French edition of his book, which appeared in 1968. There he ended with a brief meditation on the meaning of Jewish history and universal justice that had eluded "Mme. Arendt." He quoted rabbinical texts and the famous "Kaddish of Rabbi Levi-Yitshok of Berdichev," an East European Hasidic song that mingles quotations from the Aramaic-language mourner's *kaddish* prayer with Yiddish-language pleas to God to provide justice for His people. The Persians, Babylonians, Edomites, Russians, Germans, and English—all the other nations, he wrote, worshipped their kings and themselves. Only the people of Israel acknowledged God's sovereignty over the world. Now they too deserved redemption and an end to exile. Robinson quoted the song's full text to emphasize the uniqueness of the Jewish pursuit of higher law. Beyond the profane pursuit of power by empires, Jewish politics, in other words, would bring a small people justice and advance the rule of (divine) law for all humanity. But Jews could do so only if they embraced their distinctiveness rather than aping other peoples and abandoning their own roots.[57]

"Universalism is an old Jewish doctrine," Perlzweig wrote in 1966, that in modern times had received "a new meaning and a practical application" thanks to Jewish human rights activism. Then and now, Jews sought to blend pragmatism and idealism, politics and principle, and self and other in the quest for justice. He recalled his 1947 visit to Haiti a few months ahead of the UN vote on the partition of Palestine: "I was recognized by the President of that State as a man who, he said, had fought for the rights of Negroes in the United Nations. A great many people [also] said that I had fought for the rights of Jews; they were both right, I fought for human rights and . . . Jewish rights." Sustaining this twin focus was always a balancing act. But if the human rights side of the equation proved more challenging after

1948, from 1960 onward it seemed well-nigh impossible. In the new climate of Cold War decolonization, Jewish rights seemed to be in direct contradiction to human rights.[58]

At its core, the controversies over Eichmann and the swastikas revolved around the same question: the linkage between universal justice and Jewish particularism. The efforts in the 1960s to seek a legal victory over antisemitism, past and present, stumbled into the thickets of a new anticolonial universalism. The fights over the Eichmann trial pointed to a struggle over how Jews could seek justice in the international arena given the reality of Israel as a sovereign power. Combating antisemitism old and new, Jewish rights-defenders in the 1960s found themselves accused from without and within of moral parochialism. What emerged from each of the battles over antisemitism, law, and human rights in the 1960s was an image of Israel as the ultimate parochial entity, incompatible with the universalist imperatives of human rights and global justice. Those who understood the fight against antisemitism and for Holocaust justice as advancements for Jews and humanity found themselves drowned out by those who argued that, in the words of one American Protestant minister, "In the ethical sense I can see little difference between the Jew-pursuing Nazi and the Nazi-pursuing Jew."[59]

We should be careful not to overstate the clarity of this linkage. In the first half of the decade, Zionism's negative image had not fully hardened in the global human rights imagination. Indeed, international human rights in the 1960s remained an inchoate idea still largely unknown outside the rarified circles of diplomats and legal specialists. That would change dramatically over the course of the next decade. The emergence of a truly global human rights movement coincided with the departure of Jewish organizations from the world of international activism. The key event in that story came in 1967, when Jewish sovereignty and human rights were both stretched to new extremes by a sudden, brief war with long-term aftershocks.

10

Prisoners of Zion

ON SEPTEMBER 24, 1968, the second day of Rosh Hashanah, Bella Ravdin dashed off the angriest Jewish New Year card of her life. "Our people in the Head office seem not to have the slightest idea what is going on here in Israel," wrote the founder of Amnesty International's Israeli branch to her American counterpart Paul Lyons. Since the end of the previous year's Six-Day War, Israel had been rocked by Palestinian bombings at Jerusalem's Bikkur Holim Hospital, the Tel Aviv Central Bus Station, and elsewhere. The attacks left dozens dead and hundreds wounded. Yet the annual Amnesty Report "speaks of so-called terrorist organizations" and "Arab political prisoners." The Arabs held in Israeli military detention, she insisted, were hardly nonviolent prisoners of conscience. They were guerilla fighters detained under "our emergency laws for security reasons." "Placing bombs in bus stations, cinemas, cafes," she added, "is not so-called terrorism but T E R R O R I S M."

Ravdin's commitment to human rights ran deep. She had fled Nazi Germany for British Palestine in 1933 and had used her Holocaust restitution payments for the Nazi murder of her mother to help launch the Israeli branch of Amnesty. She had attended early organizing conferences in England and personally sponsored scores of prisoners from Spain to South Africa. This depth of commitment only made the sting of betrayal worse. The London leadership, she wrote, had clearly "taken a pro-Arab attitude in the whole dispute," focusing solely on allegations of abuse in Israel prisons while neglecting "the welfare of the Jews in Arab countries." Many English Jewish members had quit the organization. She now considered doing the same. When it came to Israel, Amnesty had lost its moral bearings. "We have no war and no peace," she wrote, but languish in a perpetual state of "guerrilla warfare." How could Amnesty's leaders expect them to go on "with business as usual"?[1]

What Ravdin was grasping in real time was that, with its sudden victory in the Six-Day War, Israel had switched roles in the mind of the emerging global human rights community. In a change as quick as it was baffling, the plucky David was being recast as Goliath. "The good people everywhere have decided to outlaw me," wrote Israeli leftist writer Amos Kenan in 1968. His help was no longer welcome in the global fight for justice. The new reality could be measured by one metric. As an Israeli, he observed bitterly, "I am finally and absolutely forbidden to sign petitions of all sorts for human rights."[2]

The decade after 1967 witnessed two parallel dramas: the rapid rise of human rights into global consciousness and the growing demonization of Israel in that new human rights culture. Across the long 1970s, Amnesty morphed from a struggling British grassroots movement into the premier international human rights organization. By mid-decade it approached 100,000 members across two thousand chapters worldwide. Two years later, in 1977, it was awarded the Nobel Peace Prize. Just as Amnesty was entering the human rights arena to rousing applause, veteran Jewish human rights organizations were quietly exiting in defeat. In the early 1970s, both the World Jewish Congress and the American Jewish Committee shuttered their UN offices. Their ignominious departure was hastened by a combined Soviet-Arab campaign that falsely accused them of acting as front organizations for the Government of Israel. This was followed by a steady drumbeat of hostile UN measures, culminating in the 1975 UN General Assembly Resolution 3379, which officially branded Zionism as a form of racism.

Jewish human rights activism never fully recovered from that crisis. Though there would be many more chapters in the story of Jews and human rights, they were all overshadowed by a lingering question. In a world full of unabashed autocrats and genocidal regimes, what explains the human rights community's unswerving focus on the State of Israel?

The two conventional answers to that question point to the Manichean image of Israel in international human rights today. To Israel's critics, human rights simply caught up with Zionist politics after 1967. For the sovereign Jewish state to deny self-determination and basic rights to a stateless Palestinian population was a deliberate political choice. In this view, shining a spotlight on Israel, regardless of whether its neighbors are better or worse, is precisely what human rights activists are supposed to do. Israel's claim to democracy demands that it be held to such a standard. To Israel's defenders, however, this image of Israel as a rogue regime is itself the product of an artificial searchlight powered by propaganda. The glare of a deliberately tilted klieg light distorts the features of a democracy struggling with terrorism and an endless border war. Equally damning, they charge, the nightmarish lighting creates shadows in which terrorists hide with impunity.

There can be little doubt that the unanticipated permanence of the Israeli-Palestinian conflict has tightly bound Jews into a Gordian knot of ethics and power. An ongoing military occupation is bound to result in inequities and abuses that rightly deserve the attention of the global human rights community—and a separate historical reckoning. An aggressive post-1967 Jewish settler movement further injected a toxic current of religious messianism into the mix, while providing no viable solution for how to reconcile its territorial claims against the reality of the Palestinian population living there. At the same time, even the most sympathetic observers note that Palestinian leaders have often deliberately blurred the line between moral protest and cynical manipulation of human rights activism to further authoritarian goals. Politics alone, however, cannot explain fully the story of Jews and human rights in the aftermath of the Six-Day War. If Zionism changed after 1967, so too did human rights.[3]

Despite the blossoming interest across the world in popular protest movements and global justice causes, most people in the 1960s had still never heard the phrase "human rights." But in the 1970s, an idea associated with arcane treaties and political philosophy suddenly swept into the global lexicon as a catchphrase for moral universalism. Historians have explained that change by reference to Western dissatisfaction with Cold War geopolitics and the moral bankruptcy of other grand ideologies that dominated so much of the twentieth century: the discrediting of European socialism in the aftermath of the Prague Spring in 1968; the crisis of American liberalism in the wake of Vietnam and Watergate; the tainting of nationalism by the radicalization of Third World anticolonialism; and the disturbing rise of authoritarianism in both right-wing and left-wing variants across the Global South. It is less noticed that this dramatic change in the fortunes of human rights went hand in hand with the decline of Jewish activism in that arena. This was not a coincidence.[4]

The quest for the universal always begins with a rejection of the particular. No organization embodied that truism better than Amnesty International. In the 1970s, it was Amnesty that carried human rights beyond the confines of the UN and out into the world's imagination. Its meteoric rise was fueled by a distinctive vision of human rights universalism, a transcendent ethos beyond nations and states, beyond parties, politics, and ideologies. The movement it led took the form of a religion-less religion or, more properly, a secularized global Christianity. From Peter Benenson onward, the faithful of Amnesty wished to do more than increase justice and reduce harm; they aspired to redeem the world itself. In Amnesty's hands, human rights left behind international law to become a post-legal instrument to free the minds and bodies of the unjustly imprisoned and abused. Its activists were not interested in adjudicating rights claims in the realm of law. They wished instead to elevate human rights into an ideological end in itself. That powerful ideal of moral purism is what captured the world's imagination. But to reach the universal, Amnesty had to leave behind the particular. In the post-1960s human rights imagination, the pole of stubborn particularism increasingly came to be symbolized by Zionism.[5]

Bella Ravdin foresaw this problem already in 1968. She had come to Amnesty from the Zionist movement. Concerned about social justice and renewing Jewish peoplehood, she turned to global activism. With Jewish politics as the moral starting point for her internationalist ethics, she envisioned human rights not as an uncompromising universalism but as a form of "realistic idealism." Now she believed her Amnesty colleagues, in their messianic zeal, had turned Zionism into the imaginary enemy of human rights.[6]

Ravdin's early critique of the new face of human rights did not turn her into a defensive tribalist. She believed that Israel remained entirely fallible and subject to improvement; human rights applied there too, without question. Equally importantly, the rest of the world still mattered. The Middle East was not the only place on fire. "Looking at what happened lately in Czechoslovakia, the war in Biafra," she asked in her 1968 letter, "can there still be hope that this world will not head for doomsday?" Yet she saw one bright spot on the global horizon: the upcoming American presidential election. In her disillusionment with human rights, she enunciated a new article of faith that would increasingly govern Jewish human rights philosophy from that point onward: the indispensability of American moral power. "I am wishing the U.S.A. [a] President who will be able and [equipped with] progressive thinking to tackle all the problems facing mankind." The 1970s would bring an answer to her secular New Year's prayer.[7]

"The Oldest Human Rights Organization"

Long speeches were a favorite Soviet stall tactic at meetings of the UN Commission on Human Rights. When Moscow's diplomats lacked the votes to block a threatening measure or an embarrassing line of discussion, they simply ran out the clock. On March 21, 1967, Soviet diplomat Yakov Ostrovsky set a new record by speaking for a full hour. On the table was a proposal to create a UN High Commissioner for Human Rights. Its chief sponsor was Blaustein, now working closely with Abram. Back in the 1950s, Blaustein had called for the UN to appoint a chief human rights legal officer "with an international reputation for neutrality and objectivity." This person would be authorized to hear individual petitions from around the world and to investigate alleged violations in a truly independent, apolitical manner. In 1963, he revived the idea, emboldened by the return of a Democratic president. He sought out support from the Kennedy State Department, the British Foreign Office, the UN Secretariat, and other Western NGO activists, all of whom were frustrated by the political stalemates of the UN program.[8]

Even after Kennedy's shocking death that November, Blaustein pushed on with his advocacy with the new Johnson administration. The idea picked up steam in the mid-1960s, buoyed by his promise of a $1 million donation to the secretary-general for the UN to study the "Blaustein plan." A coalition of Western states began to emerge, with discreet U.S. and British backing and public sponsorship by the government of Costa Rica. Even more striking, the network of NGOs that co-sponsored the effort included a virtual map of Jewish human rights activism up until that point. For example, a March 1966 press release in support of the measure was co-signed by six people, three of whom were Benenson, Perlzweig, and Blaustein's chief AJC aide-de-camp on human rights, Sidney Liskofsky.[9]

The moment of unity was not destined to last. For while Perlzweig and Benenson hoped the High Commissioner idea might allow human rights to circumvent Cold War tensions, Blaustein's AJC team saw the proposal as a strategic calculation. "[I]n the long run," wrote Abram, now the Johnson administration's U.S. delegate to the Commission, "the U.S. and other 'open societies,' have less to risk and more to gain from exposure to international human rights pressures than the Communist and other undemocratic nations which hide behind various types of 'curtains.'" As it turned out, his adversaries agreed. Hence Ostrovsky's spring 1967 speech devolved into an antisemitic diatribe.[10]

Over weeks of debate at the Commission that spring, Ostrovsky used every trick he could to dissuade and delay consideration of the High Commissioner proposal. Finally, in the late March session, he played his trump card. How could they take the proposal seriously, he asked, given that it came from a man who served "two masters"? The U.S. delegate was himself quite plainly a Jew, sneered Ostrovsky, "obeying the orders of the Zionists and the Jews of America." When Abram tried to lodge a protest, Ostrovsky cut him off: "You may interrupt people at a meeting of the American Jewish Committee, Mr. Abram, but this is not a meeting of . . . [that] Zionist organization of which you are president." Abram countered with his own attack on Russian hypocrisy and antisemitism: "The American Jewish Committee is the oldest human rights organization, having been founded in 1906 to fight Czarist antisemitism, and it struggles against all forms of man's inhumanity to man and for all people—regardless of race, color or creed," he declared. Surely the Soviet delegate knew this. After all, Abram had personally seen him frequently visiting the AJC's human rights library in its midtown building on East 56th Street.[11]

If there remained any doubt about the Cold War Middle Eastern geopolitical alliances, it was soon put to rest by what happened next. The Iraqi delegate, Badia Afnan, rose to defend her country's Soviet ally with a forty-five-minute tirade of her own. Iraq had just brutally repressed a Kurdish separatist uprising, leading to widespread charges of genocide. She now blasted the "Zionists" for violating the rights of Arab citizens of Israel. She was promptly rebuked by the Israeli delegate, Supreme Court Justice Haim Cohn, who answered that Israel had nothing to hide. "In contrast with some other countries," he said pointedly, "my Government pledges that Israel would admit a High Commissioner for human rights and allow him to see whatever he wanted to see and could pledge that we would listen carefully to his advice."[12]

Cohn was no stranger to human rights. Born and raised in Weimar Germany, he practiced law in Palestine after 1933, then rose to become Israel's first minister of justice and then the country's attorney-general in the 1950s. He served as a judge on its highest court throughout the 1960s and 1970s even as he co-launched the Israeli Amnesty branch with Ravdin and worked closely on Israel's human rights foreign policy with Robinson. He was fully convinced that Israel was in the right, legally and politically. In 1966, the government had lifted national security restrictions that had limited the movements and other civil liberties of certain Arab-Israeli border communities. With a clean bill of legal health, Israel was ready to go on the offensive against the Soviets and the Arabs and help flesh out the necessary infrastructure to make human rights a more effective reality.

Emboldened by the fight, both Cohn and Abram pushed forward that spring. At last we have movement on human rights, Abram wrote in a mass mailing to the 26,000 lawyers among the AJC's national membership. Along with the High Commissioner proposal, Abram relaunched the effort to ban antisemitism in the draft Convention on the Prevention of Religious Intolerance (CPRI). The 1965 Convention on the Elimination of Racial Discrimination specifically listed apartheid as the archetype of all racial discrimination, but failed to mention antisemitism at all. Now, as its sister treaty came up for consideration in May 1967, Cohn and Abram co-sponsored a joint Israeli-American amendment to list antisemitism by name as the baseline model of religious hatred. Yet before any of these votes could take place, the geopolitical landscape would be completely altered in less than a week.[13]

Tensions had risen steadily in the Middle East in the first half of 1967 after the late 1966 Jordanian-Israeli border clashes. Bellicose statements from Nasser and other Arab leaders about wiping Israel off the map and finishing the war of 1948 were accompanied that May by Egyptian, Syrian, Jordanian, and other Arab troop deployments along the Israeli borders. On May 17, Soviet MiG-21 jets strafed the Dimona nuclear reactor in the southern Negev desert. The next day, Nasser insisted that UN Secretary-General U Thant remove the UN Emergency Force troops, which acted as a buffer in the Sinai Peninsula. Four days later, Nasser closed the Straits of Tiran to Israeli shipping, a blockade that constituted a casus belli in international law. Like Jews around the world, Perlzweig anxiously watched as "the gravest crisis that has confronted the Jewish people for many years" unfolded. Whatever the outcome, he recognized, the Middle East situation placed "Israel back as #1 on the Jewish agenda." All Jewish human rights work would have to reckon with that new reality.[14]

On June 5, as Perlzweig sat writing those lines in New York, nearly two hundred Israeli aircraft fanned out over the Mediterranean Sea before swooping back in on the coast to bomb the Egyptian Air Force on the ground in a surprise preemptive attack. With devastating precision, they destroyed the greatest military weapon on their southern flank, the force of Soviet-made Egyptian jets. At the same time, Israeli troops flowed into Sinai while Arab forces began to counterattack. It was all over nearly as soon as it began. Though outnumbered in terms of sheer troop strength, Israel proved its considerable military superiority. In less than a week, the Jewish state gained full control of Jerusalem and took over large swaths of the Jordanian West Bank, Egyptian Gaza, and the Syrian Golan Heights. Jubilation now replaced panic. In the early days of postwar euphoria, few considered the looming challenge. With the land came the people in it—and the question of their shared future.

From Minority to Majority

Just days after the fighting ended, Perlzweig touched down in Israel, anxious to see the postwar situation with his own eyes. In Jerusalem he strolled across the ruins of the border wall that had formerly separated its eastern and western halves. The sights and sounds of a city reunited filled him with hope.

> I walked into the Old City and I walked into the market, and walked down the steps where there were Arab shops and I went into the shops and talked to them. I found nothing but friendliness. I was directed by Arab policemen. The officials, the Jews and the Arabs mingled together in the streets. There was no sign of fear at all. . . . After all these years of enmity and bitterness, you would never guess that a week or two ago there had been two governments and no communication.

These memories were still fresh as Perlzweig spoke these words in Geneva in early July at the World Federations of United Nations Associations Summer School. His lecture was titled "Judaism and Human Rights," part of a series on world religions and human rights, but he had little interest in talking about theology: "I have spent a great deal of my life in the fight for human rights and so when I ask you to try and consider with me the meaning of the Jewish tradition for human rights, the contribution it has made, you will understand I am not talking in theoretical terms, but . . . [rather from] daily experience." There were certain core ideas in Judaism about the dignity of the individual, he went on, but the thrust of Jewish human rights activism was not to be found in abstract doctrine but in this-world justice. As an example, he described his current assignment: "I have been engaged in what has been a rather difficult effort to secure human rights for a minority or a series of small minorities that have been overlooked in the exciting events of the last few weeks. Those minorities are the Jewish communities in a number of countries bordering on Israel." New antisemitic campaigns in Egypt, Syria, and Iraq had led to the arrest of hundreds of Jews, reports of torture, and even murder. Fears ran high, in the words of his American Reform rabbinical colleagues, that "the dark shadow of genocide again casts its pall upon the Jewish people."[15]

Beyond Jewish anxieties about the fate of other Middle Eastern Jews, Perlzweig recognized that Israel itself held a new position of power over its Arab population. "You might say a minority is always in favor of human rights," he told his Geneva audience, "What happens when it becomes a majority, when it is put to the test?" Thus far, he said proudly, Jews had acquitted themselves well. "Every Arab citizen, as an Israeli citizen, has exactly the same rights as every Jewish-Israeli citizen." Left unmentioned was the fate of the new post-1967 Palestinians, who now found themselves inside the conquered territories of the West Bank and the Gaza Strip.[16]

In July 1967, Perlzweig could afford to ignore these people. He believed their status would be swiftly resolved through Arab-Israeli peace negotiations. Blaustein shared this hope. While Perlzweig hopped between London, Geneva, and Jerusalem that July, Blaustein spent that month shuttling back and forth between Tel Aviv and New York, helping Israeli leaders and UN Secretary-General U Thant identify an Arab country willing to "quietly talk peace with Israel." None stepped forward. Meanwhile, the Israelis themselves began to rethink their eagerness for an immediate peace settlement. The terms would have to be favorable. In the end, the other side also showed little interest in peace talks. On September 1, the Arab states convened in Sudan to issue the Khartoum Resolution, rejecting negotiations of any kind with Israel. Included in that summit was the PLO, now one of a number of Marxist, anticolonial Palestinian organizations that embraced terrorism as a means of combating Israel and advancing their national cause. Under the leadership of Yasser Arafat, the PLO specifically linked its struggle for the "right of self-defense and the complete restoration of our lost homeland" to legally established "principles of human rights." The move guaranteed that the UN would become even more of a battlefield for issues concerning Jews, Arabs, and human rights.[17]

"A Simple Piece of Political Arithmetic"

The Six-Day War came just as the full impact of the new demographics of the postcolonial UN began to manifest in the arena of human rights. Emboldened by their growing numbers, Asian and African states pushed hard in the late 1960s to empower the UN human rights program. Yet they coupled this effort with a radical transformation of the very definition of human rights. One of the first signs of that change came at a fall 1967 session of the Sub-Commission on the Prevention of Discrimination and the Protection of Minorities. Perlzweig, back from his summer travels, listened in

Maurice Perlzweig (back row, center) attending a session
of the Sub-Commission on the Prevention of Discrimination
and the Protection of Minorities in the mid-1960s

Courtesy of Roberta Cohen

shock as the Tanzanian representative suggested it was time to change the
name and mandate of the body from the protection of "minorities" to the protection of "majorities." This radical demand reflected just how much the logic
of anticolonialism had transformed the meaning of human rights. This
transformation was even more visible in the two human rights covenants,
long stalled, which finally appeared in 1966. Both the International Covenant on Civil and Political Rights and the International Covenant on Economic, Social and Cultural Rights now affirmed the "right of all peoples to
self-determination" as preceding all others. Once envisioned as a tool for
taming statist nationalism in the aftermath of World War II, under its newest custodians the UN human rights system turned into a vehicle for sover-
eigntist claims of anticolonial movements.[18]

This change placed Perlzweig and other Jewish human rights activists
in a bind. On the one hand, he applauded the energy and resolve of the
Asian and African delegates who agitated for using the Commission on
Human Rights for direct investigation and enforcement of "gross violations" of human rights. Their demographic clout secured the passage of

ECOSOC Resolution 1235 in 1967, empowering the Commission on Human Rights to undertake its own investigations. For the first time ever, the UN human rights body could authorize itself to intervene in sovereign states in the quest for justice. On the other hand, Perlzweig privately worried that the new Afro-Asian "thinking on human rights is utterly different from ours." The African states' number one issue, he wrote, was anticolonialism, with the most egregious example being South African apartheid.

> Any publication on human rights which does not clearly indicate that the highest priority must be given first to the fight against apartheid, and second to the ending of colonialism, is strictly taboo. Its authors belong to the enemy camp, and are raising such terrible questions as Greece, Haiti or the Jews in the Soviet Union for the calculated purpose of diverting attention from what ought to be the main goal of all decent people.

Perlzweig was hardly a colonial apologist. He knew enough of African politics to understand the injustices of apartheid, and his Zionism alerted him to the cardinal importance of national self-determination. The problem, he explained, was twofold. First, by privileging sovereignty over individual or group protection, the new ideology distorted the moral calculus at the root of human rights.

> When Black men slaughter other Black men, it is apparently nobody's business. Perhaps I should modify this and say that when Arabs slaughter Black men as in the Sudan it is also nobody's business. Mr. Mohammed's Nigeria could dispose of 30,000 Igbos [in Biafra], in a clear case of genocide, without affecting his style when he talks about the wickedness of white governments. Even slavery cannot be examined without reference to "the slavery-like practices of apartheid and colonialism." . . . We seem to have acquiesced in a double standard, one for white and the other for colored, but inherent in this approach is the acceptance of the view that the life of colored peoples is less valuable than that of others, provided always that it is destroyed by Afro-Asians.[19]

The other danger lay in the realm of geopolitical strategy. The Arab states seized on the new anticolonial reality to broker an alliance permanently linking apartheid to Zionism. In return for Arab support on fight-

ing apartheid, African diplomats readily acceded to Arab demands to treat
Israel like a Western colonial power in all UN human rights matters. In
this context, Jewish concerns increasingly came to be seen as special pleading at best, political conspiracy at worst. The Holocaust earned no particular sympathies. To Perlzweig, this new reality was ample reason to proceed
with caution in the immediate aftermath of the Six-Day War. He informed
his WJC colleagues that the same Tanzanian delegate on three occasions
gave UN speeches in which he exclaimed that "he was not sure defeat of
the Nazis was such a good thing," since "he himself had been 'a British
object.' "[20]

Not all of Perlzweig's fellow Jewish activists took such a dark view. In spite
of the Six-Day War, Cohn and Abram entered the fall 1967 session of the
UN determined to resume where they had left off the previous spring.
Blaustein enlisted the help of Judge Arthur Goldberg, who had stepped
down from the Supreme Court to become U.S. ambassador to the UN, to
advance the High Commissioner proposal. Abram also pushed forward
the Convention on Religious Intolerance with its American-Israeli amendment on antisemitism. The first proposal went nowhere; the second produced what Perlzweig called a "humiliating defeat." When it came time to
vote, out of twelve countries that had previously supported the American-
Israeli amendment just months before, all but two now defected. Steadfast
allies such as Costa Rica, France, the Netherlands, and the United Kingdom
remained silent. Meanwhile, speaker after speaker from the Arab and Communist camps excoriated Israel for violating the religious sanctity of Jerusalem and the human rights of its Arab residents (notably without
reference to the newly conquered populations in the West Bank and Gaza).
In this acrimonious atmosphere, the entire Convention on Religious Intolerance collapsed, leaving in its wake only a stream of legal pejoratives directed at both Jews and Israel.[21]

Reviewing the failure that December, Perlzweig chastised his American
and Israeli friends for ignoring "a simple piece of political arithmetic." "There
is only one Jewish vote in the General Assembly," he wrote, "and thirteen
Arab votes, and the Arab states are able to mobilize the votes of countries
that are indifferent or apathetic in the Afro-Asian bloc in which they play a
very active part." Nor could one ignore the optics. "We have overlooked what

seems to me to be a marked change in the image which the Jews have acquired since June," he told Cohn. "For good or for ill, we are no longer the 'underdog,' and there are many places, other than Paris, in which the description 'dominateur' has become plausible." A forlorn Cohn concurred. He announced his retirement from UN work: "The Commission itself—in its enlarged composition—is becoming more and more politicized."[22]

Any lingering hopes in Perlzweig's mind for human rights died the next year in Tehran in the depressing spectacle of the UN's International Year of Human Rights Conference. The cruel irony of a global gathering on human rights held in an authoritarian police state was only the beginning. The shah's twin sister, Princess Ashraf Pahlavi, played official hostess to the event. In her remarks, she triumphantly announced the rise of Asian womanhood, even as the local Iranian press carried reports of polygamy and Savak secret police agents openly tailed the attendees. Disgusted, Perlzweig left Iran early. The whole meeting, he wrote, had been "a strictly political occasion." For Jews, it was a maddening "exercise in futility" to hear the Arabs "make it a forum for their denunciation of Israel" and "what is now the customary resolution condemning Israel for the treatment of the inhabitants of the occupied territories."

> Many of those who attended the Conference felt that this would be an occasion for mutual back-slapping. As it turned out, it proved to be an occasion for mutual nose-punching. In either case, it failed in its objective to do anything imaginative and constructive which might set forward the cause of human rights. Instead it gave encouragement to those who seek to use every discussion on human rights to exacerbate the Arab-Israeli conflict or to downgrade the discussion of human rights problems which might "detract attention" from apartheid and neocolonialism.[23]

Perlzweig was quick to recognize that the Palestinians living under the new Israeli military occupation deserved justice. He remained a subscriber to the "pure Zionist doctrine that every people is entitled to establish its own sovereign state." That solution would come after all the "oratorical flatulence" on both sides had ceased, when "a more rational dialogue" would lead to peace negotiations between the Israelis and the Arabs held, he assumed, with the tacit consent of the Soviets and the Americans. What

Perlzweig did not anticipate was that rational dialogue was nowhere in sight.[24]

The path to peace was supposed to begin with UN Security Council Resolution 242, approved in November 1967, which stipulated "land-for-peace" as the basis for a resolution of the conflict. But small-scale fighting actually continued between Israel and its Arab neighbors throughout the next three years in the so-called War of Attrition. The unceasing state of hostilities made the work of a Jewish NGO at the UN almost impossible. Thanks to Soviet-Arab propaganda, Perlzweig observed in a private lament, many Afro-Asian delegations believed "we are not really an NGO but a GO, and that we are in fact an instrument either of Israel or of the [World] Zionist Organization, which is taken to mean the same thing." Soon that charge would become official. Beginning in September 1968, the Soviet and Arab state delegations mounted a campaign to expel Jewish organizations from UN activity by revoking their legal status as official consultants. Through an exhausting series of nearly forty meetings stretching into the spring of 1969, a special ECOSOC committee reviewed all 166 NGO members to screen out and revoke the credentials of groups too closely interested in "the rights of a particular people or group." The intent was both clear and familiar: racism was a universal problem, but antisemitism was a parochial concern. The purge made no distinction among Jewish NGOs. All were attacked by Soviet diplomats, who operated under explicit orders from Moscow to denounce "international Zionism." Despite Perlzweig's decades of effort to insulate his group and Jews from the Cold War and the Arab-Israeli conflict, the WJC was labeled a "racist organization," an "arm of Israel," and "an anti-UN organization." The writing on the wall was clear. "We are living in a new world," observed Perlzweig forlornly in 1969. Jewish human rights diplomacy must confront that reality or risk perpetual failure.[25]

The events of 1967 and 1968 finally awakened Blaustein, Abram, and the other AJC leaders to the crisis confronting them. In May 1969, the AJC sponsored a conference, "The United Nations and Human Rights: What Are the Roadblocks?" The distinguished roster of speakers included Justice Goldberg, retired from his UN ambassadorship and now incoming president of the AJC; Republican lawyer Rita Hauser, newly appointed by President Richard Nixon as Abram's replacement on the Commission on

Human Rights; Roger Baldwin; and various other lawyers and former British and U.S. diplomats. Most speakers tried hard to find reasons for optimism about the long-term prospects for human rights. Many referenced Blaustein's High Commissioner idea, which though tabled remained a tantalizing prospect for restoring political neutrality. Other speakers, however, voiced much bleaker views. Andrew Onejeme, the UN representative from the new breakaway Igbo Republic of Biafra, locked in a war with Nigeria, asked poignantly, "Why are the governments so preoccupied with Southern Africa, and do nothing about the flagrant human rights violations in Biafra?" Yoram Dinstein, the Israeli international lawyer and Israeli consul in New York, all but announced the end of the road for human rights at the UN. Recent events had amply demonstrated that the organization was hopelessly compromised.

> The whole emphasis on the promotion of human rights within the framework of the UN is, therefore, wrong. To advance human rights, coping with roadblocks in the organization is not enough; the whole road must be regarded as a cul de sac. If human rights are to be seriously developed, if the world is to be humanized, the process must be deUNized.[26]

Dinstein had a radical solution in mind. At that moment, the Israeli government was engaged in a delicate and secret negotiation with another organization that also sought a path around the UN to promote human rights. It was the beginning of a strange, brief dalliance between the State of Israel and Amnesty International with lasting, profound consequences for both in the field of human rights.

"Necessarily Inadequate"

"I have always regarded Amnesty as a part of the Christian witness," wrote Benenson just weeks after the Six-Day War. Recent events had only strengthened his conviction that politics must be avoided at all costs. If Amnesty did not turn inward to focus on spiritual principles, then "we are trying to empty the sea with bottomless buckets." The ultimate goal must remain the transformation of humankind into "a single world community . . . [that] encompasses the whole earth." He added one telling comment: "I still think—more so than ever after the Arab-Israeli war—that the head-quarters should be out of England." Benenson's profession of utopian faith in one breath followed by a confession of political anxiety in the next was a revealing indication of just how much Jewish questions shaped his moral imagination. Zionism epitomized the chains of tribal politics that only a global spiritual revolution could transcend. That linkage would only grow stronger in the decade to come.[27]

Today, the long-standing rift between Amnesty and Israel looks like a classic conflict of two poles of political thought: universalism versus particularism. Yet the distance between the two belies their shared history. Their divergence began on a personal level, with Benenson's growing estrangement from Israel, and continued with a failed partnership in the aftermath of 1967. Together these forgotten events show how the crisis of human rights made for a shotgun marriage in the late 1960s, followed in just a few years by a bitter divorce. It was in that conflict that human rights and Jewish politics took their final, fateful leave of one another—while leaving their permanent mark on one another in the process.

The Six-Day War coincided with the end of the draining, months-long fight between Benenson and other senior colleagues over the allegations of MI-5 and CIA infiltration. Stepping away from the organization that spring, Benenson retired to his farm near Aylesbury to repair his health and refocus his thoughts. Yet his presence still loomed over Amnesty, as did his ambivalence about Israel. He was quick to condemn Israeli treatment of the Palestinians after 1967. "[I am] a Zionist," he told reporters, but now "I weep for Zion." He stoked controversy with periodic public calls not to visit Israel until the government "frees its subject race." In a column published the same day that three commuter buses were blown up by Palestinian terrorists in Jerusalem, Benenson dismissed Jewish concerns about security: "If the brow-beaten people of the Earth were rescued from their daily fear, terrorism would sink to insignificance. Given their situation, what have they to lose by setting off bombs?" He later championed the case of Mordecai Vanunu, the Israeli whistleblower and Christian convert who revealed the existence of the Dimona nuclear program. Given these and other comments, some of his close friends in Amnesty concluded that Benenson had become "almost anti-Jewish."[28]

The charge of self-hatred was an exaggeration. Even as Benenson vocally turned on Israel after 1967, he did not become an antisemite. He made no effort to disavow the personal ties of his family (including his outspoken mother) to Israel. He wrote affectionately if ironically about Jewish philanthropy, Israeli kibbutzim, and Jewish guilt. Most crucially, he rejected Arab attempts to deny Jews any title to historic Palestine—and to equate Zionism with South African apartheid. Jews, he wrote, were the "majority of the population," not minority rulers like the White Afrikaners, and the Jewish claim to the land of Zion was "deeply rooted in the religion of Judaism and . . . the fact that two thousand years ago Palestine was a Jewish territory." Jews and Arabs alike were entitled to their beliefs and their land. Justice required as much. Still, he bristled at Jewish clannishness and ethnic pleading, which stood in the way of the ultimate promise of global humanity unbound by difference. The problem was excessive Jewish parochialism, and his example suggested that the ideal way for Jews to practice human rights was as Jews beyond Judaism. He had little patience for the nuances of Jewish politics and the contingencies of history. After 1967, he assigned both Jews and Arabs fixed roles in the morality play of human rights. His colleagues at the helm of Amnesty soon followed his lead.[29]

The 1967 crisis at Amnesty was not only about leadership. The group was still plagued by financial struggles. Its quick initial growth after 1961 plateaued in the middle of the decade. The late 1960s saw the demise of several branches, including entire national sections in France and the Netherlands. The heavy reliance on Benenson's charisma and freewheeling style had left Amnesty struggling to exercise effective control over its mushrooming branches. It fell to Benenson's successor, Martin Ennals, to right the ship. Raised a devout Baptist in a prominent family of British politicians, Ennals had passed through leftist student politics into senior leadership roles in the British civil liberties and anti-apartheid movements. He had no public record on the Middle East conflict, save for one youthful letter to the *Times* of London contesting the 1947 UN Partition plan as a violation of Arab rights. But he had come to the attention of British intelligence authorities in the 1950s for his UNESCO work in Cairo. After taking the helm at Amnesty in 1968, Ennals quickly faced internal pressure to stake out an aggressive stance on the human rights violations in the Israeli-Palestinian conflict.[30]

In December 1968 Sir Osmond Michael Williams, a Liberal MP and Amnesty patron, traveled to Beirut for the first Arab Regional Conference on Human Rights. Years before he had done his British military service in Mandatory Palestine. Now he came for an event that was part of a broader effort by both the Arab League and the European radical left to instrumentalize human rights following the Six-Day War. At the conference Osmond met representatives of the PLO and the Popular Front for the Liberation of Palestine, who gave him reports of Arab prisoners claiming torture in Israeli prisons in the war's aftermath. Back in London, the question arose of whether to pursue the allegations. Fellow longtime Amnesty leaders Christopher Mayhew and Ian Gilmour urged Ennals to focus on this issue. Gilmour had launched his own pro-Palestinian lobbying group in the aftermath of 1967 to combat what he called the Israeli pattern of Nazi-like *"apartheid and Zionist exclusiveness."* In his opinion, "the Palestinian resistance fighters are no more terrorists than were the French maquis" (the World War II resistance fighters). Until that time, Amnesty had never sponsored a prisoner from Israel. It was high time to do so, he insisted.[31]

While Williams was visiting Beirut, Ennals attended a public evening meeting in London sponsored by the World Jewish Congress on "the plight of the Jews in Arab lands." There, he pledged that he would personally visit the Middle East in the next few months to investigate allegations of abuse on both sides. He made the trip in February 1969, touring Israel and inspecting its military prisons, after which he publicly announced in a letter to the Israeli Commissioner of Prisons "that he was favourably impressed by what he saw." In spite of his pledge, Ennals did not end up visiting any Arab country to investigate the status of Jewish prisoners. Instead, he decided to dig further into reports of Israeli torture that had surfaced in Williams's additional interviews with former Arab prisoners. Based on these testimonies, Ennals compiled a report that he then presented to the Israeli government in April 1969.[32]

Ennals hoped the report would give him leverage to expand a dialogue with the Israeli government on access to prisoners and pledges of legal reform. To

strengthen his position, he informed the Israelis that if they did not cooperate, he would be forced to turn over his materials to a new Arab-sponsored
working group within the UN Commission on Human Rights, the "UN Special Committee to Investigate Israeli Practices Affecting the Human Rights
of the Palestinian People and Other Arabs of the Occupied Territories."
Israeli diplomats protested that the allegations were baseless and likely
manufactured. The report lacked specifics on the precise times and places
of the alleged abuses. Some of the people making the charges could not
even be properly identified; others were enemy fighters or terrorists. Those
still in jail all belonged to the banned Fatah guerilla movement. Ennals's
heavy-handed tactics amounted to political blackmail.[33]

During the fall of 1969, a debate broke out within the ranks of Amnesty's
leadership over how to proceed with the Israel report. Much of it centered
on whether Amnesty should abandon its longtime policies of not sponsoring prisoners who used or endorsed violence. Five years earlier, the organization had officially voted not to adopt Nelson Mandela as a Prisoner of
Conscience because he had participated in the armed wing of the African
National Congress. Why, asked Anthony Marreco, had Amnesty now shifted
its policies? "Are we equipped to decide who is or who is not a Prisoner of
Conscience in an area of armed conflict? We have not hitherto attempted
to do so and . . . [we should consider] the danger of taking action which
may do much more harm than good." Other voices, led by Mayhew and
Gilmour, insisted that the moral imperatives of the situation in the Middle
East demanded a new approach. Besides, they claimed, Israel could never be
trusted. In the internal Amnesty newsletter, Ennals conceded that his report
was "necessarily inadequate." He and his co-authors had tried strenuously to
arrange an "overall mission of investigation in the Middle East," but this
had proven impossible. Meanwhile, given "the atmosphere of intense propaganda it is difficult to sift truth about conditions from exaggeration and
fabrication." Nonetheless, they felt they had no choice but to press forward
with some kind of further action on Israel.[34]

From Haifa Bella Ravdin vigorously disagreed. She complained that the
organization had lost its moral bearings. Disregarding the voluntary cooperation of a democratic government, they had continued to rely on hearsay
and rumor engineered by Arab states. By Amnesty's own internal num-

bers, Pakistan held 7,000 political prisoners, Iraq 3,000, and Egypt 750. Other countries held even more, such as Vietnam with 100,000 and South Korea with 50,000. Yet only Israel was singled out for this kind of scrutiny. "Are we still a humanitarian movement?" she asked in an open letter to the International Executive Committee, "Are there not vested interests [at work]? Israel smells only of oranges not of oil." In search of support she turned to her own government for help. From that point onward, the Israeli Foreign Ministry paid the travel expenses of Ravdin and other volunteers to attend Amnesty meetings in Europe.[35]

Ravdin saw nothing wrong with this coordination with her own government. Neither, it turned out, did Ennals. His solution to the 1969 crisis was to make another, even bolder appeal to the Israelis that October. If Israel joined Amnesty in conducting a joint investigation of the allegations, he proposed, his organization would table its first report and prepare a new one. To broker the deal, he turned to New York University law professor Gidon Gottlieb, a European-born Jew with family in Israel, who served as Amnesty's UN liaison. Gottlieb presented Ennals's gambit to Israeli officials in New York: "An Amnesty International enquiry at this level with [Israeli] Government cooperation would be extremely important as a precedent," the first of its kind. Together, Israel and Amnesty might create a new paradigm for international human rights.[36]

The Israelis initially professed deep skepticism. While they desperately hoped to avoid the delivery of what they saw as damaging and unfounded propaganda with Amnesty's imprimatur to the politicized chambers of the UN, they also did not trust the organization to remain objective. When Ennals suggested to Haim Cohn that he join the team, he wrote back declining on grounds that there was no need for such an investigation: "We ourselves have conducted it and it is resolved. I would not treat anything proposed by Arab governments or outsiders as valid—it's just cruel propaganda."[37]

Still, Ennals persisted. Negotiations between Ennals and Cohn stretched on for several weeks. As Israel faced growing condemnation at the UN, the Israeli Foreign Ministry slowly warmed to the idea of a cooperative effort that might neutralize Arab propaganda. Finally, in late December 1969, Ennals and Cohn struck an agreement. Amnesty would send its own team to do an inquiry in Israel. The Israeli government would appoint an independent member of the Israeli bar to review the findings. Assuming a favorable response on their part, Amnesty and Israel would co-publish the report. In the event Israel did not approve the end result, Amnesty would be entitled to release it on its own with a twenty-one-day notice. On paper, the plan sounded bold and creative. Here was a novel attempt to pioneer a method of human rights cooperation between a sovereign state and an NGO, a consensual model of addressing controversial issues in a delicate political climate. The reality turned out quite differently.[38]

"Have I Not a Right to Know?"

In January 1970, a team of three Amnesty volunteers consisting of Williams, Dublin MP and lawyer Ritchie Ryan, and Norwegian academic Arne Harland visited Israel and Jordan. Their mandate was to study Israeli policies for the detention and interrogation of prisoners by interviewing current and former Arab prisoners. At the end of January, Ennals submitted their report to the Israelis. The team found fifteen alleged cases of Israeli torture. But all the events in question had taken place three years before, in the immediate aftermath of the war, and the individuals making the accusations all now lived in Arab countries. The only documentation was statements taken from six alleged victims living in Jordan, along with nine other informal interviews conducted more than a year earlier by Williams.[39]

The Israeli diplomats immediately complained that neither the stories nor the former prisoners' identities could be verified on the basis of the interviews. This report was hardly better than the first one. Israel offered safe passage and legal representation to Arab witnesses willing to come to Israel for a formal adjudication of their claims. Ennals countered with a suggestion that they allow an international commission of legal inquiry. Negotiations again dragged on for weeks. Meanwhile, Mayhew and Gilmour accused Israel of deliberate delay and obfuscation and threatened to resign from Amnesty if Ennals did not release the report. It was plain that the Israeli diplomats had no intention of truly cooperating, they claimed. Finally, in a climate of mutual recrimination, Ennals published the report at midnight on April 1, 1970. Through what was described as an "unfortunate administrative" error, he did not inform the Israeli government in advance, as promised.[40]

The reactions were immediate and explosive. Israel's ambassador to the United Kingdom complained that Ennals had deliberately blind-sided Israel in a gross betrayal of the terms of the agreement. Cohn resigned from the Israeli section of Amnesty, joined by nearly all the other Israeli leaders. Many Jewish members of the British section also resigned in protest. The Swiss national section condemned the report. So, too, did the *Times* of London, which accused Amnesty of having "allowed itself to be dragged into the positon of becoming the vehicle for Arab atrocity propaganda, willingly or unwillingly."

> Avowed terrorists work not only with the bomb and the grenade but with big and little lies and slanders, and these are by no means the least effective of their weapons. It would be senseless to offer them a "neutral" international forum before which to proclaim their right to destroy Israel as a state.[41]

The strongest reaction of all came from the United States. An American section of Amnesty had begun in 1966 following a visit by Benenson to New York. It was now led by Mark Benenson, a prominent civil liberties lawyer and Peter's cousin. After consulting the rest of his board, in May 1970 Benenson announced that the American branch would break with London and publicly disavow the report. In a letter to the *Times* of London, he wrote, "At best, the Amnesty report reveals the zeal of the prosecutor, convinced of the defendant's guilt, who perhaps without conscious malice omits from his brief material which would help the defence." At worst, it revealed a decided lack of "impartiality" on the part of his colleagues. Amnesty declined to examine the "Arab torture of Jews" on the ground that its investigators lacked access to the countries in question. The Arab governments simply refused to accommodate them.

Meanwhile, Israel had generously cooperated beyond any reasonable standard. Its offer to take testimony from witnesses was a major concession to human rights, given that "Israel is virtually in a state of war, the Arabs concerned [are] at least the equivalent of enemy civilians and many of them had been suspected, rightly or wrongly, of terrorist activity." More broadly, Benenson wrote, Amnesty risked mission creep that would badly damage its reputation: "No doubt even guerillas have rights, but in attempting to assure them, Amnesty is neglecting its principal wards, the non-violent prisoners of conscience, and losing the confidence of the governments with which it must deal."[42]

Mark Benenson's disavowal set off a furor within Amnesty. When he and Amnesty board member Theodore Bikel showed up at the annual International Executive Committee meeting in England a few days later, the two men found themselves "virtually ostracized." Refusing to back down, they proposed a draft resolution of self-criticism regarding double standards, "one for open societies and one for closed societies." Beyond Israel, they pointed to other recent examples where Amnesty had made missteps: a series of missions to South Vietnam with none to North Vietnam, a major focus on Chile coupled with a steadfast avoidance of Cuba, and the neglect of Jewish victims in the Arab world. "By exploring in great detail allegations to torture by Israel and giving comparatively little or no attention to alleged torture by Arab countries," they wrote, "Amnesty has violated its policy of even-handedness."[43]

Another war of words ensued, and the gulf within Amnesty continued to widen. Acting on its own, the Swedish branch broke protocol and launched its own inquiry by confronting President Golda Meir during a visit to Sweden about an Arab prisoner held in security detention without trial. The West German branch tried to start its own "new special group" to focus exclusively on Arab prisoners in Israel. Struggling to maintain control, Ennals rejected these efforts as unauthorized by the leadership. Meanwhile, the Jewish and Israeli press began to question Amnesty's motivations. Hoping to quench the fire, Ennals announced in June 1971, in a letter to the editor in London's *Jewish Chronicle*, that absent new allegations of torture in Israeli prisons, they would not renew their investigation. The case file was officially closed. And yet the drawer would not shut.[44]

What explained the enduring controversy? Ennals blamed the Israelis and the media for sensationalizing the problem. Within the ranks of the Amnesty leadership in England, however, a different explanation quietly circulated: nine of seventeen members of the American group's board were Jews. One of the strongest proponents of this theory was Eleanor Aitken, an

English Quaker, longtime Amnesty volunteer, and founder of Unipal, a British organization that sent university students to volunteer in Palestinian refugee camps. She demanded to know how many Jews were on the board of Amnesty USA, and on Amnesty's newly established Borderline Committee, a special group set up to handle the most politically sensitive cases of prisoner sponsorship. Aitken insisted her intentions were pure:

> You really should not, you know, suppose that I am anti-Semitic because I asked if any of the Borderline Committee were Jewish. . . . You must, I am sure be aware of the nature of the Jewish connection with Israel? And as Jews know all too well what persecution means, there are many Jewish members of A.I. It does not follow, though, that they can always be immune from a strong emotional attachment to Israel, of which they are all at least potential citizens. *Amnesty* very properly does not allow national sections to investigate their own prisoners. I think therefore that it is not likely that a Jew would be on a Borderline Committee which has to deal with Israel and the Occupied Territories. But why should I not know for *sure*? Have I not a right to know?

Ennals was horrified by the question. He replied swiftly that he did not know who was Jewish and would not ask. Such a practice would be anathema to the principles of the organization. Yet he went on to specify his reasoning: "I think it is absolutely essential that a distinction be made between Jews, Zionists, and Israelis." It did not apparently occur to him that breaking out "Zionists" as a separate category reinforced the invidious slur overtaking the human rights imagination in the early 1970s. Judaism was a religion; Israel, a state. Zionism was a dangerous racial nationalism, the very antithesis of human rights. The corollary to that worldview was Ennals's assumption that Zionism's victims could not be judged for their actions. He admitted as much in a subsequent interview: "Terrorism comes because human rights are not granted."[45]

Despite her growing despair, Ravdin tried to repair the breach between Amnesty and Israel. Perhaps, she reasoned, if Amnesty took on the issue of the millions of Jews captive in the Soviet Union, it could redeem itself on Jewish matters. In 1971 she sponsored a resolution to amend the organization's charter to promote a focus on the right to leave one's country as a cardinal human right. Amnesty could prove its good faith by addressing the crying issue of Soviet Jewry in a comprehensive manner consistent with its own principles.[46]

In response, Ennals again displayed a tone deafness born of human rights universalism. Amnesty had long sponsored individual Jewish prisoners, he wrote back to her, but it could not possibly take on a *group* issue that involved the entire Soviet Jewish population. "Our determination to work for prisoners, Jewish or non-Jewish," he explained, extends only to "those who are in prison or under house arrest. We have never sought to turn Amnesty into a general human rights movement taking up all worthy causes." The idea that an entire Jewish population might be captive to Soviet antisemitism and in need of collective relief apparently did not occur to him. The International Executive Committee echoed the sentiment, informing Ravdin that "it is not within the purview of Amnesty to concern itself with the wider implications of immigration policies."[47]

In the summer of 1972, Ravdin arranged for Ennals to visit Israel in a last-ditch attempt to break the "deadlock." But her effort was undermined by yet another controversy. After Palestinian terrorists kidnapped, tortured, and murdered Israeli athletes at the Munich Olympics, a West German Amnesty branch registered its concern about the deportation of Arab students with alleged radical ties. It not only failed to mention the Jewish victims of the attack but actually promoted the false allegation that one Jordanian young woman born in East Jerusalem had died after being sent home via a plane to Tel Aviv. That prompted another round of outcry within Amnesty. From New York, Gidon Gottlieb wrote Ennals to announce his intention to resign, saying he could no longer stomach the group's "alarming evidence of moral obtuseness." A "climate of tolerance for inhuman acts by 'the underdog' " had made Amnesty repeatedly fail "to take a public stand on torture by anti-government forces and other groups." The zeal for universalism had produced a moral blind spot on Jewish concerns. For Ravdin, too, Munich was the last straw. She tendered her resignation with a biting epitaph: "Human Rights *ad absurdum* would have made me a traitor to my own people."[48]

The same sentiment spread among the American section leadership, both Jewish and non-Jewish. The board of Amnesty USA debated how to respond to Gottlieb's resignation. Many members felt that their earlier fears of an anti-Jewish bias or a severe "balance problem" had been fully confirmed. Mark Benenson accused Ennals of allowing Arab governments to abuse Amnesty's willful naiveté: "Neutral Amnesty is being manipulated into not so neutral a position. Rather awkward, isn't it?" Meanwhile, the head of the Anti-Defamation League, Rabbi Judah Cahn, who was also the longtime vice president of the NAACP, attacked Amnesty for an unremitting obsession with Israel. After the debacle of 1970, it had continued to take "political positions on a number of issues of special concern to Jews, positions which have at the very least placed in doubt the organization's impartiality and its adherence to stated aims."[49]

Where did the truth lie in the conflict? One person who tried hard to see both sides of the issue was the young law professor Alan Dershowitz. Back in 1970, he had conducted his own inquiry into the status of Arab prisoners in Israeli prisons via a two-month investigation. He talked his way into meetings with high-ranking Israeli officials and sat down for face-to-face interviews with several Arab prisoners, including the prominent poet and intellectual Fouzi el-Asmar. As a scholar of civil liberties, Dershowitz was troubled by the Israeli practice of "administrative detention" of Arab Israelis, which he likened to the internment of Japanese Americans during World War II. These prisoners were not under military jurisdiction in the West Bank, but Israeli citizens accused of supporting the Palestinian militants in their continued low-grade war with Israel. Dershowitz concluded that Israel should err in the direction of more respect for the rights of its Arab citizens, even if some of "those released might engage in acts of terrorism. . . . Risks to safety have always been the price a society must pay for its liberty. Israel knows that well. By detaining only two dozen of its 300,000 Arab citizens, Israeli today is taking considerable risk. Indeed, I know of no country—including our own—that has ever exposed its wartime population to so much risk in the interest of civil liberties."[50]

Dershowitz's evaluation neatly summed up the challenge of human rights for Zionism after 1967. In the eyes of those sympathetic to the Jewish state, the country was locked in a permanent war with its neighbors. This necessitated an agonizing balancing act between national security and civil liberties. Amnesty's leaders, however, tended to look at the situation and see a Jewish country stubbornly resisting the universal norms of human rights *because* of its fealty to tribal nationalism.

The argument between Amnesty and Israel never really ended. It dragged on throughout the decade, especially after the 1973 Arab-Israeli war, when the organization again tried unsuccessfully to intervene on behalf of Arab and Jewish prisoners of war. Much of the rancor derived from a nagging sense of doubt among the Amnesty rank and file about the meaning of impartiality in human rights advocacy. By the time the organization received the Nobel Peace Prize in 1977, however, a more specific perception had begun to take hold among Jews: that the organization had a special problem when it came to Jews and Israel.[51]

Ravdin, of course, did not speak for all Jews. Some held fast to their Amnesty activism, often while adopting an explicitly anti-Zionist ideology. A smaller number sought to reform the organization from within. But many Jewish members shared Ravdin's loss of faith in Amnesty and her conclusion that human rights, at least as practiced by the organization, was somehow incompatible with Jewish political loyalty. For those Jews who had left Judaism, like Peter Benenson, human rights remained a deeply attractive proposition. But to those concerned about Jewish survival and collective flourishing, Amnesty had joined the UN as a hostile forum. Amnesty, declared Ravdin, had turned the term "prisoner of conscience" into a "kind of supermarket to include many categories of prisoners." Jews were destined to lose out if human rights became a victim popularity contest. Given this reality, the only remaining way to help endangered Jews around the world and redeem human rights was through the exercise of American power.[52]

"Escape to the Homeland"

On November 15, 1970, Jacob Blaustein died at his Baltimore farm after a brief illness following complications from abdominal surgery. The very next day in Moscow, a young Jewish scholar of ancient Chinese literature named Vitaly Rubin recorded an entry in his diary:

Sakkharov, Chalidze, and Arnish Tverdokhlebov have organized a Committee for Human Rights in the USSR. . . . Terrific chaps! . . . But immediately upon hearing this, I concluded that I would not join this organization, because I do not consider myself a citizen of this country. I don't believe in the possibility of improvement here without monstrous bloodshed and I won't be here to take part in political action.[53]

Rubin admired his friends in their noble quest for freedom, but their fight was not his fight. His home lay elsewhere. Securing human rights in the Soviet Union was someone else's struggle. After visiting with Rubin and his fellow activists, American writer Herbert Gold captured their mentality: "[I]t is not their job to make things better, to help Russia save its soul. They just want to go. They see themselves as Jews and Israelis, detained in exile."[54]

Blaustein would have been sorely disappointed to hear this young Russian Jew express so little faith in international human rights, but he likely would have agreed with his conclusion about the fate of Jews in the Soviet Union. When Blaustein's colleagues gathered to memorialize him in Uppsala, Sweden, in 1972, at a conference that marked the opening of the AJC's Jacob Blaustein Institute for the Advancement of Human Rights, they chose as their theme "the Right to Leave and to Return." Nothing better captured the Jewish dilemma. After years of debate about how best to help Jews under Communism, the arguments had ended. The Jewish future henceforth depended solely on one right: the right to *aliyah*. With the UN and Amnesty both closed off as avenues of hope, international human rights seemed to have failed the Jews. Only nationhood, in the form of repatriation to Israel, could truly protect them as Jews. And crucially, though few wished to discuss it openly, talk of Jewish return inevitably raised the question of Palestinian refugees and their right of return to a national homeland as well.[55]

In 1974 the Blaustein Institute hosted another international conference on the theme of "Judaism and Human Rights." Despite the expansive title, the conference mood was best summed up by Rita Hauser, now retired from her stint as the U.S. delegate to the UN Commission on Human Rights, who eulogized Blaustein and his dream together. Under the "International Bill of Rights" envisioned in 1945, she declared, Jewish freedom was supposed to be internationally guaranteed: "Jews would be protected in the enjoyment of their rights to the extent the rights of others everywhere were similarly respected . . . [and] protected by the international institution to be created—the United Nations." At the same time, some Jews chose a different route, that of Zionism: "Their energies were directed to fulfilling a national, not an international dream, and they worked toward creating a Jewish state where the rights of Jews, by definition, would be clearly protected and dependent on none but Jews." Three decades later, she concluded, it was time for the AJC to admit failure: "The dream of protection of Jews, so long the victims of abuse by universal schemes, seems ill-fated. Jews thrive in free nations; in others, they can only hope for escape to the homeland of Israel. The Zionists of 1945 were probably right." With both the UN and Amnesty hostile to Jewish causes, international human rights would not save the Jews of Soviet Russia. Their fate, rather, lay with "escape to the homeland." International protection had ceased to be an option for the Jews.[56]

From the Israeli side, Yoram Dinstein echoed her assessment. While there were individual Jews in the Soviet dissident movement, the general campaign for freedom could not help "the struggle of Soviet Jewry." Jews were twice penalized in Soviet society, once alongside all other citizens in a totalitarian state and then further abused as an oppressed national minority. "Nothing, of course, prevents a Jew, as an individual, from fighting for the two goals together," he explained, "but it is important to recognize that the two fronts do not necessarily overlap."

> The denial to Soviet Jews—as Jews—of the substantive human rights, individual as well as collective, is so systematic and comprehensive, the discrimination against them so flagrant and all-consuming, the violation of the international undertakings of the USSR where Jews are concerned so unique, deep, and ramified, that the question almost presents itself whether a Jew can remain as a Jew within the boundaries of the Soviet Union.[57]

The Jews of the Soviet Union had their own answer. Beginning in 1968, thousands upon thousands of them applied to emigrate. That story remains little understood. While in retrospect it looks like a victory for international human rights, in reality it had much more to do with Zionism and Cold War geopolitics. There were the occasional figures like Natan Sharansky, who

linked his struggle for freedom to the larger campaign against Soviet tyranny. Yet Sharansky was a most atypical Soviet Jew, even among refuseniks, those would-be Jewish emigrants who had been denied the right to
leave. Even when refuseniks spoke of human rights, they expressed the
belief that they could best realize those rights as a nation in the context of
Israel. "It is not racial discrimination that compels us to leave the country,"
wrote a group of eighteen Georgian Jewish families in 1969 in an open
letter to the UN. Nor was it religious discrimination. Rather, their faith
and their history convinced them that they could live as Jews only in "the
land of our forefathers."[58]

The 1970s offered a repeat of the 1930s, but with a different ending. Once
again, the rising international rights scheme could not offer Jews the protection they needed, let alone the freedom to preserve their national identity with dignity. The international nature of Jewish politics again proved to
be a liability as it linked the Jewish fate under Communism to the Arab-
Israeli conflict and the Cold War. And once more, the only sure way to make
Jews safe was by removing them from the danger zones of Europe and
the Middle East to a Jewish homeland. The difference was that, this time
around, Jews found a liberal superpower willing to expend its political
capital in the international arena to act directly on their behalf.

This did not mean that the freeing of Soviet Jewry had no relation to human
rights. The 1970s saw the dawn of human rights in U.S. foreign policy.
The first signs of this interest came in 1974, when Democratic congressman Donald Fraser convened a series of hearings on U.S. policy toward
human rights abuses by foreign governments. A reluctant Nixon administration grumbled about the intrusion into its pursuit of détente with the
Soviet Union. The same year, Democratic senator Henry "Scoop" Jackson
and colleagues fashioned the Jackson-Vanik Amendment, linking Soviet-
American trade deals to freedom of emigration. By 1976, human rights
had come to be embraced, albeit in different ways and to different degrees,
by *both* the right and the left in American foreign policy. The famous Helsinki Accords, a 1975 agreement between the Warsaw Pact countries and
NATO nations to settle the borders of post–World War II Europe in exchange for trade and mutual security guarantees, contained a minor but
important mention of human rights that would prove crucial for dissidents

fighting for democratic freedom in the Soviet Union and its allied states. In 1977, President Jimmy Carter announced an explicit U.S. commitment to human rights in his inaugural address, publicly ratifying the new doctrine in U.S. foreign policy.[59]

This cascade of remarkable achievements rightly belongs in the annals of American human rights history. Historians have lately begun to explore this terrain. Some see a recovery of American idealism and political virtue after Vietnam and Watergate; others see Cold War politics driving the search for a propaganda weapon against Communism. No doubt both motives were at work to varying degrees. For our purposes, the key point is that this drama of emergent American human rights involved little of the Jewish activism that had led the effort for decades—and few of the Jewish activists. The American government, Israel, and Jewish NGOs solved the Soviet Jewish problem not via international law or the UN forum or a global appeal to conscience, but via bilateral diplomatic negotiation with the Soviet government. Beginning with Nixon, successive U.S. administrations negotiated quietly with Moscow on the question of exit visas for Soviet Jews. Both the left-wing version of U.S. diplomacy on behalf of Soviet Jews—the Jackson-Vanik Amendment—and the right-wing approach of détente and quiet negotiation ultimately derived from specifically American ideals and interests. And both approaches depended on the discretion of U.S. presidents willing to engage in bilateral negotiations with Soviets not the ideals enshrined in the UN's human rights treaties.[60]

Whether détente or Jackson-Vanik helped or hindered the freeing of Soviet Jews remains a question historians have yet to answer decisively. Nor, despite the mythologization of this event in American Jewish memory, is there yet enough hard evidence to answer the question of whether public pressure actually influenced either Soviet or American foreign policy. What is clear, in the final analysis, is that Soviet Jewish emigration took place at a time when Jews were becoming marginalized in the international human rights movement. By 1974, the AJC and the WJC had both closed down their UN offices. Perlzweig retired that year and ruefully concluded that, in the field of human rights, "the United Nations has done very little, except produce documents." He wrote that he had become, in the words of Matthew Arnold, a wanderer "between two worlds, one dead, the other powerless to be born."[61]

Also in 1974, the PLO perpetrated a series of gruesome terrorist attacks inside Israel, including the massacre of twenty-one schoolchildren. Terror had become the first instrument of choice for Palestinian rights. That November a cheering UN General Assembly welcomed to the podium Yasser Arafat, wearing an empty gun holster after having been forced to check his weapon at the door. In response, a newly retired Jacob Robinson bemoaned the triumph of "tyranny" and the "subversion of international law." In June 1975, the World Conference of the International Women's Year in Mexico City called for the "elimination of colonialism and neo-colonialism, foreign occupation, Zionism, apartheid and racial discrimination in all its forms." The participants infamously declined an Australian proposal to add "sexism" to the list. This all led up to the day, November 10, 1975, that the General Assembly voted 72 to 35 (with 32 abstentions) to approve Resolution 3379, declaring "Zionism is a form of racism and racial discrimination."[62]

The loudest American voice of protest belonged not to a Jewish spokesman but to a rising Democratic political star, U.S. ambassador to the UN, Daniel Patrick Moynihan. He understood the marginalization of the Jews and the ideological distortion of human rights as two sides of the same coin: both represented simultaneous challenges to liberal values and American power. The UN's anti-Zionism measure, Moynihan asserted, was more than an immoral act enshrining "antisemitism in international law." It was also a "totalitarian" manipulation of human rights into an attack "aimed at Jews everywhere and liberal democracy everywhere."[63]

Where Moynihan saw in the defense of Israel a chance to redeem America, the Israeli ambassador to the UN, Chaim Herzog, recognized a larger process at work. An international lawyer who had trained under Lauterpacht at Cambridge and then married his niece, Herzog saw how modern Israel had once again become a symbol in the world's imagination of itself.

> Over the centuries it has fallen to the lot of my people to be the testing agent of human decency, the touchstone of civilization, the crucible in which enduring human values are to be tested. A nation's level of humanity could invariably be judged by its behavior towards its Jewish population. It always began with the Jews but never ended with them.

So it would be with the UN and human rights. Israel had become a symbol of the triumph of politics over international law. Herzog only hoped that this moral nadir would lead to a historical turn in world affairs. To prove his point, he quoted the same passage from Prophet Isaiah that his wife's uncle had invoked twenty-five years earlier in his speech at the Hebrew University: "And it shall come to pass in the last days . . . for out of Zion shall go forth the law, and the word of the Lord from Jerusalem."[64]

In the aftermath of the Six-Day War, Jewish human rights activists coined the nickname "Prisoners of Zion" to refer to the endangered Jewish communities of the Arab Middle East and Soviet Europe. The phrase neatly captured how Israel was both the source of heightened Jewish vulnerability and the best solution to it. Compromised by their ties to Zion, real or imaginary, these Jews could only find justice and freedom in Zion. In retrospect, however, the label applied more broadly. After 1967, Jewish human rights activists could no longer avoid being ensnared in the political web of claims and counterclaims about Israel and human rights. Whether they wished to fight for the rights of Jews, Palestinians, or others, they were forced to answer for Israel's sins, again real or imagined.

Nor, finally, was this predicament limited to Jews. Amnesty, too, became a Prisoner of Zion, captive to its own brand of utopian universalism in which Zion played a unique role. And beyond Amnesty, the 1975 debacle at the UN demonstrated that, in the broader human rights imagination, Zion had come to signify the ultimate parochialism. That mental bondage would endure through the decades, even as the events of the 1970s faded into obscurity. Its legacy remains even today as Jews and others grapple with the entangled braids of American power, Jewish sovereignty, and human rights.

EPILOGUE: THE PRECIOUS GIFT

ONE OF THE MOST REVEALING DEBATES in the history of Jewish human rights took place not in a UN meeting or a Jerusalem courtroom, but via a brief exchange of letters between Hannah Arendt and Gershom Scholem in the summer of 1963. When word of the publication of *Eichmann in Jerusalem* reached Israel, Scholem angrily accused Arendt of cold indifference to her own people. "In the Jewish tradition," he wrote, "there is a concept, hard to define and yet concrete enough, which we define as *ahavat yisrael*: love of the Jewish people. . . . With you, my dear Hannah, as with so many intellectuals coming from the German left, I find no trace of this." Scholem criticized her heartless "mockery" of Zionism. Arendt shot back:

> You are quite right—I am not moved by any "love" of this sort. . . . I have never in my life "loved" any people or collective—neither the German people, nor the French, nor the American, nor the working class or anything of that sort. I indeed love "only" my friends and the only kind of love I know of and believe in is the love of persons.[1]

On its face, the contretemps mapped perfectly onto the well-etched binary of particularism and universalism. Arendt's cutting words painted Jewish peoplehood as an exercise in moral parochialism. Group identity invalidated universal ethics. National belonging blinkered the sovereign mind. While the Israeli professor of religion might cling sentimentally to nationhood, the proud diaspora philosopher cast off tribal loyalties in the name of global justice.

Except that Scholem and Arendt agreed much more than they disagreed. Scholem had long criticized Zionism's chauvinist excesses and moral missteps. Arendt had many times proclaimed the essential tie between roots and rights. "Justice for a people," she wrote in 1942, "can only mean national justice. One of the inalienable human rights of Jews is the right to live and if need be to die as a Jew. A human being can defend himself only as the person he is attacked as. A Jew can preserve his human dignity only if he can be human as a Jew." In this and other passages, she praised Zionism as the very model of rooted cosmopolitanism. Far from enemies, she stressed, the particular and the universal were inextricably and necessarily linked. Why, then, had she changed her mind?[2]

Students of Arendt—and there are many—have offered various explanations for her change of heart. They range from internalized self-hatred to personal hubris to righteous anger over the Arab-Israeli conflict. But the best explanation is the one she offered herself. In place of *ahavat yisrael,* she had found a new love: *amor mundi*—the love of the world. The Latin phrase, the private name she gave her 1958 magnum opus, *The Human Condition,* reflected her deep longing to be one with all of humanity, to embrace the entire world. Roman love's speedy promise of limitless universalism trumped Israel's modest march through history. In that sense, her harsh, cynical words, pronounced with Stoic detachment, concealed a rich vein of hungry idealism. Like many human rights activists past and present, she dreamed of one humanity, undivided. Much like Peter Benenson, she had lost patience with the limits of nationhood. Her vision, of almost messianic immediacy, was also a flight from the painful tedium of Jewish politics.[3]

The phrase "[to] be human as a Jew" reads like an oxymoron today. It smacks of special pleading or relativism. Human rights are supposed to transcend difference, not affirm it. Yet this is not the only way to define human rights. The Jewish political tradition, of which Arendt was once a prime exponent, recognized national politics as a precondition of international justice. To survive as a minority required political self-definition, which in turn meant collective politics. As she wrote in 1940, "a people can be a minority somewhere only if they are a majority somewhere else."[4]

Seven decades after the founding of modern human rights and the State of Israel, fifty years after the start of the Israeli Occupation, many Jews have also grown impatient with the practice of collective politics. The distance between *ahavat yisrael* and *amor mundi* in the Jewish imagination has never seemed wider. On the Jewish right, loud voices malign human rights as the very antithesis of Zionism. These people seek to wish away the hard choices about the fate of the Palestinians and Israeli democracy by vilifying the entire human rights movement. The current Israeli government treats foreign and local human rights organizations as threats to the national security of the Jewish people. On the Jewish left, angry spokespeople herald human rights as a redemptive universalism that demands the dissolution of the Jewish nation-state. Post-Zionism, in the minds of many, promises liberation from the burden of nationhood. A Jewish democracy to them is a contradiction in terms.

This polarization has had a crippling effect on the small, embattled Israeli human rights NGO community. It has led both to the demonization of human rights activists as *sonei Yisrael,* haters of Israel, and to a mirror image of Zionists as *hostis humani generis,* enemies of humankind. In some activist circles, that schism has also reinforced binational fantasies of solving the Israeli-Palestinian conflict via a single secular, democratic state. But wishing away the national identities of Jews and Palestinians will not lead to a more just society in the shared land between the Jordan River and the Mediterranean. Until a two-state solution is realized, Israeli human rights activism will continue to struggle with what Lauterpacht called the question that "lies so conspicuously on the borderline of law and a most intractable problem of politics."

If Israeli Jews are deeply split over human rights, American Jews exhibit their own profound ambivalence. Nothing exemplifies this condition better than the American Jewish Committee. In the early 1970s, even as the AJC shuttered its formal UN operations, its board quietly funded the start of a pioneering Israeli NGO, the Association for Civil Rights in Israel.

Likewise, the Jacob Blaustein Institute for the Advancement of Human Rights began discreetly providing technical assistance to a succession of UN secretaries-general and other UN human rights officials—work that it continues today. But though its offices are housed in the AJC's main headquarters, the Blaustein Institute's name is frequently left off official AJC publications, and vice versa. What is more, in 2001 the AJC began sponsoring UN Watch, an organization started by Morris Abram to expose antisemitism and anti-Israel bias in the UN human rights program. Based in Geneva, UN Watch has garnered both acclaim and criticism for its confrontational approach to the UN human rights program. It was instrumental in the U.S.-led decision in 2006 to force a reorganization of the UN Commission on Human Rights into the Human Rights Council, an effort to temper its anti-Israel bias. The entire raison d'etre of UN Watch, then, is to critique the kind of work supported by the Blaustein Institute. The presence of two diametrically opposed initiatives under the same roof suggests a Jewish organization at war with itself over the meaning of international human rights.[5]

The wider the mental gulf grows between Jewish politics and human rights, the more a false dichotomy between particularism and universalism overtakes the Jewish historical imagination. Lauterpacht died in 1960, Robinson in 1977, Perlzweig in 1985, and Benenson in 2005. Few Jews today remember these founding fathers of human rights, let alone their political backstories. Fewer still know the story of the Jewish fight for minority rights that preceded and helped define the rise of human rights after World War II. Blaustein's name adorns a Jewish institute that barely exists in the contemporary Jewish political consciousness. Hardly anyone remembers that he championed the idea of a UN High Commissioner for Human Rights and sought an early peace between Arabs and Jews. While Amnesty continues to inspire controversy in the Jewish world, Benenson's Jewish odyssey and Amnesty's failed experiment in cooperation with Israel are also completely forgotten.[6]

What unites both the left and the right in the human rights world today—Jewish and at-large, Israel and diaspora—is a collective amnesia about the historical relationship between Jewish politics and human rights. Time and again, Zionism is imagined as clannish self-love; human rights are ascribed a sacral status as moral universals. As a result, when Jews look backward, they see the same story of particularism and universalism in conflict, repeating itself over and over again in an endless loop. The real political and moral dilemmas confronting Jews today—global antisemitism, the Israeli-Palestinian conflict, the memory of the Holocaust, the attenuation of Jewish collective identity—are conflated with a lazy dichotomy between nationhood and cosmopolitanism. We are left with a human rights universalism that pretends to come from nowhere and a Jewish nationalism that is positioned in opposition to the world.

The same rigidity defines those secular Jewish human rights activists who operate outside the framework of the Jewish community. Many Jewish activists today would define themselves as Arendt's heirs to an *amor mundi* that need not reckon with the burden of Jewish politics. Pioneering figures like Arieh Neier and Kenneth Roth, and their peers in Amnesty International, Human Rights Watch, and similar organizations, have long defined themselves strictly by their universalist commitments. Other prominent international lawyers, such as Richard Goldstone and Philippe Sands, valorize their own Jewish cosmopolitanism by direct reference to the Holocaust as the sole source of their—and our—modern human rights. Once again, these ahistorical reveries conscript their Jewish forebears into mythical roles as either selfless cosmopolitans or tragic victims. Left out of these accounts are their politics, the starting point for Jewish responses to injustice and the source for the Jewish imagination of human rights. Writing Jews back into the history of human rights fulfills a Jewish imperative to look backward into the past in order to rethink the future. This rich legacy opens up a repertoire of ideas for moving beyond the impasse we have reached today.[7]

And not only for Jews. We live in a world that has never been more aware and more concerned about human rights and yet has never felt more powerless in the face of war, the refugee crisis, and genocide. In recent years there has been growing talk of the "endtimes" and the "failure" of human rights as a whole. Critics point not only to the politicization of the UN human rights system but also to the persistence of genocide and other mass atrocities that are creating a global refugee crisis. They ask whether human rights treaties actually do anything to prevent the violations and atrocities they are supposed to stop—or the underlying inequities that fuel conflict. This larger crisis of human rights leaves us at an uncertain juncture in the history of the world's first universal ideology.[8]

What is missing, especially on the global left, is a sense of political proportion. Faced with exclusionary nationalism, the professional human rights community speaks the language of long-distance solidarity and global cosmopolitanism. This well-meaning activism is impatient of context and suspicious of governments. It sees injustice, crisis, and atrocity and favors networks and crowds instead of nations and states. For human rights activists today, there are often only atomized individuals and one interconnected humanity, the face of the refugee and the twitterverse, with no institutions in between. Human rights no longer live in the realm of the political. That larger flight from the core questions of political liberalism is as unfortunate as it is dangerous. The historical legacy of Jewish human rights activism offers a sober reminder that idealism and power must always be considered in the same frame, or else we risk hollow gestures and futile advocacy.

In one of his last public appearances, at a conference in Tel Aviv in the 1970s, Jacob Robinson was asked to assess the fate of Jews and human rights across the very full century he had lived. At the end of a lengthy set of remarks, he returned to the question that still haunted him three decades after he had fled Lithuania: "Were minority rights 'an experiment that failed?'" His answer was a riddle of sorts: "Perhaps one may use the Talmudic expression, 'Lo ikhshar dara,' which, freely translated, means that a precious gift was given to a generation which proved to be insufficiently mature to weave it into its social fabric."[9]

Lo ikhshar dara. What Robinson had in mind as the precious gift of minority rights he did not say. He might have meant a solution to the question of Israel's own Arab minority. How to accommodate the national identity of Arab citizens in the State of Israel was and remains a challenge at the heart of the Jewish nation-state. Or he could have been dreaming of a day when two sovereign states existed side by side, one Israeli and one Palestinian, with minority rights conferred on those Arabs and Jews who wished to remain in their homes while receiving the protection of their kin-state.

But what he had in mind was far less likely a specific policy prescription than a Jewish sensibility about the proper balance between individual and group, nation and state, politics and law. On a larger level, Robinson's fabled gift represented the elusive meeting point between idealism and realism, the place where rootedness and cosmopolitanism collapsed into one.

The generation of Robinson and his fellow Jewish human rights activists was not yet ready to receive the gift of which he spoke. Ours is perhaps not ready either. But the gift lives on, waiting to be rediscovered, reopened, and reimagined.

ABBREVIATIONS

ACLU   Princeton University, Mudd Library, American Civil Liberties Union
          Papers, 1912–1990

AIAO   Amnesty International Archives Online, www.amnesty.org

AIUSA   Columbia University, Rare Book and Manuscript Library, Amnesty
          International of the USA Papers, National Office Records, 1966–2003

AJA   American Jewish Archives (Cincinnati), World Jewish Congress
          Collection, MS-361

AJCA   American Jewish Committee Archives (New York)

AJCO   American Jewish Committee Online Digital Archives, www.ajcarchives
          .org

AJHS   American Jewish Historical Society Archives (New York)

BNA   British National Archives

CEIP   Columbia University, Rare Book and Manuscript Library, Carnegie
          Endowment of International Peace Archives

CJH   Center for Jewish History (New York)

CUA   Columbia University Library, Columbia Center for Oral History

CZA   Central Zionist Archives (Jerusalem)

ECA   Eton College Archives

ESP   University of Virginia Library Special Collections, Edward Stettinius, Jr.
          Papers, #2723-Z

GFA   Greenberg Family Private Archive (Sudbury, Massachusetts)

HHC   Hull History Centre, Papers of Justice (British Section of the
          International Commission of Jurists, U DJU)

HL   Hersch Zvi Lauterpacht

HP   Buffalo & Erie County Historical Society, Philip Halpern Papers, C66-3

HUA   Harvard University, Schlesinger Library Archives, Papers of
          Caroline K. Simon, MC 370

IBP	Johns Hopkins University Archives, Special Collections, Sheridan Libraries, Isaiah Bowman papers, Ms. 58
ICSJ	Hebrew University of Jerusalem, Institute for the Study of Contemporary Jewry, Oral History Project
IISG	International Institute of Social History (Amsterdam), Amnesty International Collection, ARCH01331
IS	*Idishe shtime* (Kovno, Lithuania)
ISA	Israel State Archives (Jerusalem)
JBP	Johns Hopkins University Archives, Special Collections, Sheridan Libraries, Jacob and Louis Blaustein Collection, Ms. 400
JHP	University College London, Institute of Commonwealth Studies, Jack Halpern Papers, ICS28
JR	Jacob Robinson
JTA	Jewish Telegraphic Agency
LBJ	Lyndon Baines Johnson Presidential Library, Library Oral Histories
LFA	Lauterpacht Family Archive (Cambridge, England)
LMA	London Metropolitan Archive, Papers of the British Board of Jewish Deputies, ACC/3121
LNA	League of Nations Archive (Geneva)
LOC	Library of Congress, Manuscript Division
MAP	Emory University, Manuscript, Archives, and Rare Book Library, Morris B. Abram Papers, MS-514
MBA	National Library of Israel, Martin Buber Archive
MP	Maurice Perlzweig
NARA	National Archives and Records Administration (College Park, Maryland)
ND	*Nowy Dziennik*
NYPL	New York Public Library, International League for Human Rights Collection, Mss Col 1518
PB	Peter Benenson
RGANI	Russian State Archive of Contemporary History (Moscow)
SUA	University of Southampton, Special Collections, Anglo-Jewish Archive, World Jewish Congress, Institute of Jewish Affairs Papers, MS-237
TPL	Harry S. Truman Presidential Library & Museum, Presidential Papers
UNA	United Nations Archives
USHMM	United States Holocaust Memorial Museum, Jacob Robinson Papers, RG 2013.506.1
WA	Weizmann Institute, Chaim Weizmann Archives (Rehovot, Israel)
WW	New York Public Library, William E. Wiener Oral History Library of the American Jewish Committee
YIVO	YIVO Institute for Jewish Research (New York)
YVA	Yad Vashem Archives (Jerusalem)

NOTES

Prologue

1. Natan Gelber, *Toldot ha-tenu'ah ha-tsiyonit be-Galitsyah, 1875–1918* (Jerusalem: Ha-Sifriyah ha-Tsiyonit be-hotsa'at R. Mas, 1958), 2:838; Ezra Mendelsohn, *Zionism in Poland: The Formative Years, 1915–1926* (New Haven, CT: Yale University Press, 1982), 88–91; "Ha-veidah ha-mukdemet," *Ha-tsefirah*, Jan. 9, 1919; Alexander Prusin, *Nationalizing a Borderland: War, Ethnicity, and Anti-Jewish Violence in East Galicia, 1914–1920* (Tuscaloosa: University of Alabama Press, 2005), 85.

2. Elihu Lauterpacht, *The Life of Hersch Lauterpacht* (Cambridge: Cambridge University Press, 2010), 21–24; David Horowitz, *In the Heart of Events—Israel: A Personal Perspective* (Jerusalem: Turtledove Publishers, 1980), 30–31; Prusin, *Nationalizing*, 74–91.

3. Quoted in Nathan Feinberg, "Recognition of the Jewish People in International Law," in N. Feinberg and J. Stoyanovsky, eds., *Jewish Yearbook of International Law* 1 (1949): 1.

4. "'What Remains? The Language Remains': A Conversation with Gunter Grass," in Hannah Arendt, *Essays in Understanding* (New York: Schocken Books, 1994), 12.

5. Linda Kerber, "We Are All Historians of Human Rights," *Perspectives on History* (Oct. 2006): 3. For the essential critique of this approach, see Samuel Moyn, *The Last Utopia: Human Rights in History* (Cambridge, MA: Harvard University Press, 2010).

6. For other important correctives, see Nathan Kurz, "A Sphere above the Nations? The Rise and Fall of International Jewish Human Rights Politics, 1945–1975" (PhD diss., Yale University, 2015); Abigail Green, "The British Empire and the Jews: An Imperialism of Human Rights?" *Past & Present* 199 (May 2008): 175–205;

Michael Galchinsky, *Jews and Human Rights: Dancing at Three Weddings* (Lanham, MD: Rowman & Littlefield, 2008).

7. Samuel Moyn, "The Universal Declaration of Human Rights of 1948 in the History of Cosmopolitanism," *Critical Inquiry* 40 (Summer 2014): 365–84.

8. Tony Judt, "Edward Said: The Rootless Cosmopolitan," *The Nation*, July 1, 2004; Philippe Sands, *East-West Street: On the Holocaust and Crimes against Humanity* (New York: Knopf, 2016); Jeff Greenfield, "The Ugly History of Stephen Miller's 'Cosmopolitan' Epithet," http://www.politico.com/magazine/story/2017/08/03/the-ugly-history-of-stephen-millers-cosmopolitan-epithet-215454. For earlier nuanced discussions of "rooted cosmopolitanism," see Michael Walzer, *Nation and Universe* (Oxford: Oxford University Press, 1989); David Hollinger, *Postethnic America: Beyond Multiculturalism* (New York: Basic Books, 1995); Michael Miller and Scott Ury, "Cosmopolitanism: The End of Jewishness?" *European Review of History* 17, no. 3 (June 2010): 337–48; Arie Dubnov, "Anti-cosmopolitan Liberalism: Isaiah Berlin, Jacob Talmon and the Dilemma of National Identity," *Nations and Nationalism* 16, no. 4 (Oct. 2010): 559–78; and Natan Sznaider, *Jewish Memory and the Cosmopolitan Order* (Cambridge: Cambridge University Press, 2011).

Part 1. Emergence

Y. L. Peretz, *Lider un baladn* (Vilnius: B. Kletskin, 1927), 24; HL, "Zgoda na niezgodę," *ND*, Aug. 25, 1925; *Sitzungsbericht des Kongresses der Organisierten Nationalen Gruppen in den Staaten Europas: Genf, 26. bis 28. August 1929* (Vienna: Wilhelm Braumüller Universitäts-Verlagsbuchhandlung, 1930), 70; Uri Zvi Greenberg, "Uri Tsvi farn tseylem," *Albatros* 2 (1922): 3–4, translated by the author.

Chapter 1. A Jewish Magna Carta

1. Yosef Tenenboym, *Tsvishn sholem un milkhome: Yidn oyf der sholem-konferents nokh der ershter velt-milkhome* (Buenos Aires: Tsentral-Farband fun Poylishe Yidn in Argentine, 1956), 245; U.S. Department of State, *Papers of the Paris Peace Conference* (Washington: U.S. Government Printing Office, 1946), 6:624–29; Arthur Link, ed., *The Deliberations of the Council of Four* (Princeton, NJ: Princeton University Press, 1992), 2:524–27.

2. Link, *Deliberations*, 2:54.

3. Peter Yearwood, *Guarantee of Peace: The League of Nations in British Policy, 1914–1925* (Oxford: Oxford University Press, 2009), 3–5.

4. HL, "The Mandate under International Law in the Covenant of the League of Nations" [1921], in Hersch Lauterpacht, *International Law, Being the Collected Papers of Hersch Lauterpacht* (Cambridge: Cambridge University Press, 1977), 3:39–40.

5. Susan Pederson, *The Guardians: The League of Nations and the Crisis of Empire* (Oxford: Oxford University Press, 2015), 277–82; Mark Mazower, *No Enchanted Palace: The End of Empire and the Ideological Origins of the United Nations* (Princeton, NJ: Princeton University Press, 2009), 28–65; Frank Trentmann, "After the Nation-State: Citizenship, Empire and Global Coordination in the New Internationalism, 1914–1930," in Kevin Grant, Philippa Levine, and Frank Trentmann, eds., *Beyond Sovereignty: Britain, Empire and Transnationalism, c. 1880–1950* (New York: Palgrave, 2007), 34–53; and Glenda Sluga, *Internationalism in the Age of Nationalism* (Philadelphia: University of Pennsylvania Press, 2013), 45–78.

6. Martti Koskenniemi, *From Apology to Utopia: The Structure of International Legal Argument* (Cambridge: Cambridge University Press, 2005).

7. Lauterpacht, *Life*, 19–20; Horowitz, *Heart of Events*, 31.

8. Quoted in "Irving Howe Interviews Gershom Scholem. 'The Only Thing in My Life I Have Never Doubted Is the Existence of God,'" *Present Tense* 8, no. 1 (Aug. 1980): 56.

9. "Rezolucye wiecu żydowskiej młodzleży akad. we Lwowie," *ND*, Oct. 24, 1918; "Zjazd organ 'Hechaluc' dla Galicyi wsch. we Lwowie," *Chwila*, Dec. 9, 1919.

10. Quoted in David Roskies, *Against the Apocalypse: Responses to Catastrophe in Modern Jewish Culture* (Cambridge, MA: Harvard University Press, 1986), 267–68.

11. Carole Fink, *Defending the Rights of Others: The Great Powers, the Jews, and International Minority Protection, 1878–1938* (Cambridge: Cambridge University Press, 2004), 112–30.

12. Israel Cohen, "The Lemberg Pogrom," YIVO, Israel Cohen Papers, RG 448, Box 2, Folder 19; Rosa Bailly, *A City Fights for Its Freedom: The Rising of Lwow in 1918–1919* (London: Leopolis, 1956), 350; Arthur Lehman Goodhart, *Poland and the Minority Races* (London: Allen and Unwin, 1920), 141–42.

13. Horowitz, *Heart of Events*, 30–31; "Tseir'ei Tsion. Ha-heḥlatot she-nitkablu be-ve'idah ha-artzit ha-rishonah shel 'Tseir'ei Tsion' be-Folin," *Ha-tsefirah*, Oct. 31, 1918; "Z Żyd. Tow. Szkoły Ludowej i Średniej we Lwowie," *Chwila*, Feb. 7, 1919.

14. Henry Morgenthau, *All in a Life-Time* (Garden City, NY: Doubleday, 1922), 322–23.

15. "Drishot ha'am ha-ivri," *Ha-tsefirah*, Oct. 31, 1918, 1; Lawton Kessler, Aaron Alperin, and Jack Diamond, "American Jews and the Paris Peace Conference," *YIVO Annual of Jewish Social Science* 2/3 (1948): 235.

16. James Loeffler, "'The Famous Trinity of 1917': Jacob Robinson and Zionist Internationalism in Historical Perspective," *Jahrbuch des Simon-Dubnow-Instituts* 15 (2016): 211–38. See also Dimitry Shumsky, *Beyond the Nation State: The Zionist Political Imagination from Pinsker to Ben-Gurion* (Philadelphia: University of Pennsylvania Press, 2018); and Yosef Gorny, *From Binational Society to Jewish State: Federal Concepts in Zionist Political Thought, 1920–1990, and the Jewish People* (Leiden: Brill, 2006).

17. *Proceedings of the 1916 American Jewish Congress* (New York: American Jewish Congress, 1916), 37; Louis Brandeis, "The Jewish Problem—How to Solve It,"

Maccabean 26, no. 6 (June 1915): 106; James Loeffler, "Nationalism without a Nation? On the Invisibility of American Jewish Politics," *Jewish Quarterly Review* 105, no. 3 (Summer 2015): 367–98.

18. Quoted in Egle Bendikaite, "The Lithuanian Zionist Conference, Vilnius, 5–8 December 1918," in Vladas Sirutavičius and Darius Staliūnas, eds., *A Pragmatic Alliance: Jewish-Lithuanian Political Cooperation at the Beginning of the 20th Century* (Budapest: Central European Press, 2011), 264–65; Fink, *Defending the Rights of Others*, 3–38.

19. Link, *Papers of Woodrow Wilson*, 46:322; *Report of the Proceedings of the American Jewish Congress* (Philadelphia: American Jewish Congress, 1919), 13; Ilya Grunberg, *Les Juifs à la Conférence de la Paix* (Geneva: Édition Atar, 1919), 12–14.

20. Letter from Leon Reich to the Eastern Galician Delegation of the Jewish National Council in Vienna, Apr. 7, 1919, CZA, F3/55; Mark Levene, *War, Jews and the New Europe: The Diplomacy of Lucien Wolf, 1914–1919* (Oxford: Oxford University Press 1992), 262–83; Tenenboym, *Tsvishn sholem un milkhome*, 68.

21. Letter from M. P. Ringel to Eastern Galician Delegation of the Jewish National Council in Vienna, Apr. 14, 1919, CZA F3/55; *Report of the Proceedings of the American Jewish Congress*, 25, 82, 95–96; *Papers of the Paris Peace Conference*, 5:397–99.

22. Letter from Leo Motzkin to Eric Drummond, June 16, 1919, quoted in David Engel, "Manhigim yehudim, takhnun 'estregi ve-ḥazirah ha-beinl'eumit li-aher milḥemet ha-'olam ha-rishonah," *Mikhael* 16 (2004): 155–68; Comité des Délégations Juives auprès de la Conférence de la Paix, "Memorandum concernant les droits des Minorités," (May 10, 1919), quoted in Nathan Feinberg, *La Question des Minorités a la Conférence de la Paix de 1919–1920 et l'action Juive en Faveur de la Protection Internationale des Minorités* (Paris: Comité des Délégations Juives, 1929), 45.

23. Tenenboym, *Tsvishn sholem un milkhome*, 245; *Papers of the Paris Peace Conference*, 5:680–81 and 6:624–29; Link, *Deliberations*, 1:439 and 2:89–91.

24. American Jewish Congress, *Proceedings of Adjourned Session of American Jewish Congress including Report of Commission to Peace Conference and of Provisional Organization for Formation of American Jewish Congress* (New York: Provisional Organization for Formation of the American Jewish Congress, 1920), 29; Fink, *Defending the Rights of Others*, 209–10.

25. Matthew Silver, *Louis Marshall and the Rise of Jewish Ethnicity* (Syracuse, NY: Syracuse University Press, 2014), 359; Fink, *Defending the Rights of Others*, 211, 246.

26. Fink, *Defending the Rights of Others*, 364–68; *Report of the Proceedings of the American Jewish Congress*, 84.

27. "Program Personalnej autonomji narodowej Żydów w państwie polskiem," *Gazeta Żydowska*, Jan. 1, 1919; "Memoryał" (1919), CZA, F3/79; "Memoryał," CZA,

F3/56; "Posłuchanie deputacyi lwowskiej żyd. młodzieży akad. u ministra Łukasiewicza," *Chwila*, Sept. 12, 1919; Yehoshua Thon, "Al ha-perek," *Ha-tsefirah*, June 3, 1919; Letter from Joseph Tenenbaum to Eastern Galician Delegation of the Jewish National Council, May 14, 1919, CZA, F3/55.

28. *The Pogroms in the Ukraine under the Ukrainian Governments (1917–1920): Historical Survey with Documents and Photographs* (London: Bale & Danielsson, 1927), xi–xii.

29. Quoted in Morgenthau, *All in a Life-Time*, 373–74.

30. "Zjazd syońskich korporacyi akademickich Malopolski (H. A. Z.) w Przemysłu," *ND*, Feb. 20, 1920.

31. "Memoryał," and "Protokoll," Dec. 8, 1920, CZA, F3/58.

32. Letter from Arieh Tartakower to Rachel Lauterpacht (June 11, 1960), LFA; Dorothy Stone, "Sir Hersch Lauterpacht; Teacher, Writer and Judge—A Presidential Address," *Transactions of the Jewish Historical Society of England* 28 (1984): 102.

33. Lauterpacht, *Life*, 29–35; Letter from HL to Michael and Gittel Steinberg, Feb. 7, 1923, LFA.

34. Letters from HL to London Zionist Office, June 23, 1920, Norman Bentwich to Rachel Lauterpacht, Sept. 7, 1960, and Shabtai Rosenne to Stephen Schwebel, Apr. 3, 1983, LFA; Mendelsohn, *Zionism in Poland*, 260; Eli Lauterpacht, "Memorandum for the Lauterpacht Bio File," LFA; Letter from HL to Rachel Lauterpacht, Feb. 7, 1923, LFA; Interview with Arnold McNair, Aug. 16, 1967, LFA; HL, "O uniwersytet żydowski," *Nowe Życie* 1, no. 1 (June 1924): 122.

35. "Der erste weltkongress der jud. Studentenschaft," *La Tribune Juive*, May 16, 1924, 220; "Jewish Students' World Congress," *Jewish Chronicle*, May 9, 1924, 17; HL, "Z miesiąca na miesąc," *Nowe Życie* 1, no. 2 (July 1924): 271–74; Zwi Lauterpacht, "The World Union of Jewish Students and the Congress in Antwerp," *Inter-University Jewish Federation Bulletin* 1, no. 1 (Aug. 1924): 15–16.

36. HL, "The World Union of Jewish Students [1924]," mss. in LFA.

37. "Der Weltkongress juedischer Studenten," *Juedische Rundschau*, May 9, 1924; HL, "World Union"; Aryeh Tseytlin, "1-er alveltel. idish. studenten-kongres," *Haynt*, May 13, 1924; Dawid Fajgenberg, "Wszechświa towy zjazd studentów-Żydów w Antwerp," *Nowe Życie* 1, no. 1 (June 1924): 276.

38. HL, "World Union"; HL, "List z Londynu," *ND*, Sept. 5, 1925.

39. HL, "In Plea of a Syllabus," mss. in LFA; HL, "The Mandate," 30, 68–69; Interview with Arnold McNair.

40. Hersch Lauterpacht, *The Function of Law in the International Community* (Oxford: Oxford University Press, 1933); Lauterpacht, *Life*, 66; "University Zionist Federation, Report of the First Executive Meeting" [Mar. 1924], LFA; Letter from Julius Stone to J. M. Rich, Nov. 16, 1926, LMA, ACC 3121, Folder B4/I/10; HL, "Ofenzywa z 77 Great Russell Street," *ND*, Apr. 8, 1926.

41. Letter from HL to Secretary of the Zionist Federation, Feb. 15, 1925, LFA; "Diary of the Palestine Tour," *Magazine of the WUJS* 1, no. 3 (June 1925): 5.

42. HL, "Sprawa węglowa w Anglji," *ND*, Jan. 28, 1926.

43. Michael Brecher, *The World of Protracted Conflicts* (Lanham, MD: Lexington Books, 2016), 204; HL, "Nastroje angielskie po Locarno," *ND*, Nov. 9, 1925; Anna Cienciala and Titus Komarnicki, *From Versailles to Locarno: Keys to Polish Foreign Policy, 1919–25* (Lawrence: University of Kansas Press, 1984), 10.

44. HL, "The Mandate," 84; Michael Cohen, *Britain's Moment in Palestine: Retrospect and Perspectives, 1917–1948* (London: Routledge, 2014), 94–212; Benjamin White, *The Emergence of Minorities in the Middle East: The Politics of Community in French Mandate Syria* (Edinburgh: University of Edinburgh Press, 2011), 2–4.

45. Hillel Cohen, *1929: Year Zero of the Arab-Israeli Conflict* (Waltham, MA: University Press of New England, 2015), xvii–xix.

46. Benny Morris, *Righteous Victims* (New York: Knopf, 1999), 110–17; Cohen, *Britain's Moment*, 215–20; Tom Segev, *One Palestine, Complete: Jews and Arabs under the British Mandate* (New York: Metropolitan Books, 2000), 295–332.

47. Martin Kolinsky, *Law, Order and Riots in Mandatory Palestine, 1928–1935* (London: Palgrave Macmillan, 1993), 31–122.

48. HL, "Opinja angielska wobec zajść w Palestynie," *ND*, Sept. 2, 1929.

49. HL, "Opinja angielska."

50. HL, "Opinja angielska."

51. HL, "Carr on International Morality," mss. in HL, *Collected Papers*, 2:90.

52. HL, "Rządy Labour Party przyczynia się do pacyfikacji świata," *ND*, June 22, 1929.

53. "Tsu ale yidn in Lite!" *IS*, Sept. 10, 1929; Petition from Jacob Robinson to the Permanent Mandates Commission, Sept. 3, 1929, LNA, R2282, 6A/14036/224.

Chapter 2. The Cry of the Peoples

1. Yitshok Grinboym, "In teg fun umru un payn (A briv fun zheneve)," *IS*, Sept. 11, 1929.

2. Noyekh Prilutski, "Oyf dem minderheyts-kongres," *Der Moment*, Oct. 30, 1925.

3. Interview with Daniel Greenberg, July 17, 2016.

4. JR Interview by Daniel Greenberg (Heb.), Nov. 15, 1975, GFA [Hereafter JR Interview (DG)].

5. Israel Bartal, *Kozak u-bedui* (Tel Aviv: Am Oved, 2007), 188–205; Simon Rabinovitch, *Jewish Rights, National Rites: Nationalism and Autonomy in Late Imperial and Revolutionary Russia* (Stanford, CA: Stanford University Press, 2014), 15–78.

6. JR, *Yedi'at 'amenu. demografyah ve-natsiologyah* (Berlin: "Ajanoth," 1923), 133.

7. JR Interview (DG).

8. Joseph Stalin, *Natsional'nyi vopros i marksizm* (St. Petersburg: Izdatel'stvo "Priboi," 1914); Antonio Cassesse, *Self-Determination of Peoples: A Legal Appraisal* (Cambridge: Cambridge University Press, 1995), 11–23.

9. JR Interview (DG); JR, "Memorandum, March 9, 1943," AJA, C12/3.
10. JR Interview (DG); E. B. [JR], "Di folkistishe atake," *IS*, Sept. 29, 1926.
11. JR Interview (DG).
12. Mendel Sudarsky, "Yidn in der umaphengiker Lite," in Mendel Sudarsky and Uriah Katzenelenbogen, eds., *Lite* (New York: Jewish-Cultural Society, 1951), 1:133–35; Leyb Shimoni, "Tsu der geshikhte fun linke 'poaley-tsion' in Lite," in Ch. Leikowicz, *Lite* (Jerusalem: I. L. Peretz Publishing House, 1965), 2:130; "Di tsveyte tsyonistishe konferents in Lite," *IS*, Jan. 4, 1920; Dov Levin, *The Litvaks: A Short History of the Jews in Lithuania* (Jerusalem: Yad Vashem, 2000), 119.
13. JR Interview (DG).
14. See http://biblio-archive.unog.ch/Dateien/3/D16777.pdf, copy of official telegram from Kovno, Oct. 17, 1920; Natan Feinberg, *Pirkei ḥayim ve-zikhronot* (Jerusalem: Keter, 1985), 46; Vladas Sirutavičius and Darius Staliūnas, "Introduction," in Sirutavičius and Staliūnas, *Pragmatic Alliance*, 13–15.
15. JR, "Araynfir," in JR, ed., *Barikht fun der idisher seym-fraktsye fun II Litvishn seym (1923–1926)* (Kovno: Idisher Seym-Fraktsye, 1926), 6–8.
16. JR, "Tsienizm un land-politik," *IS*, May 8, 1926, 13; JR, "Dover Robinson"; JR, *Yedi'at 'amenu*, 2, 107; JR, "Der hebreyisher kultur-kongres in lite," *IS*, Sept. 29, 1926; Sudarsky, "Virbaln," *Lite*, 1:1641.
17. JR, "Der hebreyisher kultur-kongres in lite," *IS*, Sept. 29, 1926; Sudarsky, "Virbaln," 1641.
18. On Robinson's parliamentary activities, see JR, "Di fraktsye un di algemeyne un idishe minderhaytn-bavegung," in JR, *Barikht*, 77–83.
19. JR, "Di fraktsye," 81–82.
20. JR, "Tsienizm," 13; Egle Bendikaite, "Politician without a Party: A Zionist Appraisal of Jacob Robinson's Activities in the Public Life of Lithuania," in Egle Bendikaite and Dirk Roland Haupt, eds., *The Life, Times and Work of Jokubas Robinzonas—Jacob Robinson* (Sankt Augustin: Academia Verlag, 2015), 39–66. See also Egle Bendikaite, *Sionistinis sąjūdis Lietuvoje* (Vilnius: LII leidykla, 2006) and Šarūnas Liekis, *A State within a State? Jewish Autonomy in Lithuania, 1918–1925* (Vilnius: Versus Aureus, 2003).
21. JR Interview (DG).
22. Levin, *Litvaks*, 128; JR Interview (DG); JR, "Der khurbn fun undzer avtonomye," *IS*, Sept. 23, 1924.
23. JR, "Tse hobn minderheytn rekht tsu klogn zikh in felker-bund?" *IS*, Nov. 9, 1926; JR, "Der farshlag fun Galvanuskas umtsubeytn di minderheyt-traktatn af eyn opmakh tsvishn ale melukhes," *IS*, Sept. 27, 1925; Giuseppe Motta, *Less than Nations: Central-Eastern European Minorities after WWI* (Newcastle upon Tyne: Cambridge Scholars Publishing, 2013), 1:265; E. B. [JR], "Der geheymnisfuler tsirkulyar," *IS*, Sept. 23, 1925.
24. JR Interview (DG); Fink, *Defending the Rights of Others*, 295; Rudolf Michaelsen, *Der Europäische Nationalitäten-Kongreß 1925–1928: Aufbau, Krise und Konsolidierung* (Frankfurt am Main: Lang, 1984), 85–87; David Smith and John Hiden,

Ethnic Diversity and the Nation State: National Cultural Autonomy Revisited (London: Routledge, 2014), 70–75.

25. JR Interview (DG); Moshe Landau, *Ha-brit she-hikhzivah: Yehudim ve-Germanim be-Kongres ha-mi'utim ha-Eropi, 1925–1933* (Tel Aviv: University of Tel Aviv Press, 1992), 63–104.

26. *Sitzungsbericht der ersten Konferenz der organisierten nationalen Gruppen in den Staaten Europas im Jahre 1925 zu Genf* (Vienna: W. Braumüller Universitäts-Verlagsbuchhandlung, 1925), 78; "Funem kongres fun di natsionalen minderhayten in Zheneve. Di rede fun doktor Robinzon," *Der moment*, Oct. 23, 1925; JR Interview (DG); Sabine Bamberger-Stemmann, *Der Europäische Nationalitätenkongreß 1925 bis 1938. Nationale Minderheiten zwischen Lobbyistentum und Großmachtinteressen* (Marburg: Verlag Herder-Institut, 2000).

27. "Le IV Congres des Nationalités Européenes," *Cri des Peuples* 1, no. 15 (Sept. 5, 1928): 17; Viktor Zinghaus, *Führende köpfe der Baltischen Staaten* (Kaunas: Ostverlag der Buchhandlung Pribacis, 1938), 90.

28. Smith and Hiden, *Ethnic Diversity*, 29–30; Alfonsas Eidintas, *Antanas Smetona and His Lithuania: From the National Liberation Movement to an Authoritarian Regime (1893–1940)* (Leiden: Brill, 2015), 188, 281; Letter from JR to M. W. Beckleman, Oct. 2, 1942, AJA, C7/3; Speech by Josef Griliches, Dec. 12, 1977, USHMM, Box 4/6.

29. Feinberg, *Pirkei ḥayyim*, 54–111; Frank Nesemann, "Minderheitdiplomatie— Leo Motzkin zwischen Imperien und Nationen," in Dan Diner, ed., *Synchrone Welten: Zeitenräume jüdischer Geschichte* (Göttingen: Vandenhoeck & Ruprecht, 2005), 147–71; Levene, *War*, 310; Fink, *Defending the Rights of Others*, 286–89; *Report of the Secretary and Special Delegate of the Joint Foreign Committee on Jewish Questions Dealt with by the First Assembly of the League* (London: The Committee and the Association, 1921), 14.

30. JR Interview (DG); Gershon Bacon, "Polish Jews and the Minorities Treaties Obligations, 1925: The View from Geneva (Documents from the League of Nations Archives)," *Gal-Ed* 18 (2002): 145–76.

31. Quoted in Melvin Urofsky, *A Voice That Spoke for Justice: The Life and Times of Stephen Wise* (Albany: SUNY Press, 1982), 294; Max Heller, *The Zurich Conference for Jewish Rights* (New York: American Jewish Congress, 1927), 6; "Full Report on Jewish Rights at Zurich," *Wisconsin Jewish Chronicle*, Aug. 26, 1927.

32. Urofsky, *Voice*, 293–96; "Full Report on Jewish Rights at Zurich"; "Opponents Scored at Zurich Conference on Jewish Rights," Jewish Telegraph Agency, Aug. 19, 1927; Letter from JR to Zvi Aberson, Oct. 30, 1927, CZA, A139/220.

33. "Le Discours de Jacob Robinson," *Cri des Peuples* 1, no. 19 (Oct. 3, 1928): 18–19.

34. JR, "Tse hobn minderheytn"; Letters from JR to Zevi Aberson, Mar. 28, 1928, and June 30, 1929, and Letter from Ewalde Ammende to JR, Apr. 4, 1928, CZA, A139/220; Jacob Robinson and Herbert Kraus, eds., *Das Volkerrecht der Uebergangszeit. Grundlagen der voelkerrechtlichen Beziehungen der Union der Sowjetrepubliken von E. A. Korowin* (Berlin: Grunewald, 1929); JR Interview (DG); Martyn Housden, *On Their Own Behalf: Ewald Ammende, Europe's National Mi-*

norities and the Campaign for Cultural Autonomy, 1920–1936 (Amsterdam: Rodopi, 2014), 199–211.

35. "Idishe miutim in der gantser velt apelirn tsum felker-bund vegn Erets-Yisroel," *IS*, Sept. 10, 1929; "Tsu ale yidn in Lite!" *IS*, Sept. 10, 1929; Petition from JR to the Permanent Mandates Commission, Sept. 3, 1929, LNA, R2282, 6A/14036/224; Natasha Wheatley, "Mandatory Interpretation: Legal Hermeneutics and the New International Order in Arab and Jewish Petitions to the League of Nations," *Past and Present* 227, no. 1 (2015): 229; Fink, *Defending the Rights of Others*, 308–16; Christoph Kimmich, *Germany and the League of Nations* (Chicago: University of Chicago Press, 1975), 133–49.

36. *Sitzungsbericht des Kongresses der Organisierten Nationalen Gruppen in den staaten Europas, Genf, 3. Bis 6. September 1930* (Leipzig: Braumüller, 1931), 71–75.

37. Jacob Robinson, Oscar Karbach, Max Laserson, Nehemiah Robinson, and Mark Vishniak, eds., *Were the Minorities Treaties a Failure?* (New York: Institute of Jewish Affairs, 1943), 256.

38. JR Interview (DG); N. Feinberg, "Perishat ha-yehudim mi-kongres ha-miutim," in *Masot bi-she'elot ha-zeman* (Jerusalem: Dvir, 1980), 108; John Hiden, *Defender of Minorities: Paul Schiemann, 1876–1944* (London: Hurst, 2004), 212–17; Landau, *Ha-brit she-hikhzivah*, 126–59; Housden, *On Their Own*, 296–310.

39. Quoted in Carl Voss, ed., *Stephen S. Wise: Servant of the People: Selected Letters* (Philadelphia: Jewish Publication Society of America, 1970), 170, 185–86.

40. Adolf Hitler, *Mein Kampf* (Munich: Eher Verlag, 1925), 162–63.

41. Quoted in Raphael Gross, *Carl Schmitt and the Jews: The "Jewish Question," the Holocaust, and Legal Theory* (Madison: University of Wisconsin Press, 2007), 32, 61; Charles Frye, "Carl Schmitt's Concept of the Political," *Journal of Politics* 28, no. 4 (Nov. 1966): 818; William Scheuerman, *Carl Schmitt: The End of Law* (Lanham, MD: University Press of America, 1999), 141–74; Hersch Lauterpacht, *International Law and Human Rights* (New York: Columbia University Press, 1950), 17; Carl Schmitt, *Constitutional Law*, trans. and ed. Jeffrey Seitzer (Durham, NC: Duke University Press, 2008), 198.

42. JR, *Kommentar der Konvention über das Memelgebiet vom 8. Mai 1924* (Kaunas: Spaudos Fondas, 1934).

43. Philipp Graf, *Die Bernheim-Petition 1933: jüdische Politik in der Zwischenkriegszeit* (Goettingen: Vandenhoeck & Ruprecht, 2008), 104; Letter from JR to Leo Motzkin, Apr. 1, 1933, CZA A126/616; Paul Doerr, *British Foreign Policy, 1919–1939* (Manchester: University of Manchester Press, 1998), 124.

44. Fink, *Defending the Rights of Others*, 302–7.

45. Quoted in Feinberg, *Masot*, 78.

46. Comité des Délégations Juives, *La Société des Nations et L'Oppression des Juifs en Allemagne* (Paris: Librarie Arthur Rousseau, 1933); Fink, *Defending the Rights of Others*, 331.

47. Report to Administrative Committee by JR, July 2, 1945, AJA, C98/14; League of Nations Information Session #6455, May 30, 1933, in AJA, C125/2.

48. Comité des Délégations Juives, *La Société des Nations*, 9.

49. Quoted in Speech by Eduard Benes, Chicago, 1933, in AJA, C125/2.

50. Quoted in Mark Mazower, *Dark Continent: Europe's Twentieth Century* (New York: Knopf, 2000), 58.

51. Letter from JR to Natan Feinberg, Apr. 20, 1933, quoted in Graf, *Bernheim-Petition*, 222; JR, "Jews and Minority Rights: Confusions and Clarification [1942]," AJA, C127/5.

52. Jacob Robinson, "International Protection of Minorities: A Global View," *Israel Yearbook on Human Rights* 1 (1974): 73.

53. JR, "Jews and Minority Rights."

Chapter 3. Golden Shackles

1. PB, "Appeal to Rescue Jewish Youth from Germany" [1938], ECA; Flora Solomon, *From Baku to Baker Street* (London: Harper Collins, 1986), 168.

2. Michael Cohen and Martin Kolinsky, "Introduction," in M. Cohen and M. Kolinsky, eds., *Britain and the Middle East in the 1930s: Security Problems, 1935–39* (New York: Palgrave, 1992), xvi; Dan Diner, "Ambiguous Semantics: Reflections on Jewish Political Concepts," *Jewish Quarterly Review* 98, no. 1 (Winter 2008): 99–102; Fink, *Defending the Rights of Others*, 346–53; Zara Steiner, *The Triumph of the Dark: European International History, 1933–1939* (Oxford: Oxford University Press, 2011), 359; Gil Rubin, "The Future of the Jews: Planning for the Postwar Jewish World, 1939–1946" (PhD diss., Columbia University, 2017).

3. MP, "Comments," *New Judea* 15, no. 6 (Mar. 1939): 109.

4. Joseph Roth, *The Wandering Jews* (New York: W. W. Norton, 2001), 126–28.

5. Maurice Perlzweig, *Perlzweig: Human Rights Pioneer. A Memoir*, ed. Suzi Peel (Washington, DC: n.p., 2015), 100–102 [Hereafter Perlzweig, *Memoir*]; Norman Rose, *The Gentile Zionists* (London: Cass, 1973), 72–79.

6. Perlzweig, *Memoir*, 258; "Jewish National Movement," *Jewish Chronicle*, Jan. 3, 1919; Cohen, *Britain's Moment*, 5–37; Geoffrey Alderman, *The Jewish Community in British Politics* (Oxford: Oxford University Press, 1983), 102–7.

7. Interview with Roberta Cohen, Jan. 10, 2013; "Men and Matters," *Young Zionist* 11, no. 10 (Nov. 1932): 5; "These Names Make the News," *Daily Express*, July 17, 1933.

8. Perlzweig, *Memoir*, 55, 82–83.

9. Perlzweig, *Memoir*, 115; MP, "Zionist Affiliations: 'Liberal' Judaism and Jewish Nationalism," *Jewish Chronicle*, May 20, 1921; MP, "Liberal Judaism and Zionism: Conflict or Co-Operation?" *Pioneer* 1, no. 5 (Oct. 1928): 9; "Zionist Affiliations," *Jewish Chronicle*, May 6, 1921.

10. "The Jew To-Day and To-Morrow," Apr. 3, 1931, AJA, B34/12; MP, "The Liberal Jewish Congress in Berlin. A Zionist Comment," *New Judea* 4, no. 4 (Sept. 29, 1928): 6–7; I. R., "The Jewish Mission," *Young Zionist* 3, no. 2 (Feb. 23, 1928): 2.

11. Perlzweig, *Memoirs*, 195; Hallam Tennyson, *The Haunted Mind: An Autobiography* (London: Andre Deutsch, 1984), 44.

12. Craig Raine, "Peter Benenson," *New Review* 4, no. 47 (1978): 27; Solomon, *From Baku*, 43–44; "Grigori Benenson, Noted Financier," *New York Times*, Apr. 6, 1939.

13. Solomon, *From Baku*, 29, 35, 41–42, 49–50, 77; Raine, "Peter Benenson," 27–28; Manya Harari, *Memoirs, 1906–1969* (London: Harvill Press, 1971), 16.

14. A. Lissack, "Mr. Harold J. Solomon, O.B.E., M.C.," *Jewish Chronicle*, Aug. 15, 1930; Solomon, *From Baku*, 87–93; "Palestine at Wembley," *Jewish Chronicle*, Sept. 24, 1924; "Report of the High Commissioner," *Palestine Bulletin*, June 26, 1925; "Colonel Harold J. Solomon," *Palestine Bulletin*, Aug. 19, 1930; Cohen, *Britain's Moment*, 94–212.

15. Solomon, *From Baku*, 98–99, 101, 106–10; "Homeland Gossip," *B'nai B'rith Messenger*, Mar. 24, 1922.

16. Raine, "Peter Benenson," 28.

17. "Undaunted," *Daily Express*, May 24, 1929; Maurice Sorsby, "Mr. Harold J. Solomon, O.B.E., M.C.," *Jewish Chronicle*, Aug. 15, 1930; "Colonel Harold J. Solomon," *Palestine Bulletin*, Aug. 19, 1930; "Jewish National Fund," *Jewish Chronicle*, May 13, 1927; "Jewish National Fund," *Jewish Chronicle*, June 17, 1927; A. Lissack, "Mr. Harold J. Solomon, O.B.E., M.C.," *Jewish Chronicle*, Aug. 15, 1930; Harry Defries, *Conservative Party Attitudes to Jews, 1900–1950* (London: Routledge, 2001), 118.

18. "Peter Benenson," *Jewish Chronicle*, Apr. 5, 2005; Richard Abraham, *Alexander Kerensky: The First Love of the Revolution* (New York: Columbia University Press, 1990), 361; George Weidenfeld, *Remembering My Good Friends: An Autobiography* (New York: Harper Collins, 1994), 187; Raine, "Peter Benenson," 28; Interview with PB, IISG, AI 982–83.

19. Betty Sargeant, "The Desperate Mission of Stefan Lux," *Georgia Review* 55, no. 4/56, no. 1 (Winter 2001/Spring 2002): 187–201.

20. Leon Kubowitzki, ed., *Unity in Dispersion: A History of the World Jewish Congress* (New York: World Jewish Congress, 1948), 51; "Bro. Perlzweig's Stirring Address," *Jewish Chronicle*, Nov. 25, 1932; "The Palestine Movement: Zionism-Communism," *Jewish Chronicle*, Feb. 1, 1935; *Protocole du premier congrès juif mondial* (Geneva: World Jewish Congress, 1936), 158.

21. Alderman, *Modern British Jewry*, 282–83; Perlzweig, *Memoir*, 137, 363; Gisela Lebzelter, *Political Anti-Semitism in England, 1918–1939* (Oxford: Oxford University Press, 1978), 136–54; M. L. Perlzweig, "International Defence of Jewish Rights," *Zionist Review* 6, no. 6 (June 9, 1938): 13–14; "Palestine," *The Guardian*, July 23, 1936; "Jews of Eastern Europe," *The Guardian*, July 25, 1936.

22. Quoted in Aaron Klieman, ed., *The Rise of Israel: Zionist Evidence before the Peel Commission, 1936–1937* (New York: Garland, 1987), 18.

23. Helen McCarthy, *The British People and the League of Nations: Democracy, Citizenship, and Internationalism, c. 1918–45* (Manchester: University of Manchester Press, 2011), 212–13.

24. Cohen, *Britain's Moment*, 287.

25. Segev, *One Palestine, Complete*, 414–17; Cohen, *Britain's Moment*, 272–77; "Minority Status Unthinkable," *The Guardian*, Jan. 17, 1938; "16th Century Trying to Shut out 20th," *The Scotsman*, Oct. 27, 1938; "Statement by the Rev. M. L. Perlzweig," May 31, 1936, AJA, B34/12.

26. John P. Fox, "British Attitudes to Jewish Refugees from Central and Eastern Europe in the Nineteenth and Twentieth Centuries," in Werner Mosse, ed., *Second Chance: Two Centuries of German-Speaking Jews in the United Kingdom* (Tubingen: Mohr Siebeck, 1991), 484.

27. Raine, "Peter Benenson," 28–29; Interview with Marlys Deeds, 1985, IISG, File 985; P. J. H. Solomon, "College Annals 'Obituary,' 1938," ECA; Solomon, *From Baku*, 168.

28. Letter from PB to Provost, Nov. 25, 1938, ECA; PB, "College Annals"; Ari Joshua Sherman, *Island Refuge: Britain and Refugees from the Third Reich* (Berkeley: University of California Press, 1973), 215–16; Interview with PB, IISG, File 985; Bernard Wasserstein, *Britain and the Jews of Europe: 1939–1945* (London: Leicester University Press, 1994); Vera Fast, *Children's Exodus: A History of the Kindertransport* (Portland: I. B. Tauris, 2010), 18–26; Norman Bentwich, *They Found Refuge: An Account of British Jewry's Work for Victims of Nazi Oppression* (London: Cresset Press, 1956).

29. Alderman, *Modern British Jewry*, 275–79; Sherman, *Island Refuge*, 183.

30. Solomon, *From Baku*, 164, 169, 172–75, 200; Abraham, *Alexander Kerensky*, 365–67, 380; Maureen Cleave, "Solomon's Zeal," *Observer Magazine*, July 1, 1984; Weidenfeld, *Remembering My Good Friends*, 192; Interview with George Weidenfeld, July 6, 2015.

31. Interview with Maurice Perlzweig, Jan. 31, 1983, CUA; "The Rev. M. L. Perlzweig. Tributes at London Luncheon," *Zionist Review* 7, no. 1 (May 9, 1940): 11; "Rights of Jews in Romania," *Times* (of London), Jan. 17, 1938.

32. Bela Vago, *The Shadow of the Swastika: The Rise of Fascism and Anti-Semitism in the Danube Basin, 1936–1939* (London: Saxon House, 1975), 55.

33. Vago, *Shadow of the Swastika*, 267–68, 289.

34. Gerhart Riegner, *Ne Jamais Désespérer* (Paris: Cerf, 1999), 253–56.

35. Perlzweig, *Memoir*, 276; Letter from MP to Alex Easterman, May 22, 1951, AJA, B54/9.

36. Quoted in Martin Gilbert, *Churchill and the Jews: A Lifelong Friendship* (New York: Holt, 2008), 157.

37. "Jews Reject New Plan for Palestine," *Birmingham Daily Post*, May 15, 1939; MP, "Comments," *New Judea* 15, no. 6 (Mar. 1939): 109; Cohen, *Britain's Moment*, 212.

38. Perlzweig, *Memoir*, 266–76; Vago, *Shadow of the Swastika*, 412–14.

39. Perlzweig, *Memoir*, 293.

40. Perlzweig, *Memoir*, 287, 296.

41. Lewis Namier, "In the Margin of Events," *Zionist Review* 1, no. 22 (June 27, 1941): 6.

Part 2. Convergence

Morris D. Waldman, "A Bill of Rights for All Nations," *New York Times*, Nov. 19, 1944 (emphasis in original); American Jewish Conference, *Proceedings of the American Jewish Conference* (New York: American Jewish Conference, 1945),

2:45; Robert Marcus, "Human Rights: A Jewish View," *Congress Weekly* 16, no. 2 (Jan. 10, 1949): 7–9; MP Speech, Jan. 19, 1952, AJA, B3/4.

Chapter 4. Jewish Human Rights

1. Quoted in Sidney Liskofsky, "International Protection of Human Rights," in Louis Henkin, ed., *World Politics and the Jewish Condition* (New York: Quadrangle Books, 1972), 277.
2. JR, Memorandum, Oct. 30, 1944, AJA, B86/2; Letter from JR to Vera Micheles Dean, Dec. 29, 1941, AJA, C7/3.
3. Louis Holborn, ed., *War and Peace Aims of the United Nations*, 2 vols. (Boston: World Peace Foundation, 1948), 1:427–28, cited in A. W. Brian Simpson, *Human Rights and the End of Empire* (Oxford: Oxford University Press, 2004), 160.
4. YIVO RG 347.17.10, Box 106, Folder "AJC Declaration—Comments, 1944–1945" [Hereafter "AJC Comments"].
5. James Loeffler, "The Particularist Pursuit of American Universalism: The American Jewish Committee's 1944 'Declaration on Human Rights,'" *Journal of Contemporary History* 50, no. 2 (Oct. 2014): 274–95.
6. "Report on the Institute for Jewish Affairs Origins and Activities, 1941–1947," AJA, C132/3; "The Institute for Contemporary Jewish Research. Proposal Presented to the World Jewish Congress by JR, Apr. 29, 1939" and "Speech of MP at the Hotel Biltmore, Atlanta, Feb. 3, 1941," AJA, C71/27.
7. Letter from JR to Alexander Abramson, Feb. 27, 1941, AJA, C8/6; JR Interview (DG); "Institute of Jewish Affairs, meeting minutes, 1940–1945," AJA, C68/5.
8. Elizabeth Borgwardt, *A New Deal for the World: America's Vision for Human Rights* (Cambridge, MA: Harvard University Press, 2009), 53–56; Mark Bradley, *The World Reimagined: Americans and Human Rights in the Twentieth Century* (Cambridge: Cambridge University Press, 2016).
9. Letter from JR to A. L. Easterman, Jan. 21, 1942, AJA, C11/6; Report on American Society for International Law, Apr. 24–26, 1941, AJA, C4/7; Letter from JR to Nahum Goldmann, June 25, 1942, AJA, C12/6; Meeting Minutes, May 2, 1942 and Meeting Agenda, Mar. 26, 1942, AJA, C1/2; Letter from JR to Quincy Wright, Oct. 26, 1942, AJA, C96/13; "International Safeguards for Human Rights," AJA, C104/5; Letter from JR to Stephen Wise, Maurice Perlzweig, Nahum Goldmann et al., May 13, 1943, AJA, C10/1.
10. Letter from JR to James Murdock, Feb. 4, 1942, AJA, C3/73; Transcript of Meeting of Carnegie Endowment for International Peace Post-War Planning Conference, Feb. 28–Mar. 1, 1942, AJA, C6/9.
11. Letter from MP to JR, AJA, C10/1; Letter from Stephen S. Wise to JR, May 17, 1943, AJA, C6/3.
12. JR, Memo [1943], AJA, C97/4; "International Protection of Minority Rights," Sept. 17, 1942, AJA, C15/12; JR, Memo [1944], AJA, C128/7; Mark Mazower, "The Strange Triumph of Human Rights, 1933–1950," *Historical Journal* 47, no. 2 (2004): 387.

13. "Jewish Peace Aims, 1941–42," Nov. 23, 1941, AJA, C95/16; JR, Memo, Feb. 24, 1943, AJA, C6/1; MP, Memo, June 13, 1944, AJA, C175/16; Jacob Robinson, *Human Rights and Fundamental Freedoms in the Charter of the United Nations: A Commentary* (New York: World Jewish Congress, 1946), 1.

14. "Jacob Blaustein? Who's He?" *Forbes* 102, no. 6 (Sept. 15, 1968): 26; Victor Bienstock, "War-Time Jewish Leaders," *Wisconsin Jewish Chronicle*, Oct. 15, 1943.

15. Loeffler, "Nationalism without a Nation?" 367–98.

16. JB Speech, Apr. 16, 1950, JBP, Box 2.5, Folder A-3-1.

17. Morris Waldman, Memo, Sept. 13, 1943, YIVO RG 347.1.29, Box 42, Folder 13.

18. "Latest Opinion Trends in the USA" (May 3, 1945), ESP, Box 343; Howard Sachar, *A History of the Jews in America* (New York: Penguin, 1992), 791.

19. Report of JB, Oct. 24, 1943, JBP, Box 2.3, Folder A-2-9; Speech of John Slawson, JBP, Box 1.199, Folder 285; Ben Halpern, "The Committee Discovers a Cure-All," *Jewish Frontier* 11 (Sept. 1944): 32–36.

20. Hersch Lauterpacht, "The Legal Aspect," in C. A. W. Manning, ed., *Peaceful Change: An International Problem* (London: Macmillan, 1937), 135–68.

21. Quoted in Lauterpacht, *Life*, 192, 199.

22. "American Federation Proposed: Lauterpacht Offers Postwar Solution," *Daily Tar Heel*, Oct. 23, 1940; Letter from HL to Robert Jackson, Jan. 15, 1941, LFA; Lauterpacht, *Life*, 181.

23. Letters from HL to Eli Lauterpacht, Apr. 15, 1943, Aug. 26, 1943, and Sept. 14, 1943, LFA.

24. Lauterpacht, *An International Bill of the Rights of Man* (Oxford: Oxford University Press, 1945), preface, xvii, 16–17, 26–28, 49.

25. Lauterpacht, *International Bill of Rights*, 119.

26. Letter from HL to JR, Oct. 5, 1944, AJA, C98/11; Lauterpacht, *International Bill of Rights*, 139, 141, and 144.

27. Letter from JR to Clyde Eagleton, Apr. 10, 1945, LOC, Pasvolsky Papers, Box 2, Folder "International Organization, 1945"; Memo, Aug. 21, 1943, LOC, Pasvolsky Papers, Box 3, Folder 7; Rowland Brucken, *A Most Uncertain Crusade: The United States, the United Nations, and Human Rights, 1941–1953* (DeKalb: University of Northern Illinois Press, 2013), 53–55.

28. Lauterpacht, *International Bill of Rights*, 215; Marco Duranti, *The Conservative Human Rights Revolution: European Identity, Transnational Politics, and the Origins of the European Convention* (Oxford: Oxford University Press, 2016).

29. Aide-Memoire, Mar. 21, 1944, JBP, Box 2.128, Folder "AJC 1944"; Zohar Segev, *The World Jewish Congress during the Holocaust: Between Activism and Restraint* (Oldenbourg: Brill, 2014), 44–104; Marc Lee Raphael, *Abba Hillel Silver: A Profile in American Judaism* (New York: Holmes & Meier, 1989), 97–102; Richard Breitman and Allen Lichtman, *FDR and the Jews* (Cambridge, MA: Harvard University Press, 2013), 257–60.

30. Memo, June 21, 1944, JBP, Box 2.128, Folder P-2-26.

31. Interview with Joseph M. Proskauer, Jan. 25, 1961, CUA; Jerold Auerbach, "Joseph M. Proskauer: American Court Jew," *American Jewish History* 69, no. 1 (Sept. 1, 1979): 1–16; FDR Papers, The President's Official File, Part 1, OF 76—Church Matters, Box 9, "76c—Jewish, August, 1943–1945."

32. American Jewish Conference Statement on an International Bill of Rights, July 31, 1944, CZA, C7 460/2; Meeting Minutes, Mar. 21, 1942, AJA, C95/16.

33. Letter from MP to JR, Sept. 11, 1944, AJA, C10/1; "Worldwide Bill of Rights," *Detroit Free Press*, Aug. 21, 1944.

34. Memo, YIVO RG 347.17.10, Box 106, Folder "Drafts of Declaration of Human Rights," 7–8; quoted in Casey Nelson Blake, *Beloved Community: The Cultural Criticism of Randolph Bourne, Van Wyck Brooks, Waldo Frank and Lewis Mumford* (Chapel Hill: University of North Carolina Press, 1990), 31.

35. Drafts of the Declaration, YIVO RG 347.17.10, Box 106, Folder "Drafts of Declaration of Human Rights"; Loeffler, "Particularist Pursuit."

36. Memos, Nov. 14, 1944, Nov. 24, 1944, YIVO RG 347.17.10, Box 106, Folder "AJC Declaration on Human Rights, 1944"; "Answer to Tyranny," Radio Script, Nov. 28, 1944, YIVO RG 347.14.10, Box 107, Folder "Declaration of Human Rights. Publicity."

37. Memos, JBP, Box 1.26, Folder 373.

38. "A World 'Bill of Rights,'" *New York World-Telegram*, Dec. 15, 1944; "AJC Comments"; Eleanor Roosevelt, "Talks with Students," *New York World Telegram*, Dec. 20, 1944.

39. "AJC Comments."

40. "AJC Comments"; Wright Patterson, "Grassroots," *Menard News*, Dec. 21, 1944; Charles Tobey, "Wake up America! The Hour Is Late," in *Vital Speeches of the Day* 7 (1941): 748–51; quoted in Glenn H. Smith, *Langer of North Dakota: A Study in Isolationism, 1940–1959* (New York: Columbia University Press, 1979), 93, 96; Mark Sullivan, "World Bill of Rights Might Insure Mankind Real 'Peace on Earth,'" *Washington Post*, Dec. 24, 1944; Mark Sullivan, "'Anti-Bias' Measure: National Importance," *Washington Post*, Mar. 7, 1945; Samuel Moyn, *Christian Human Rights* (Philadelphia: University of Pennsylvania Press, 2015), 65–100.

41. "AJC Comments"; YIVO RG 347.17.10, Box 106, Folder "Declaration of Human Rights," Memo on Publicity (Nov. 24, 1944); National Catholic Welfare News Service Press Release, Dec. 15, 1944; "The Poles Are Also People with Human Rights," *Washington Post*, Dec. 25, 1944.

42. Gedaliah Bublick, "Di foderung far glaykhe rekht iz a vofn inem kamf kegn Tsien," *Morgn-zhurnal*, Dec. 29, 1944; "AJC Comments."

43. "Now Is the Time," *Changing World* 17 (Jan. 1945): 5; American Jewish Committee, *To the Counselors of Peace: Recommendations of the American Jewish Committee* (New York: American Jewish Committee, 1945), 15, 23–24.

44. Interview with Joseph Proskauer.

Chapter 5. Unfinished Victory

1. L. D. Hotchkiss, "Hollywood Air Marks Opening of Conference," *Los Angeles Times*, Apr. 26, 1945.

2. Letter from Samuel Goldsmith to Jacob Robinson, Apr. 8, 1945, AJA, C7/4; Escott Reid, *On Duty: A Canadian at the Making of the United Nations, 1945–1946* (Kent, OH: Kent State University Press, 1983), 24.

3. "Dumbarton Oaks Report," AJA, B96/11.

4. "Remarks at Temple Emanu-El, Apr. 3, 1945," JBP, Box 2.134, Q-1-8.

5. Jane Evans, "Notes from San Francisco, #1, Apr. 25, 1945," CEIP, Box 215, Folder 5.

6. "For World Peace: The Nations Gather," *New York Times*, Apr. 29, 1945; Willard Edwards, "First Session Is All over in Half an Hour," *Chicago Daily Tribune*, Apr. 26, 1945.

7. Reid, *On Duty*, 33, 50; "San Francisco Side-Show," *The Economist*, May 26, 1945; Boris Smolar, "Between You and Me," *American Israelite*, May 3, 1945; Mrs. Henry Monsky and Maurice Bisgyer, *Henry Monsky: The Man and His Work* (New York: Crown Publishers, 1947), 103.

8. Perlzweig, *Memoir*, 359. Geoffrey Wigoder, ed., *American Jewish Memoirs: Oral Documentation* (Jerusalem: Magnes Press, 1980), 270–72; Monsky and Bisgyer, *Henry Monsky*, 103, 114; "Report on San Francisco," AJHS I-67, Box 3, Folder 14; AZEC Meeting Notes, May 30, 1945, AJA, B96/13; Elihu Elath, *Zionism at the UN: Diary of the First Days* (Philadelphia: Jewish Publication Society of America, 1976), 34–37.

9. Letter from Archibald Cox to ERS, May 7, 1945, ESP, Box 313, Folder C.

10. Neil Smith, *American Empire: Roosevelt's Geographer and the Prelude to Globalization* (Berkeley: University of California Press, 2003), 246–47; Tara Zahra, *The Great Departure: Mass Migration from Eastern Europe and the Making of the Free World* (New York: W. W. Norton, 2016), 161–62; Monty Penkower, *The Holocaust and Israel Reborn: From Catastrophe to Sovereignty* (Urbana: University of Illinois Press, 1994), 208–9; Jason Kalman, "Dark Places around the University: The Johns Hopkins University's Admissions Quota and the Jewish Community, 1945–1951," *Hebrew Union College Annual* 81 (2010): 233–79; "Meeting of American Delegation," IBP, Box 17.6, Folder "May 27–28, 1945"; "FBI Report, May 3, 1945" and "Calendar Notes, May 1, 1945," ESP, Box 317, Folder "SF Conference-FBI" and Box 244, Folder "Calendar Notes."

11. Memorandum," May 29, 1945, YIVO RG 347.1.29, Box 40, Folder 41; Record, ESP, Box 246, "ERS Record, Sections 9–10."

12. "Verbatim Proceedings, Apr. 4, 1945," ESP, Box 289, Folder 1; Letter from I. L. Kenen to Meir Grossman, May 1, 1945, CZA, C7/213; Notes for Speech, June 2, 1945, JBP, Box 2.3, A-2-8.

13. Memo, Mar. 30, 1945, JBP, Box 1.29, Folder 396; *Charter of the United Nations: Report to the President on the Results of the San Francisco Conference by the Chairman of the United States Delegation, the Secretary of State, June 26, 1945* (Washington,

DC: U.S. Government Printing Office, 1945), 28–31; Letter from Edward Stettinius to Harry Truman, Apr. 19, 1945, www.trumanlibrary.org; "Promotion of Respect for Human Rights and Fundamental Freedoms," Apr. 9, 1945, NARA RG 59, Box 208, Folder "Respect for Human Rights."

14. Transcript of Meeting with Consultants, ESP, Box 291, Folder "May 2, 1945"; Remarks by Frederick Nolde, June 20, 1955, JBP, Box 2.78, Folder K-1-13.

15. Letter from Joseph Proskauer to John Slawson, May 3, 1945, JBP, Box 1.28, Folder 390; James Loeffler, "'The Conscience of America': Human Rights, Jewish Politics, and American Foreign Policy at the 1945 United Nations San Francisco Conference," *Journal of American History* 100, no. 2 (Sept. 2013): 401–28.

16. JB, Report on San Francisco, JBP, Box 2.3, Folder A-2-9.

17. "Proskauer's Eleventh Hour Action Achieved Human Rights in Charter," *Committee Reporter* 2, no. 7 (July 1945): 2; Letter from Archibald MacLeish to Edward Stettinius, May 2, 1945, ESP, Box 291, Folder "May 2, 1945"; Transcript of Administrative Committee Meeting, June 5, 1945, JBP, Box 2.121, Folder O-3-20; "Memorandum," May 3, 1945, IBP, Box 17:6; JB, Report on San Francisco, JBP, Box 2.3, Folder A-2-9; Carol Anderson, *Eyes off the Prize: The United Nations and the African American Struggle for Human Rights, 1944–1955* (Cambridge: Cambridge University Press, 2003), 50–51.

18. JB Speech, June 12, 1945, JBP, Box 2.3, Folder A-2-8.

19. JR, Report to Administrative Committee, July 2, 1945, AJA, C98/14.

20. Letter from I. L. Kenen to Meir Grossman, May 3, 1945, CZA, C7/213; Letter from I. L. Kenen to Meir Grossman, May 24, 1945, CZA, C7/213, 161; JR, Report to Administrative Committee, July 2, 1945, AJA, C98/14.

21. JR, Report to Administrative Committee.

22. Elath, *Zionism at the UN*, 37; JR, Interim Report on Paris Peace Conference, Sept. 1946, AJA, C133/8.

23. JR, General Report, Dec. 6, 1945, AJA, C14/16.

24. JR, Remarks on War Crimes, July 22, 1943, AJA, C101/8; Minutes, Sept. 24, 1943, AJA, C68/6; JR, "The Jewish Tragedy at Nuremberg," *Hadassah Newsletter* 26 (Dec. 1946): 9.

25. Minutes, Sept. 24, 1943, AJA, C68/6; Mark Lewis, *The Birth of the New Justice: The Internationalization of Crime and Punishment, 1919–1950* (Oxford: Oxford University Press, 2014), 151, 154; Letter from Alex Easterman to MP, May 14, 1942, AJA, C174/6; Letter from JR to MP, Jan. 22, 1943, AJA, C174/10; Memo, July 22, 1943, AJA, C101/8; Y. Robinson, "Poshei ha-milḥamah veha-oneshatam," *Ha-tzofeh*, Apr. 6, 1945.

26. Martti Koskenniemi, "Hersch Lauterpacht and the Development of International Criminal Law," *Journal of International Criminal Justice* 2 (2004): 817; Kerstin Von Lingen, "Setting the Path for the UNWCC: The Representation of European Exile Governments on the London International Assembly and the Commission for Penal Reconstruction and Development, 1941–1944," *Criminal Law Forum* 25 (2014): 45–76; Lauterpacht, *Life*, 204–6, 212–15.

27. Letter and Memo from HL to Alex Easterman, May 1, 1944, AJA, A71/5; IJA Meeting Minutes, Mar. 28, 1944, AJA, C68/6; Letter from MP to JR, Aug. 2, 1944, AJA, C175/16.

28. Letter from Alex Easterman to MP, Aug. 1, 1944, AJA, B1/7; MP Memo, June 13, 1944, AJA, C175/16.

29. www.trumanlibrary.org/whistlestop/study_collections/nuremberg/documents/index.php?pagenumber=4&documentid=C106-16-5&documentdate=1945-06-12&studycollectionid=nuremberg&groupid=; Michael Marrus, "A Jewish Lobby at Nuremberg: Jacob Robinson and the Institute of Jewish Affairs, 1945–1946," *Cardozo Law Review* 27, no. 4 (2006): 1651; Lewis, *Birth,* 150–80; Jonathan Bush, "Nuremberg and Beyond: Jacob Robinson, International Lawyer," *Loyola International and Comparative Law Review* 39, no. 259 (2017): 271–79.

30. Letter from HL to Chaim Weizmann, July 29, 1945, in WA, 12-2956; Lauterpacht, *Life,* 272; Jacob Robinson, "The International Military Tribunal and the Holocaust. Some Legal Reflections," *Israel Law Review* 7, no. 1 (Jan. 1972): 3.

31. Letter from HL to Chaim Weizmann, July 29, 1945, in WA, 12-2956; Letter from HL to Chaim Weizmann, Aug. 12, 1945 in WA, 3-2599; Letter from I. L. Kenen to Meir Grossman, Oct. 28, 1945, CZA, C7/26; Letter from HL to Patrick Dean, Aug. 20, 1945, LFA.

32. Letters from I. L. Kenen to Meir Grossman, Nov. 6, Nov. 15, and Nov. 19, 1945, CZA C7/26; JR, General Report, Dec. 6, 1945, AJA, C14/16.

33. Koskenniemi, "Hersch Lauterpacht," 817; HL to Rachel Lauterpacht, Nov. 30, 1945, LFA.

34. Robinson, "Jewish Tragedy," 9.

35. James Loeffler, "Becoming Cleopatra: The Forgotten Zionism of Raphael Lemkin," *Journal of Genocide Research* 19, no. 3 (Summer 2017): 340–60.

36. Robinson, "Jewish Tragedy," *Hadassah,* 9; JR, Private Report, Dec. 10, 1945, AJA, C14/16; Letter from I. L. Kenen to Meir Grossman, Oct. 28, 1945, CZA, C7/26.

37. Aide-Memoire, Sept. 19, 1945, JBP, Box 2.128, Folder P-2-27.

38. Aide-Memoire, Sept. 19, 1945.

39. Letter from JB and Joseph Proskauer to Harry Truman, July 15, 1946, JBP, Box 1.37, Folder 5-65.

40. Mordekhai Dantsis, "Di yidishe tragedye oyf der fridens-konferents, vos efent zikh haynt," *Der Tog,* July 29, 1946; Aron Alperin, "Gerekhtigkayt un glaykhhayt—ober nit far unz, yidn," *Der Tog,* Nov. 3, 1945.

41. I. L. Kenen, Memo, Oct. 25, 1946, CZA, C7/360.

42. Letter from JB to Byrnes, July 25, 1946; Letter from Francis Russell to JB, July 27, 1946, AJCO, Folder "War and Peace/Paris Peace Conference."

43. Letter from David Wahl to Meir Grossman, Aug. 14, 1946, CZA, C7/121; Letter from I. L. Kenen to Meir Grossman, July 29, 1946, CZA, C7/399; Meeting Minutes, Oct. 26, 1946, AJA, B63/16.

44. I. L. Kenen, Memo, Oct. 25, 1946, CZA, C7/360.

45. Letter from Zach Shuster to John Slawson, Aug. 17, 1946; Aide-Memoire, Aug. 6, 1946, AJCO, Folder "War and Peace/Paris Peace Conference"; I. L. Kenen, "In No-Man's Land," *New Palestine* 37, no. 4 (Dec. 13, 1946): 12; Statement of Louis Lipsky, Sept. 12, 1946, Statement on Peace Treaties, June 27, 1946, C7/121; Letter from Max Gottschalk to John Slawson, Aug. 1, 1946, Folder "War and Peace/ Paris Peace Conference"; Letter from David Wahl to Meir Grossman, Aug. 14, 1946, CZA, C7/399; Kurz, "Sphere," 134–36; Nathan Kurz, "In the Shadow of Versailles: Jewish Minority Rights at the 1946 Paris Peace Conference," *Jahrbuch des Simon-Dubnow-Instituts* 15 (2016): 187–210.
46. Letter from JB to John Slawson, Sept. 30, 1946, JBP, Box 1.199, Folder 285; Letter from I. L. Kenen to Meir Grossman, Aug. 21, 1946, CZA, C7/399.
47. Letter from I. L. Kenen to Meir Grossman, Aug. 8, 1946, CZA, C7/399; JR, Interim Report, Sept. 11–13, 1946, AJA, C133/8.
48. Alex Easterman, Memo, Dec. 14, 1946, AJA, B2/1.
49. JB, Speech, June 1948, JBP, Box 2.3, Folder A-2-8; JB, "Freedom Is Indivisible," June 15, 1947, Box 2.3, Folder A-2-9; Meeting Minutes, Jan. 1947, JBP, Box 2.135.
50. Letter from JR to Meir Grossman, Sept. 18, 1945, CZA, C7/360; Meeting Minutes, Oct. 20, 1946, AJA, B63/16.
51. Maks Lazerson, "Farvos der Erets-Yisroel teylungs-plan iz far unz beser vi a federatsye," *Der Tog*, July 27, 1946; Jesse Lurie, "Report on Paris," *Palestine Post*, Sept. 9, 1946.
52. Jacob Robinson, "Unfinished Victory," *Jewish Affairs* 1, no. 8 (Sept. 15, 1946): 3–15.

Chapter 6. The Failed Partitions

1. MP Statement, AJA, B93/5.
2. MP, Note on the Right of Petition, June 15, 1949, AJA, C23/1.
3. Hannah Arendt, *The Origins of Totalitarianism* (New York: Schocken Books, 1973), 299; Hannah Arendt, "The Rights of Man; What Are They?" *Modern Review* 3, no. 1 (1949): 31.
4. Letter from JR to Stephen S. Wise, June 12, 1946, AJA, C6/3.
5. Robinson, *Human Rights*, 71–73, 104–6; Mark Vishniak, "A Commentary on Human Rights," *Jewish Frontier* 13, no. 6 (June 1946): 41; JR, "International Human Rights and International Human Duties, Nov. 1946," AJA, C109/6.
6. IJA Meeting Minutes, 1946, AJA, C68/8; Letter from JR to Philipp Friedman, Dec. 13, 1946, AJA, C16/2; Memo, LOC, Charles Malik Papers, Box 76, Folder 7; Johannes Morsink, *The Universal Declaration of Human Rights: Origins, Drafting, and Intent* (Philadelphia: University of Pennsylvania Press, 2010), 4–6; Mary Ann Glendon, "John P. Humphrey and the Drafting of the Universal Declaration of Human Rights," *Journal of the History of International Law* 2 (Nov. 2000): 250–60.

7. Mary Anne Glendon, *A World Made New: Eleanor Roosevelt and the Universal Declaration of Human Rights* (New York: Random House, 2002), 53–78.

8. JR Interview (DG).

9. JR Interview (DG); JR, Memo, Dec. 30, 1946, AJA, B108/12.

10. Letter from JR to Quincy Wright, Oct. 8, 1946, AJA, C19/5; JR Memo, Mar. 26, 1947, ISA, File 72.27.1.1.

11. Letter from JR to F. N. Foerster, Apr. 16, 1947, AJA, C16/5.

12. UN General Assembly Official Records, Transcript of 78th Plenary Meeting, UN Doc A/PV.78 (May 14, 1947); Raja Choueri, *Charles Malik: Discours Droits de l'Homme et Onu* (Beirut: Edition Felix Beryte, 1998), 387–93.

13. JR, Memo, Mar. 26, 1947, ISA File 72.27.1.1; JR, Memo, Feb. 2, 1948, ISA, File 74A.

14. JR, *Palestine and the United Nations* (New York: Public Affairs Press, 1947); JR Interview by Menachem Kaufman (Heb.), Dec. 14, 1973, ICSJ; JR, Memos, Mar. 26, 1947 and Sept. 27, 1947, ISA, File 72.27.1.1.

15. JR, Memo, Sept. 27, 1947, ISA, File 72.27.1.1; MP, Memo, Jan. 2, 1948, AJA, B34/2; JB, Speech, Jan. 17, 1948, JBP, Box 2.10, B-1-37.

16. Sidney Liskofsky, "International Events," *American Jewish Year Book* 48 (1946–1947): 424–41.

17. Letter from J. Green to D. Sandifer, May 21, 1953, NARA RG 59, Box 8; Simpson, *Human Rights and the End of Empire*, 250–52, 350.

18. Hersch Lauterpacht, "A Bill of Human Rights," *Times* (of London), July 1947; Hersch Lauterpacht, "Towards an International Bill of Rights," *The Listener*, Nov. 3, 1949; Hersch Lauterpacht, "The Universal Declaration of Human Rights," *British Yearbook of International Law* 25 (1948): 354–81.

19. Jay Winter and Antoine Prost, *René Cassin and Human Rights: From the Great War to the Universal Declaration* (Cambridge: Cambridge University Press, 2013), 221–64; Samuel Moyn, "René Cassin, Human Rights, and Jewish Internationalism," in Jacques Picard, Jacques Revel, Michael P. Steinberg, and Idith Zertal, eds., *Thinking Jewish Modernity: Thinkers, Artists, Leaders, and the World They Made* (Princeton, NJ: Princeton University Press, 2016), 278–91; Glendon, *World Made New*, 172; Eric Beckett, Memo, Aug. 6, 1948, BNA 371/72810; Letter from HL to K. Das, Dec. 16, 1948 quoted in Lauterpacht, *Life*, 262.

20. Nehemiah Robinson, "Memo," May 13, 1948, AJA, B119/5; John Humphrey, *On the Edge of Greatness: The Diaries of John Humphrey*, ed. A. J. Hobbins (Montreal: McGill-Queen's University Press, 1994), 1:36 and 3:90.

21. Eliav Lieblich and Yoram Shachar, "Cosmopolitanism at a Crossroads: Hersch Lauterpacht and the Israeli Declaration of Independence," *British Yearbook of International Law* 84, no. 1 (2014): 7–10.

22. Hersch Lauterpacht, "Memorandum to Jewish Agency," 1947, ISA, 93.3/3/70; Hersch Lauterpacht, *Recognition in International Law* (Cambridge: Cambridge University Press, 1947); Hersch Lauterpacht, "Act of Independence," LFA.

23. Lauterpacht, "Act of Independence."

24. Lieblich and Shachar, "Cosmopolitanism," 11–51.

25. Letter from JR to HL, July 16, 1948, LFA.

26. Hersch Lauterpacht, "Memo to the Provisional Government of Israel," July 1948, LFA.

27. Letter from HR to Shabtai Rosenne, July 28, 1948, ISA, 130.4.1.161.

28. Richard Yaffe, "Arab Pogroms Endanger 800,000 outside Palestine," World Jewish Congress, New York, Jan. 18, 1948; Letter of Robert Marcus to Trygve Lie, Jan. 8, 1948, AJA, B13/4; Press Releases, Apr. 5 and June 21, 1948, AJA, B34/2; Press Release, Oct. 12, 1948, AJA, B140/29.

29. Letters from Oscar Karbach to Robert Marcus, Jan. 26, 1948 and Nehemiah Robinson to MP, Feb. 18, 1948, B13/4; Press Release, Jan. 9, 1948, AJA, B34/2.

30. Memo, Dec. 1948, AJA, C29/10; Nehemiah Robinson, Memo, Apr. 1948, AJA, C29/10.

31. Memo, Jan. 19, 1948, AJA, B13/4.

32. Jacob Robinson, Memo, Apr. 13, 1949, ISA, 93.3.1.247; Statement, June 21, 1948, AJA, B23/1; Report, Mar. 16, 1948, AJA, C129/3; Letter from MP to Nehemiah Robinson, Feb. 20, 1948, AJA, B13/4; Memo, Jan. 19, 1948, AJA, B13/4; Memo, May 19, 1948, AJA, B28/1.

33. Report, Apr. 6, 1948, AJA, B140/14; Memo, May 19, 1948, AJA, B28/1; Letter from Felix Bienenfeld to MP, June 10, 1949, AJA, B118/6.

34. Humphrey, Edge of Greatness, 1:64 and 3:32.

35. Humphrey, Edge of Greatness, 3:90.

36. Benny Morris, 1948. A History of the First Arab-Israeli War (New Haven, CT: Yale University Press, 2009).

37. UN General Assembly Organization Records, General Assembly Resolution 194 (III) 7/97, UNA Doc A/RES/194 (III) (Dec. 11, 1948).

38. Press release, Dec. 10, 1948, AJA, B34/2.

39. Press release, Jan. 7, 1949, AJA, B34/2.

40. Nahum Goldmann, "Israel Will Not Interfere outside Palestine," Jewish Affairs 2, no. 11/12 (Nov.–Dec. 1948): 2.

41. UN ECOSOC Records, Resolution 214 (VIII) B (Feb. 14, 1949).

42. MP Statement (Sept. 1949), AJA, B93/5; MP Speech (May 1949), AJA, B140/38.

43. Perlzweig, Memoir, 361–62; UN General Assembly Organization Records, UN Conciliation Commission for Palestine, A/AC.25/W/29 (Oct. 28, 1949); MP, Statement (1949), AJA, B93/5; MP Speech, May 2, 1949, AJA, B140/38.

44. MP, "The Menace of War," Dec. 26, 1947, AJA, B34/2; Letter from MP to Moises Goldman, AJA, B86/4.

45. Letter from MP to Leon Kubowitski, Apr. 11, 1950, AJA, B27/6; Letter from MP to A. Steinberg, Dec. 20, 1951, AJA, B127/1.

Part 3. Divergence

Quoted in Nahum Sokolow, *History of Zionism: 1600–1918* (London: Longmans, Green and Company, 1919), 1:259; Memo, AJA, C8/14; Letter from MP to Julius Stone, June 26, 1967, AJA,B26/3.

Chapter 7. The Limits of Neutrality

1. JR, Memo, Dec. 1951, ISA, 130.4/1-182; Michael L. Hoffmann, "U.N. Nations Cool to Refugee Bill," *New York Times*, July 5, 1951.
2. Isaac London [JR], "Days of Anxiety: A Chapter in the History of Soviet Jewry," *Jewish Social Studies* 15, no. 3/4 (July–Oct. 1953): 275; Jacob Robinson, "Metamorphosis of the United Nations," *Recueil des Cours de l'Academie de Droit International de la Haye* 94 (1958): 512, 580–81.
3. "Shavu'a ḥagigat meḥatzit ha-yovel shel ha-universitah ha-'ivrit," *Hed-ha-mizraḥ*, May 5, 1950.
4. HL, "International Law after the Second World War," *Collected Papers*, 2:159; HL, "State Sovereignty and International Law," *Collected Papers*, 3:426.
5. HL, "International Law," 163, 167.
6. HL, "State Sovereignty," 429.
7. *Report of the Commission on Human Rights* (New York: United Nations, 1947); Humphrey, *Edge of Greatness*, 3:84; HL, *International Law*, 229–30.
8. Report (Nov. 1953), AJA, B102/11; Memo, Apr. 10, 1950, AJA, B111/3; Letter from MP to Alex Easterman, June 28, 1951, AJA, C23/2; HL, "State Sovereignty," 421.
9. HL, "International Law," 167, 170; Nathan Kurz, "Jewish Memory and the Human Right to Petition, 1933–1953," in Simon Jackson and Alanna O'Malley, eds., *The Institution of International Order: From the League of Nations to the United Nations* (New York: Routledge Press, forthcoming).
10. Lauterpacht, *Life*, 339.
11. Letter from JR to Shabtai Rosenne, May 31, 1950, ISA, 130.4.1.194; Letter from HL to Shabtai Rosenne, May 29, 1950, ISA, 130.4.1.194.
12. Letter from JR to Shabtai Rosenne, May 31, 1950, ISA, 130.4.1.194.
13. Letter from Shabtai Rosenne to HL, June 26, 1950, ISA, 130.4.1.194.
14. Lauterpacht, *Life*, 355; Feinberg, *Pirkei ḥayyim*, 160; Rotem Giladi, "'A Historical Commitment'? Identity and Ideology in Israel's Attitude to the Refugee Convention, 1951–4," *International History Review* 847 (2014): 13; Stephan Wendehorst, *British Jewry, Zionism, and the Jewish State, 1936–1956* (Oxford: Oxford University Press, 2012), 347–55; "Ha-poresh," *Maariv*, Sept. 9, 1957.
15. Letter from HL to Shabtai Rosenne, Jan. 6, 1958, LFA; Letter from HL to Helen Werians, Mar. 12, 1952, NYPL, Box 9.
16. Memo, May 18, 1949, ISA, 93.3.1.247; Letter from JL to Yekutiel Gordon, June 5, 1950, ISA, 130.4.1.183; Letter from JR to Shabtai Rosenne, Apr. 24, 1952, ISA, 130.4.1.163; Rotem Giladi, "Not Our Salvation: Israel, the Genocide Convention, and the World Court 1950–1951," *Diplomacy and Statecraft* 26, no. 3 (2015): 473–93.

17. Letter from JR to Moshe Sharett, Jan. 9, 1951, ISA, 130.4.1.250; Letter from JR to Shabtai Rosenne, Jan. 23, 1950, ISA, 130.4.1.251.

18. Giladi, "'A Historical Commitment?'"

19. Robinson, *Metamorphosis*, 543–45.

20. Letter from JR to Moshe Sharett, Jan. 9, 1951, ISA, 130.4.1.250; Report, Dec. 1951, ISA, 130.4.1.182; Letter from JR to Shabtai Rosenne, May 9, 1951, ISA, 130.4.1.180; Report, June 3, 1953, ISA, 130.4.1.181.

21. Aide-Memoire, 1952, JBP, Box 1.37, Folder 5-65N.

22. Yosef Hayim Yerushalmi, "Servants of Kings and Not Servants of Servants: Some Aspects of the Political History of the Jews," in David Myers and Alexander Kaye, eds., *Faith of Fallen Jews: Yosef Hayim Yerushalmi and the Writing of Jewish History* (Waltham, MA: University of New England, 2015), 245–76.

23. Speech, Jan. 17, 1948, JBP, Box 2.10, Folder B-1-37; Speech, Apr. 16, 1950, JBP, Box 2.5, Folder A-3-1.

24. American Jewish Committee, *Israel through American Eyes* (New York: American Jewish Committee, 1949).

25. Executive Committee Meeting Minutes, May 7–8, 1949, AJCO; Zvi Ganin, *An Uneasy Relationship: American Jewish Leadership and Israel, 1948–1957* (Syracuse, NY: Syracuse University Press, 2005), 32, 156, 171–72; Report, Aug. 1, 1951, ISA, 93.38.1.31; Gabriel Sheffer, *Moshe Sharett: Biography of a Political Moderate* (Oxford: Oxford University Press, 1995), 370–94.

26. Letter from JB to Harry Truman, Sept. 17, 1948, TPL; Letter from JB to Harry Truman, Sept. 1950, JBP, Box K-1-10.

27. Ganin, *Uneasy Relationship*, 161–63, 172; Letter from MP to Stephen Roth, Jan. 12, 1953, AJA, B56/1.

28. Aide-Memoire, Dec. 16, 1949, JBP, Box 2.121, Folder O-3-11; Interview with Edwin M. Wright, July 26, 1974, TPL.

29. Ganin, *Uneasy Relationship*, 175, 179; Memos on meetings with Truman, Eisenhower, and Dulles, 1952–54, JBP, Box 2.78, Folder K-1-11; Letter from Abba Eban to JB, Dec. 16, 1949, Box 2.121, Folder O-3-11; Aide-Memoire, 1952, Box 1.37, Folder 5-65N; "Jacob Blaustein," 30.

30. Speech, 1954, JBP, Box 2.128, Folder P-2-10.

31. Frank Holman, *The Life and Career of a Western Lawyer* (Baltimore: Port City Press, 1963), 416; Simpson, *Human Rights*, 460.

32. AJC, *A World Charter for Human Rights* (New York: American Jewish Committee, 1948); Radio and Television Report (Jan. 1, 1949), AJCO; Letter to Membership, Sept. 11, 1950, AJCA, FAD Series 1, Box 2, Folder 2; Meeting Minutes, May 1948, JBP, Box 1.14, Folder 201; Memo, Jan. 7, 1949, JBP, Box 1.14, Folder 201; Memos, 1947–1950, AJCA, FAD Series 1, Box 6, Folder 4.

33. AJCA, FAD, Series 1, Box 13, Folder 5, Minutes (1952); AJA, B111, F3, "Memo," Apr. 10, 1950; JBP, Box 2.3, Folder A-2-9 Year, File #2, 1949, Speech, Feb. 1946.

34. Brucken, *Uncertain Crusade*, 132–70.

35. Aide-Memoire, Jan. 21, 1952, JBP, Box 1.37, Folder 5-65-N; Aide-Memoire, Mar. 30, 1953, JBP, Box 4.65, Folder Q-1-4.

36. Letter from JB to Morris Waldman, Dec. 27, 1952, JBP, Box 1.21, Folder 286; Letter from JB to Harry Truman, Feb. 12, 1953, TPL; Letter from JB to Dwight Eisenhower, June 11, 1954, JBP, Box 2.78, Folder K-1-10.

37. Letter from JB to John Foster Dulles, May 3, 1953, JBP, Box 2.78, Folder K-1-11.

38. Letter from MP to Will Maslow, May 13, 1955, AJA, B88/11; Philip Halpern Speech, Oct. 24–25, 1953, HP, MSS-C66-3, Box 8, Folder "Bricker Amendment, Personal Correspondence, July 2, 1953–Apr. 8, 1955"; Memo, Oct. 9, 1953, JBP, Box 2.90, Folder L-2-13; Memo (1953), JBP, Box 2.128, Folder P-2-10.

39. Caroline Simon Speech, Aug. 16, 1948, HUA, MC 370, Folder "International Bar Conference Association."

40. Jacob Blaustein, *The Fight for Freedom . . . Problems and Prospects* (New York: American Jewish Committee, 1954), 6; "Far from Ready," *Buffalo Evening News,* Oct. 23, 1953; Letter from JB to John Slawson, Nov. 2, 1953, JBP, Box 2.90, Folder L-2-13; CCJO Board Meeting Minutes, Apr. 3, 1954, JBP Box 2.109, Folder N-2-19A; Memo (1953), AJA, B113/4.

41. Sheffer, *Moshe Sharett,* 750–55.

42. Ganin, *Uneasy Relationship,* 195–97; Sheffer, *Moshe Sharett,* 758.

43. Ganin, *Uneasy Relationship,* 195–97.

44. Letter from John Slawson to Simon Segal, Jan. 17, 1955, AJCO.

45. Letter from John Slawson to Simon Segal, Jan. 17, 1955; Letter from Easterman to MP, Dec. 21, 1954, AJA, B50/8; Letter from MP to Alex Easterman, Dec. 24, 1954, AJA, B55/3; Telegram from MP to Alex Easterman, Jan. 5, 1955, AJA, B55/4.

46. Letter from John Slawson to Simon Segal, Jan. 17, 1955.

47. Letter from Roger Baldwin to Gamal Nasser, Jan. 31, 1955; Letter from Roger Baldwin to Simon Segal, Jan. 29, 1955, AJCO.

48. Memo, Jan. 17, 1955, AJA, C26/3; Memo, Apr. 4, 1955, AJCO; *The Story of Zionist Espionage in Egypt* (Cairo: Ministry of National Guidances, 1954).

49. Ganin, *Uneasy Relationship,* 209; Aide-Memoire, Feb. 9, 1957, JBP, Box 2.109, Folder N-2-29; Interview with Henry Byroade, TPL.

50. Speech, Apr. 1957, JBP, Box 1.114, Folder 2489.

51. Letter from Moses Moskowitz to JB, JBP, Box 1.42, Folder 745; David Horowitz, "With the U.N.," *Jewish Advocate,* Sept. 29, 1955; Letter from JB to Fred Robin, May 21, AJCO; Letter from John Slawson to JB, May 23, 1956, JBP, Box 2.52, Folder G-1-15; Meeting Minutes, Oct. 4, 1955, HP, Box 13; Letter from JB to Arthur Goldberg, July 26, 1965, JBP, Box 2.52, Folder G-1-15.

52. Letter from JR to Gideon Rafael, Mar. 31, 1954, ISA, 130.4.1.170; Letter from JR to Jacob Tzur, Apr. 16, 1955, ISA, 130.4.1.201.

53. Jacob Robinson, "A Democracy in an Autocratic World," in Moshe Davis, ed., *Israel: Its Role in Civilization* (New York: Harper and Brothers, 1956), 150.

54. G. H. Hansen, *Zionism, Israel and Asian Nationalism* (Beirut: Institute for Palestine Studies, 1971), 250–60; Roland Burke, *Decolonization and the Evolution of International Human Rights* (Philadelphia: University of Pennsylvania Press, 2011), 95.
55. Letter from Yaakov Tzur to JR, Apr. 16, 1955, ISA, 130.4.1.201.
56. Letter from Yaakov Tzur to JR, Apr. 16, 1955.
57. Letter from JR to Yaakov Tzur, Apr. 18, 1955, ISA, 130.4.1.201.
58. Letter from JR to Shabtai Rosenne, Oct. 11, 1954, ISA, 130.4.1.164.
59. Abba Eban, *An Autobiography* (New York: Random House, 1977), 221–22.

Chapter 8. The Road to the Kingdom

1. Peter Benenson, "The Scene in Cyprus," *The Spectator,* Nov. 9, 1956; Peter Benenson, "Stagnation in Cyprus; Seeds of Dissension," *Manchester Guardian,* Jan. 23, 1957; Charles Foley, *Island in Revolt* (London: Longmans, 1962), 110.
2. Benenson, "Stagnation in Cyprus," 6.
3. Foley, *Island in Revolt,* 110; Benenson, "Scene in Cyprus," 8.
4. Peter Benenson, "Amnesty—the First 25 years," *The Observer,* May 25, 1986.
5. Tom Buchanan, "'The Truth Will Set You Free': The Making of Amnesty International," *Journal of Contemporary History* 37, no. 4 (2005): 575–97; Letter from MP to Charles Malik, Dec. 5, 1958, in AJA, B4/3.
6. Moyn, *Last Utopia,* 130–48; Stephen Hopgood, *Keepers of the Flame; Understanding Amnesty International* (Ithaca, NY: Cornell University Press), 52–72.
7. Interview with Marlys Deeds, IISG, AI 985.
8. Foley, *Island,* 111, 125–27.
9. "University News," *Jewish Chronicle,* July 12, 1940; Ivo Elliott, ed., *The Balliol College Register, 3rd ed., 1900–1950* (Oxford: Oxford University Press, 1953), 394–95; Tony Kushner, *The Persistence of Prejudice: Antisemitism in British Society during the Second World War* (Manchester: Manchester University Press, 1989), 59–62; Raine, "Peter Benenson," 30; Hallam Tennyson, "Appreciation," *The Guardian,* Mar. 1, 2005; Tennyson, *Haunted Mind,* 125, 136–39.
10. Peter Benenson, "Spanish Trial Notebook: Packing the Court," *The Observer,* Apr. 11, 1954; Letter from PB to *Manchester Guardian,* Dec. 24, 1956, HHC U DJU/1/2; Kirsten Sellars, "Human Rights and the Colonies: Deceit, Deception and Discovery," *Round Table* 93, no. 377 (Oct. 2004): 709–24.
11. Foley, *Island,* 127–28.
12. Peter Benenson, *Gangrene* (London: Calderbooks, 1959), 9.
13. Peter Benenson, "Oman Rebellion," *The Times,* Aug. 13, 1957.
14. Lola Hahn Warburg, "Flora Solomon," *Association of Jewish Refugees Information* 29, no. 9 (Sept. 1984): 7; Maureen Cleave, "Solomon's Zeal," *The Observer Magazine,* July 1, 1984, 57, 61.
15. "Social and Personal," *Palestine Post,* Apr. 7, 1949; Telegram from Peter and Margaret Benenson, Flora Solomon, and Benjy and Maidie Weizmann to Chaim and Vera Weizmann, Jan. 2, 1949, WA, 12-44A; Solomon, *From Baku,* 198, 200,

207; Interview with George Weidenfeld; Richard Crossman, *The Diaries of a Minister* (London: Hamish-Hamilton, 1976), 2:282, 355–59.

16. "The General Election," *Jewish Chronicle,* May 20, 1955; "Social and Personal," *Jewish Chronicle,* May 8, 1959.

17. Peter Benenson, "The Voter at Home: A Candidate's Discoveries," *The Guardian,* May 20, 1955; Benenson, *Gangrene,* 38.

18. Lawrence Black, *The Political Culture of the Left in Affluent Britain, 1951–64* (London: Palgrave Macmillan, 2003).

19. Benenson, "Palestine in Cyprus"; Solomon, *From Baku,* 207, 215–16; "Sixty Jewish Candidates," *Jewish Chronicle,* Sept. 11, 1959; "Results of the General Election," *Jewish Chronicle,* June 3, 1955; "Social and Personal," *Jewish Chronicle,* May 8, 1959; Peter Benenson, "Blunt Soldier," *The Spectator,* Mar. 1, 1957.

20. Letter from PB to Eric Baker, Mar. 4, 1960, IISG, AI 1163.

21. Letter from PB to Eric Baker, Mar. 26, 1960, IISG, AI 1163.

22. Solomon, *From Baku,* 17–18, 155, 229.

23. Bernard Sharratt, "English Roman Catholicism in the 1960s," in Adrian Hastings, ed., *Bishops and Writers: Aspects of the Evolution of Modern English Catholicism* (Wheathampstead: Anthony Clarke, 1977), 129; Peter Benenson, "Problems of the Catholic Lawyer," *Wiseman Review* 237, no. 497 (Autumn 1963): 274–75.

24. Benenson, "Problems," 277; Tom Buchanan, "Peter Benenson," *Oxford Dictionary of National Biography* (Oxford, 2009) (accessed online Jan. 1, 2017); Peter Benenson, "On Mater Mundi and Universal Compassion," Feb. 28, 1989, IISG, AI 982-83; Peter Benenson, "The Natural Law and Statute Law: A Lawyer's View," in Franz Bockle, ed., *Understanding the Signs of the Times* (New York: Paulist Press, 1967), 47–48.

25. Alan Segal, *Paul the Convert: The Apostolate and Apostasy of Saul the Pharisee* (New Haven, CT: Yale University Press, 1990).

26. "Jewish Law Society Formed to Study Jurisprudence," *Jewish Chronicle,* Apr. 29, 1955; PB, Memo (1962), IISG, AI 1025; Letter from PB to Eric Baker, Feb. 15, 1961, IISG, AI 1163;

27. Interview with Tom Sargant, IISG, AI 991; Interview with PB, IISG, AI 982–83.

28. Letter from PB to Ricard Aragno, Nov. 18, 1961, IISG, AI 1030; MP, *Memoirs,* 199–200.

29. Letter from MP to J. Linton, Aug. 23, 1960, AJA, B4/6; Letter from MP to Nahum Goldmann, Nov. 9. 1964, AJA, B8/6; Letter from MP to Nahum Goldmann, Oct. 10, 1956, AJA, B127/11.

30. MP, *Memoirs,* 200; Letter from MP to Arieh Tartakower, Jan. 8, 1963, AJA, B5/2; Letters from Sara Denzen to MP, Aug. 5, 1960, and MP to Nahum Goldmann, Dec. 8, 1960, AJA, B4/6.

31. Letter from MP to Will Maslow, Oct. 9 1956, AJA, B4/7; MP, *Memoirs,* 200.

32. MP, *Memoirs,* 199.

33. Letters from MP to Wade Pinckney, Feb. 29, 1960, and Russell Blades, Mar. 4, 1960, AJA, B89/13.

34. "The Forgotten Prisoners," *The Observer,* May 28, 1961.

35. "The Forgotten Prisoners"; Tom Read, "Abdul Is 'Prisoner of the Year,'" *Daily Mirror*, Dec. 10, 1962.

36. Letter from Hugh Gaitskill to PB, May 30, 1961, IISG, AI 1023.

37. Bernard Levin, "All Those in Favour," *The Spectator*, June 1, 1961; Amnesty International, *Annual Report, 1963–64* (London: Amnesty International, 1964), 3, 10.

38. PB to Eric Baker, Jan. 13, 1961, IISG, AI 1008.

39. Raine, "Peter Benenson," 29.

40. PB to Eric Baker, Mar. 27, 1962, IISG, AI 1064.

41. Binyamin Pinkus, *Tehiyah u-tekumah le'umit: Ha-tsiyonut veha-tenu'ah ha-tsiyonit bi-verit ha-mo'atsot, 1947–1987* (Sede Boker: Ben-Gurion University Press, 1993), 234–38; N. Erlikh, "Sionizm—maska dlia shpionov," *Trud*, Jan. 19, 1962.

42. "Leningrad Leader Pleads Not Guilty," *Jewish Telegraphic Agency*, Dec. 7, 1961; "Russian Reject Charges of Antisemitism," *Jewish Telegraphic Agency*, Nov. 24, 1961, 52; Letter from MP to Israel Goldstein, Dec. 12, 1961, AJA, B12/5.

43. Letter from PB to the Chief Rabbi of Israel, Mar. 30, 1962, IISG, AI 1026; "'Remember Jews in Russia': Chief Rabbi's Passover Plea," *Jewish Chronicle*, Apr. 20, 1962; Letter from MP to Alex Easterman, Feb. 19, 1962, AJA, B5/1; MP Memo, (1961), AJA, B4/7.

44. Letter from Bella Ravdin to Martin Buber, Nov. 19, 1963 in MBA, Ms. Var. 350 008 611a; Letter from Jack Halpern to Sean MacBride, Oct. 16, 1964; Letter from Jack Halpern to Neta Eran, Nov. 11, 1964, JHP, 11.E.8.

45. Ian Gilmour, "Zionism and Anti-Semitism," *The Spectator*, June 23, 1960; Letter from PB to Eric Baker, Jan. 27, 1962, IISG, AI 1164; Peter Benenson, "Amnesty Looks East," *The Observer*, June 17, 1962.

46. H. A. R. Philby, "The Threatened Vision of Musa Alama," *The Observer*, May 28, 1961; H. A. R. Philby "Nasser's Pride and Glory," *The Observer*, July 22, 1962.

47. Solomon, *From Baku*, 225–26.

48. Letter from PB to Walter Padley, Dec. 13, 1964, BNA, FO 1110/2112; Memo, Mar. 24, 1965, BNA, FCO 1110/1992; Memo, May 9, 1967, BNA, LCO 2/8097.

49. International Executive Committee Meeting Minutes, July 4, 1964, JHP, ICS 28/11/A/13;

50. Tom Buchanan, "Amnesty International in Crisis, 1966–7," *Twentieth Century British History* 15, no. 3 (2004): 267–89; S. Rastgeldi, "Aden Report," Dec. 1966, AIAO; *Hansard Commons* 738 (Dec. 19, 1966): cols. 1005–8.

51. Peter Calvoressi, Report (Mar. 1967), AIUSA, Box I.3 6, Folder 4.

52. Phillip Knightley, "Amnesty Row as Chief Quits, Fights Back," *Times* (of London), Feb. 26, 1967; Letter from PB to Gerald Gardiner, Jan. 6, 1967, BNA, LCO 2/8097.

53. Memo, Jan. 9, 1967, BNA, LCO 2/8097.

54. "Last Minute Compromise Saves Amnesty," *Times* (of London), Mar. 13, 1967.

55. Yaacov Roi and Boris Morozov, eds., *The Soviet Union and the June 1967 Six Day War* (Washington, DC: Woodrow Wilson Institute, 2008).

Chapter 9. The Swastika Epidemic

1. WJC Press Release (1960), AJA, B15/20; WJC Internal Report (June 1961), AJA, C149/13; Sidney Liskofsky, "International Swastika Outbreak," *American Jewish Yearbook* 62 (1961): 209; "1,000 Incidents of Anti-Semitism," *Times* (of London), Jan. 25, 1960.
2. "Sandburg Favors Death for Swastika Painters," *New York Times,* Jan. 7, 1960.
3. JR Speech, Oct. 10, 1945, AJA, C14/21.
4. MP and Alex Easterman, "Problems and Prospects in International Affairs" (1959), AJA, B29/12; Letter from MP to Nahum Goldmann, Jan. 7, 1960, AJA, B8/12.
5. Letter from MP to Nahum Goldmann, Jan. 7, 1960, AJA, B8/12.
6. WJC Memo (1952), AJA, B13/2; Nathan Lerner, *The Crime of Incitement to Group Hatred* (New York: World Jewish Congress, 1965), 12–26.
7. Letter from Philip Halpern to Eustace Seligman, Mar. 23, 1960, HP, Box 1, Folder 3; Philip Halpern, Speech, Mar. 16, 1956, HP, Box 22, Folder 1.
8. Letter from MP to Will Maslow, Oct. 20, 1960, AJA, B8/12; WJC Statement on Discrimination against the Jewish Minority in the Soviet Union, (1960), AJA, B4/3; World Jewish Congress, *Proceedings* (London: World Jewish Congress, 1959), 50.
9. UN Report of the 12th session of the Sub-Commission on Prevention of Discrimination and Protection of Minorities to the Commission on Human Rights, New York, Jan. 11–30, 1960, UNA Doc UN E/CN.4/800.
10. UN Report of the 12th session of the Sub-Commission on Prevention of Discrimination and Protection of Minorities to the Commission on Human Rights, New York, Jan. 11–30, 1960, UNA Doc UN E/CN.4/800.
11. Philip Halpern Speech, Oct. 21, 1961, HP, Box 11, Folder 17; UN E/CN.4/800; Gerhard Jacoby, Memo, Feb. 5, 1960, AJA, B117/8.
12. Letter from MP to Nahum Goldmann, Sept. 30, 1960, AJA, B89/13.
13. Letter from MP to Nahum Goldmann, Sept. 30, 1960; Letter from Monty Jacobs to MP, Jan. 25, 1960, AJA, B87/7; Letters from Philip Halpern to Dorothy Crook and Sidney Liskofsky, Mar. 21, 1961, HP, Box 11, Folder 7; Letter from MP to Nahum Goldmann, Jan. 11, 1960, AJA, B87/7; AJC, *As the UN Probes Prejudice* (New York: American Jewish Commitee, 1960), 18.
14. Michael F. Scholl, "Active Measures and Disinformation as Part of East Germany's Propaganda War, 1953–1972," in Kristie Macrakis, Thomas Wegener Friis, and Helmut Müller-Enbergs, eds., *East German Foreign Intelligence: Myth, Reality and Controversy* (London: Routledge, 2010), 114–15; John Barron, *KGB: The Secret Work of the Soviet Secret Spies* (New York: Readers Digest Press, 1974), 172–74; Christopher Andrew, *The Sword and the Shield: The Mitrokhin Archive and the Secret History of the KGB* (New York: Basic Books, 2000), 292–321; Christopher Andrew and Oleg Gordievsky, *KGB: The Inside Story of Its Foreign Operations from Lenin to Gorbachev* (New York: HarperCollins, 1990), 463.

15. M. Polikanov, "Svastika vyglianula iz podvorotni," *Pravda*, Jan. 8, 1960; E. Pal'di, "Pylkie simpatii k svastike," *Literaturnaia Gazeta*, Feb. 6, 1960; L. Sedin, "Fashistskoe podpol'e 'Svodbodnogo Mira,'" *Literaturnaia Gazeta*, Feb. 4, 1960.

16. Memo, June 2, 1961, AJA, C149/13; Memo, June 27, 1960, YVA, O.65, File 46.

17. Hanna Yablonka, *Medinat Yisra'el neged 'Adolf 'Aykhman* (Tel Aviv: Yediot Achronot, 2001), 44–55.

18. "Jungle Law," *Washington Post*, May 27, 1960.

19. JR, "Jungle Law," *Washington Post*, June 20, 1960.

20. JR, "Placing Eichmann on Trial," *New York Times*, June 6, 1960.

21. JR, "Eichmann and the Question of Jurisdiction," *Commentary* 30, no. 1 (July 1, 1960): 1.

22. Telegram from Maximo Yagupsky to Eugene Hevesi, Aug. 22, 1960, AJCO; Moshe Pearlman, *The Capture and Trial of Adolf Eichmann* (New York: Simon and Schuster, 1963), 78–79.

23. "The Man in the Cage," *Time* 77, no. 17 (Apr. 21, 1961): 24; Interview with Daniel Greenberg.

24. Telford Taylor, "Large Questions in the Eichmann Case," *New York Times*, Jan. 22, 1961; Letter from Roger Baldwin to Alan Reitman, June 25, 1961, ACLU, Series 3, Box 1160, Folder 6; Richard Crossman, "The Faceless Bureaucrat," *New Statesman* 61 (Mar. 31, 1961): 503; "Crossman Modifies His Views on Trial," *Jewish Chronicle*, Apr. 14, 1961.

25. Deborah Lipstadt, *The Eichmann Trial* (New York: Nextbook/Schocken, 2012), 34; MP, *Memoirs*, 370.

26. Marianne Sanua, *Let Us Prove Strong: The American Jewish Committee, 1945–2006* (Waltham, MA: Brandeis University Press, 2007), 97–98; "Use of AJC's Name on Programmatic Material," Apr. 25, 1958, AJCO; "The American Public and the Eichmann Trial: A Reanalysis of Data from the Gallop Poll of May, 1961," AJCO.

27. JR, Memo, 1961, YVA, Box 8/6.

28. Quoted in Ariel Feldenstein, *Ben-Gurion, Zionism and American Jewry: 1948–1963* (New York: Routledge, 2007), 134.

29. "In the Dock," *Time* 77, no. 16 (Apr. 14, 1961): 33.

30. Gideon Hausner, *Mishpat yerushalayim* (Tel Aviv: ha-Kibuts ha-mc'uḥad, 1980), 2:307.

31. JBP, Aide-Memoire (1960), Box 2.78, Folder K-1-18; Interview with David Ben-Gurion, WW, Box 207, #3.

32. Press Release (1961), JBP, Box 1.120, Folder 2644; "Jacob Blaustein Confers with President Kennedy," *Jewish Telegraph Agency*, Apr. 18, 1961; Aide-Memoire, JBP, Box 2.121, Folder O-3-15; Statement of JB and David Ben-Gurion, Apr. 23, 1961, JBP, Box 2.2, Folder A-1-22.

33. Judith Vogt, "When Nazism became Zionism—an Analysis of Political Cartoons," in Shmuel Ettinger, ed., *Anti-Semitism in the Soviet Union: Its Roots and Consequences* (Jerusalem: Hebrew University of Jerusalem, 1983), 159–94, 182;

Nati Cantorovich, "Soviet Reactions to the Eichmann Trial: A Preliminary Investigation 1960–1965," *Yad Vashem Studies* 35, no. 2 (2007): 103–42.

34. Haim Gouri, *Facing the Glass Booth: The Jerusalem Trial of Adolf Eichmann* (Detroit: Wayne State University Press, 2004) 300–303; "Proper Court Trial Asked for Eichmann," *Chicago Daily Tribune*, Mar. 23, 1962; Nehemiah Robinson, "The Eichmann Trial. Some Reactions and Attitudes," May 1, 1961, AJA, B15/1.

35. MP, Memo (1964), AJA, B29/16.

36. Moyn, *Last Utopia*, 84–119.

37. MP and Alex Easterman, "Problems and Prospects"; Stephen Jensen, *The Making of International Human Rights: The 1960s, Decolonization, and the Reconstruction of Global Values* (Cambridge: Cambridge University Press, 2017); MP, Memo (1964), AJA, B29/16.

38. UN GA Resolution 1781 (XVII) (Dec. 7, 1962), UNA Doc A/RES/1781(XVII).

39. Letter from MP to Nahum Goldmann, Dec. 12, 1962, AJA, B5/1.

40. Letter from MP to Nahum Goldmann, Oct. 22, 1965, AJA, B5/7.

41. Letter from MP to Nahum Goldmann, May 21, 1964, AJA, B87/10.

42. Natan Lerner, *The U. N. Convention on the Elimination of All Forms of Racial Discrimination* (Leiden: Brill, 1970), 2; Egon Schwelb, "The International Convention on the Elimination of All Forms of Racial Discrimination," *International and Comparative Law Quarterly* 15, no. 4 (Oct. 1966): 1012; Statement of Morris Abram, Jan. 16, 1964, AJA, B6/1; Memo, Nov. 11, 1965, AJCA, Box 3, Folder 11.

43. "Judaism without Embellishment," *Jews in Eastern Europe* 2, no. 5 (July 1964); Letter from Morris Abram to Boris Ivanov, Apr. 3, 1963, MAP, Box 93, Folder 3.

44. Memo, Nov. 11, 1965, AJCA, Box 3, Folder 11; Schwelb, "The International Convention," 1012; Roberta Cohen, Memo, Jan. 10, 1966, AJA, B6/1.

45. Roberta Cohen, Memo, Jan. 10, 1966, AJA, B6/1.

46. Memo, Oct. 25, 1965, CZA, S110/2; Ofra Friesel, "Equating Zionism with Racism: The 1965 Precedent," *American Jewish History* 97, no. 3 (July 2013): 304; Ofra Friesel, *'Aflayah giz'it, ma'azan ha-emah ve-antishemiyut: sipur ledatah shel amanat zekhuyot adam* (Jerusalem: Nevo, 2011).

47. Letter from MP to Nahum Goldmann, Oct. 22, 1965, AJA, B13/15; MP, Report (June 1966), AJA, B91/4.

48. Letter from MP to Stephen Roth, Jan. 9, 1967, AJA, B26/8; Letter from MP to Alex Easterman, Nov. 11, 1964, AJA, B8/6.

49. Memo, Oct. 25, 1965, CZA, S110/2; Michael Brecher, *The Foreign Policy System of Israel: Setting, Images, Process* (London: Oxford University Press, 1972), 236–37.

50. JR, Memo (1964), USHMM, Box 8/3.

51. Morris Abram Oral History Interview II, May 3, 1984, by Michael L. Gillette, Internet Copy, LBJ Library.

52. Hannah Arendt, *Eichmann in Jerusalem* (New York: Viking Press, 1963), 7, 269.

53. Daniel Maier-Katkin, *Stranger from Abroad: Hannah Arendt, Martin Heidegger, Friendship and Forgiveness* (New York: W. W. Norton, 2010), 268–84; Eli Lederhendler, *New York Jews and the Decline of Urban Ethnicity* (Syracuse, NY: Syra-

cuse University Press, 2001), 59–60; JR, "A Report on the Evil of Banality: The Arendt Book," *Facts* 15, no. 1 (July-Aug. 1963): 263–70.

54. JR, "Report."

55. JR, *And the Crooked Shall Be Made Straight* (New York: Macmillan, 1965), 100; JR, Statement, Mar. 8, 1964, USHMM, Box 7, File 9.

56. Hannah Arendt, "'The Formidable Dr. Robinson': A Reply," *New York Review of Books*, Jan. 20, 1966.

57. Jacob Robinson, *La tragédie juive sous la croix gammée à la lumière du procès de Jérusalem: (le récit de Hannah Arendt et la réalité des faits)* (Paris: Centre de documentation juive contemporaine, 1968), 348–49.

58. MP, Memo (June 1966), AJA, B29/22; *World Jewish Congress Fourth Plenary Assembly Proceedings* (Geneva: World Jewish Congress, 1959), 48.

59. Peter Papadatos, *The Eichmann Trial* (London: Stevens, 1964); Milton Himmelfarb, "Some Attitudes towards Jews," *Commentary* 35, no. 5 (May 1, 1963): 425.

Chapter 10. Prisoners of Zion

1. Letter from Bella Ravdin to Paul Lyons, Sept. 24, 1968, AIUSA, Box II, Folder 5 11/1; Bella Ravdin, ed., *Looking Back in Content: A Factual Report* (Haifa: n.p., 1975), 3.

2. Amos Kenan "A Letter to All the Do Gooders," *Yediot Achronot*, Mar. 22, 1968, repr. in translation in Isi Leibler, ed. *The Case for Israel* (Sydney: Executive Council of Australian Jewry, 1972), 146.

3. Lori Allen, *The Rise and Fall of Human Rights: Cynicism and Politics in Occupied Palestine* (Stanford, CA: Stanford University Press, 2013).

4. Samuel Moyn, "Louis Henkin, Human Rights, and American-Jewish Constitutional Patriotism," in James Loeffler and Moria Paz, eds., *The Law of Strangers: Jewish Lawyers and International Legal Thought in Historical Perspective* (Cambridge: Cambridge University Press, forthcoming); Barbara Keys, *Reclaiming American Virtue: The Human Rights Revolution of the 1970s* (Cambridge, MA: Harvard University Press, 2014); Michael Barnett, *The Star and the Stripes: A History of the Foreign Policies of American Jews* (Princeton, NJ: Princeton University Press, 2016), 183–85.

5. Hopgood, *Keepers of the Flame*, 52–72; Moyn, *Last Utopia*, 120–75.

6. Letter from Bella Ravdin to Israel Goldstein, Feb. 7, 1961, MBA, Ms. Var. 350 008 611a.

7. Letter from Bella Ravdin to Paul Lyons, Sept. 24, 1968, AIUSA, Box II, Folder 5 11/1; Letter from Bella Ravdin to Marc Schreiber, May 23, 1969, publ. in Ravdin, *Looking Back*, 18.

8. Letter from JB to Louis Sohn, May 3, 1965; Memo, "UN High Commissioner for Human Rights [ca. 1970], JBP, Box 4.113.

9. Letter from MP to Nahum Goldmann, Mar. 22, 1966, AJA, B91/4; Telegram, Mar. 2, 1966, AJA, B91/4.

10. Conversation Memo of JB and Sidney Lisofsky, Jan. 11, 1966, JBP, Box 2.52, Folder G-1-13 1967; Memo on CHR 1968, "International Conference on Human

Rights [1968], BNA FCO 61/194; Letter from MP to Gregorio Shapiro, May 11, 1967, AJA, B10/15; Humphrey, *Edge of Greatness*, 4:77, 160–62.

11. Statement by Morris Abram, Mar. 21, 1967, MAP, Box 61/4.

12. Burke, *Decolonization* 74, 129–33; Quoted in Z. H. Druckman, "UN Human Rights Body Gives Anti-Bias Provision Approval," *Jewish Floridian*, Mar. 31, 1967; Statement by Morris Abram, Mar. 21, 1967, MAP, Box 61/4.

13. Letter from Morris Abram to Harlan Cleveland, Jan. 7, 1965, MAP, Box 94/8; Letter from Morris Abram to Seymour Halpern, Feb. 11, 1966, AJCA, Box 2, Folder 3; Memo, "ABA and Human Rights Conventions [1967], AJCA, Box 2, Folder 3; Jensen, *Making of International Human Rights*, 139.

14. Letter from MP to Nahum Goldmann, May 31, 1967, AJA, B6/7; Letter from MP to G. M. Riegner, June 5, 1967, AJA, B6/7.

15. MP, "Human Rights and Responsibilities in Judaism," *Bulletin of the Federation of United Nations Associations* 22 (1967): 24–26; Letters from MP to U Thant and Alex Easterman, June 16, 1967, AJA, B6, F7; Letter from Andre Jabes to MP, June 27, 1967, and Statement of the Central Conference of American Rabbis, June 21, 1967, AJA, B13/13.

16. MP, "Human Rights," 27.

17. Aide-Memoires of July 28, July 29, and Aug. 3, 1967, JBP, Box 1.140, Folder 3100; Avi Raz, *The Bride and the Dowry: Israel, Jordan, and the Palestinians in the Aftermath of the June 1967 War* (New Haven, CT: Yale University Press, 2012), 136–64; Itamar Rabinovich and Jehuda Reinharz, eds., *Israel in the Middle East: Documents and Readings on Society, Politics, and Culture* (Waltham, MA: University Press of New England, 2008), 244.

18. MP Memo, Apr. 1968, AJA, B91/5; Moyn, *Last Utopia*, 84–119.

19. Howard Tolley, *The U.N. Commission on Human Rights* (Westport, CT: Greenwood Press, 1987), 63; Letter from MP to Andres Aguilar, Mar. 9, 1971, SUA, MS 239/T3/28.

20. MP Memo, Dec. 20, 1968, AJA, B7/2.

21. Letter from JB to Arthur Goldberg, Sept. 18, 1967, AJC Papers, FAD Series 1, Box 14, Folder 1; Letter from MP to Nahum Goldmann, Nov. 21, 1967, AJA, B6/8; David Marmor, "Netziv ha-'um lezekhuyiot 'adam—Irgunim yehudiim b'artzot ha-brit" [July 19, 1966], ISA, File 93.38.1.175.

22. Letter from MP to Nahum Goldmann, Nov. 21, 1967, AJA, B6/8; Letter from MP to Haim Cohn, Dec. 22, 1967, AJA, B10/11; Letter from Haim Cohn to MP, Dec. 31, 1967, AJA, B6/8.

23. Letter from MP to Nahum Goldman, May 27, 1968, AJA, B28/5.

24. Letter from MP to Julius Stone, June 26, 1967, AJA, B26/3; Letter from MP to M. Ashkenazy, June 23, 1967, AJA, B26/3.

25. MP Memo (May 1969), AJA, B13/19; Michael Berlin, "Soviet-Led Drive Hits UN's Jewish Groups," *New York Post*, Apr. 28, 1969; RGANI, "Zapiska v TsK KPSS [1969] and "Zapiska v TsK KPSS [1974]," fond 89, op. 19, d. 5, 7; MP Memo (May 1969), AJA, B130/9.

26. Sidney Liskofsky, comp., *The United Nations and Human Rights: What Are the Roadblocks?* (New York: American Jewish Committee, 1969), 28, 41.

27. Letter from PB to Eric Baker, July 21, 1967, IISG, AI 1008; PB, "Problems of the Catholic Lawyer," 274–75; Hopgood, *Keepers of the Flame*, 8, 71.

28. Jenni Frazer, "Rights and Wrongs," *Jewish Chronicle*, May 17, 1991; PB, "Amnesty—the First 25 Years," *The Observer*, May 25, 1986; Judith Antonelli, "Human Rights Level in Israel Debated," *Jewish Advocate*, Feb. 4, 1988; Interview with Tom Sargant, IISG, AI 991; Letter from PB et al., to *The Independent*, Feb. 24, 1997.

29. PB, "Review: Collaboration with Tyranny in Rabbinic Law," *Natural Law Forum* 11, no. 135 (1966): 135; PB, *The Other Face* (Lausanne: Non-Ti-Scordar-Di-Me, 1977), 17–19, 62; PB, "Political Dissent in Developing Countries," *Views* 3 (Autumn/Winter 1963): 121; PB, "Review: Selected Essays: 1934–43, by Simon Weil," *Blackfriars* 44, no. 513 (Mar. 1963): 135–36; PB, "I diritti dell'uomo fondamento della pace," in Matteo Perrini, ed., *Primo: I Diritti Dell'uomo* (Brescia: Morcelliana, 1985), 20; Interview with PB, IISG, AI 978; Letter from Eric Baker to the British Sections, Feb. 26, 1967, AIUSA, Box I.3 6, Folder 4.

30. Jan Eckel, "The International League for the Rights of Man, Amnesty International, and the Changing Fate of Human Rights Activism from the 1940s through the 1970s," *Humanity* 4, no. 2 (Summer 2013): 183–214; Wendy Wong, *Internal Affairs: How the Structure of NGOs Transforms Human Rights* (Ithaca, NY: Cornell University Press, 2012), 84–114; Victor Orebi and Martin Ennals, "Palestine: International Law and the United Nations," *Times* (of London), Dec. 9, 1947; Metropolitan Police Report, July 10, 1950 on Martin F. A. Ennals, BNA, KV2/4043, 43; Letter from A. E. Davidson to J. H. Money, Jan. 19, 1956, BNA K2/2044.

31. David Forsythe, "The Arab League," in D. Forsythe, ed., *Encyclopedia of Human Rights* (Oxford: Oxford University Press, 2009), 3:312–16; Paul Kelemen, *The British Left and Zionism: History of a Divorce* (Manchester: University of Manchester Press, 2012), 203–204; Report on Sir Osmond Williams's Activities in 1969–1970, IISG, AI 1029; Ian Gilmour, "Zionist Doctrine and Israeli Expansionism," *Times* (of London), June 25, 1969; Ian Gilmour, "Arab-Israeli Dispute," *Times* (of London), Apr. 10, 1969; Letter from Eric Baker to Martin Ennals, Jan. 4, 1970, IISG, AI 1220.

32. "Prisoners in Israel Report [Apr. 1969]," AIUSA, Box II.5 11/1; Amnesty International, "Amnesty in Action," *Annual Report* (London, 1968), 5; "Middle East Probe by Amnesty," *Jewish Chronicle*, Dec. 6, 1968; "Israel," *Amnesty International Review* 30 (Feb. 1970): 2; Ravdin, *Looking Back*, 17.

33. "Israel," *Amnesty International Review* 30 (Feb. 1970): 2; "Amnesty Notebook," *Amnesty International Review* 28 (Aug. 1969): 2; Letters from Martin Ennals to Ra'anan Sivan, Nov. 14 and Dec. 29, 1969, in IISG, AI 1220; "Co-Operation Withheld from Amnesty," *Jewish Chronicle*, Dec. 12, 1969, 11; Letter from Paul Lyons to Mark Benenson, Nov. 26, 1969, AIUSA, Box II.5 11/1.

34. Letter from Anthony Marreco to Martin Ennals, Jan. 6, 1970, IISG, AI 1225; "Torture and Truth," *Jewish Chronicle*, Aug. 15, 1969; AI Press Release, Sept. 1969, AI 1220; "Research Department," *Annual Report, 1968–1969* (1970), 16; Ravdin, *Looking Back*, 27.

35. Ravdin, *Looking Back*, 21; Letter from PB to M. Townson, Apr. 24 1963, IISG, AI 1030.

36. Letter from Martin Ennals to Netanel Lorch, Oct. 6, 1969, IISG, AI 1220.

37. Letter from Haim Cohn to Martin Ennals, Nov. 7, 1969, IISG, AI 1120.

38. Letter from Martin Ennals to Haim Cohn, Dec. 31, 1969, Summary Notes of Amnesty-Israel Meeting [Dec. 1969], and Letter from Martin Ennals to Ra'anan Sivan, Jan. 27, 1970, IISG, AI 1220; Report on Sir Osmond Williams's Activities, AI 1029.

39. Report on Sir Osmond Williams's Activities, AI 1029.

40. Letter from Israeli Ministry of Foreign Affairs to Martin Ennals, Jan. 26, 1970, and letters from Martin Ennals to Ra'anan Sivan, Jan. 27 and Feb. 10, 1970, IISG, AI 1029; Amnesty Report on the Treatment of Certain Prisoners under Interrogation in Israel, Apr. 1970, IISG, AI 1029; Cable from Yoram Dinstein to Ministry of Foreign Affairs, Mar. 31, 1970, ISA 197.21.

41. "Amnesty and Atrocities," *Sunday Times*, Apr. 5, 1970; Ravdin, *Looking Back*, 27; Interview with Diana Redhouse, May 1984, IISG, AI 990; Israeli Press Statement, Apr. 2, 1970, IISG, AI 1029; Naomi Shepherd, "Israel and the Amnesty Affair," *New Statesman* 70 (Apr. 17, 1970): 537–38.

42. Keys, *Reclaiming American Virtue*, 1; Letter from Mark Benenson and Nelson Bengston, *Times* (of London), Apr. 17, 1970; Letter from Nathan Perlmutter to Mark Benenson, Apr. 2, 1970, AIUSA, Box II.5 11/2; Draft Letter from Martin Ennals to the *Times* (of London), Apr. 20, 1970, IISG, AI 1220.

43. Letter from Mark Benenson to Board of Directors, May 16, 1971, AIUSA, Box I.1 1, Folder 7.

44. Letter from Mark Benenson to AIUSA Board, May 25, 1970, AIUSA, Box II.5 11/2; Yaacov Friedler, "Amnesty Int'l Marks 10th Anniversary Striving to Liberate All Men of Peace—Except the Jews," *Jerusalem Post*, May 28, 1971.

45. Letter from Eleanor Aitken to Anne Burley, Nov. 1, 1974, IISG, AI 1185; Interview with Martin Ennals, July 11, 1977, CJH; AIUSA Board Meeting Minutes, Mar. 7, 1970, AIUSA, Box I.1.1, Folder 6; Brian Cashinella, "Amnesty Split on Report," *Times* (of London), Apr. 4, 1970; Letter from Martin Ennals to Eleanor Aitken, Nov. 5, 1974, IISG, AI 1185.

46. Ravdin, *Looking Back*, 26.

47. Ravdin, *Looking Back*, 9.

48. Letters from Gidon Gottlieb to Martin Ennals, Nov. 9, 1972, Gidon Gottlieb to IEC, Nov. 9, 1973, Martin Ennals to Gidon Gottlieb, Nov. 15, 1972, and Martin Ennals to the IEC, May 16, 1972, AIUSA, Box I.3 6, Folder 4; Ravdin, *Looking Back*, 7, 31–33.

49. Draft Resolution, Dec. 17, 1974 and David Hawk, Memo on Balance [1974], AIUSA, Box I.3 6, Folder 4; Letter from Mark Benenson to Martin Ennals, Apr. 4,

1972, AIUSA, Box II.5 11/2; Judah Cahn, "Amnesty International and Jewish Questions," *ADL Israel Backgrounder*, Feb. 1972, 4.

50. Alan Dershowitz, "Terrorism and Administrative Detention: The Case of Israel," *Commentary* 50, no. 6 (Dec. 1, 1970): 78.

51. Yetta Lackner, "Analysis of AI's Treatment of Israel [1975]," AIUSA, Box II.1 3, Folder 17; "Amnesty Unbalanced," *Jewish Chronicle*, Apr. 18, 1975; Leo Mindlin, "Another Noble Prize Bites the Dust," *Jewish Floridian*, Nov. 11, 1977; Stephen Miller, "Politics and Amnesty International," *Commentary* 65, no. 3 (Mar. 1, 1978); 57–61; Bradley, *World Reimagined*, 221–22.

52. Ravdin, *Looking Back*, 22; Draft Letter from David Ives to *Jewish Chronicle*, Apr. 22, 1975, AIUSA, Box II.1 3, Folder 17.

53. Vitaly Rubin, *Dnevniki, pis'ma* (Tel Aviv: Biblioteka-Alii'a, 1988), 250.

54. Herbert Gold, "Life among the Refuseniks," *New Republic* 171, no. 8 (Aug. 24, 1974), 16; Moshe Decter, ed., *Redemption! Jewish Freedom Letters from Russia* (New York: American Jewish Conference on Soviet Jewry, 1970), 14–17, 33–35; Interview with Moshe Decter, Feb. 22, 1990, WW.

55. Karl Vasak and Sidney Liskofsky, eds., *The Right to Leave and to Return* (New York: Jacob Blaustein Institute, 1976); Ad Hoc NGO Joint Statement to the Commission on Human Rights [Feb. 1971], ISA, File 130.3.5.100; Kurz, "Sphere," 348–57; Moria Paz, "'A Most Inglorious Right': René Cassin, Freedom of Movement, Jews and Palestinians," in Loeffler and Paz, *Law of Strangers*.

56. Rita Hauser, "International Human-Rights Protection: The Dream and the Deceptions," in David Sidorsky, ed., *Essays on Human Rights* (Philadelphia: Jewish Publication Society of America, 1979), 29.

57. Yoram Dinstein, "Soviet Jewry and International Human Rights," in Sidorsky, *Essays*, 129, 140.

58. Sarah Snyder, *Human Rights Activism and the End of the Cold War: A Transnational History of the Helsinki Network* (Cambridge: Cambridge University Press, 2011), 58–59; Lillia Belen'kaia and Boris Zinger, *Naperekor: Evreiskoe natsional'noe dvizhenie v SSSR i ego ideologiia: 1945–1976 gg.* (Minsk: MET, 2004), 244; Pinkus, *Tehiyah u-tekumah*.

59. Barnett, *Star and the Stripes*, 176–83.

60. Barnett, *Star and the Stripes*, 184; Noam Kochavi, *Nixon and Israel: Forging a Conservative Partnership* (Albany: SUNY Press, 2009); Anatoly Adamishin and Richard Schifter, *Human Rights, Perestroika, and the End of the Cold War* (Washington, DC: United States Institute of Peace Press, 2009), 45–47, 61–67; Keys, *Reclaiming American Virtue*, 109–26; Henry Feingold, *"Silent, No More": Saving the Jews of Russia, the American Jewish Effort, 1967–1989* (Syracuse, NY: Syracuse University Press, 2007), 187–226; Pauline Peretz, *Let My People Go: The Transnational Politics of Soviet Jewish Emigration during the Cold War* (New Brunswick, NJ: Transaction Publishers, 2015), 245–95; Letter from Sidney Liskofsky to Morris Abram, May 23, 1979, AJHS, P-874, Box 27, Folder 12; Interview with Morris Abram, May 3, 1984, LBJ.

61. Baruch Gur-Gurevitz, *Open Gates* (Jerusalem: Jewish Agency for Israel, 1996), 11; MP, *Memoirs*, 365, 382.

62. Letter from JR to Chaim Herzog, Aug. 11, 1977, USHMM, Box 10, Folder 10; Moses Moskowitz, *The Roots and Reaches of United Nations Actions and Decisions* (Rockville, MD: Sijthoff and Noordhoff, 1980), 113–70.

63. Gil Troy, *Moynihan's Moment: America's Fight against Zionism as Racism* (New York: Oxford University Press, 2013), 106–7, 133–34.

64. Rabinovich and Reinharz, *Israel*, 350–51.

Epilogue

1. Letters from Gershom Scholem to Hannah Arendt and Arendt to Scholem, June 23, 1963, and July 24, 1963, in Ron Feldman, ed., *The Jew as Pariah* (New York: Schocken Books, 1978), 240–51.

2. Hannah Arendt, "A Way toward the Reconciliation of Peoples," in Jerome Kohn and Ron Feldman, eds., *Hannah Arendt: The Jewish Writings* (New York: Schocken Books, 2007), 261; Sznaider, *Jewish Memory*.

3. Hannah Arendt, *The Human Condition* (Chicago: University of Chicago Press, 1958), 242.

4. Hannah Arendt, "The Minority Question (Copied from a Letter to Erich Cohn-Bendit, Summer 1940)," in *Hannah Arendt, The Jewish Writings*, 126–29.

5. American Jewish Committee, *The Jacob Blaustein Institute for the Advancement of Human Rights of the American Jewish Committee, 1971–1992* (New York, 1992), 30–31; Michael Galchinsky, "The American Jewish Committee and the Birth of the Israeli Human Rights Movement," *Journal of Human Rights* 5, no. 3 (July–Sept. 2006): 303–21.

6. Rosa Doherty, "Amnesty Rejects Call to Campaign against Antisemitism," *Jewish Chronicle*, Apr. 12, 2015; Bush, "Nuremberg and Beyond," 264–66.

7. Richard Goldstone, "From the Holocaust: Some Legal and Moral Implications," in Alan Rosenbaum, ed., *Is the Holocaust Unique? Perspectives on Comparative Genocide* (Boulder, CO: Westview Press, 1996), 47–53; Sands, *East-West Street*.

8. Stephen Hopgood, *The Endtimes of Human Rights* (Ithaca, NY: Cornell University Press, 2013); Eric Posner, *The Twilight of Human Rights Law* (Oxford: Oxford University Press, 2014); Samuel Moyn, *Not Enough: Human Rights in an Unequal World* (Cambridge, MA: Harvard University Press, 2018).

9. Robinson, "International Protection of Minorities," 90.

ACKNOWLEDGMENTS

"I once heard Winston Churchill expatiate on one of his favorite themes, which was that the Greeks and the Jews were the two most political and argumentative peoples in history, and as far as possible he would like to avoid any conflict with them," Maurice Perlzweig recalled. "I asked him whether he had ever come across what I regarded as an even more ferocious species, namely Greek Jews. It was probably my heated imagination, but it seemed to me that he visibly paled at the thought."

Researching the history of Jews and human rights these past several years has often felt like an argument with Perlzweig's fabled Greek Jews. Both Jewish history and international law are fields full of heated quarrels and passionate politics. Both rarely intersect, too, though happily that situation has recently begun to change. Each requires careful, methodical treatment when it comes to controversial topics such as human rights, Zionism, and antisemitism. I therefore owe an enormous debt to those institutions, friends, and colleagues who have helped make this book possible.

That debt begins with the Andrew W. Mellon Foundation for the Humanities, in partnership with the University of Virginia, for generously supporting me with a New Directions Mid-Career Fellowship that allowed me to study international law for the 2013–2014 year at the Georgetown University Law Center. Associate Dean Greg Klass welcomed me there as a Dean's Visiting Scholar, while Professor David Luban warmly shared his insight and erudition. Carlos Vazquez, David Stewart, Mark Feldman, and my former fellow historian Adam Levitan graciously tolerated my incursions into the legal realm.

Stints as a Robert A. Savitt Fellow at the Jack, Joseph and Morton Mandel Center for Advanced Holocaust Studies of the United States Holocaust Memorial Museum and a Kluge Fellow at the John W. Kluge Center of the Library of Congress provided further time, space, and scholarly community in which to deepen the research base for this project, as well as access to expert reference teams to help guide my inquiries. I thank the staffs of the Africa and Middle East Reading Room, especially the Judaica section; the Law Library; and the Manuscript Division of the Library of Congress and the Library, Research Collections, and Photo Archives at the Holocaust Museum.

The research in Washington, DC, was one part of a global journey through archives and libraries across Europe, the Middle East, and the United States. I thank the staff and leadership of the following institutions for their expert help in response to all my requests and entreaties: the American Jewish Archives, and Gary Zola, Kevin Profitt, and Joe Weber; the American Jewish Committee Archives, and Desiree Guillermo and Charlotte Bonelli; the American Jewish Historical Society; the Amnesty International Archives; the British Library; the British National Archives; the Buffalo & Erie County Historical Society; the Center for Jewish History; the Central Zionist Archives; the Columbia University Library Special Collections Division and Center for Oral History; the Emory University Manuscript, Archives, and Rare Book Library; the Eton College Archives, and Sally Jennings; the George Washington University I. Edward Kiev Judaica Collection, and Brad Sabin Hill; the Harvard University Library Judaica Division, and Charles Berlin and Elizabeth Vernon; the Harvard University Schlesinger Library Archives; the Israel State Archives; the Hebrew University of Jerusalem Institute for the Study of Contemporary Jewry and Truman Oral History Archives; the Hull History Centre; the Indiana University League of Nations Archive; the International Institute of Social History; the Jagellonian University Library; the Johns Hopkins University Archives, and James Stimpert; the League of Nations Archive; the London Metropolitan Archive and the British Board of Jewish Deputies; the Lyndon Baines Johnson Presidential Library; the National Archives and Records Administration; the National Library of Israel; the New York Public Library; the Princeton University

Mudd Library; the Russian State Archive of Contemporary History (RGANI); the Stanford University Hoover Institution Archives; the Tel Aviv University Library and Stephen Roth Institute for the Study of Contemporary Antisemitism and Racism; the Harry S. Truman Presidential Library; the United Nations Archives; the United States Holocaust Memorial Museum, and Edna Friedberg; the University College London Institute of Commonwealth Studies; the University of Cambridge Squires Law Library, and Lesley Dingle; the University of Southampton Library, Special Collections, Anglo-Jewish Archive; the University of Virginia Library, Inter-Library Loan Office, and Special Collections; the Weizmann Archive; the University of Oxford Balliol College Archives, and Anna Sander, and the Kressel Archive, and Milena Seidler; the Yad Vashem Archives; and the YIVO Institute for Jewish Research.

The travel to many of these destinations was supported by the Andrew W. Mellon Foundation, the Columbia University Libraries Research Award, the University of Virginia Center for International Studies, the University of Virginia Buckner W. Clay Endowment, and the American Council for Learned Societies/National Endowment for the Humanities/Social Science Research Council Combined Postdoctoral Fellowship for Research on Eastern Europe and Eurasia.

Invaluable research assistance was provided by Nikita Bezrukov, Vivien Chang, Yael Gilead, Anne Grant, Jon Grinspan, Stefanie Halpern, Lisa Hoelle Marie, Maryam Ismail, Hamutal Jackobson, Kobi Kabalek, Jessica Kirzane, Ilya Kolmanovsky, Rhonda Konig, Isabelle Levy, Alyssa Masor, Matthew Stefanski, Anat Vaturi, and Weronika Zalewska.

I have learned an enormous amount about the lives of the people in this book from conversations and interviews with a handful of very special individuals. Roberta Cohen and Suzi Peel generously shared their memories and personal archives related to Maurice Perlzweig. The late George Weidenfeld shared his recollections of Flora Solomon and Peter Benenson. Daniel and Chana Greenberg warmly opened their home and entrusted me with precious materials and memories related to Jacob Robinson. Likewise, the late Sir Elihu Lauterpacht, whom I met thanks to the good graces of Peter Trooboff, shared his memories and provided me access to his family's private archive.

For permission to use photographs and quote from unpublished material, I am very grateful to Daniel Greenberg, Conor Lauterpacht, the late Elihu Lauterpacht, and Suzi Peel. I thank as well the editors and publishers of the *Journal of Contemporary History,* the *Journal of American History,* the Oxford University Press, and Sage Publications for permission to reuse materials previously published in their journals.

Making sense of all of this historical material has been a welcome challenge. It has required me to lean heavily on the generosity of friends and colleagues around the world, including Michael Berkowitz, Leora Bilsky, Daniel Blumenthal, Michael Brenner, Jonathan Brent, Rivka Brot, Menachem Butler, Ariel Cohen, Alon Confino, Kevin Cope, Jeremy Dauber, Gaston De Los Reyes, Dan Diner, Carrie Filipetti, William Forbath, Carl Gershman, Sarah Gershman, Eric Goldstein, Peter Gordon, William Hitchcock, Amos Hochstein, Stephen Jensen, Martti Koskenniemi, Neal Kozodoy, Charles Krauthammer, Robyn Krauthammer, Ned Lazarus, Melvyn Leffler, Assaf Likhovsky, Erik Linstrum, Yair Listokin, Dahlia Lithwick, Dirk Moses, Derek Penslar, Martin Peretz, Noam Pianko, Matthew Price, Simon Rabinovitch, Sophia Rosenfeld, Zvi Septimus, Dimitry Shumsky, Michael Shurkin, Michael Silber, Daniel Silverberg, Michael Stanislawski, Elizabeth Thompson, Scott Ury, Annette Weinke, Melissa Weintraub, and Tara Zahra. I thank as well colleagues who invited me to present this work in progress at George Washington University, Georgetown University, Harvard University, the Library of Congress, Tel Aviv University, the United States Holocaust Memorial Museum, the University of Chicago, the University of Virginia, and annual conferences of the Association for Jewish Studies and the Law and Society Association.

For sharing valuable research materials and stimulating ideas, I thank Israel Bartal, Egle Bendikaite, Tom Buchanan, Jonathan Bush, Arie Dubnow, David Engel, Rotem Giladi, Jaclyn Granick, Stephen Hopgood, Nathan Kurz, Kenneth Moss, David Myers, Gil Rubin, Joshua Rubinstein, Mira Siegelberg, Sarah Snyder, Jeffrey Veidlinger, Natasha Wheatley, and Phillip Zelikow.

Michael Barnett, Abigail Green, David Luban, Moria Paz, Daniel Schwartz, Eliyahu Stern, and Leon Wieseltier each offered trenchant comments and thoughtful critiques of the manuscript. Lisa Leff read far too many drafts and doled out brilliant advice and unflagging encouragement. From the beginning, Samuel Moyn has been a most generous and incisive reader. I cannot thank him enough for his extraordinary support. Karen Naimer introduced me to many of the forgotten heroes in this book and showed me how they live on in her own tireless pursuit of global justice. Jeremy Eichler has turned what would otherwise have been a solitary quest into an extraordinary running conversation about ideas and craft, and graced me with the gifts of his abiding friendship and writerly wisdom.

Don Fehr and his team at Trident have superbly guided me through the publishing process and, along the way, taught me much more than I never knew there was to know. William Frucht has showed me that truly great editors do still exist, and we are lucky to have them. Debbie Masi, Karen Olson, and Mary Pasti have expertly shepherded the manuscript into print. I am very grateful to the Natan Fund, Felicia Herman and Adino Poupko, the Jewish Book Council, and Miri Pomerantz Dauber, Carolyn Starman Hessel, and Naomi Firestone-Teeter for their generous support of this book's publication.

My family has been enormously supportive of this book's slow gestation. I thank my parents for their patient encouragement and I am grateful for my mother's keen eye as an historian and visual scholar. My brother and sister-in-law, Charles and Amy, supplied good cheer and great advice. My wife Rachel has had to live with this book-in-progress for some time now. The extended journey has given me a chance to benefit from her passion for moral clarity and intellectual precision. I dedicate this book to my children, David, Eli, and Talia. They have taught me many lessons, among them that the best questions are the simplest ones.

INDEX

Page numbers in italic type indicate photographs or illustrations.

Abraham, Morris (General "Two-Gun" Cohen), 117
Abrahams, Israel, 63
Abram, Morris, 250–54, 256, 265–67, 273, 275, 298
Aden, 225–26
Adenauer, Konrad, 238, 245
Afnan, Badia, 267
Afro-Asian coalition, 172, 184, 198, 250, 270–73, 275
Agayants, Ivan Ivanovich, 238
Agudat Yisrael, 236
Aitken, Eleanor, 284–85
AJC. *See* American Jewish Committee
Alliance Israélite Universelle, 188
Alperin, Aron, 137
American Bar Association, 90, 187–88
American Civil Liberties Union, 178, 194
American Federation of Labor, 85
American-Israel Public Affairs Committee, 120
American Jewish Committee (AJC), 13, 85–87, 95–99, 102–12, 118–23, 134, 136–38, 153, 183, 187, 188, 190–92,

196–97, 243, 246, 250, 266–67, 275, 289–90, 292, 297–98
American Jewish Conference, 83, 96, 104–5, 110
American Jewish Congress, 90, 96, 119–20
American Jews: conservative, 190–91; criticism of, 86; and human rights, 88, 97, 191, 297–98; influence of, 22, 44, 47; and Israel, 183, 184, 186, 246; reaction of, to Arendt's *Eichmann in Jerusalem,* 257
American Law Institute, 92–93
American Oil Company (AMOCO), 85
American Revolution, 91
American Society for International Law, 90
Ammende, Ewald, 44
Amnesty International: Borderline Committee, 285; crisis of, 225–28, 277–78; criticisms of, 261–62, 280–81, 283–88; divisions within, 283–87; finances of, 278; founding of, xiii, 58, 204–5, 215–19; growth of, 219, 262; human rights